The Disability Rights Movement

The Disability Rights Movement

From Charity to Confrontation

Doris Zames Fleischer and Frieda Zames

TEMPLE UNIVERSITY PRESS

PHILADELPHIA

Temple University Press, Philadelphia 19122
Copyright © 2001 by Temple University
All rights reserved
Published 2001
Printed in the United States of America

Library of Congress Cataloging-in-Publication Data

Fleischer, Doris Zames.
    The disability rights movement : from charity to confrontation / by Doris Z. Fleischer and Frieda Zames.
        p. cm.
    Includes bibliographical references and index.
    ISBN 1-56639-811-8 (cloth : alk. paper) — ISBN 1-56639-812-6 (pbk. : alk. paper)
    1. Handicapped—Civil rights—United States. 2. Discrimination against the handicapped—United States. I. Zames, Frieda, 1932- . II. Title.
    HV1553 .F58 2000
    323.3—dc21

                                                                00-039282

To our mother and father, Pauline and Joseph Zames

Contents

Personal Notes

IN THE EARLY 1950s I attended Brooklyn College, located on a campus built in the 1930s in the pseudo-Georgian style of the 1830s. In order to enter the two main buildings, Boylan Hall and Ingersoll Hall—mirror images facing each other across a central quadrangle—I had to go up two steps. On rainy days I was terrified of falling because my crutch tips would slip. Snowy or icy days were worse. Never once at Brooklyn College did I think that those two steps in any way could be changed. I had to make do as best I could. I thought that it was my responsibility to fit in. I felt lucky just going to college since relatively few people with disabilities had such an opportunity at that time. It never occurred to me to ask for anything, certainly not to make demands—not even for a banister.

Why did most people with disabilities of my generation and many that followed—some of whom even gained considerable prominence in the modern disability rights movement—make the same assumption that I did? What caused the leap in consciousness of people with disabilities in the 1970s? How did this new vision give birth to a civil rights movement for people with disabilities? How has this civil rights movement affected people with disabilities as well as the wider society? These are the questions that inform this book.

—Frieda Zames

The most important thing that ever happened to me occurred two years before I was born. My sister (and now my coauthor) contracted polio. Despite her stay in a hospital and convalescent home during my first five years, she was always a presence in my life. In our home, my entire family and our circle of friends celebrated every one of my absent sister's birthdays. My parents even "conned" me into thinking that each of the frequent long train and bus rides that we took to visit her was a treat. Although I was too young to be allowed into the hospital, I loved standing outside and waving to her, for to me she was Rapunzel high up in the tower. When she came home and solved my problems and taught me how to fight back, I imagined myself the hero for rather absurdly holding up my five-year-old fingers to traffic in the middle of the rather empty streets near our house as she slowly crossed using her crutches and braces.

The much publicized Chair in Bioethics at Princeton's Center for Human Values, Peter Singer, wrote in *Practical Ethics,* a book he assigned in his course at the university: "When the death of a disabled infant will lead to the birth of another infant with better prospects of a happy life, the total amount of happiness will be greater if the disabled infant is killed." If my parents somehow could have known that at two and a half my sister would become disabled, and had they chosen the path that Professor Singer prescribes, would his Benthamesque vision of the greatest good for a greatest number have been achieved? To respond to this question, I think of the many nondisabled people I know who have not lived lives as productive or fulfilling or happy as my sister's. When I consider her social roles as mathematics professor and disability rights activist, her loving personal relationships, and the daily lessons in living I have learned from her, I don't know about that other sibling who might have taken her place. And the point is, neither does Professor Singer. But I do know one thing for certain. I'm not ready to trade her in.

    —Doris Zames Fleischer

Preface

IN THE ANATOMY OF PREJUDICE (1996),[1] Elisabeth Young-Bruehl analyzes what she believes to be "*the* four prejudices that have dominated American life and reflection in the past half-century—anti-Semitism, racism, sexism, and homophobia."[2] No reference is made to disability discrimination. Misrepresented as a health, economic, technical, or safety issue rather than discrimination, prejudice based on disability frequently remains unrecognized.

Although disability bias impacts upon a great many people, often with devastating consequences, Young-Bruehl's omission is not surprising. R. C. Smith, author of *A Case About Amy* (1996)[3]—an analysis of the 1982 Supreme Court ruling that denied a public school accommodation of a full-time sign-language interpreter for Amy Rowley, an extremely intelligent, profoundly deaf child—observes:

> Unkind words against homosexuals, African-Americans, Hispanics, and other minorities at least prompt rebuke from people who, though not members of these stigmatized groups, still recognize the prejudice. But prejudice against individuals with disabilities commonly goes undetected by a general public too unaware of its own feelings to recognize what has been said or written as prejudicial.[4]

Perhaps this oversight stems from a collective fear of disability since everyone is subject to illness, accident, the declining powers of advanced age—all forms of human vulnerability. "Handicapism," also referred to as "ableism," is the only "ism" to which *all* human beings are susceptible.[5]

This denial of the reality of disability results in stereotypes that continue to prevail. Films present people with disabilities either condescendingly as "inspirational," endeavoring to be as "normal" as possible by "overcoming" their limitations, or as disfigured monsters "slashing and hacking their way to box office success."[6] The inspirational figure hearkens back to Tiny Tim from Dickens's *A Christmas Carol,* a receptacle for the pity of those who did not have poor Tim's misfortune. In fact, "in the nineteenth century notion of charity, afflicted [the term used at the time for the disabled] people might be said to be created in order to provide opportunities for Christian folk to exercise their Christian virtue."[7] In the process, the lucky nondisabled could surreptitiously celebrate their superiority while simultaneously imagining that, by means of their charity, they were imitating the life of Christ.

When the authors of this book began their work over five years ago, the issue of disability rights had not yet entered into the public consciousness. Although President George Bush had signed the Americans with Disabilities Act (ADA) in 1990, which gave people with disabilities many of the same civil rights won by other groups, the struggle of the disability community to secure these rights appeared to lack the drama of the struggles of African Americans or women and indeed did lack the media attention. Even the controversy regarding an appropriate memorial for Franklin Delano Roosevelt, which did attract media attention, pointed to the surprising *invisibility* of disability and to a lack of awareness of the profound separation of images of power (the Presidency) and images of disability (the wheelchair). Disappointing as actor Christopher Reeve's emphasis on spinal cord regeneration, rather than disability rights, has been to many in the disability community, his struggle—after an accident left him quadriplegic—did catch the attention of a public watching a superman who once flew, but now cannot walk, re-create his life.

Until recently, the media did not seem cognizant of the significant number of people with disabilities in the United States (not to mention the rest of the world), nor the degree to which "invisible disabilities" such as psychiatric disorders, heart disease, diabetes, cancer, and learning disabilities predominate over visible ones. According to 1994–1995 data, over 20 percent of Americans—fifty-four million—were disabled, with almost half of them having severe disabilities.[8] As a consequence of medical and technological progress, the disability and the aging populations will continue to grow. It is not surprising that as people age, the probability increases that they will become disabled, and the likelihood of that impairment being severe also increases. What is surprising is the prevalence of disability for specific age groups: almost one-fourth of people forty-five to fifty-four, over one-third of those fifty-five to sixty-four, almost one-half of those sixty-five to seventy-nine, and almost three quarters of those eighty years and above.

The public's avoidance of acknowledging the ever-threatening possibility—and after a certain age, probability—of disability is not unexpected. Yet, the results of a 1998 study—indicating that even for adults with disabilities, only 54 percent have heard of the ADA[9]—reveals that despite the social and political gains achieved by disability activists in the past twenty years, the educational challenges ahead are significant. For example, the failure to select a handicapped-accessible site for the December 3, 1997, Presidential Conference on Race in Akron, Ohio, illustrates how often the pervasiveness of disability is unappreciated; officials did not consider that people with disabilities are included among racial minorities.

Almost a decade after passage of the ADA, this landmark legislation fueled by the civil rights movement is being seriously challenged in the courts. In 1999, the U.S. Supreme Court ruled in three separate employment cases that physical impairments that can be controlled by medication or assistive devices did not constitute a "disability" under the Americans with Disabilities Act. More threatening, however, to the viability of the ADA are challenges to the constitutionality of Title II of this law. In the year 2001, the Supreme Court is expected to rule in *Garrett v. University of Alabama* on whether Congress has the authority under the "equal protection" clause of the Fourteenth Amendment to ban discrimination by states against individuals with disabilities. In 2000, the Court, in *Kimel v. Florida Board of Regents*, invoking the doctrine of "sovereign immunity" as embodied in the Eleventh Amendment, held that Congress lacked the power to require states to pay damages for violations of another federal statute—the Age Discrimination in Employment Act. A decision against plaintiff Garrett could eliminate Title II's ban on discrimination against people with disabilities by state or local governments in any sphere—employment, access to public services, education, health care, or other programs administered by states and localities.[10]

Because many people with disabilities require "reasonable accommodation"[11] under the ADA in order to achieve equality, civil rights for this population are in jeopardy. While critics of the ADA overestimate the cost of such accommodation, they also underestimate the cost of discrimination, not only to individuals with disabilities, but also to society in general. The U.S. Senate recognized this frequently untapped potential in people with disabilities when, on June 16, 1999, it passed by a vote of 99 to 0 the long-overdue Work Incentives Improvement Act permitting those who require health care benefits to work without losing such benefits. On that occasion Senator Edward M. Kennedy (D-Mass.) declared, "We must banish the patronizing mind-set that disabled people are unable. In fact, they have enormous talent, and America cannot afford to waste an ounce of it."[12] This book is an effort to document the enormous talent that brought forth the disability rights movement.

Acknowledgments

WE WOULD LIKE TO acknowledge the valuable contributions of the following people: Samuel W. Anderson, Michael Auberger, Rims Barber, Sylvia Bassoff, Kim Baxter, Elizabeth Benjamin, Philip Bennett, Marcia Bernstein, Frank Bowe, Marca Bristo, Dale Brown, Paul Camacho, Dennis Cannon, Daniel Carr, Judi Chamberlin, James Cherry, Ira Cochin, Judith Cohen, Diane Coleman, Gerald R. Costa, Alice Crespo, Justin Dart, Anne Davis, Jim Davis, Mary Delgado, Susan Dooha, Marya Doonan, Melinda Dutton, Anne Emerman, Tod Ensign, Robert Fasano, Fred Fay, Keith Frank, Eunice Fiorito, Barbara Fisher, A. E. Foster, Lex Frieden, Tim Fuller, Martin Gensler, Ellen Gerson, Stephen Gold, Karen Luxton Gourgey, John C. Gray, Mark Green, Richard Greer, John Gresham, Rachelle Grossman, Joe Harkins, Florence Haskell, Eileen Healy, Paul Hearne, Nelson Hendler, Ilse Heumann, Judith E. Heumann, Alan Hevesi, Olga Hill, Catherine Huynh, Paul Jendrek, Blanche Kwas Johnson, Susan Jouard, Lois Kaggen, Martin Katzen, Bruce Alan Kiernan, Sherry Lampert, Nadina LaSpina, Martin Leff, Robert and Toby Levine, Edward Lewinson, Diane Lipton, Edward Litcher, Paul Longmore, Kitty Lunn, Robert Lynch, Nicholas M. and M. M., Sandra Marlow, Carr Massi, Rosemarie McCaffrey, Michael McCann, John M. McNeil, Terence Moakley, Marilyn Newman, Raphael Nisan, Ellen Nuzzi, Roxanne Offner, Marcia Osofsky, Celeste Owens, Harvey Pacht, Sandra Parrino, Gary Pitts, Keisha Powell, Rami Rabby, James Raggio, Daniel Robert, Edward Roberts, Nancy Rolnick, Phyllis Rubenfeld, Lani Sanjek, Marilyn Saviola, Susan Scheer, Robert Schoenfeld, Carmen Silver, William Skawinski, Eleanor Smith, Mary Somosa, Richard Spiegel, Marvin Spieler, Steven Stellman, Jean Stewart, Paul Sullivan, Karen Tamley, Arthur Teicher, Marvin Wasserman, James Weisman, Judith Wessler, Harry Wieder, Charles Winston, Barry Winthrop, Arthur Wohl, Sidney Wolinsky, Alexander Wood, Deborah Yanagisawa, Ernest Zelnick, Barbara Zitcer, Gerry Zuzze.

Special thanks to Michael Ames, for his wise editorial counseling and his continuing encouragement and support; Leonard Fleischer, without whom this book could not have been written—like Faulkner's Dilsey, he endured; Michael Imperiale, for providing us with supplies and the nourishment we needed to take on and complete this project; the helpful people at Temple University Press—Charles Ault, Jennifer French, Tamika Hughes, and Irene Imperio; and Yvonne Ramsey, for her patience, editing acumen, and good humor.

Chronology

1817   The first school for deaf students in the United States is established in Hartford, Connecticut.

1829   Louis Braille invents the raised dot system for the blind known as Braille.

1841   Dorothea Dix begins her efforts to improve conditions for people with disabilities incarcerated in jails and poorhouses.

1864   The National Deaf-Mute College—known as Gallaudet College in 1954 and later Gallaudet University—is established.

1880   The Congress of Milan bans the use of sign language in schools for deaf people.

——   The National Association of the Deaf is founded.

1903   Helen Keller publishes her autobiography, *The Story of My Life*.

1904   Winifred Holt Mather establishes Lighthouse No. 1 for blind people in New York City, the first of many throughout the world.

1909   Clifford Beers, author of *A Mind That Found Itself,* organizes The National Committee for Mental Hygiene, later known as The National Mental Health Association.

1914   The War Risk Insurance Act becomes law.

1917   The Smith-Hughes Vocational Education Act becomes law.

1918   The Smith-Sears Veterans Rehabilitation Act becomes law.

1920   Disabled American Veterans of the World War is founded—later known as Disabled American Veterans.

——   The Smith-Fess Vocational Rehabilitation Act becomes law.

1921   The American Foundation for the Blind is founded.

——   Franklin Delano Roosevelt contracts polio.

——   The United States Veterans Bureau is established—later known as the Department of Veterans Affairs.

1922   Edward F. Allen establishes the National Easter Seal Society in Elyria, Ohio.

1923   Henry Kessler, a pioneer in rehabilitation medicine, initiates surgical techniques that allows muscular control of artificial limbs.

1927   Franklin Delano Roosevelt co-establishes the Warm Springs Foundation.

1929   Dorothy Harrison Eustis and Morris Frank found Seeing Eye, the first guide dog training school in the United States.

—	National Easter Seal Society establishes Rehabilitation International.
1932	Franklin Delano Roosevelt is elected President of the United States.
1935	The League of the Physically Handicapped is organized; it disbands in 1938.
—	The Social Security Act, providing federal old age benefits and grants to the states for assistance to blind people and children with disabilities, becomes law.
1937	The March of Dimes is founded.
—	The National Foundation for Infantile Paralysis is founded.
1940	Jacobus tenBroek organizes the National Federation of the Blind in Wilkes-Barre, Pennsylvania.
1943	The Barden-LaFollette Act dealing with vocational rehabilitation becomes law.
1947	Paralyzed Veterans of America is organized.
1948	Tim Nugent initiates services and a sports program for students with disabilities at the University of Illinois, and the university institutes a paratransit system on its wheelchair accessible campus.
1949	United Cerebral Palsy Association, uniting all local cerebral palsy organizations in the United States, is founded.
1950	Elizabeth Boggs forms a parents' group working for improved services for children with developmental disabilities.
—	Gunnnar Dybwad and others organize the Association of Retarded Citizens, which later develops branches throughout the United States and the world.
1951	Howard Rusk opens the Institute of Rehabilitation Medicine at the New York University Medical Center in New York City.
1955	Jonas Salk develops the first successful polio vaccine.
1956	A law is enacted enabling people aged fifty or older to qualify for Social Security Disability Insurance.
1960	The Social Security disability program is amended to allow people under fifty to quality for Social Security Disability Insurance.
—	William Stokoe's paper on *Sign Language Structure* legitimizes American Sign Language and ushers in the movement of Deafness as culture.
1961	Former members of the National Foundation for the Blind found a new organization, the American Council of the Blind.
1962	Edward Roberts sues to gain admission to the University of California, the same semester that James Meredith requires a lawsuit to become the first black person to attend the University of Mississippi.
1964	The Civil Rights Act, which will impact significantly on subsequent disability rights legislation, becomes law.
1965	The Social Security Act is amended, establishing Medicare and Medicaid.
1968	The federal Architectural Barriers Act becomes law.
—	Prodded by Harold Willson, the California state legislature guarantees that the Bay Area Rapid Transit system will be the first rapid transit system in the United States to accommodate wheelchair users.
1970	Judith E. Heumann organizes Disabled In Action in New York City.
—	The Urban Mass Transportation Assistance Act becomes law.
1971	The Mental Patients Liberation Project is initiated in New York City, and similar projects begun by "psychiatric survivors" emerge throughout the nation.

1972   Amendments to the Social Security Act allow recipients of disability benefits under the age of sixty-five to qualify for Medicare.

—   The appalling conditions at Willowbrook State School in New York City for people with developmental disabilities are exposed as the result of a television broadcast from the facility.

—   Demonstrations are held in Washington, D.C., by disability activists protesting President Nixon's veto of what will become the Rehabilitation Act of 1973.

—   Guide Dog Users is organized in New York City.

—   Passage of amendments to the Social Security Act creates the Supplemental Security Income program.

—   Edward Roberts establishes the Center for Independent Living in Berkeley, California—a symbol of the Independent Living Movement emerging throughout the nation and the world.

—   U.S. District Court for the District of Columbia decides in *Mills v. Board of Education* that every school-age child is entitled to a free public education regardless of the nature or severity of the individual's disability.

1973   The Architectural and Transportation Barriers Compliance Board—later known as the Access Board—is established under the Rehabilitation Act of 1973 to enforce the Architectural Barriers Act of 1968.

—   The Rehabilitation Act of 1973, including Section 504, becomes law.

1974   The first convention of People First—the largest U.S. organization of and led by people with developmental or cognitive disabilities—is held in Salem, Oregon.

1975   The American Coalition of Citizens with Disabilities is organized in Washington, D.C.

—   Wade Blank relocates adults with severe disabilities from a nursing home into apartments, initiating what will become the Denver, Colorado, Atlantis Community.

—   The Education for All Handicapped Children Act, later known as the Individuals with Disabilities Education Act, becomes law.

—   Edward Roberts becomes director of the California Department of Rehabilitation.

1976   James Cherry wins lawsuit (*Cherry v. Mathews* in U.S. District Court for the District of Columbia) requiring that the Secretary of Health, Education, and Welfare develop and promulgate Section 504 regulations.

—   *Disabled In Action of Pennsylvania v. Coleman* (known as the Transbus lawsuit) is filed in the Eastern District of Pennsylvania.

1977   Following nationwide demonstrations by disability activists, HEW Secretary Joseph Califano signs the regulations for Section 504 and the Individuals with Disabilities Education Act.

—   *Lloyd v. Regional Transportation Authority* is decided in U.S. Court of Appeals for the Seventh Circuit, establishing a private right of action under Section 504.

1979   U.S. Supreme Court decides *Southeastern Community College v. Davis,* a suit impacting on accessible public transportation.

—   Disability Rights Education and Defense Fund is founded in Berkeley, California.

—   The National Alliance for the Mentally Ill is founded in Madison, Wisconsin.

1980   Black Deaf Advocates is founded.

1981   The year is designated as the International Year of Disabled Persons by the United Nations.

1982   The U.S. Supreme Court decides in *Hendrick Hudson Central School District v. Rowley* that there is "no Congressional intent to achieve strict equality of opportunity or services" in the Individuals with Disabilities Education Act.

1983   ADAPT, denoting American Disabled for Accessible Public Transit, is organized.

—   Edward Roberts and Judith E. Heumann (together with Joan Leon) organize the World Institute on Disability in Oakland, California.

1984   The National Council on Disability becomes an independent federal agency.

1986   The U.S. Supreme Court decides in the Baby Jane Doe case (*Bowen v. American Hospital Association*) that parents' refusal of needed surgery does not violate Section 504.

—   Irving Zola founds the Society for Disability Studies.

1988   The Gallaudet University uprising results in its first deaf president, I. King Jordan.

—   The Fair Housing Act is amended to include people with disabilities.

—   Civil Rights Restoration Act becomes law, in effect overturning the U.S. Supreme Court's 1984 *Grove City College v. Bell* decision regarding the discrimination on the basis of sex in federally assisted education programs or activities.

1989   *ADAPT v. Skinner*—decided by the U.S. Court of Appeals for the Third Circuit—helped pave the way for accessibility of public transportation.

—   Ralf Hotchkiss establishes the Wheeled Mobility Center at San Francisco State College, from which his International Wheelchair Program emanates.

—   Ronald Mace establishes the Center for Universal Design in Raleigh, North Carolina.

—   *Daniel R. R. v. State Board of Education* (Fifth Circuit) in Texas—the first of four significant inclusion cases (from 1989 to 1994) involving children with developmental disabilities—results in consistent legal decisions that the Individuals with Disabilities Education Act mandated the integration of these children into regular classes with full supports.

1990   ADAPT now denotes American Disabled for Attendant Programs Today as the organization focuses on a new primary purpose.

—   President George Bush signs the Americans with Disabilities Act into law.

1995   The American Association of People with Disabilities is established in Washington, D.C.

—   Diane Coleman and others organize Not Dead Yet to oppose Jack Kevorkian and supporters of physician-assisted suicide.

—   Justin Dart and others organize Justice For All in Washington, D.C.

—   Billy Golfus's film, *When Billy Broke His Head*—a personal view of the disability rights movement—premiers on public television.

1996   The paradigm shift in scientists' characterization of the development of AIDS begins the process of changing AIDS from a fatal disease into a chronic one.

—   Veterans Health Care Eligibility Reform Act (dealing with Vietnam veterans) becomes law.

1997   The U.S. Supreme Court validates the state prohibition on physician-assisted suicide in *Vacco v. Quill* and *Washington v. Glucksberg*, while deciding that this issue is properly within the jurisdiction of the states.

1998   Persian Gulf War Veterans Act becomes law.

—   The U.S. Supreme Court decides in its first Americans with Disabilities Act case, *Bragdon v. Abbott*, that the act's definition of disability includes asymptomatic HIV.

—   The U.S. Supreme Court decides in *Pennsylvania Department of Corrections v. Yeskey* that the Americans with Disabilities Act covers state prisons.

1999   The U.S. Supreme Court decides in *Carolyn C. Cleveland v. Policy Management Systems Corp., et al.* that people receiving Social Security disability benefits are protected against discrimination under the Americans with Disabilities Act if and when they are able to return to the work force.

—   The U.S. Supreme Court decides in *Olmstead v. L.C. and E.W.* that individuals with disabilities must be offered services in the "most integrated setting."

—   The U.S. Supreme Court decides in three employment cases, *Sutton et al. v. United Air Lines, Inc., Murphy v. United Parcel Service, Inc.,* and *Albertsons, Inc. v. Kirkingburg* that individuals whose conditions do not substantially limit any life activity and/or are easily correctable are not disabled according to the Americans with Disabilities Act.

—   The Work Incentives Improvement Act, allowing to work those who require health care benefits, becomes law.

Abbreviations and Acronyms

AAPD	American Association of People with Disabilities
AARP	American Association of Retired People
ABA	Applied Behavioral Analysis
ACB	American Council of the Blind
ACCD	American Coalition of Citizens with Disabilities
ACLU	American Civil Liberties Union
ACRMD	Association of Children with Retarded Mental Development
Act-Up	AIDS Coalition To Unleash Power
ADA	Americans with Disabilities Act
ADAPT	American Disabled for Accessible Public Transit, later American Disabled for Attendant Programs Today
AFB	American Foundation for the Blind
AHCA	American Health Care Association
AHRC	Association for Help of Retarded Children
AIDS	autoimmune deficiency syndrome
ALS	amyotrophic lateral sclerosis
AMA	American Medical Association
ANSI	American National Standards Institute
APTA	American Public Transit Association
ARC	Association of Retarded Citizens (currently known as The Arc)
ASL	American Sign Language
BART	Bay Area Rapid Transit
BCID	Brooklyn Center for Independence of the Disabled
BCIL	Boston Center for Independent Living
BDA	Black Deaf Advocates
CARR	Committee Against Right on Red
CHIP	Child Health Insurance Program
CIA	Central Intelligence Agency
CIDNY	Center for Independence of the Disabled in New York
CIL	Center for Independent Living (Berkeley, California)
DAV	Disabled American Veterans

DAVWW	Disabled American Veterans of the World War
DIA	Disabled In Action
DNR	do-not-resuscitate (order)
DREDF	Disability Rights Education and Defense Fund
DSP	Disabled Students Program
EEOC	Equal Employment Opportunity Commission
EPSDT	Early Periodic Screening, Diagnosis and Testing
EPVA	Eastern Paralyzed Veterans Association
ERB	Emergency Relief Bureau
FAHA	Federal Aid Highway Administration
FDA	Food and Drug Administration
GMHC	Gay Men's Health Crisis
HCFA	Health Care Financing Administration
HEW	U.S. Department of Health, Education, and Welfare
HILC	Harlem Independent Living Center
HMO	health maintenance organization
HPLSU	Handicapped Persons Legal Support Unit
HUD	U.S. Department of Housing and Urban Development
ICD	Institute for the Crippled and Disabled, later International Center for the Disabled
IDEA	Individuals with Disabilities Education Act
IEP	individualized educational plan
IL	independent living
ILC	independent living center
ILRU	Independent Living Research Utilization (program)
IYDP	International Year of Disabled Persons
JFA	Justice For All
JOB	Just One Break
LD	learning disability
LIU	Long Island University
LRE	least restrictive environment
MiCasa	Medicaid Community Attendant Services Act
MiCassa	Medicaid Community Attendant Services and Supports Act
MSA	Medical Savings Account
MTA	Metropolitan Transportation Authority (New York City)
NAAV	National Association of Atomic Veterans
NAD	National Association of the Deaf
NAMI	National Alliance for the Mentally Ill
NCD	National Council on Disability
NFB	National Federation of the Blind
NIH	National Institutes of Health
NMHA	National Mental Health Association
NOD	National Organization on Disability
NYLPI	New York Lawyers for the Public Interest
NYSCPD	New York State Coalition of People with Disabilities
OVR	Office of Vocational Rehabilitation

PARC	Pennsylvania Association for Retarded Children
PH	physically handicapped
PVA	Paralysed Veterans of America
QILC	Queens Independent Living Center
SABE	Self Advocates Becoming Empowered
SDS	Society for Disability Studies
SILC	Statewide Independent Living Council
SKIP	Sick Kids Need Involved People
SSDI	Social Security Disability Insurance
SSI	Supplemental Security Income
TAB	temporarily ablebodied
TDD	telecommunication device for the deaf
TT	text telephone
TTY	teletypewriter
UCP	United Cerebral Palsy (local organizations)
UCPA	United Cerebral Palsy Association (national organization)
UMTA	Urban Mass Transportation Administration
USDOT	U.S. Department of Transportation
VA	Veterans Administration
VESID	Vocational and Educational Services for Individuals with Disabilities
WID	World Institute on Disability
WIIA	Work Incentives Improvement Act
WIN	Wheelchair Independence Now, later Win Independence Now
WPA	Works Progress Administration

The Disability Rights Movement

Chapter One

"Wheelchair Bound" and "The Poster Child"

"HOPE FOR THE CRIPPLED" was the name of a postage stamp issued in 1970, said Judith E. Heumann, current Assistant Secretary of the U.S. Department of Education and quadriplegic wheelchair user, in her 1980 testimony to the United States Commission on Civil Rights.[1] The stamp pictured "a person seated in a wheelchair rising to a standing position [that] indicated what people thought of a disabled individual in a wheelchair.... You are not considered to be a whole person; however, once you are in this standing position—that is normality." In January 1999, the nation saw another image on their TV screens. Defending President Clinton from impeachment, the President's Chief Counsel Charles Ruff took center stage in the Senate chambers *in his wheelchair*. How have our images of people with disabilities (until recently called "the disabled") changed in the last fifty years?

FDR, the "Cured Cripple"

The ability to stand and to walk was unnecessary for Franklin Delano Roosevelt—who had contracted polio eleven years before he was elected to his first of four terms as President—to be one of the most significant political figures of the twentieth century. Yet both the nation and the man had an obsession with the myth of his total recovery. FDR had to be seen, and had to see himself, as a "cured cripple,"[2] not a person diminished by disability. As his wife Eleanor observed, however, the disability may have been a "blessing in disguise,"[3] steeling and sensitizing the man. According to historian Doris Kearns Goodwin:

> The paralysis that crippled his body expanded his mind and his sensibilities. After what Eleanor called his "trial by fire," he seemed less arrogant, less smug, less superficial, more focused, more complex, more interesting. He returned from his ordeal with greater powers of concentration and greater self-knowledge. "There had been a plowing up of his nature," Labor Secretary Frances Perkins observed. "The man emerged completely warmhearted, with new humility of spirit and a firmer understanding of profound philosophical concepts." No longer belonging to his old world in the same way, he came to empathize with the poor and underprivileged, with people to whom fate had dealt a difficult hand.[4]

The extent to which the public was aware of Roosevelt's disability varied widely. While for many people with disabilities FDR engendered faith in their own possibilities, the general public preferred not to see their President's physical impairment. Although some did not know, others refused to learn, and still others refused to tell that the President was disabled. *New York Times* columnist Maureen Dowd describes her father's experience:

> In the 30's my father, a D.C. police detective, traveled to the Deep South to bring back a prisoner for trial. As he waited at the railroad station to come home, some nasty-looking vagrants surrounded him.
> "You're from Washington," one said to him. "Do you see the President?"
> "Yes," replied my father, who worked on protective details for President Roosevelt.
> "There are some ugly rumors going around that the President is a cripple," the bum growled. "We're going to kill any man says that's true."
> "The President," my father lied pleasantly, "is a fine, athletic man" [which unbeknownst to Dowd or her father had some element of truth since Roosevelt swam frequently].[5]

Of the many who were cognizant of the President's contraction of polio, only a privileged few knew the degree to which it limited his mobility.

The continuing public self-deception regarding Roosevelt's disability is dramatically illustrated by the decision to create a Washington, D.C., memorial depicting FDR as though he were not a wheelchair user. Karl E. Meyer in the *New York Times* "Editorial Notebook" indicated that "there will be no visual reminder of this fact [Roosevelt's inability to stand unassisted] in the FDR memorial due to be dedicated next spring [1997]. On the contrary, he is to be shown standing tall in one of the three sculptures planned for the seven-acre site on the banks of the Potomac."[6] Although Meyer's article was critical of this alteration of the truth about FDR, two letters to the editor expose the persistent public unwill-

ingness to confront the reality of Roosevelt's disability:

> Roosevelt's being crippled was hardly what made him one of our greatest Presidents. Memorials exaggerate in visual terms the features of those paid this granite homage. Wouldn't representing him in a wheelchair have the effect of overplaying his being crippled?

> President Roosevelt was seen by all but a few as not being disabled. His memorial should so depict him, as he was perceived and is remembered. To do otherwise is a form of revisionism.[7]

"Lester Hyman, a Memorial Commission member, said that they had decided not to display a wheelchair or braces in order to show Roosevelt as people then knew him."[8] Although Maureen Dowd appeals for an honest depiction of the President as he really was, her language and attitude reveal her limited understanding of disability. Her reference to Roosevelt as "wheelchair bound"—rather than a "wheelchair user"—is a melodramatic construction no longer accepted by people with disabilities, for the phrase is an anachronism of a pre-accessible society. This reference, more than a quibble about political correctness,[9] demonstrates how the language perpetuates common misconceptions about people with disabilities.

Although Dowd concludes that Roosevelt's concealment of his disability stemmed from his courage, more likely his political savvy told him that as President of a nation in the throes of a disabling economic depression and devastating world conflict, he needed to be perceived as a forceful and vigorous leader. At that time, power and disability were felt in a visceral way to be mutually exclusive. More indicative of Dowd's as well as the popular misconception is her assumption that what people with disabilities need are the following: first, to gain inspiration, from a "supercrip" like Roosevelt, to overcome their impairments; and second, like Tiny Tim, to serve as an inspiration to nondisabled people.

Worthwhile as these symbolic roles may be, they are not the major needs of people with disabilities, as John Gliedman and William Roth discovered in their study, *The Unexpected Minority*.[10] Their research on children with disabilities led the authors to an unanticipated conclusion: this population's most urgent need was a *political movement* to remove social impediments. Not burdened by stigma, discrimination, or inaccessibility, many people with disabilities, like most other people, would be resourceful enough to recognize and fulfill their own potential. Perhaps the one overriding purpose for portraying Roosevelt as he really was is to reassert the historical truth with which the nation has never fully come to terms: for many years, from 1932 to 1945, what was arguably the most demanding job in the world was accomplished from a wheelchair.

There were two public occasions when FDR deliberately permitted people to see the severity of his disability.[11] These incidents suggest his awareness of the relationship between coping with bias (because of disability or race) and transcending obstacles (physical and attitudinal). In 1936, at the request of Mordecai Johnson, president of Howard University, Roosevelt allowed the audience to observe his physical vulnerability at the dedication of a new building on campus: "He let himself be lifted from the car and set down in full public view, and then he proceeded to walk slowly and painfully to the podium."[12] Appreciating the crippling effects of prejudice, especially in this period when racial barriers were sanctioned by law, Roosevelt was willing to appear before the student body as a model of achievement in the face of great odds.

Six years later, he presented himself in his wheelchair at a hospital as a means of asserting his identification with the injured and the amputees. As Roosevelt aide Sam Rosenman remembered:

> At one of the hospitals [Oahu, Hawaii], . . . the President did something which affected us all [Roosevelt's entourage] very deeply. He asked a secret service man to wheel him slowly through all the wards that were occupied by veterans who had lost one or more arms and legs. He insisted on going past each individual bed. He wanted to display himself and his useless legs to those boys who would have to face the same bitterness. . . .
>
> With a cheering smile to each of them . . . and a pleasant word at the bedside of a score or more, this man who had risen from a bed of helplessness ultimately to become President of the United States was living proof of what the human spirit could do.[13]

At Warm Springs, Georgia, a rehabilitation center established by Roosevelt before his Presidency, he also revealed what his wife called "an understanding of the suffering of others."[14] There new "polios" had the opportunity to see old "polios" living productive lives in a noninstitutional setting, alive with intellectual stimulation, spontaneity, and fun.[15] As FDR biographer Hugh Gregory Gallagher puts it, "There was flirting, falling in love, sexual hanky-panky—and much gossip about it all."[16] Demonstrating an insight into the deepest needs of other "polios," many of whom were adolescents or young adults, FDR was known affectionately as "Dr. Roosevelt" at Warm Springs.[17] Under his direction, the establishment attended not only to paralyzed limbs, with newly devised treatments, but also to injured self-images.

Roosevelt chose Fred Botts—an early patient at Warm Springs who had a serious disability—as registrar in charge of admissions and, informally, as representative of patients' interests.[18] Sharing FDR's vision of the operation, Botts served as the "guardian of the spirit" of Warm Springs. The removal of Botts from his post after Roosevelt's death signaled the loss of patient primacy at

Warm Springs and its transformation into a more conventional institution controlled by professional medical administrators.

For the most part, however, as historian Paul Longmore indicates, FDR lived according to a bargain that misrepresented the nature of disability:

> This Bargain could only be struck in a society that viewed disability as a transgression, something the disabled person could, with effort, "manage" and control—"a private, emotional or physical tragedy best dealt with by psychological coping," Longmore says. This view of disability has been called the "medical model": it sees the disability itself as the problem, to be dealt with in private, something between doctor and patient.... "The Bargain," Longmore points out, "disallows any collective protest against things like prejudice or discrimination."[19]

Doris Kearns Goodwin in *No Ordinary Time* describes the "unspoken code of honor" adhered to by White House and press photographers as well as newsreel film makers:

> In twelve years, not a single picture was ever printed of the President in his wheelchair. No newsreel had ever captured him being lifted into or out of his car. When he was shown in public, he appeared either standing behind a podium, seated in an ordinary chair, or leaning on the arm of a colleague. If, as occasionally happened, one of the members of the press corps sought to violate the code by sneaking a picture of the President looking helpless, one of the older photographers would "accidentally" block the shot or gently knock the camera to the ground. But such incidents were rare; by and large, the "veil of silence" about the extent of Roosevelt's handicap was accepted by everyone—Roosevelt, the press, and the American people.[20]

In the Shadow of Polio, a description by Kathryn Black of her mother's struggle with polio, "an embarrassing rebuke to all the heroic 'can-do' propaganda of the period," confirms Longmore's sense of the distorted social view of "disability as a transgression": "Because some patients did recover, and a few recovered spectacularly, those who did not came to be perceived as having somehow failed the test of American wholesomeness. If only they had tried a little harder, surely they would have made it from iron lung to rocking bed, from bed to braces, from braces to crutches, from crutches to the 100-yard dash."[21]

Though FDR and his circle strove to deceive a public that invited the deception, the President fell victim to the same dissembling that he was perpetrating: disability equals weakness; therefore, he is in fact not "really" disabled. The fiction the public was fed that he *could* walk without a great deal of human or mechanical aid became the internalized hoax that he *would* walk without assistance. The symbolic value placed on walking, inappropriate as it may have been, was given dramatic expression in Dore Schary's 1958 play and 1960 film, *Sunrise at Campobello.* The heroic ending, signifying FDR's re-entrance into political life after his "victory" over polio, is represented by his walking with crutches to the platform to nominate Al Smith at the 1924 Democratic Convention.

The image of walking is not merely Schary's metaphor. It is a collective symbol, as in the "Riddle of the Sphinx" in Sophocles' *Oedipus:* "What walks on four legs in the morning, two in the afternoon, and three at night?" The answer—man—refers to the human condition, for a person crawling in infancy on all fours or hobbling in old age with a cane, as if with three legs, represents dependency; but a man at the height of his powers walks on his own two legs. A problem arises, however, when metaphor is confused with reality. With TV reporting making a Roosevelt-like "splendid deception" impossible today, disability stigma—despite the passage of the Americans with Disabilities Act—is still so pervasive that it is improbable that anyone with an impairment as severe as FDR's could be elected President.[22]

League of the Physically Handicapped

While FDR, the press, and the public were denying the President's disability, the League of the Physically Handicapped, at the same time, was making disability discrimination visible. One of the first disability organizations to articulate its purpose in unequivocally political terms, the league was a militant group formed in the 1930s to oppose discrimination in government and private employment.[23] The 1935 Social Security Act, while providing income support and vocational rehabilitation for people with disabilities, did not completely serve the needs of those capable potential employees who were able to compete in the workforce if given the opportunity. The original nucleus of the league, six individuals who formed a sit-in protest at the New York City office of the Emergency Relief Bureau (ERB) director, Oswald W. Knauth, from May 29 to June 6, 1935, were convinced that their physical disabilities were being used as an excuse to treat them as if they were unemployable. Thus, they perceived themselves as a minority unprotected by the law rather than "medical models" victimized by physical impairments.

Although most of its members were mobility-impaired, the league demonstrated the value of coalition of individuals with different disabilities. Among its members were people with a variety of disabilities resulting from childhood poliomyelitis (also known as infantile paralysis), cerebral palsy, heart conditions, and tuberculosis, as well as from accidents. Florence Haskell, who contracted polio in 1916, the year of the first major polio epidemic in the United States,

was "politicized and radicalized" when she was informed that she would have to pass a physical examination in order to obtain a secretarial job for which she was "perfectly qualified."

Haskell recognized that the physical examination would unjustly doom her employment chances even though her disability would not interfere with her performance. In fact, her disability was not even discovered until she was in fifth grade, and then only accidentally. Other highly capable individuals with diverse physical disabilities had similar experiences; frequently, they were rejected for less qualified nondisabled workers. On those unusual occasions when they were hired, they were often paid wages well below the regular salary for their occupation regardless of their competence.

Despite the selection by Home Relief Agencies of a number of recipients for government jobs, records of people with disabilities were stamped "PH" (physically handicapped), disqualifying those candidates from consideration. The Wednesday, May 29, 1935, occupation of the ERB director's office was an impromptu reaction, resulting from the six protesters' frustration at being unable to confront Knauth directly to demand employment opportunities. The press was unaware of the protest until the following afternoon when the wife of one of the demonstrators brought a huge crowd of supporters, later joined by even more onlookers, to the building. Emboldened, the occupiers not only insisted on an audience with the director, but also added new demands: fifty jobs would have to be offered to league members immediately, and ten more jobs made available each week; salaries would have to be no less than twenty-seven dollars for married employees and twenty-one dollars for single employees; workers with disabilities would have to be integrated with, rather than segregated from, nondisabled workers.

Although the exact date of the league's formation is unknown, Haskell remembers it as occurring shortly after this nine-day protest and the ensuing trial. Up to that point, most of the activities of those who would later become league members were ad hoc responses to events. The most dramatic of these events was a ten-day near-comic trial of eleven ERB picketers—some sit-in protesters joined by other demonstrators—arrested on June 6, 1935. Besides asking Mayor Fiorello La Guardia to preside over the trial, the unorthodox and erratic judge, Overton Harris, compared himself to Christ, expressed his desire to escape to Tahiti, and urged the defendants to be practical and forget their constitutional and human rights. Newspaper accounts, such as "Crippled Pickets 'Torture' Harris," indicated that the press noted the farcical quality of the trial.[24] The publicity the members received from this trial, as well as political actions such as demonstrations, picket lines, sit-ins, and hunger strikes, inspired them to organize formally. They raised enough money to rent office space, where they elected officers and regularly discussed tactics.

Despite their success in eliminating the "PH" category and acquiring Works Progress Administration (WPA) jobs for themselves and others in New York City, league members recognized that their task was incomplete. Job discrimination because of disability was still accepted nationwide. On the first of their two trips to Washington, D.C., on May 8, 1936, thirty-five members traveled in a flatbed truck for over thirteen hours in order to appeal to FDR, the disabled President, to provide access to government employment for people with physical disabilities throughout the country. The league's occupation of the offices of the WPA served two purposes: first, it dramatized members' determination to meet with, if not President Roosevelt, then at least with a major figure in his administration; second, it served as respite for the weary travelers.

When they met with Harry L. Hopkins, head of the WPA, on the following day, they insisted on a permanent jobs program for—as well as a national census of—people with physical disabilities. A census was required to verify the league's contention that there were many qualified potential workers with physical disabilities. The protesters demanded that the census be paid for by the WPA, but supervised by the league, for they wanted to be certain that the project was carried out properly. The *Washington Star* described the league members as seeking "not sympathy—but a concrete plan to end discrimination against employment of the physically handicapped on WPA projects":

> The 21-year-old girl president [Sylvia Flexer, later Sylvia Flexer Bassoff] of the youthful League of the Physically Handicapped—lame from infantile paralysis since she was fourteen months old—is tired of stock phrases which lead nowhere, she declared today.
>
> She and her companions, who laid 24-hour siege to a WPA headquarters Saturday in a successful attempt to arrange an interview with Administrator Harry L. Hopkins, are sick of the humiliation of poor jobs at best—often no work at all. "We are looking to the Federal Government because we know the States would turn us over to local agencies and we'd be right back where we started," she declared.[25]

In August 1936, the league sent Roosevelt and Hopkins a "Thesis on Conditions of Physically Handicapped," a ten-page document making the case for government intervention in employing people with physical disabilities.

At this point, the attention of the League of the Physically Handicapped returned to obtaining WPA jobs for people with physical disabilities in New York City. The League for the Advancement of the Deaf joined in this effort. Whatever concessions the League of the Physically Handicapped received were more than negated by numerous layoffs, which spurred the league again to go to Washington in August 1937 in order to urge Hopkins to secure jobs for workers with physical disabilities. Limited by meager funds, league members slept the first night on the WPA lawn and the second on the grounds of the Washington Monument. Meeting with no success, they once again sought government job opportunities in New York City for workers with disabilities. Ultimately, many of the league leaders were employed by civil service.

Because of the personal success of many of the members, as well as the dissension triggered by the red-baiting of a small minority, the League of the Physically Handicapped gradually ceased to exist. During its approximately four years of activism, from 1935 to about 1938, its achievements were noteworthy. Imbibing the 1930s spirit of social agitation, refusing to remain invisible, league members broke the stereotype regarding disability. Rather than evoking pity, they were impelled by their anger to risk social disapproval. Armed with a sense of solidarity with other unemployed workers with disabilities, they struggled against discrimination that unjustly limited their job opportunities. Considering the number of manual labor jobs at that time and the lack of access for workers with disabilities to private-sector jobs, league members believed that government had an obligation to employ people with disabilities. The actions and accomplishments of members changed their self-perception, for, as Haskell says, "People faced the public for the first time, not with self-consciousness, but with honor. We were able to work, marry, and have children. We could do what others do in our society." Because their legacy was not known, later generations of disability activists would have to reinvent their vision.

Public and governmental reaction to the League of the Physically Handicapped re-vealed contradictory assumptions. Members were described both as Communists and Communist dupes, unable to organize their own protests without guidance from outside agitators. New York City WPA director Victor Ridder first acknowledged the validity of the league's contention that government owed jobs to people with physical disabilities because of the employment barriers they encountered. Shortly after, however, he labeled league activists "troublemakers who were mentally as well as physically disabled." Although disabled veterans were given priority in employment, civilians with similar disabilities were considered unemployable. ERB director Knauth claimed that New York City had no obligation to give unemployable people work, so they should seek jobs in private industry.

On their first trip to Washington, when Hopkins denied the league's claim that the WPA was discriminating against workers with disabilities, he advised members to provide proof of their assertion. Despite the league's submission of the "Thesis," which included an analysis—with some statistical evidence—of the disability employment situation in New York City, as well as a recommendation for a national census, the document was ignored. The most blatant contradiction, however, was that FDR, the leader of the government that was designating these workers with disabilities as unemployable, was himself disabled.

The March of Dimes

Employing the slogan "Dance—that others may walk,"[26] Birthday Balls, held from 1934 through 1945, celebrated the birthday of the President who was more severely disabled than many of the workers denied jobs because of their disabilities. Attended by over three million Americans, by 1937 there were seven thousand Birthday Balls funding

Warm Springs and programs in communities where the money was raised.[27] Even on January 30, 1945, while the President was on an arduous ocean voyage to meet Churchill and Stalin at Yalta, Mrs. Roosevelt was attending the rounds of yearly Birthday Balls to support the March of Dimes.[28] In order to remove politics from the efforts to deal with the polio epidemics, and because the Birthday Balls were not raising enough money, the National Foundation for Infantile Paralysis and its fund-raising arm, the March of Dimes, were both initiated in 1937. Despite the overwhelming support for the March of Dimes, the National Foundation for Infantile Paralysis drew criticism for being radical because it provided whatever the polio patient required, from medical care to equipment, without means-testing. "Conservative medical opinion found this policy to be a dangerous precedent—perhaps even communistic in concept."

Nonetheless, several factors contributed to the success of the foundation in its eighteen-year struggle against polio, from the organization's inception in 1937 to the development of the Salk vaccine in 1955. Profoundly dedicated to providing care for those affected by polio, Roosevelt also was determined to eradicate the disease. Basil O'Connor, the President's former law partner who "used the prestige of the presidency to fight a germ,"[29] was selected as director of the foundation. Capable and resolute, O'Connor was willing to take whatever risks necessary to serve the purposes of the foundation. When O'Connor realized that success seemed imminent, he allowed the foundation to go into debt to finance the final research required to develop the Salk vaccine. His "passionate" devotion to his task became almost "obsessive" when his daughter, a mother of five, told him after she contracted the illness, "I've gotten some of your polio."

A wordplay on the newsreel "The March of Time," the March of Dimes campaign was comedian Eddie Cantor's master stroke.[30] Using his coast-to-coast radio show, Cantor asked listeners to send their dimes directly to the White House. Two days after the appeal, the results seemed disastrous. A White House aide complained to the March of Dimes committee, "You fellows have ruined the President; all we've got is $1,700.50. The reporters are asking us how much we've got. We're telling them we haven't had time to count it." Over the next days, however, more than two hundred thousand letters arrived and the message from the White House changed dramatically: "The White House was buried under an avalanche of mail. The White House mail chief reported, 'The government of the United States darn near stopped functioning.'" This initiative, providing the financial base of the National Foundation for Infantile Paralysis, launched what eventually proved to be the successful effort to discover a polio vaccine.[31] The work of Dr. Jonas Salk, who produced the killed virus injected vaccine, and of Dr. Albert Sabin, who developed the live virus oral vaccine, was entirely funded by the March of Dimes.[32]

Parent-Initiated Childhood Disability Organizations

In 1958, with polio having virtually disappeared in the United States, the March of Dimes took on a new challenge: confronting the complex array of childhood disabilities known as birth defects.[33] Although the 1937–1958 March of Dimes predated the other organizations that served children with specific disabilities, it was an anomaly, for it was not parent-initiated.[34] Furthermore, the development of the polio vaccine, the extraordinary achievement of this March of Dimes—a concerted effort of government, volunteers, and scientists to find a means of preventing polio—has not served as a paradigm for coping with other childhood conditions that still exist. Unlike polio, which is caused by three specific viruses, many of the other childhood disabilities—such as muscular dystrophy, spina bifida, Down syndrome, and cerebral palsy—are congenital ailments that occur for a great variety of reasons.

Like many other groups of its kind, United Cerebral Palsy (UCP) was begun by parents of children with cerebral palsy who advertised in a local newspaper, seeking other parents in similar situations.[35] UCP's original purpose was to make physicians aware of the inadequacy of services for children with disabilities. The first UCP, originating in New York City as a result of an advertisement placed in the *New York Herald Tribune* in March 1946, was a model for the many UCPs formed in numerous cities throughout the country. By 1949, all the UCPs had joined together into one national entity, the United Cerebral Palsy Association.

Today, local UCPs provide direct services to children and adults with cerebral palsy and their families, including evaluation and treatment, parent counseling and family support programs, residences and camps, day treatment and workshops, and career development and advocacy. National UCP deals with advocacy on the federal, state, and local levels, promoting legislation and programs that benefit people with cerebral palsy and other disabilities. The UCP Research and Educational Foundation conducts research on the causes and prevention of cerebral palsy as well as on improving the motor functions of people with cerebral palsy.

Another example of a parent group, the New York Association for Help of Retarded Children (AHRC), was founded in 1949 by Ann Greenberg, the mother of a child with Down syndrome, who placed advertisements in the *New York Post* in an effort to find parents who shared her concerns. In 1951, Ida Rappaport, formerly of AHRC, formed her own organization, Association of Children with Retarded Mental Development (ACRMD) because of a policy disagreement with Ann Greenberg. Perhaps because of her own son's condition, Greenberg wanted to devote the energies of her organization primarily to those with profound developmental disabilities, while Rappaport chose to focus on those, like her child, with moderate developmental disabilities.

During the 1950s, parents and a few others, in particular Gunnar Dybwad of ARC, the Association of Retarded Citizens (now known as The Arc), organized in 1950 by a group of parents and friends of people with delayed development, "began to liberate people confined in . . . custodial institutions."[36] These activists learned more than anyone had known before about the abilities and potential of people with developmental disabilities when they are treated as full human beings. Although ARC was initiated mainly by parents, the acronym acquired new meanings as people with developmental disabilities became increasingly involved with the organization. For example, the former Tulsa ARC is now known as Tulsa Advocates for the Rights of Citizens with Developmental Disabilities.

The National Easter Seal Society was formed in 1922 in Elyria, Ohio, by Edgar F. Allen after his teenage son and fifteen others were killed in a streetcar accident.[37] Realizing that all of the sixteen who died might have been saved if a hospital had been located near the accident, Allen first founded a hospital and later spearheaded a drive to create a medical facility for children with disabilities. Allen was strongly influenced by his own survey indicating that many children with mobility impairments were hidden away by their parents, who feared detection could result in their children's

institutionalization. Yet, these children ur-
gently needed medical and educational services. Joining with Rotary Clubs and other
volunteers, Allen organized the National
Society for Crippled Children, later known
as the National Easter Seal Society, which
became the prototype for state programs established after the 1935 Social Security Act.

Although originally serving as a national
clearinghouse for disability information, by
1929 the National Easter Seal Society developed a separate international organization. Renamed Rehabilitation International
in 1972, this arm of the society provides
for dissemination of information and exchange of ideas in many parts of the world.
Modeling its funding campaign after the
Christmas Seal effort to combat first tuberculosis, and then respiratory illnesses,
the National Easter Seal Society, reflecting middle-American values, has remained
more compatible with small-town church
groups than with cosmopolitan urban centers.[38] While maintaining a presence in each
state in the union, the National Easter
Seal Society has continued projects from
speech therapy to elimination of physical barriers for people with motor impairments.[39] Extending his mission to include
adults, Allen demonstrated his farsighted-
ness in the 1920s and 1930s by presenting economic arguments for education and
employment—rather than charity—for people with disabilities so as to allow them to
achieve equality and independence. Because
of its origins, the society has been associated with rehabilitation, housing, transportation, and accessibility for people with
a *variety* of disabilities, especially mobility impairments.

The Poster Child and the Telethon

Except for Easter Seal, organizations that
served people with mobility impairments

tended to focus on a *specific* disability, such
as the 1937–1958 March of Dimes for polio,
the United Cerebral Palsy Association, and
the Muscular Dystrophy Association. These
organizations concentrated on the *cause* of
the disability, not its *effect*. One significant
factor influencing this fragmentation was
that each of these organizations focused on
the search for a cure for, or prevention of,
the particular disability. The success of the
Salk and later Sabin vaccines in preventing
the acute infectious disease of polio seemed
to justify this approach.

Emphasizing children proved to be an
effective way of raising funds. The poster
child was probably inspired by the "exploitation of touching photographs of crippled
children," used as early as 1933 in fund-
raising efforts for Warm Springs, predating
the cleverly-devised and attention-grabbing
March of Dimes campaign (as the funding arm of the polio foundation).[40] This
concept was imitated by other childhood
disability groups, as the child selected for
the year to represent the organization of a
particular disability was always physically
appealing, a symbol of vulnerability evoking sympathy. One unstated, though er-
roneous, message communicated by these
posters was that disability was somehow
limited to children.

Whatever public misconceptions arose
out of the fund-raising strategies employed
by these organizations, the techniques used
in later years by the telethons were far more
blatant and undignified. Real children with
disabilities were paraded across the stage as
objects of pity, while the amount of money
raised was flashed on the television screen.
The implication that somehow this money
would be used to cure these particular children, and children like them, was misleading. For example, a 1993 article reported that
much of the money collected as a result of
the Jerry Lewis Muscular Dystrophy Association Telethon has always gone toward

the cost of the telethon itself.[41] Another use of this money is not widely known: "Much of Jerry's money goes into investigating genetic screening to prevent people with MDA [sic] from even coming into the world. Jerry's kids are people in wheelchairs on television raising money to find a way to prevent their ever having been born."[42]

The public images put forth by the poster children and the telethons negated the reality of adults with disabilities. It is almost amusing to record both the Pollyannaish and macabre assumptions of disabled youngsters who had little awareness of the existence of adults with disabilities. Some thought that all children with disabilities were cured as adults; others thought that they all died before reaching adulthood. Later, adults with disabilities took on the task of questioning their absence from all these public relations strategies. How could children with disabilities mature into productive adults if they had no models? How could adults with disabilities participate in society if they were invisible? Was the money acquired by means of telethons worth the damaging misconceptions? In response to these questions, these adults determined that the principal need of children with disabilities is not the services to which telethons contribute, but rather a civil rights movement diminishing "society's role in handicapping disabled people."[43]

Changing Views of Disability in the United States

Such a widespread movement was inconceivable until the 1960s, considering the legacy of segregation of people with disabilities that dates back to the Thirteen Colonies:

> Disabled individuals were prohibited from settling in the towns and villages of

our Thirteen Colonies unless they could demonstrate ability to support themselves independently.... Immigration policy effectively forbade entrance into the country of persons with physical, mental, or emotional disabilities. Because popular perceptions equated disability with inability [within the colonies and later the states], existence of a disability appeared reason enough to deny a person the right to participate in societal life. Within families, persons with disabilities were hidden, disowned, or even allowed to die through the withholding of life-support services. Within disabled individuals, self-perception inevitably reflected prevailing social attitudes, keeping people from even attempting to become self-reliant.[44]

With an expanding U.S. population, pressure mounted first for institutionalization, and later rehabilitation, of people with disabilities. In the early decades of the twentieth century, however, the work of writer and social critic Randolph Bourne—who had "a highly visible [physical] disability" that "involved little functional impairment"—was described by the renowned poet, Amy Lowell, with this caustic remark: "His writing shows he is a cripple. Deformed body, deformed mind."[45] When Bourne related his experience as a person with a disability, especially in his "often quoted and so little understood" essay entitled "The Handicapped," he placed "his psychological struggle to achieve 'self-respect'... within the context of a society that [devalued] him because of his disability. From the stigmatized social condition that had isolated him as an adolescent and had kept him unemployed as an adult, he knew of 'no particular way of escape.'"

Longmore notes why Bourne's story is so significant: "When devaluation and discrimination happen to one person, it is biography, but when, in all probability, similar experiences happen to millions, it is social history." Like Longmore, sociologist Irving Zola points out the necessity for a recorded history of people with disabilities:

> The reason that people with disabilities are often thought to have had no history is really that they've had no recorded history. Only recently have there been any histories of disability. It's been partly because society has denied that there was anything important to be learned. It was partly because, as with any minority group, the people were so of the Other that they were never given any of the tools to record any aspects of their history: "history" would be, supposedly, only one of successes, of the heroes of the society, not those who had difficulty, in some ways, fitting in. So, people with disabilities have followed the paths of people with color, and women, of trying to reclaim what has long been lost.[46]

The early twentieth century, the period in which Bourne lived, was "an era when prejudice and discrimination against disabled people seemed to have been intensifying sharply":

> If in New York City he [Bourne] was rejected as a luncheon guest because of his "unsightliness," in Chicago he might have been arrested for showing up at all. A [1911] city ordinance [repealed in 1974] warned: "No person who is diseased, maimed, mutilated, or in any way deformed so as to be an unsightly or disgusting object or improper person to be allowed in or on the public ways or other public places in this city, shall therein or thereon expose himself to public view."

Bourne's opportunity to get an education was unusual, for most children with disabilities were treated more like the boy with cerebral palsy who, in 1919, was expelled from public school in Wisconsin, despite his ability to keep up with the class academically, because "the teachers and other children found him 'depressing and nauseating.'" In fact, "segregation and sterilization of deaf people, blind people, people with developmental disabilities, even people like Bourne who had tuberculosis" was

proposed by eugenicists and professionals who dealt with people with disabilities:

> In 1912, the eugenic section of the American Breeders' Association, later renamed the American Genetics Association, drafted a model sterilization law to be applied to these "socially unfit" classes. By the beginning of World War I, sixteen states had adopted sterilization statutes. A few eugenicists even advocated the mercy killing of individuals with epilepsy or mental handicaps, especially those who were mildly mentally retarded.

The eventual recognition that people with disabilities are not only capable of participating in the workforce, but also entitled to benefits, was expressed by changes in laws, such as the 1918 rehabilitation legislation:

> From the beginning [of the nation], institutions for mentally and emotionally impaired persons were custodial rather than educational. Persons with sensory and physical disabilities were more likely to be taught at least fundamental academic material, but instruction was less to prepare these individuals for vocations than to satisfy religious and societal expectations and to resolve ethical concerns.... It was not until large numbers of veterans returned from the First World War, however, that any Federal initiative [training and employing veterans with disabilities] emerged.[47]

The 1935 Social Security Act establishing "old age and survivors benefits, unemployment compensation, and programs for disabled youth and adults" reflected the realization "that assistance to disabled individuals was as much a matter of social justice as charity."[48]

During World War II defense plants desperately needed workers, so "government propaganda urged employers to get past their prejudices" against people with disabilities as is evident in this war film monologue:

> Sure enough, blind. But they can do it as well as anybody, and they volunteered, releasing

workers with eyes for other duties.... All through the factory now you may glimpse things like this, an unobtrusive limp that means only one good leg. Or like this, of course you really don't need more than one arm for this job.... Maybe a man might be a better worker without his hearing with all this noise. But the point is, whereas, industry started out to make it possible for these physically handicapped people to help themselves, now it ends up that these handicapped people are helping their country.[49]

Of course, like Rosie the Riveter employees with disabilities lost their jobs after the war to make room for the returning soldiers. She was sent back to the kitchen while people with disabilities were once again considered unemployable.

Furthermore, because government still failed to provide many of the supports required by people with disabilities, private agencies developed, each serving individuals with specific impairments. Most of the service-provider disability organizations for people with motor impairments, however, did not recognize the common requirements of their clients—a barrier-free environment and wheelchair-accessible transportation. By the 1970s, people from different disability groups began to realize that working together would be more beneficial for everyone than working separately or competitively. Consequently, a new concept emerged: the idea of disability as a social and political force. What perhaps was revolutionary was what underlay this new awareness. The predominant issues for blind people—literacy—and for deaf people—language—had primarily involved changes in *people with disabilities*. However, the creation of universally accessible surroundings necessitated a redesigning of society for *everyone*.

Chapter Two

Seeing by Touch, Hearing by Sign

SINCE BLIND PEOPLE HAD access to spoken language, they needed a tactile alphabet, such as Louis Braille's 1829 elegant raised dot method for reading and writing. Following the logic of English grammar and word order, the Braille system served to integrate blind people into the larger society. On the other hand, deaf people required a visual syntax, necessitating a form of communication that tended to separate them from the hearing world. Integration for deaf people has required them to concentrate on speaking and lip-reading, which too often have been Herculean tasks requiring effort that they could have more productively spent on acquiring sign language—the key to their ability to learn and to communicate.

Blindness and Deafness: A Comparison

Blind people, like those with other disabilities, have had to prove their *capability;* deaf people have had to prove their *humanity.* In *Seeing Voices,* Oliver Sacks suggests that the common assumption that deafness is less problematic than blindness may be mistaken:

Whether deafness is "preferable" to blindness, if acquired in later life, is arguable; but to be born deaf is infinitely more serious than to be born blind—at least potentially so. For the prelingually deaf, unable to hear their parents, risk being severely retarded, if not permanently defective, in their grasp of language unless early and effective measures are taken. And to be defective in language, for a human being, is one of the most desperate of calamities, for it is only through language that we enter fully into our human estate and culture, communicate freely with our fellows, acquire and share information. If we cannot do this, we will be bizarrely disabled and cut off—whatever our desires, or endeavors, or native capacities. And indeed, we may be so little able to realize our intellectual capacities as to appear mentally defective.[1]

Under Roman law, deaf people were treated as though they were "retarded"; they "were generally outcasts, considered uneducated and ineducable, and outside the privileges and obligations of the law."[2] In modern times, because of the obstacles to communication between the hearing world and the deaf, the phrase "deaf and dumb," in which "dumb" originally meant simply the inability to speak, came to mean deaf and stupid.[3] In mid-sixteenth century Spain most deaf people were deprived of their birthright, their legacy.[4] In order to circumvent the legal hurdles, a Spanish priest, Pedro Ponce de Leon, devised oralism, a means of teaching deaf nobility the capacity to approximate speech well enough to satisfy the requirements of inheritance law. Ironically, oralism would become "the grand tragedy against which modern 'Deaf' culture [not to be confused with 'deafness' as disability] has constructed itself."[5]

Oralism is available to only a small percentage of those who are profoundly deaf, most often the postlingually deaf. Generally, people who are hard-of-hearing use speech while those who are profoundly deaf use sign language. Since the ability to speak was traditionally a source of political influence in the deaf community, those who used sign language were disadvantaged. The 1988 uprising at Gallaudet University, the world's only institution of higher education for people who are deaf or hard-of-hearing, signaled a change. After the protest, deaf advocacy was no longer solely a province of the oral deaf. Being a deaf child of deaf parents, relying on American Sign Language, gained currency in the new radical deaf community.

In contrast, blind people have long held leadership roles in organizations for the blind, such as the American Foundation for the Blind (AFB) founded in 1921.[6] Robert Benjamin Irwin, the first full-time executive director of AFB (from 1929 to 1948), was blind from the age of five, supported himself through college and graduate school, and strongly advocated integration of blind people in all aspects of life, including education and employment.[7] Partially sighted at birth and blind by the age of twenty-three, Henry Latimer, executive secretary of the Pennsylvania Association for the Blind, made the following incisive remark in his speech nominating Irwin for his new role at AFB:

In the event that Mr. Irwin's physical blindness is offered as an obstacle to the proper exercise of the duties of this office, I submit that such an objection, in light of his manifest ability and success, is wholly unworthy of consideration by those who, like ourselves, are constantly teaching, preaching and professing to believe in the capabilities of blind people.

Leadership in organizations for deaf people dramatically differed from leadership in organizations for blind people, especially after the 1880 Congress of Milan.[8] A victory for the oralists, this congress of educators of deaf people, where deaf teachers were excluded from voting, banned the use of sign language in schools. Notables such as Alexander Graham Bell, Samuel Gridley Howe, and even the "patron saint of progressive education," Horace Mann,[9] spearheaded the oral movement in the United States. The result of their efforts was to make deaf and dumb—signifying mental deficiency, as well as inability to speak—a self-fulfilling prophecy. Approximately one hundred years of oral education for deaf children resulted in a large alienated, illiterate, and powerless deaf population, one that had internalized the negative self-image the educational system had imposed on them. Therefore, it is not surprising that deaf people did not insist on gaining leadership roles in organizations that served them until the 1980s.

Sign Language and Oralism

Advocates of oralism did not recognize that in prohibiting deaf children's use of sign language, they were depriving these learners of their inherent biological adaptive mechanisms for communication. For the hearing world, the channel of communication is "mouth-to-ear"; for the deaf, the channel is "manual and facial gestures" to eye.[10] A few unusual deaf children may eventually learn "spoken" English by a combination of lip-reading and partial hearing capacity. Most prelingually deaf children lacking accessibility to sign language, however, will attain no, or limited, language ability. On the other hand, Nora Ellen Groce's *Everyone Here Spoke Sign Language: Hereditary Deafness on Martha's Vineyard* demonstrated how deaf people can blend successfully with the rest of the community, even achieve distinction, when the sign language for which they have a natural predilection is regarded as any other language and allowed to flourish.[11] Because of the high incidence of deafness on Martha's Vineyard, one in four by the mid-nineteenth century, "the entire community learned Sign, and there was free and complete intercourse between the hearing and the deaf. Indeed the deaf were scarcely seen as 'deaf,' and certainly not seen as at all 'handicapped.'"[12]

Two factors reveal how the oral educators were inadvertently creating a functional form of retardation in individuals whose potential, had they been encouraged to acquire a first language—Sign—will never be known. First, there is a specific and early time frame—"up to the age of six,... steadily compromised from then until shortly after puberty"—for language acquisition on the human maturation clock.[13] Once the critical period has passed without the proper stimulation, language learning is usually impaired forever. Second, inhibiting rather than fostering language, as the oralists were heedlessly doing by barring Sign, frequently results in the failure of children to develop cognitive skills completely.

If the cognitive scientists who describe language as a "mental organ" are correct, then language is not a "cultural artifact" but a "biological birthright," an instinct as organically linked to being human as web-spinning is to being a spider.[14] Thus, when the educators at the Congress of Mi-

lan sought to impose "spoken" language on deaf children, they were tampering, unwittingly, with the composition of the learners' brains. Moreover, these educators of deaf children were violating the deaf community's particular expression of what modern linguists call the "Universal Grammar"—that innate plan natural to all evolving languages. Supporting the concept of a Universal Grammar, researchers have found that very young deaf children from different cultures use gesture in similar ways as they progress from simple to more complex combinations, developing a type of gestural grammar.[15] Even if the intention of the Congress of Milan was to integrate deaf people into the greater community, its method was misguided, for languages, spoken and signed, are not deliberate inventions. They are intricate systems, designs that unconsciously develop as a process, historically, over generations, to suit the biologically distinctive attributes of a group.[16]

The oralism that began in the 1880s was a regressive movement in deaf education. In the 1750s, the abbé de l'Epée realized that in order to teach religion to the impoverished Parisian deaf, he would have to function as if he were a missionary in a foreign land, learning the street sign language of the deaf.[17] Thomas Gallaudet, an American, finding no cooperation in England in his quest for a procedure for teaching language to his neighbor's deaf child, discovered de l'Epée's successful method in Paris.[18] Since Gallaudet neither knew sign language nor had experience as an educator, he persuaded Laurent Clerc, a teacher of deaf students, to accompany him to America to establish a school for the deaf in Hartford, Connecticut, in 1817.[19] Clerc, who was profoundly deaf, was trained at the National Institute for Deaf-Mutes, founded by de l'Epée in Paris.[20] The abandonment of oralism in American deaf education until the 1880 Congress of Milan was propitious, an accidental result of Gallaudet's discouragement by the English oralist educators.

A natural, uniquely North American sign language evolved from the merging of the Parisian sign language with American English. As an indication of the progress being made in the education of the deaf, President Abraham Lincoln signed legislation in 1864 authorizing the seven-year-old Columbia Institution for the Deaf, Dumb, and Blind to confer college degrees with Dr. Edward M. Gallaudet (the son of Thomas H. Gallaudet, founder of the first school for deaf students in the United States) as president of the institution.[21] Although deaf people were attaining success and becoming integrated in the hearing society in the nineteenth century, oralism gained ascendancy in the education of deaf children.[22] The effect was increased segregation of deaf people in socialization and employment, a consequence of reduced educational achievement by deaf students who had been deprived of their natural language.

Although the American delegation at Milan voted against the pure oral method, by 1900 oralism had undermined deaf education in America and rendered many deaf educators unemployed.[23]

> Deaf people were well organized in the mid-nineteenth century, with their own newspapers, clubs, unions, and congresses. But as popular misconceptions of Darwinism and the theories of eugenics spread, social theorists argued that by their "clannish" behavior the deaf were going to marry only each other and produce ever larger numbers of deaf children. (In fact most children of deaf parents can hear.) To break up the deaf communities and integrate deaf people into hearing society, leading educators of the deaf demanded that sign language be suppressed and that the deaf learn to speak. The vigorous objections of deaf people were ignored—how could they know what was best for them?[24]

Oralism took about twenty years to take firm root in the United States because there was a countervailing ethos vigorously supporting the teaching of sign language. The National Association of the Deaf (NAD), originally called the National Convention of Deaf-Mutes, held its first meeting in Cincinnati at about the same time as the Milan Congress.[25] Drafting a constitution and electing a deaf educator, Robert P. McGregor, as its first president, this group of educated and successful deaf people, representing twenty-one states, formed an association that still plays a significant role in deaf politics. Americans, including a professor at the National Deaf-Mute College (later known as Gallaudet College) and the president of NAD, were delegates at the first International Congress of the Deaf, organized in Paris in 1889, one hundred years after de l'Epée's death, in response to the demeaning proscription of sign language.[26]

Frequently alienated from the rest of society because of a communication barrier, deaf people were inclined to form separate clubs where they could socialize with others like themselves. Despite the directive requiring oralism in the schools, in the clubs deaf people used the form of expression that was natural to them, sign language. Although these clubs served an essential purpose—encouraging human interaction, providing required information, and forging deaf consciousness—they tended to isolate generations of deaf people from the world around them. Although most people join homogeneous groups, this proclivity among deaf people has been exacerbated by the demoralizing effects of oralism. Their own language, Sign, and the culture that emanates from their language found expression only clandestinely in the deaf clubs. Because many deaf people incorporated the sense of shame fostered by their oral education, their natural language became a secret burden shared only among themselves. Once a source of private humiliation for a great number of deaf people, sign language only recently is becoming visible in public places.

The great potential of this language, fostered by new technology, is evident in the growing academic interest in Sign:

> With its usual kinetic visual mode, sign presents an artistic form that is at once ancient in its oral (nonwritten) tradition and postmodern in its exploration of visual media. ASL [American Sign Language] literature provides a unique *postmodern bardic tradition*. The stories, poetry, and folkloric language games of the Deaf have been passed on for years by "sign of hand" (as in "word of mouth"). But, as oral traditions may be recorded and preserved, so ASL may now be produced and reproduced in mass quantity thanks to the development of video technology. While the impact of visual technology on ASL literature is analogous to the impact of the printing press on written literature, it may be too early to discern the implications of that technology. At the very least, video has enabled the works of leading Deaf poets and storytellers to become nationally recognized and analyzed.[27]

Many deaf people before the 1980s were limited because of misconceptions about their language and their learning potential. On Martha's Vineyard or an isolated village in the Yucatan or in other locations, when sign language, carrying no stigma, was treated as different but equal to spoken language, deafness was not a drawback.[28] However, most people do not live in environments as inclusive as these. At best, even when deaf people are integrated in a community, they operate in a language different from the majority. Blind people functioning in the same language as the rest of society did not have the kind of obstacles that deaf people had to overcome. Yet, until the introduction of touch systems for written language, blind people had limited access to reading and writing.

Braille and Talking Books

Just as deaf people gravitated to sign language before educators recognized its value, blind students at the Missouri School for the Blind embraced Braille in 1854 before it was accepted by their teachers.[29] At last, a touch system was available that enabled blind people to write as well as read, for other touch systems made only reading possible. Because of the simplicity of Braille, blind people could use their fingers to read and a stylus to write.

In 1829, Louis Braille, a young blind teacher and former student at the Royal Institute for Blind Children in Paris, published his modification of Charles Barbier's technique.[30] Barbier's phonetic scheme consisted of twelve-unit cells, while Braille's alphabetic method consisted of six-unit cells. An officer in the Napoleonic Army, Barbier created his raised-dot secret military code for night writing, employing a hinged frame for holding paper and a pointed implement for punching dots. When Barbier demonstrated his invention at the institute where Braille was working, the young educator recognized not only the value for blind people of an embossed dot code for reading, but also of a frame and stylus for writing.

Braille's legacy to blind people has been both his appreciation of the requirement for an easy tactile formulation—combining the features necessary for reading and writing—and his skill in devising such a methodology.[31] Since each Braille six-unit cell has sixty-three potential combinations, it is possible to have a specific combination for each of the letters of the alphabet and the individual marks of punctuation, as well as for frequently used words. Braille's design is so versatile that the arrangement can be applied not only to language, but also to any ordered sequence, such as musical notation, the periodic chemical table, or mathematical systems.

Despite France's official recognition of Braille in 1854, it took England until 1905 and the United States until 1932 to formally accept a uniform version of Braille as the medium for reading and writing for blind people.[32] Invented in 1890 by Frank Hall, the Braillewriter—a six-keyed Braille typewriter in which each letter is a combination of keys similar to a musical chord—eventually helped promote standardization of Braille.[33] Yet, the United States required a long time to adopt a consistent Braille code because different schools and different localities employed diverse touch systems, as well as variations on Braille's original method. In the "war of the dots"—this competition between these incompatible schemes—blind people were the losers, for they could read only the limited number of books published in the particular code that they knew.[34] A nationally accepted Braille system, the natural key to literacy for blind people,[35] was comparable to an established sign language, the natural means to cognition and communication for deaf people.

While Braille gives blind people access to only a limited number of books, Thomas Edison's 1877 invention of the phonograph augmented the books available to blind people by utilizing recorded texts, which by 1934 under the auspices of the American Foundation for the Blind evolved into "talking books."[36] Unlike most technological advances, long playing (LP) records were used by blind people before they were used by the general public, for talking books preceded commercial LPs by fourteen years. People with voices appropriate for selected recordings, many of whom were famous actors, offered their services despite the small remuneration.

In order to make the potentiality of talking books a reality, the American Foundation for the Blind (AFB) hired an electrical engineer to develop inexpensive, durable records and playback machines, usable by blind people. Besides convincing Congress to appropriate funds for talking books, the AFB also contended with the copyright protection of writers and speakers by restricting the equipment to blind people. Responding to Helen Keller's request, FDR issued a 1935 executive order allowing the Works Progress Administration to manufacture playback machines.[37] By lowering the cost of the machines, the President's decree made them obtainable by an increasing number of blind people. More suitable than Braille for certain publications, talking books expanded learning possibilities for blind people. Years later talking books would become valuable not only to blind people, but also to people with a variety of other impairments, such as certain learning or motor disabilities.

Sheltered Workshops

The effort to make deaf people function as if they were *not* deaf was evident in the oralist movement. It was assumed for blind people, however, that accommodations *had* to be made. Considered able to travel independently and capable of performing menial tasks, deaf people were employed more often than blind people. Separate occupation-oriented facilities that employ people with disabilities, known as "sheltered workshops," were created for blind workers since they were regarded as unemployable in the general workforce.

An outgrowth of the work departments located in special residential schools for blind children, sheltered workshops prepared graduates, as well as newly-blinded adults, to earn a living. In 1840, Samuel Gridley Howe founded the work department at the Perkins Institution in Massachusetts, a facility that became the model for the sheltered workshop.[38] Howe's intention was to foster a sense of self-respect and self-reliance in the blind workers, not to provide profit for the institution. Yet critics argue that the workshops were basically flawed, for they did not encourage integration of their workers into the general workforce, and, in slack times, they retained only their best employees. Furthermore, some workshops exploited their workers, too often paying them far less than minimum wage and offering no fringe benefits.

The Lighthouse

Winifred Holt Mather, the founder of the Lighthouse movement, quoted a French commanding officer addressing soldiers blinded in battle during World War I: "The greatest menace to the blind is the short-sightedness of the seeing."[39] This aphorism expressed the prophetic vision that led Mather to recognize as early as 1904 the possibility for and significance of independence for blind people. Well-traveled and fluent in four languages, she was instrumental in establishing Lighthouses offering services to blind people in such places as New York, Paris, Bordeaux, Rome, Calcutta, Canton, Osaka, Kyoto, and Cuba.[40]

Her progressive notion of a movement for blind people, in a context not confined by national limits, anticipated the international movement for people with disabilities that would not receive prominence until the 1980s. Despite being reprimanded for immodesty and arrogance by representatives of the public and the medical profession for not appreciating her supposed limitations as a woman and a nonprofessional, she persevered in her efforts to prevent blindness, to provide services and training for blind people, and to encourage their integration into the outside world. Decrying the error of institutionalizing blind people, she realized that their inclusion in the wider society would serve not only them, but also the communities that would have the wisdom to accept them.

Mobility for Blind People: Guide Dogs and White Canes

For blind people, unlike deaf people, mobility was the key to independence, the opportunity "to forgo the comfort of sheltered lives and move out into the bustling traffic of their sighted peers."[41] Blind people seem to have always used staffs and animals, especially dogs, as guides. Prior to World War I, however, American leaders in the blind community, because of their effort to make blindness unobtrusive, exhibited a lack of enthusiasm for the guide dog movement.[42] After World War I, dogs were used as guides in Germany, first for soldiers blinded in the war, then for blind civilians. The 1926 visit of wealthy Philadelphia socialite Dorothy Harrison Eustis to a German school where guide dogs were trained inspired her 1927 *Saturday Evening Post* article that caught the attention of young and recently-blinded Morris Frank. Following his trips throughout the country, where he demonstrated the independence that guide dogs accord blind people, Frank joined Eustis in 1929 in establishing the first United States guide dog training school, Seeing Eye.

By tapping their staffs as they walked, blind people were able to signal others regarding their presence and also generate echoes providing necessary information about their surroundings.[43] The replacement of clattering horses' hooves and noisy iron wheels by high-speed, quiet, rubber-tired automobiles required that blind people use the clearly visible, red-tipped white cane. With support from the Lions Club of Peoria, Illinois, in 1930, a city ordinance was enacted mandating that motorists yield the right-of-way to people who presented themselves as blind by displaying their white canes.[44] After this so-called White Cane Law was passed in 1931, Lions Clubs throughout the nation worked effectively toward the passage of similar laws in other states. Spurred by the accidental death of Thomas D. Schall, the blind Minnesota senator who was fatally injured by a car in 1935, the AFB advocated for the white cane movement and also offered canes at wholesale prices.

By the 1960s, mobility instruction—a specialized discipline for teaching blind people how to use the cane as a mobility tool—had become a formal profession. Although the pencil-tipped cane, tapped from side to side by the blind traveler, has been the traditional mobility device used by blind people, since the late 1980s a small but growing percentage of this population has been successfully introduced to the constant-contact rolling-tip cane.[45] The rolling-tip cane is less likely to get stuck and offers more information about the surface of the ground than the traditional cane.

Jacobus tenBroek and the National Federation of the Blind

The increased mobility and independence that blind people experienced with the use of dogs and canes expanded their educational and vocational opportunities, as well as enabled them to organize to promote their economic well-being. Although the 1942 annual convention of the National Federation of the Blind (NFB) dealt with employment problems—including exploitation of blind workers in sheltered workshops—the original focus of the organization was Social Security benefits for blind people.[46] Founded in November 1940 in Wilkes-Barre, Pennsylvania, by Jacobus tenBroek, NFB, in its first convention, called for a national pension for blind people, without means testing, as part of the Social Security Act.[47] In his 1944 address, tenBroek

explained "that we oppose a system of relief which insists upon the means test, budgeting, individual need individually determined, and large social worker discretion, which in our experience have been veritable instruments of oppression."[48]

TenBroek described NFB as comparable to the American Federation of Labor: "Because we [NFB] are trying to do for our people what organized labor is trying to do for its people, because of the similarity in organizational structure, in purpose and in work, and because of the laboring man's inherent sympathy for the underprivileged and the conditions under which they live, organized labor has responded more than generously, materially, morally, and with political support." Without the right to organize, however, workers in sheltered workshops still have neither the protection of minimum wage laws nor unemployment compensation. Although many of these workers could function in a competitive environment, they are trapped in workplaces devoid of opportunity or hope because of discrimination rather than lack of ability.

Though most civil service examinations were not open to blind candidates until the early 1960s, NFB, from its inception, opposed exclusion of blind people from civil service employment. The members of the late 1930s League of the Physically Handicapped fought for their inclusion in the civil service workforce at a time when people with even minor disabilities were relegated to either dependence on family or work in segregated shops. However successful they were in their ambitious endeavor, their goal was limited and once achieved, the League of the Physically Handicapped disbanded. On the other hand, NFB, perceiving its struggle in a civil rights context before the 1960s civil rights movement, is still a vital organization working for social change.

Some of tenBroek's goals anticipated specific objectives articulated by disability activists three decades later. He exhorted his audience to strive for legislation amending the Civil Service Act of the United States so that discrimination on account of blindness would be prohibited. He called blind people's "demand for equality" one of the "fundamental principles underlying our [NFB's] program and guiding our activities . . . because it is not based upon any notion that all men are physically or mentally equal, but that they have an equal right to insist upon opportunities for which they are properly qualified."

Differentiating NFB from the agencies purporting to serve the blind, tenBroek announced that "the National Federation of the Blind is not an organization speaking for the blind; it is the blind speaking for themselves." Although the 1957 Kennedy-Baring Bill, ensuring blind workers the right to organize and bargain collectively in the workshops without intimidation, was unsuccessful, the publicity surrounding the failed legislation brought NFB national recognition.[49] The January 11, 1958, issue of *The New Yorker* presented a favorable profile of President tenBroek as a representative of the movement he was leading:

> Most of the country's three hundred and twenty-five thousand blind people who work are employed in the special sheltered shops that society—with the best and most charitable intentions—has set up for us, where we can make baskets and such, and come to no harm. Only about two or three percent of us are holding normal jobs out in the world. My organization is convinced [that] at least twenty times that many could be doing so if they had the chance. What we seek for the blind is the right to compete on equal terms. . . . Actually, I can't say what the limits are. Every time I think I have hit on some job that a blind man couldn't conceivably hold, I find a blind man holding it.[50]

TenBroek did not minimize the problems inherent in blindness, however, or romanti-

cize the special powers supposedly engendered by blindness. Recognizing the effort necessary to deal with the loss of a vital sense, he focused on the determination and tenacity required to compensate. In an attempt to demystify blindness, he described it as "nothing more or less than the loss of one of the five senses and a corresponding greater reliance upon the four that remain— as well as upon the brain, the heart, and the spirit."[51] Echoing a phrase used by tenBroek, Kenneth Jernigan, who succeeded the first NFB president in the late 1960s,[52] argued in a speech entitled "Blindness— Handicap or Characteristic" that "blindness is *only* a characteristic . . . *nothing more or less* than that."[53] Although appearing to be an affirmation of tenBroek's position, Jernigan's assertion represented a conceptual leap. Rami Rabby, an NFB officer, indicated that Jernigan meant that blindness would be only a characteristic and not a disability if blind people were properly trained and social attitudes were appropriately modified.[54] Yet the New York City subway gate issue of the 1970s and 1980s revealed the implications of Jernigan's approach.

NYC Subway Gates: A Controversy in the Blind Community

When the New York City chapter of the American Council of the Blind (ACB) sued the Metropolitan Transportation Authority (MTA) in 1983 for the 1970 purchase of subway cars, the R-44 and R-46, which lacked gates protecting people from falling onto the tracks, NFB objected. When blind riders use the subway, they tap their canes along the side of the train until they reach the entrance door. Without these gates, blind passengers easily can mistake the space between the cars for the subway door and, as a result, fall onto the tracks. NFB's rationale for taking issue with ACB's legal action was based on the assumption that since blindness is only a characteristic, a properly trained blind person had no need for special accommodation. ACB and NFB have not hesitated to take contrary positions publicly; in fact, ACB was born in 1961 out of an internal conflict in NFB.

Though several blind people who were seasoned travelers were killed or maimed because there were no gates between the subway cars, NFB firmly maintained its position. In 1970 a blind woman fell from the subway platform into the space between the ends of the cars and onto the tracks. When the train moved on, she lost both her legs and an arm. Another tragedy concerned a blind newsdealer who had been a subway user for thirteen years. In 1974, he walked from the subway platform into what he thought was the door opening of the subway car. Amidst screaming fellow passengers, he fell between two subway cars onto the tracks. The engineer, unaware, moved on, killing the man. ACB sought an effective response to these tragedies, even taking to the streets in a July 1974 demonstration.

In the early 1980s, ACB organized Concerned Citizens for Subway Safety, a coalition of provider and consumer groups of blind and partially-sighted people determined to get the MTA to take action to prevent people from falling onto the subway tracks. When the former director of the Blind Veterans Association, David Schnair, fell between two cars onto the tracks, he was saved from serious injury or death by a bystander. As a consequence of the unemployed bystander's actions, he not only acquired a job but also received a congratulatory call from President Reagan. This kind of rescue, however, was an exception. A week later, on December 27, 1982, a well-known and well-liked employee of the Lighthouse, Bert Zimmerman, was killed by a moving train after he fell onto the subway tracks. Dorothy Matano, president of ACB, noted that "Bert was an experienced and able traveler who used the subway for many years. These death traps for the blind cover twenty percent of the subway system."[55] On January 26, 1983, a second demonstration was called by ACB in front of the MTA office in order to focus public attention on the MTA's criminal negligence. Groups representing people with a variety of disabilities endorsed the demonstration, and over two hundred individuals participated in the protest.

Reluctant to take legal action until this last accident, Concerned Citizens for Subway Safety finally became persuaded that only the threat of a lawsuit by ACB would compel the bureaucratic MTA to take the steps necessary to make the R-44 and R-46 subway cars safe for blind passengers. While the private law firm—LeBoeuf, Lamb, Greene & MacRae—representing ACB pro bono was negotiating with the MTA in order to acquire the protective gates, NFB's Rabby appeared on a television news program insisting that blind people did not need gates to use the subway system safely. Rabby's argument was that subway gates, which were actually for the protection of all passengers, were considered as serving the needs of *only* blind passengers. Rabby feared that the public's assumption that blind people required special treatment would adversely affect their participation in society—for example, in employment, housing, and transportation. The conflict between the two major national organizations *of* blind people left policymakers bewildered. ACB won its Section 504 of the Rehabilitation Act of 1973 lawsuit against the MTA in 1985, as the U.S. District Court in New York considered the lack of subway gates to be discriminatory against blind people.

NFB: Trailblazer for Sections 504 and 501

Although the president of NFB tends to determine the organization's general principles and specific agenda, NFB president Kenneth Jernigan's lack of enthusiasm for coalition did not preclude NFB from using its unique lobbying capability to support Sections 504 and 501 of the Rehabilitation Act of 1973—the first federal civil rights law and affirmative action law, respectively, for people with disabilities. When John Nagle, director of NFB's Washington office, testified on January 10, 1973, before the Senate Subcommittee on the Handicapped of the Committee on Labor and Public Welfare on the proposed Rehabilitation Act, he was the only witness to comment specifically on Section 504. Demonstrating his recognition of the potential significance of Section 504 before most other representatives of disability groups did, and transcending the NFB's traditional position focusing on the rights of the blind, Nagle manifested his solidarity with all people with disabilities: "The provision [Section 504] . . . is of major consequence to all disabled people. . . . It establishes that because a man is blind or deaf or without legs, he is not less a citizen, that his rights of citizenship are not revoked or diminished because he is disabled."[56] Moreover, Nagle indicated his early appreciation of the legal ramifications of Section 504: "It gives him [a person with a disability] a legal basis for recourse to the courts that he may seek to remove needless barriers, unnecessary obstacles and unjustified barricades that impede or prevent him from functioning fully and in full equality with all others."

As a significant force in NFB, Rabby used Section 501 of the Rehabilitation Act of 1973 and the support of his organization to become the first blind diplomat in the Foreign Service of the State Department.[57] After repeatedly passing the required Foreign Service examination, each time with a higher grade, Rabby was judged "noncompetitive" in 1987 because of his "serious lack of visual acuity." When disability attorney Tim Cook, disabled as a result of polio, saw Rabby on "Good Morning America" debating George Vest, director general of the Foreign Service, on the feasibility of a blind person serving in the job Rabby was seeking, Cook offered to represent Rabby in a Section 501 lawsuit. At Minnesota Congressman Jerry Sikorski's congressional hearing on this issue, the room was stacked with about two hundred members of NFB. "Anyone who walked into this buzz saw could see that the disability discrimination of the Foreign Service was about to end," Rabby notes as he recalls his difference with the State Department:

> They argued that a Foreign Service Officer is expected, for example, to be able to go anywhere the Service decides. It's called "the principle of worldwide availability." Since I'm blind, there may well be places I can't go. But there are places that sighted people can't go also because of their language limitations, the needs of their families, and so on. Discrimination takes a form of employers applying unrealistically demanding standards that they would like to apply to everyone, but apply only to the person with a disability. A year or two after I filed my successful lawsuit, Edward Perkins, an African American, replaced Vest and changed the discriminatory policy of the Service against women, minorities, and people with disabilities.

The approach of both Nagle and Rabby was an anomaly for NFB because the organization tends to focus *solely* on issues related to blindness. Still, NFB, the most significant civilian disability rights group until the early 1970s, exhibited its understanding, from the 1940s, of two characteristics of the modern disability rights movement. First, not only did NFB's struggle concern *equality* for blind people, but second, equality could be achieved only if blind people *advocated for themselves*. However, with few exceptions, the third characteristic, the concept of *coalition* with different disability groups, has been antithetical to the spirit of NFB since Jernigan's emergence as its leader. While Jernigan feared that blind people lose political clout when they affiliate with other disability groups, ACB has always supported coalition.

NFB and ACB: Different Approaches to Blindness

NFB and ACB offer different reasons for the emergence of the dissident NFB faction that eventually became ACB in mid-1957. NFB claims that the new faction was a puppet of nonprofit and government service agencies, many of which benefited from the same workshops that NFB sought to reform by organizing the workers. According to NFB, when dissenters lost elections held from 1957 to 1960, they decided to form their own opposing group, ACB. On the other hand, ACB contends that the split emanated from NFB's authoritarian leadership and undemocratic policies, resulting in the national organization's arbitrary expulsion of four NFB state delegations, as well as the dismissal of several high-ranking NFB officials.

Even more than twenty years later, issues continue to divide ACB and NFB. For example, NFB fiercely defends the right of blind passengers to sit in emergency evacuation seats on airplanes and to keep their long canes at their seats rather than in baggage compartments. Often using folding long canes, ACB members do not consider either of these matters to be of paramount concern. Another issue that aggravates the rift between the two groups involves "detectable warning strips," truncated domes joined together in a long narrow ground

cover several feet wide at the edge of subway and train platforms.[58] While ACB argues that these strips prevent blind people from falling onto the tracks, NFB claims that properly trained blind people do not need this special accommodation.

ACB's Karen Luxton Gourgey, formerly a member of NFB, considers what she calls NFB's "tyrannical" position on warning strips "an expression of self-hatred," a refusal to allow blind people "a margin for error."[59] Crediting NFB with having "political savvy, good Washington connections, as well as admirable membership drives and fundraising strategies," Gourgey nonetheless judges the organization's approach, since Jernigan's leadership, as "a betrayal of the original NFB vision: It's okay to be what you are." Gourgey observes that NFB, fearing that blind people will be viewed as incompetent, "is more worried about projecting the 'wrong' image or burdening the taxpayers than about safety."

Rosemarie McCaffrey, president of Guide Dog Users in New York, notes that her organization could thrive only in ACB since NFB considers the use of guide dogs as "a too dependent way of traveling."[60] On the contrary, McCaffrey points out that she finds the use of a guide dog liberating: "I can walk faster with a guide dog than with a cane. With a cane, I almost have to walk into something I'll have to detour around, but the dog takes me around the obstacle in the first place. I certainly feel safer traveling at night with a dog, so I'm less limited than I've ever been before."[61] Because NFB President Jernigan himself used a sighted companion, his wife, for traveling, McCaffrey indicates that she is mystified by his organization's position on this matter.

In 1972, some ACB members in New York City who were using guide dogs worked together to pursue their own issues, joining Guide Dog Users, Inc. (founded in New York in 1969), an organization that would remain independent of, but affiliated with, ACB. After spreading to almost twenty states, Guide Dog Users—supported by members of ACB—initiated two projects: a national lawsuit dealing with Hawaii's noncompliance with the Americans with Disabilities Act and a New York City effort known as "Operation Refusal." Because there were no reported cases of rabies in Hawaii, all dogs, even guide dogs, were prohibited from being brought into the state. The Hawaii affiliate of Guide Dog Users won the Americans with Disabilities Act lawsuit contesting this ban, just as Guide Dog Users in New York, using police officers as decoys in New York City, were successful in discouraging taxicab drivers from refusing to pick up blind people with guide dogs. Despite its significant role in disability politics, NFB requires that its members conform to the position of the leadership, while ACB offers its members the freedom to use their own judgment regarding their participation in disability advocacy.

Although for many years after the division the dispute between NFB and ACB remained bitter, by the 1980s the two organizations were occasionally working together on specific issues. For example, NFB and ACB joined together to save blind people's right to send mail without postage, known as Free Matter for the Blind, as well as to support a new library for the blind in New York City, the Andrew Heiskell Library for the Blind and Physically Handicapped. In addition, the two organizations united in support of a separate agency—the New York State Commission for the Blind and Visually Handicapped—to serve the vocational needs of blind people so that they would not have to be accommodated by the vocational agency for the general disability population, the New York State Vocational and Educational Services for Individuals with Disabilities.

Yet recriminations on both sides have not abated, and when problems occur affecting blind people, the different approaches of the two organizations often rekindle old antagonisms. The public strife between NFB and ACB not only confused supporters of the disability rights movement, but also continues to serve the purposes of those unsympathetic to the movement who argue that there is no way to satisfy the contradictory demands of disability groups. For example, Philip K. Howard asks in *The Death of Common Sense*, "Why is it appropriate to handle [disability] issues as a 'right'" if, as the director of New York's Office for the Disabled is reported to have said, "You can't please everybody?"[62]

Although differences between NFB and ACB may support Howard's argument, in most cases even when two disability groups have favored different accommodations, a compromise has been negotiated that satisfied both sides. To illustrate, corner-curb cuts required by wheelchair users present a problem for blind people who no longer have a step to warn them that they are in the street. One solution that emerged in the mid-1990s was a "detectable warning strip" across curb cuts, cautioning blind people that they are approaching the edge of the sidewalk. At the same time as a sense of unity was being forged *between* different disability groups in the late 1960s, the seeds of dissension became increasingly apparent not only *within* the blind community but also the deaf community.

Deafness as Culture

Just as NFB defines blindness as a "characteristic," many deaf people, especially those who became deaf prelingually, refer to themselves as Deaf people (with a capital "D") in order to assert their identity as a linguistic minority with their own culture. To disability activists working to consolidate their movement, the efforts of these subgroups—NFB and Deaf people—to distinguish themselves from the disability community seems to be an attempt to escape the stigma of disability. The view of Deafness as *culture* instead of *disability* is given credibility by noted deaf linguists, Carol Padden and Tom Humphries, in *Deaf in America*,[63] and by Oliver Sacks, professor of clinical neurology, in *Seeing Voices*.[64]

Nadina LaSpina, president of Disabled In Action (DIA) of Metropolitan New York, presents an opposing view:

> It's obvious that Deaf people have accepted the nondisabled majority's definition of disability. They do not want to be defined as disabled because they don't want to shoulder all the negative baggage that comes with the territory. Well, neither do we. That's why we're working hard to free ourselves and them from all that baggage. By separating themselves from us, by calling themselves members of a linguistic minority and calling us disabled, all they are doing is perpetuating the notion that disability is bad. And they're not really helping themselves since the nondisabled majority is still going to think of them as disabled.[65]

Professor Frank Bowe, who is deaf and a member of the Department of Counseling, Research, Special Education and Rehabilitation at Hofstra University, argues that the "Deaf culture advocates cannot have it both ways."[66] Indicating the contradiction in their position, Bowe points out that "they cannot on the one hand benefit from the IDEA [Individuals with Disabilities Education Act], Section 504 [of the Rehabilitation Act of 1973], the ADA, etc., provisions guaranteeing free public education, social services, and protection against discrimination—all of which costs money, and at the same time hold themselves apart from others who also benefit from such provisions."

American Sign Language

The culture of Deaf people emanates from and remains centered on their language, American Sign Language.[67] Oliver Sacks suggests that William Stokoe's 1960 "'bombshell' paper on *Sign Language Structure*, the first-ever serious and scientific attention paid to 'the visual communication system of the American deaf,'" ushered in the movement of Deafness as culture.[68] Barbara Kanapell, founder in 1972 of Deaf Pride, an organization devoted to Deaf consciousness-raising, credits Stokoe's work with fostering a special linguistic identity.[69] Sacks affirmed Kanapell's insight: "It took Stokoe's [1965] dictionary, and the legitimation of Sign by linguists, to allow the beginnings of a movement... toward deaf identity and deaf pride," as well as "a discovery or rediscovery of the cultural aspects of deafness."

Deaf people who identify themselves with Deaf culture do not perceive themselves as belonging to a disability group; rather, they consider themselves as members of an ethnic group with an inherited language and a culture "in the traditional sense of the term, historically created and actively transmitted across generations."[70] Bowe explains the rationale of Deaf people with the following illustration:

> Were a deaf person to walk into a hotel at which two conventions were being held—one of individuals with physical and mental disabilities, and the other of people speaking languages other than English—at which would this deaf person feel most at home? The leaders of the Deaf culture movement say the second—the meeting of people who speak different languages. Those people need interpreters to help them to understand people who speak different languages. Those people need interpreters to help them to understand people who speak English; so do Deaf people. Those people would have difficulty reading and writing English, not

only in speaking and understanding speech in it; so do Deaf people. On the other hand, individuals with physical and mental disabilities usually have no problems using English, and do not need interpreters.[71]

To the dismay of most hearing people, "so strong is the feeling of cultural solidarity that many deaf parents cheer on discovering that their baby is deaf."[72] Learning they could choose to abort if their fetus had inherited their predisposition to deafness, some deaf couples indicate, on the contrary, that they would choose to abort if the fetus did *not* inherit their deafness. Because their inability to communicate with the hearing world caused many deaf people to feel isolated and excluded, they created their own community, as well as a legacy that they wished to pass on to their children. President of the National Association of the Deaf, Roslyn Rosen, a deaf daughter of deaf parents and a mother of deaf children, explains why she would prefer not to be cured of her deafness: "I'm happy with who I am. . . . Would an Italian-American rather be a WASP?"

Unlike Rosen, however, more than 90 percent of deaf children in the United States are born to hearing parents, a statistic distinguishing Deaf culture from most other cultures.[73] In fact, critics argue that the focus on Deaf culture has been excessive, given the almost eleven million Americans, age fifteen and older, who have difficulty hearing ordinary conversation (even with the help of a hearing aid), and the relatively small number who use American Sign Language, roughly one-half million.[74] Moreover, giving Deaf culture minority status is fraught with potential problems: Since Sign is the first language of hearing children of Deaf parents, should these children be considered Deaf? Should deaf children be removed from their hearing parents so that they may be raised in a family of their own appropriate culture, Deaf? It is unlikely that advocates of Deaf culture really want these questions answered in the affirmative.[75]

The Gallaudet University Uprising

Focusing on Sign and Deaf culture as the inspiration for the movement that culminated in the 1988 uprising at Gallaudet University from March 6 through March 13, Sacks seems to have underestimated the pivotal role of the disability rights movement in the students' demands. Although Sacks sees the Gallaudet protest emanating out of the 1960s rights movements, he treats the struggle of people with disabilities as just *one* of the contributing factors, equal to the others. He perceives Deaf culture as a movement in itself, not as part of an overarching movement for people with all types of disabilities.

The primary grievance that ignited the student demonstration was the fact that Gallaudet, dedicated to the higher education of people who are deaf or hard of hearing, never had a deaf president since its founding in 1864. Sacks quotes a Gallaudet professor exhorting the protesters: "Virtually every black college has a black president, testimony that black people are leading themselves. Virtually every women's college has a woman as president, as testament that women are capable of leading themselves. It's long past time that Gallaudet had a deaf president as testimony that deaf people are leading themselves."[76] In fact, the action at Gallaudet culminated not only in the appointment of its first deaf president, I. King Jordan, but also in setting the stage for the 1990 Americans with Disabilities Act.[77]

Sacks mentions contributing factors to the Gallaudet revolt: "the mood of the '60s, with its special feeling for the poor, the disabled, minorities—the civil rights movement, the political activism, the varied 'pride' and 'liberation' movements."[78]

Yet, consistent with the proponents of Deaf culture, Sacks does not view the Gallaudet struggle as arising out of an ongoing movement of individuals with all varieties of disabilities to advocate for themselves. Disability rights advocates, however, representing the broad spectrum of disabilities, embraced the rebellion at Gallaudet, not only as an integral part of their struggle, but also as the continuation of an already established precedent. An at least equally dramatic event, though less publicized than the Gallaudet eruption, had occurred in 1977—the twenty-five day sit-in by disability rights activists at the San Francisco headquarters of the Department of Health, Education, and Welfare to demand the signing of the groundbreaking regulations implementing Section 504 of the Rehabilitation Act of 1973.

In addition, leaders of this 1977 victory, perhaps the most significant ever for people with all kinds of disabilities, included deaf people. In fact, one of the prime movers of the Section 504 demonstrations was Frank Bowe. While in *No Pity* Joseph Shapiro describes the Gallaudet demonstration as "a defining moment for the disability rights movement" because of the media attention it captured, he characterizes the 1977 protest as "a blip on the screen of the national consciousness."[79] Still, the San Francisco sit-in—the culmination of the nationwide demonstrations for the signing of the Section 504 regulations—was the first major coordinated political action by people with different disabilities to affect the general disability population as well as the wider society. Furthermore, this 1977 sit-in resulted in the implementation of major disability legislation of which the Americans with Disabilities Act was the logical extension. Unlike legislation dealing with other classes, the federal civil rights protection for people with disabilities is embodied in *two* separate acts: Section 504 of

the Rehabilitation Act of 1973 and the ADA of 1990.

Black Deaf Advocates

Just as members of Deaf culture did not appreciate that their movement was part of a broader disability rights movement, they failed to recognize the extent to which they accepted general public values. Not only did Gallaudet mirror the racial segregation of the time, but also as late as 1980, many black deaf people felt so alienated, culturally and linguistically, from the mainstream deaf community that they formed their own political group, Black Deaf Advocates. In *Stigma: Notes on the Management of Spoiled Identity*, Erving Goffman points out that "it should come as no surprise that in many cases he who is stigmatized in one regard nicely exhibits all the normal prejudices held toward those who are stigmatized in another regard."[80] One effect of racial segregation, legal and de facto, was that the sign language of black deaf people deviated enough from the sign language of white deaf people that signed communication between the two populations was difficult.[81]

Because of this segregation, few black deaf people belonged to the National Association of the Deaf (NAD), founded in 1880 as the political organization to oppose the onset of oralism. Since many of the black deaf individuals who joined NAD felt alienated from the white majority, they assembled informally after the NAD meetings to discuss their own issues. By 1980, one hundred years after the formation of NAD, these informal gatherings developed into Black Deaf Advocates (BDA). Consisting of twenty-two chapters, including the New York City chapter established in 1983, national BDA meets annually in different locations throughout the United States.

Sign language interpreters for black deaf people are often their own hearing children. Since the interpreters who are "certified"[82] according to the standards of the educated white deaf majority are not sufficiently comprehensible to many black deaf people, black deaf people require interpreters who can employ signs familiar to them. These interpreters, although they lack certification,[83] perform a vital function. Yet, they do not have the status or the imprimatur of legitimacy of the "certified" interpreters. Issues that concern the black deaf population also apply to other minority deaf groups, such as Native American deaf people. Moreover, the problems are complicated by ethnic deaf groups who use American sign languages other than American Sign Language, as for example Latino deaf people and the variety of Asian deaf populations.[84]

Funding has become available to improve the skills of minority interpreters in order to enable them to become "certified." To illustrate, LaGuardia Community College in New York City received a 1996 grant that mandated that the institution's interpreter program include the training of black interpreters. Yet Celeste Owens, a member of Minority Interpreters for the Deaf, indicates that little effort has been focused on the limited comprehension of many minority deaf people: "They may prepare minority interpreters very well, but if the community is not being kept up, these wonderful signers will not be understood by the people for whom they are signing."

Education of Deaf Children

An increasing awareness of the variety of ethnic deaf communities was fostered by a new respect for sign language evident in the gradual change from oralism to signing in the American school system. The experiences of Marcia Bernstein, who taught deaf children from kindergarten through high school, illustrates the evolution in the modern education of the deaf.[85] Bernstein taught deaf children at the Lexington School for the Deaf in Manhattan from 1965 to 1966 and at St. Joseph's School for the Deaf in the Bronx from 1967 to 1969. She says she felt "brainwashed" into thinking that sign language was "ugly, barbaric, and bad" for deaf children. Oralism was the teaching method at the time.

After leaving St. Joseph's in 1969, Bernstein resumed teaching at the school in 1978, at which point she discovered that the educational method had changed to "total communication," a technique using spoken English and signed English concurrently. Signed English is English with the vocabulary of sign language and the word order and grammar of spoken English. The theory was that employing this method, deaf children learned sign language and English at the same time. According to Bernstein, "It didn't work. English and sign language have different grammars and structures. Also, unlike English, 90 percent of sign language is body language and facial expression." Judith Cohen, executive director of Access Resources, an organization providing training on disability access issues including deafness, offers this comparison: "While English is linear, sign language is visual and three-dimensional. Although sign language has some iconic features, it is also an abstract language like English."[86]

Bernstein says that studies in the early 1980s proved that deaf children of deaf parents understood the grammar and concepts of language better than deaf children of hearing parents. The reason for this phenomenon was that "deaf children of deaf parents were exposed to the complete use of language through sign from birth, while deaf children of hearing parents were learning the most primitive gestures." As a result of these studies, American Sign Language (ASL) has become a significant tool in educating deaf children. Bernstein believes that deaf children are ready and able to acquire English as a second written language once they concretely and conceptually understand the grammar, syntax, and vocabulary of a sign language, such as ASL, as a first language. Unlike signed English, which uses sequential word order as in spoken English, ASL communicates in a systematic, ideogrammatic performance. Now Bernstein believes that she uses "total communication" more effectively than she did before studying ASL, for she employs ASL as the medium for explaining the concepts essential for comprehending English. In fact, Bernstein maintains that "ideally teachers of deaf people should be thoroughly proficient in ASL."

Following the lead of a handful of state-supported schools—in places like California and Indiana, and charter schools in Minnesota and Colorado—a New York City public school for the deaf instituted a landmark change, in March 1998, requiring all teachers to instruct primarily in ASL. As the *New York Times* reported:

> They [educators and advocates for deaf children] say deaf students should be treated like bilingual students, not disabled ones. In their view, students first need a primary language—American Sign Language—before they learn a second language, in this case, English. . . . In 1867, all twenty-six schools for the deaf used ASL. By 1907, all 139 such schools had forbidden its use in an effort to make the deaf more like hearing people. Instead, they were taught to read lips or [*sic*] to speak. New York's embrace of American Sign Language reflects a pendulum swing back.[87]

Consistent with this bilingual approach to teaching deaf students, a growing number of colleges and universities—such as Brown, Georgetown, Chicago, Yale, and the California state system—have accepted ASL in fulfillment of foreign language requirements.[88]

Despite the antagonism of deaf purists, the ability to speak and lip-read offers the deaf person the advantage of the entry into the hearing world. Book editor and columnist of the *Chicago Sun-Times*, Henry Kisor, postlingually totally deaf and completely oral, disparages ideologues of both camps—signers and oralists. Making a case for tailoring the teaching methods to the specific needs of the individual deaf learner, Kisor fears the "New Orthodoxy," ASL, is merely replacing the "Old Orthodoxy," oralism.[89] Supporting Kisor's position, Keith Muller, executive director of the League for the Hard of Hearing—the nation's oldest and largest hearing rehabilitation and service league—maintains that "there is no single method by which all deaf kids can be educated."[90]

Helen Keller, the Social Reformer

With the removal of barriers to education and improved teaching techniques, people with significant sensory disabilities—even dual disabilities such as Helen Keller's deaf-blindness—increasingly have been able to contribute to society. A pioneer in the struggle for disability rights, Keller was a highly-gifted hard worker who used her appealing personality and physical attractiveness to raise money internationally for blind people.[91] But she also had the good fortune to have both the resources of a well-connected family and the innovative educational strategies of an inspired teacher, Anne Sullivan.

Who can forget such moments in Keller's autobiography, *The Story of My Life*, as the way Keller learns, and delights in, the experience of language, first comprehending the meaning of the concrete term "water" and later the abstract concept "love"?[92] One lesson evident from Keller's education is that by means of an intermediary, a kind of translator similar to the modern "facilitated communicator"—as well as existing technological devices—children like Keller can be taught. Helen Keller has been mythicized, almost sanctified, and thus too infrequently remembered as "the social reformer, the activist who tried so desperately to use her celebrity to tell the truth of disability." That truth has less to do with the blind learner's literacy problem or the deaf learner's language obstacle than, as Keller noted, it has to do with "poverty, oppression, and the restriction of choices."[93]

Chapter Three

Deinstitutionalization and Independent Living

THE TREND IN THE late 1950s and early 1960s toward deinstitutionalization allowed people with severe physical disabilities to begin entering the mainstream, bringing a new population to the developing disability rights movement. Nearly all people with serious physical impairments had trouble coping with a physical environment so ill-adapted to their needs, and many were spurred into activism by the discrimination and lack of understanding they encountered.

Deinstitutionalization

An early experiment in deinstitutionalization occurred at New York City's Goldwater Memorial Hospital, a long-term chronic care institution, where it was anticipated that people would remain their entire lives. Although hospital officials assumed that these individuals, most of whom had severe motor impairments, could not function in the mainstream, in 1958 a twenty-one-year-old quadriplegic wheelchair user, Anne Emerman, was selected as a test case in independent living for this population. When she requested the opportunity to at-

tend college after graduating from high school, she was told by a social worker that "this idea is a fantasy, and fantasy can lead to mental illness."[1] Emerman, however, not only graduated from college and earned a master's in social work at Columbia University, but she also became a psychiatric social worker at Bellevue Hospital. By 1990, Emerman was a wife, a mother, and director of the Mayor's Office for People with Disabilities in New York City. Others like Emerman, who would become significant players in the disability rights movement, would follow this first test case out of Goldwater to live independent lives.

Among them was Marilyn Saviola, also a quadriplegic wheelchair user, who in her late teens organized a separate ward for young adults at Goldwater:

[Previously] a young person might be next to a dying octogenarian. "This was where the people the world wanted to forget about were thrown," Ms. Saviola said. Then she and other young people took the social activism of the 1960s to heart and pressed for their own ward. "We fought very hard to get that place," said Hermina Jackson, a quadriplegic who [also] later left Goldwater to become active in the disability rights movement. "I don't think a lot of us knew how much potential we had until we moved over there."[2]

More like a college dormitory than a unit in a chronic care hospital, the young adults ward had brightly painted walls, "a recreation room with a stereo, a kitchen where residents pitched in to prepare dinners and [to arrange] expeditions to Broadway shows." Chosen for their compatibility with young people, hospital personnel in this new ward did not wear uniforms, and an elected council of residents advocated for the ward. Despite the many residents who used respirators or ventilators, the atmosphere of the unit was typical for coeds of the 1960s: "There was rock music, late night bull sessions and experiments with smoking and alcohol," as well as "romance." One of the young nurses in the unit, Deri Duryea, explained, "They were sent there to die, and suddenly they had life."

Saviola began her emergence from institutional life in 1965 by being the first patient to attend college while still residing at Goldwater.[3] Because New York State Vocational and Educational Services for Individuals with Disabilities (VESID) claimed that she was incapable of working, she was unsuccessful the first time she tried to get financial assistance for college. Yet Saviola was not discouraged. As she explains,

> I appealed to Senator Javits, and he interceded on my behalf, referring to the federal Vocational Rehabilitation Act. As a result, VESID gave me a semester's tuition on a probationary basis. After I got a bachelor's from Long Island University and a master's in rehabilitation counseling from New York University, I figured out a way to live independently. I rented my own apartment in 1973. Medicaid paid for my 24-hour live-in personal assistance services attendant, a van, and a driver, so that I was able to work as a rehabilitation counselor at Goldwater. But to keep Medicaid, I had to live at a subsistence level.

Still required to live at a subsistence level, ten years later, in 1983, Saviola became executive director of the Center for Independence of the Disabled in New York (CIDNY), the first independent living center in New York State.

Reflecting a new federal objective of including people with severe disabilities and expanding its coverage to include individuals who might not be able to secure employment, but who could live independently, the term "vocational" was eliminated from the title of new legislation, which when enacted was simply called the Rehabilitation Act of 1973. Advancing the deinstitutionalization process, this more expansive view of rehabilitation services focused on self-direction, rather than employment. Yet, as disability policy expert Edward D. Berkowitz noted, "By the late 1970s, those identified as severely disabled [people like Saviola] accounted for more than half of the vocational rehabilitation caseload."[4]

Many formerly institutionalized people with significant disabilities residing in the community lived in dread of being forced to return to institutions when their caretakers could no longer provide for them. Paralyzed by polio at ten years of age, Bernice White, a highly intelligent and beautiful woman in her early twenties, prepared a lethal dose of pills in the late 1950s to ensure that she would die before she would be institutionalized again. Although by 1960 she was married and living in her own home, she was not alone in preferring death to "incarceration" in a nursing home.[5]

In the late 1970s, Lyn Thompson of California, immobilized by muscular dystrophy, was told she was not disabled according to Medicaid law because she earned more than two hundred and forty dollars a month operating an answering service from her home.[6] Consequently, she lost her income maintenance, her health coverage, and her personal attendant. Informed that she would be forced to enter an institution (at a considerably increased cost to taxpayers), Thompson could not accept the loss of independence she had established with such difficulty. Despite her effort to be a productive member of society, Lyn Thompson, penalized by archaic laws, took her own life in February 1978. The September 30, 1978, CBS-TV broadcast of "60 Minutes" focused nationwide attention on this tragedy.

Thompson was not informed about a personal assistance services program evolving at that time in California that may have prevented her suicide. Ironically, on March 1, 1978, less than one month after Thompson's death, a new California law allowed people with severe physical disabilities to receive full support services while employed. Moreover, in 1977 after a reevaluation of a New York City program permitting employed consumers of personal attendant care to receive these services, the New York City Human Resources Administration decided not only to continue the program, but also to extend it to future consumers who would be employed.

Earlier, in 1976, New York City established the Independent Contractor Home Care System, a program enabling self-directing consumers of personal assistance services to hire, train, supervise, and fire their own attendants.[7] Because the program paid only the minimum wage without withholding taxes and provided no employee benefits, the Independent Contractor System failed to comply with various state and federal regulations. Furthermore, the system did not offer support to the non-self-directing and frail elderly. As a result, New York City initiated a "vendor" program in 1979—a new system in which the city contracted with nonprofit, community-based agencies to manage the employment, training, and supervision of home care employees—thus depriving self-directing consumers of their previous autonomy. Implementation of the new "vendor" system galvanized these consumers into banding together to form a unique personal assistance program, complying with all government regulations, in which they maintain their independence.

Founded in 1980, this new program, Concepts of Independence,[8] has grown from serving four consumers in the five counties of New York City to serving more than a thousand consumers in twelve counties, seven of which are outside the city. If these consumers had used traditional home care in 2000 rather than Concepts of Independence, the services would have cost the state an additional $28 million. Joining with groups such as the Alzheimer's Association and Sick Kids Need Involved People (SKIP), Concepts of Independence began in November 1997 to include consumers who required surrogates—usually family members—to direct personal assistance services. To ensure that the program is appropriate for those who use personal assistance services, most board members are long-term Concepts of Independence consumers.

Chairing the board from its inception until her death in 1994, Sandra Schnur—quadriplegic as a result of polio and director of the New York City Office of Half-Fare Transportation for People with Disabilities—initiated and guided the program utilizing her organizational skills and political connections.

Marvin Wasserman, Schnur's husband, describes his wife:

In 1952, Sandra, a wheelchair user who had just graduated from high school, was advised by OVR [the Office of Vocational Rehabilitation, which later became Vocational and Educational Services for Individuals with Disabilities] to become a basket-weaver. Considering that she had weak hands because of polio, this job was a poor choice, especially for a person with *her* intelligence. When she asked to go to college instead, she was told that she was uncooperative, and her OVR case was closed. Thirteen years later, when OVR offered to send her to college, she needed two years of tutoring in mathematics, science, and foreign language to make up for the inadequate home instruction she had received. After graduating from college, Sandra earned her master's in rehabilitation counseling. Among her many accomplishments, she wrote *New York with Ease,* an accessibility guide for wheelchair users in New York City—maybe the first of its kind—published by the Easter Seal Society in 1963. But she considered her contribution to Concepts of Independence her greatest achievement.[9]

Programs like Concepts of Independence revealed that many people with severe disabilities could live independent, self-directed lives in the community more economically and productively than in nursing homes.

Early Accessibility Efforts in the Colleges

The story of Dr. John E. King—who in 1953 became president of Emporia State Teachers College, now Kansas State Teachers College—also illustrates how, when people with severe disabilities are given opportunities, common assumptions about their limitations may be dispelled:

Dr. King first seriously considered the idea of educating the handicapped at a regular college campus when he was the provost at the University of Minnesota's campus at Duluth. He recalls that a Hungarian English professor at the school discovered a youth in Duluth who was extremely able, but was almost totally paralyzed. Believing in the boy's mental ability, the school hired two football players to carry him, feed him, and tend to all his wants.

"At first we felt we were exploiting the boy," King said. "You know, helping a

person is sometimes almost an invasion of their privacy. But that boy did so well and turned out to be so fiercely independent that he made a believer out of me," he added.

King said he then began to realize the inadequacies of the educational programs for the handicapped. And, when he became president of the college here in 1953, he set about attempting to correct those inadequacies, at least at his own school. "We are blessed here with a campus without hills and not so large that the handicapped students can't get around," he said. "We'll gradually get this campus so that a student can go anywhere day or night whether he is blind or paralyzed." Years later, King said, "We've had no disciplinary problems with handicapped students except for one boy who ran his wheelchair too fast down a campus walk."[10]

After the first of these students graduated in the late 1950s, enrollment of students with severe disabilities steadily increased at Kansas State Teachers College.[11]

One of the first college programs specifically geared for people with disabilities was established in 1948 on the wheelchair accessible campus of the University of Illinois.[12] Since in World War II paraplegic soldiers survived combat for the first time, they required accommodations never before provided, such as a barrier-free college environment, in order to participate in activities on an equal basis with other students. Because of the foresight of Tim Nugent, founder and director of the Division of Rehabilitation Education Services, the University of Illinois developed services and programs designed for students with disabilities. An accessible paratransit system—a method of transportation using lift-equipped vans—was devised for the limited area of the campus. Furthermore, Nugent initiated a sports program, which has evolved into a multifaceted curriculum allowing students with a variety of disabilities to engage in athletic competition.

The University's acceptance of students with increasing degrees of disability necessitated the provision of independent living services. By the fall of 1962, students with severe disabilities shared responsibility for the operation of the newly established University of Illinois residence, the Guy M. Beckwith Living Center, renamed Beckwith Hall in 1992. Until the 1970s, the University of Illinois was one of the only major universities with both a wheelchair-accessible campus and programs specifically designed for students with disabilities.[13]

While the veterans' disabilities were all war-related, the reasons for civilians' disabilities varied greatly—from polio to cerebral palsy to accidents and innumerable other causes. Since they needed alterations for accessibility in the built environment, these individuals were motivated to seek alternatives to preconceived notions—for example, regarding transportation and architecture—as well as to consider legal and political tactics to accomplish these goals. Early programs developed on college campuses for students with disabilities were initiated by nondisabled people. However, by 1971 in Houston, 1972 in Berkeley, 1974 in Boston, and later in other localities, people with different disabilities would establish and direct their own centers for independent living—sometimes forming coalitions with like-minded groups—as they began to demand social change that would enable them to participate in the wider society.

Ed Roberts and the Independent Living Movement

The counterculture activism of the stormy Berkeley campus of the 1960s and early 1970s resonated in Edward Roberts's energetic, anti-institutional biases. Severely disabled by polio at the age of fourteen and encouraged by a feisty mother, he overcame his own self-doubt and the general skepticism concerning the opportunities that would be available to him.[14] Roberts recalls:

> I had a serious fever, and in twenty-four hours, I was paralyzed and in an iron lung. Within earshot, my mother asked the doctor whether I would live or die. "You should hope he dies, because if he lives, he'll be no more than a vegetable for the rest of his life. How would you like to live in an iron lung twenty-four hours a day?" So I decided to be an artichoke—a little prickly on the outside but with a big heart. . . .
>
> The transition was hard. . . . Everyone made the outlook [seem] bleak. I decided that I wanted to die. Now it's very hard to kill yourself in a hospital with everything set up to save your life. But the mind is a powerful thing. I stopped eating. They started to force-feed me. It was really demeaning. I dropped to fifty-four pounds.
>
> My last special duty nurse left, and the next day I decided I wanted to live. You see, that was a big turning point. Up until then, these nurses were available and doing things for me around the clock. I didn't have to make any decisions for myself because they were always there. When they all finally left, that's when I realized that I could have a life, despite what everyone was saying. I could make choices, and that is freedom. I started to eat again.[15]

Although Roberts completed his first three years of high school at home by means of a telephone connected to the classroom, both his mother and his social worker told him during his senior year that if he did not leave the house then, he never would. Roberts describes his first experience attending school with other students:

> I had taught myself glossopharyngeal breathing—frog breathing, where you swallow air into your lungs, so I had been spending time out of the iron lung before. But I was scared to go out and be seen by people.
>
> I remember that day very clearly. I arrived during lunch time. My brother lowered me out of the back of the station wagon, and it was like a tennis match—everyone turned

to look at me. I looked at someone, right in the eyes, and they turned and looked away. That was when I realized that maybe it wasn't my problem; maybe it was their problem. I checked myself out, and I realized two things. First, their looking at me didn't hurt, physically, and secondly I realized, hey, this is kind of like being a star—and I've been a star ever since.[16]

Deciding on a career in political science, Roberts acted on his mother's suggestion that he select a university based not primarily on accessibility, but on academic excellence in his field. "Armed with self-esteem and a portable respirator, [Roberts] broke the disability barrier to higher education, by insisting that he had a right to an education, by insisting that the doors to the University of California at Berkeley be opened."[17] Roberts had to sue to gain admission to the University of California in 1962, just as in the same semester James Meredith required a lawsuit to become the first black person to attend the University of Mississippi.[18] "When I first began talking with the administration," Roberts explains, "they told me, 'We tried cripples, and they don't work.'"[19]

After his successful lawsuit against the university, Roberts still had the formidable task of arranging for appropriate housing. Because of the severity of his disability, he was attended to at the Berkeley Infirmary, Cowell Hospital, by orderlies doing public service as an alternative to military service in Vietnam.[20] Steeped in the political milieu of this makeshift dormitory, Roberts recollects how he and the quadriplegics that followed him to the Berkeley campus created a spirited atmosphere on the third floor of Cowell Hospital.

They [the university administrators] didn't know where to put me. The dorms weren't accessible, and we had to find a place that would accommodate my eight hundred-pound iron lung. They finally decided that I could live in a certain ward of Cowell Hospital, on the edge of the campus. Soon there were a bunch of us crips at Berkeley. It was an exciting time. The protests and student movements were rising all around us, and we were right there. John Hessler [another Cowell resident] and I used to roll right up to the front of the demonstrations and stare down the police. What could they do? When they threatened to arrest us, we just asked them, "How are you going to get us there? Do you have an iron lung in your prison?" That's one drawback of the Americans with Disabilities Act I guess, because they didn't have accessible jails back then, which meant they didn't arrest us.[21]

Influenced to some degree by the impact of the 1963-1964 Berkeley Free Speech Movement, Roberts and his followers were more profoundly affected by the eruption at People's Park in Berkeley in late 1964, as well as the students' reaction against the overwhelming police presence in the university town.[22] Yet Roberts also acknowledges his debt to the Women's Movement:

I learned a lot from the Women's Movement. They used to let me go to their meetings; I guess they saw a connection between our experiences. I remember them talking about how to deal with stereotypes of weakness and passivity that society placed on them. I heard women talk about how they had manipulated men by capitalizing on these stereotypes. I realized that disability is actually a strength. If someone comes up to me and doesn't look me in the eye, if all they see is my ventilator and my chair, I can tell right away. If they don't see me as a human being, if they only see my equipment, I know that I can get whatever I want out of them. As long as this is not used pathologically, but to create beneficial change for others, it is a strength. Disability can be very powerful. We used the power of disability in political strategies many times.[23]

As Roberts reveals, not all civil rights activists, however, recognized the connection between their causes and his cause: "I remember meeting with Leonard Pelletier [the Native American activist] before he was arrested. I met with Stokely Carmichael and others in the Black Power movement. When I told them that we were all fighting the same civil rights battle, they didn't believe me; they didn't understand our similarities. I did. Even now, many people don't realize it."

Invited by his former college adviser, Jean Wirth, to assist her in developing a nationally-funded pilot project for minority university students, Roberts submitted a grant proposal for people with disabilities as a minority. After being funded, this proposal became known as the Disabled Students Program (DSP) at Berkeley. Establishing an agenda that suited these students' needs—wheelchair repair, accessible housing, attendant care—they formed the Rolling Quads, a political group that would make wheelchairs commonplace in the Berkeley community. Roberts comments:

My mother Zona managed the attendant pool. I remember we sent someone to visit with a high ranking military official who was responsible for the conscientious objectors. Edna Brean [DSP representative] met with him and told him about what attendants do for people with disabilities and that conscientious objectors would be ideal for the job. This official was enthusiastic; he thought this was like a punishment for these people who refused to fight. So, we got them signed up. These were the kind of people we wanted to work with. We were very lucky.

Struggling against the agency mentality that fostered dependence, the Rolling Quads worked toward achieving a barrier-free campus, one significant component of their effort to become self-reliant. Impelled by their desire to be in charge of their own lives, the Rolling Quads moved out of the hospital and into the Berkeley community. Spearheaded by Roberts, they organized an agency in 1972 governed *by* and *for* people with disabilities, the Center for Independent Living (CIL) that eventually gained national and even international prominence. Roberts explains:

Most people never thought of independence as a possibility when they thought of us. But we knew what we wanted, and we set up CIL to provide the vision and resources to get people out and into the community. The Berkeley CIL was revolutionary as a model for advocacy-based organizations; no longer would we tolerate being spoken for. Our laws said that at least 51 percent of the staff and board had to be people with disabilities, or it would be the same old oppression. We also saw CIL as a model for joining all the splintered factions of different disability organizations. All types of people used and worked in our center. This was the vision we had for the future of the movement.[24]

Carr Massi, a leading organizer of the first independent living center in New York City, the Center for the Independence of the Disabled in New York (CIDNY), relates her impressions of the CIL in 1977:

The Center for Independent Living in California, which I visited in September, is an impressive operation.... Some people have the impression that CIL is a "village" of people with disabilities. It is not. It deals in services, counseling, and training.... There is peer counseling, legal assistance, job development, training in independent living skills, and health maintenance. The CIL degree program is the only one in the United States that focuses on the psychology of disability, using the peer counseling approach practiced at the center. All this is funded by private foundations and by the government.[25]

Influenced by the CIL, Berkeley was referred to by the *New York Times* as the "mecca for the handicapped,"[26] the city where people with disabilities were accepted as an integral part of the community. Also, given the diversity of Berkeley, people with various disabilities looked just like one other unusual group that populated the area. Roberts notes:

We secured the first curb cut in the country; it was at the corner of Bancroft and Telegraph Avenue. When we first talked to legislators about the issue, they told us, "Curb cuts, why do you need curb cuts? We never see people with disabilities out on the streets. Who is going to use them?" They didn't understand that their reasoning was circular. When curb cuts were put in, they discovered that access for disabled people benefit many others as well. For instance, people pushing strollers use curb cuts, as do people on bikes and elderly people who can't lift their legs so high. So many people benefit from this accommodation. This is what the concept of universal design is all about. Now Berkeley is a very accessible city. We [people with disabilities] are visible in the community because we can get around everywhere fairly easily....

I look around, and I notice that a lot of us are getting gray. As we get older, we realize that disability is just a part of life. Anyone can join our group at any point in life. In this way, the disability rights movement doesn't discriminate. So those of us who are temporarily able-bodied and working for access and accommodation now get older, and the changes they make will benefit them as well.[27]

Two personal experiences evoke the atmosphere of the Bay Area in the 1970s.[28] Simi Kelley, a wheelchair user, describes her summer in Berkeley in 1975:

Rounding the corner to my street, I see three or four beautiful, blond California women surrounding a young handsome man sitting in a wheelchair. They're out there on the street throwing yogurt at one another and laughing like they'll never stop.

I go out to the store. I don't stop and think about it; I just go. There are curb cuts on every corner, so I don't have to deliberate over every maneuver.

There are many disabled people in Berkeley (often called Berzerkeley), and they are such an outgoing, active group that the ground has been broken. A whole different attitude toward people, and therefore toward disabled people, exists.

I found people helpful but not over-solicitous. In restaurants, hotels, and shops, people are more used to seeing people in chairs and understand how to best serve their needs.

Jane Wipfler, a founding member of the New York Metropolitan Chapter of the National Paraplegia Foundation, expresses her feelings about living in northern California, where she moved to from New York City in 1975:

The most exciting news I have to share is the attitude of people out here. Everywhere I go, I see "wheelies"—rock concerts, flea markets, movies, grocery stores, on the streets.... Many buildings display the wheelchair accessible emblem, and the front seats of all buses are reserved for the elderly and the handicapped. I've seen quadriplegics literally fly down some fairly steep hills in Berkeley without attracting much attention. It really heartens me to see the handicapped as part of the community.

As founder of the Berkeley CIL, Roberts became the embodiment of the principle of self-determination for people with disabilities. Roberts indicates how he harnessed his anger so that it fueled his creative energies:

Most psychiatrists and service professionals who work with us tell us that anger is a bad thing—a stage to get over or something that we need to overcome. But anger is a powerful energy. We don't need to suppress or get over our anger; we need to channel it into making change for the greater good. We need to make sure that we don't turn our anger in on ourselves or our loved ones, but focus it on removing obstacles and making things happen.... I get angry all the time. I'm angry that people with disabilities are second-class citizens in this country. I get angry at how 97 percent of the billions of federal dollars spent either perpetuate our dependency on the system or increase it.[29]

In order to foster independence for people with severe disabilities, the original CIL was the model, not only for the satellite agencies in each of the twenty-eight California counties, but also for the hundreds throughout the United States and in other parts of the world. Assistant Secretary of Education Judith E. Heumann, who in 1978 was senior deputy director of the CIL, relates the accomplishments of members of the CIL by engaging in an imaginary dialogue between observers of the CIL and CIL representatives:

"There's something that's going right. They're producing more rehabs than rehab, and why is that happening?" We are saying it is very simple: Disabled people know what disabled people need and want. (That is not true for all of us, but it is for many.) As a result of that, we are able to help people move on. We are peers. We are role models. That is critical. When we go into most "establishment" organizations, we hardly meet any disabled individuals; there are no peers that we can look up to. I never met a disabled professional until I was in my twenties. I had only nondisabled role models—who are not role models to me because I am not nondisabled. That oppression, which goes on, on a day-to-day basis, is something that we in the independent living programs have been able to change.[30]

Acquiring his bachelor's and master's degrees, as well as an appointment in political science, at the University of California at Berkeley, Roberts struggled against the prevailing assumption that his disability negated his intellectual capacity and his employment potential. When Jerry Brown was elected governor of California in 1975, he appointed Roberts director of the State Department of Rehabilitation. Roberts recounts:

When I finally met him [Governor Jerry Brown], he asked, "Are you one of the leaders of this [the landmark disability rights sit-in of 1977]?" I told him that I was, and he listened. Not only did he hire me, but he never cut program funding for people with

disabilities while I was there. If he ever had a question, he would come to me directly. . . . I went straight from being on welfare to this state government position. People asked me if I was going to become a bureaucrat. I told them, "No, I think I'll be an 'advocrat.'"[31]

In this position, which he held for eight years, Roberts was responsible for twenty-five hundred employees and a budget of $140 million. Robert Levine, San Francisco Bay Area Accessible Transportation Planner, who contracted polio when he was fourteen, remembers Roberts:

When Ed became the head of the Department of Rehabilitation in California in the seventies, he was like a kid who had slipped into the establishment. The faithful would go up to Sacramento and talk about how it was to be on the inside. Ed developed countywide CILs around the state, such as the San Francisco one at 812 Mission Street, where many of us joined together to discuss issues and plan strategies.

I also remember Ed speaking in New York in 1991. It was the annual meeting of disability organizations held at the Republic Bank, and Ed gave a great speech on why we should be proud to be disabled. It was a rousing tour de force. Later he was asked to name the three things most important to the disability community. He answered, "Advocacy, advocacy, and advocacy." When I saw him at Gracie Mansion the following year, he was, as usual, seeking money for the World Institute on Disability. "Hi Bob, how are you doing?" he said, and I was impressed. Ed hardly knew me, and if he remembered my name, he must have remembered thousands of others. A good trick if you're trying to get money.[32]

In 1983, Roberts and Heumann founded the Oakland California World Institute on Disability (WID), a nonprofit public policy, research, and training institute established to achieve independence and improved quality of life for people with disabilities. WID works collaboratively with a local, national, and international network of people with disabilities as well as policy-makers, corporations, and nonprofit organizations.[33] In order to raise public awareness of disability issues and the independent living concept, Roberts traveled to Russia, Australia, Japan, and France. His 1984 MacArthur Foundation Award helped fund many of his WID activities.

A unique and innovative force in the modern disability rights movement, Roberts was mourned throughout the world by many people, including the disability community, when he died at the age of fifty-six of cardiac arrest in Berkeley, California, on March 14, 1995. Although several independent living centers (ILCs) were initiated before the Berkeley CIL, Roberts deserves credit for being the founder of the ILCs because of his success in establishing a nationwide, and even a worldwide, Independent Living Movement. Dr. Frank Bowe, professor at Hofstra University, tells about Roberts's effect on people:

> I think Ed had a "visionary" bent that people found inspiring. He had the ability to think in very broad terms and to speak in an all-encompassing way so that everyone who listened to him felt included in what he had to say and encouraged to do more and better. He was one of the first to get the idea that it was not just his job to "deal with" his disability; rather, society had some obligations, too. In the 1960s, the very concept that the University of California at Berkeley and the City of Berkeley had responsibilities to accommodate for Ed's needs and for those of other students like him was radical. Certainly, it never occurred to me in four years of college that Western Maryland College should accommodate my needs [as a deaf student]. I just never thought of it that way. I saw a college that worked the way it worked, and I thought my job was to adjust to that way—or get out. But once someone like Ed introduces a new way of thinking, it can spread—as it did! I was one of many who benefited.[34]

Lucy Gwin, editor of the bimonthly magazine *Mouth: The Voice of Disability Rights*, remembers Roberts as the person to whom she was directed when she had questions about disability rights history. She was told that "Ed Roberts has all the answers," but she did not see him that way:

> Ed didn't, as he was the first to admit, have all the answers. But there was genuine treasure imbedded in his tales of the early days of IL [Independent Living]. He had stories enough to make me wish, today, that I'd recorded every one of them. Both Billy Golfus [writer and director of the well-received documentary film about the disability rights movement, *When Billy Broke His Head*] and I say we miss him most late in the evening. That's when Emperor Ed the Head held phone court from the iron lung where he spent his nights.
>
> Ed sent me a video about the first Center for Independent Living, the CIL in Berkeley that he helped to found. That video was a sixties period piece showing the IL guys wearing so-stylish bell bottoms and stringy long hair. The founders of IL were bright white male students of a prestigious university who grew up in homes where families could describe themselves as "comfortable." In the '40s and '50s, polio had knocked down those families' most-likely-to-succeed kids like bowling pins. America's best and brightest . . . had been transformed over night into second-class citizens by a microscopic organism with a long Latin name. . . .
>
> What caused them to question their second-class status? They'd hatched out of privilege and protection into a world that was changing radically. A people's cry for liberty and justice was visible, audible, and haunting America on its nightly news. The nation sat witness while solemn black people stood their ground as sheriffs set dogs on them for having the nerve to sit down at lunch counters, go to schools, or both. . . . Black pride arose from white oppression and black poverty.
>
> The independent living revolution arose from among privileged white boys. And, bless them, those boys stormed the barricades to free us [people with disabilities] from *the medical model*. They fought tooth and nail for curb cuts and restaurant access, and a new,

improved vocational rehabilitation system. . . . Ed Roberts did, later, rise above his privileges to spend the last years of his life touring the country for Partners in Policymaking. He spoke then of freedom for *everyone.*[35]

Proliferation of the Independent Living Concept

Berkeley was a harbinger for what was to come, and what is still in the process of happening, as other cities become increasingly accessible, though the climate, transportation, and culture may not be as hospitable to people with disabilities in other locales as they are in the Bay Area. The Boston Center for Independent Living was established in 1974 by Fred Fay, a quadriplegic disability activist and a Ph.D. in psychology; Paul Corcoran, a physician in rehabilitation medicine; and Robert McHugh, a rehabilitation counselor.[36] After Fay broke his neck in 1960 at the age of sixteen as a result of a fall from a trapeze, he spent two years rehabilitating at Warm Springs, Georgia, where he experienced people with disabilities serving as board and staff members. Fay received his undergraduate and graduate degrees from the University of Illinois, an institution noted for being receptive to and accessible for students with severe disabilities. With his vision of the potential of disability independence encouraged by Warm Springs and the University of Illinois, Fay initiated a halfway house in a Boston nursing home for people with severe disabilities who had no family or friends to provide care.

Perceiving these nursing home clients as people who were "incarcerated against their will," Fay indicates that "their only crime was needing attendant care in the morning and at night; otherwise they were pretty much independent for the rest of the day." Disillusioned by this experience, Fay obtained funding from the State Rehabilita-

tion Agency to cofound the Boston Center for Independent Living (BCIL) in order that people with severe disabilities could function autonomously outside an institution. Like the Berkeley CIL, BCIL provides peer counseling, personal care attendant services, advocacy, and employment referrals, as well as information regarding community-based housing and assistive devices.

Experiencing disability discrimination after he broke his neck in a 1967 car accident, Lex Frieden became an advocate for disability rights and independent living.[37] When Frieden, a wheelchair user, was refused admission to the completely wheelchair-accessible Oral Roberts University in 1968, he indicates how he became aware of the similarity between racial prejudice and prejudice based on disability:

The school was built according to 1960s architectural standards—level with wide doorways—so although wheelchair accessibility was not deliberate, it seemed a good place for me to go to school. When they wouldn't accept me because they said my presence in a wheelchair would be an imposition on the other students, at first I was disheartened. But in a few days I realized that this was discrimination—just like the discrimination people of color had to deal with—for a characteristic over which they had no control and for which there was no logic.

The next school I applied to, the University of Tulsa, was built according to 1930s Ivy League standards with many steps, so the dean of admissions had to meet me in the parking lot. He told me that the new building would have level entrances, and if I would plan my schedule early, all my classes would be in that building until other buildings became accessible. This was reasonable accommodations before the term was invented. Then he said that the University of Tulsa would be honored to have me. After I filed a 1976 complaint against Oral Roberts, I received an apology and an invitation to attend the institution. Some of my colleagues suggested that perhaps Oral

Roberts University had originally rejected me because I would have been an embarrassment considering Oral Roberts's reputation as a faith healer.

While at the University of Tulsa in 1968, Frieden helped organize a disability rights organization, Wheelchair Independence Now (WIN), but the name was soon changed to Win Independence Now: "We realized that not all people with disabilities were in wheelchairs, and we shared common issues." About the same time that Roberts founded the CIL in Berkeley, Frieden organized Cooperative Living, an independent living center in Houston, Texas, "that attempts to bridge the gap between hospital and community by means of a six-week program that teaches independent living skills."[38] In 1975, the same year that he was elected as the first secretary of the national disability rights organization, the American Coalition of Citizens with Disabilities (ACCD), he formed the Coalition for Barrier Free Living, an organization focusing on accessibility issues.

Founded by Frieden in 1977, the Independent Living Research Utilization (ILRU) program, the think tank for the Independent Living Movement, defined the concept of independent living.[39] Serving as a national center for information, training, research, and technical assistance in independent living, ILRU incorporated independent living provisions in the Rehabilitation Act of 1978. ILRU's staff, mainly people with disabilities, develop techniques for accumulating, synthesizing, and distributing information concerning independent living for national and international rehabilitation and educational agencies and institutions, consumer organizations, and other independent living centers and councils. Similar to the World Institute on Disability, ILRU's goal is to increase and disseminate knowledge and understanding of independent living, as well as to advance the use of research project results.

Two accessible apartment complexes—Creative Living I and II—built in 1974 and 1986 in Columbus, Ohio, served as temporary independent living environments for young adults with severe physical disabilities who were pursuing educational or vocational training or beginning employment.[40] These programs, funded by the Department of Housing and Urban Development (HUD), prepare quadriplegic wheelchair users for self-sufficient futures. However expensive the cost of subsidizing these residents may appear, approximately thirty thousand dollars a year for six years per person, the investment is prudent because of the long-term dividends. If recipients of Creative Living Services become gainfully employed rather than totally dependent on Medicaid, society benefits by both their professional and economic contribution.

When the Rehabilitation Institute of Chicago organized an independent living committee in 1978 in order to set up an ILC, the institute's plan was to establish transitional housing for recently-disabled people who had completed rehabilitation.[41] A member of the committee, Marca Bristo, newly rehabilitated following a spinal cord injury, asked a provocative question: "Where do we go after we leave transitional housing when there's no accessible housing?" Having just attended a conference in Berkeley on sexuality and disability, Bristo was keenly aware of the variety of disability accommodations being provided in the San Francisco Bay Area. Supporting Bristo in her concern, other members of the committee pointed out that what was really needed was accessible, affordable housing, where people with disabilities could live independently alongside nondisabled people. "We don't want to live in segregated, special housing," asserted Bristo, expressing the sense of the committee. Responsive to the committee's recommendations, the institute abandoned its original plan, and instead in 1980 established Access Living, the independent living center of Chicago.

President and CEO of Access Living since its inception, Bristo has helped to create a model independent living center that serves all of Chicago.[42] Access Living provides the four core ILC services: information and referral, peer counseling, independent living training, and advocacy. Unlike many of the other centers, however, Access Living treats litigation of disability lawsuits as a significant aspect of advocacy. With a civil rights team consisting of two staff attorneys and two technical assistants, Access Living deals with a variety of disability issues including access to transportation and to schools, discrimination in housing, availability of home services, and denials of sign language interpreters for the deaf. With the exception of housing cases, the center's focus has been on large-scale cases to achieve systemic change.

Consistent with its initial purpose, Access Living supports lawsuits filed against violators of the federal Fair Housing Amendments Act of 1988, which not only protects people with disabilities against housing discrimination but also requires that housing developers comply with the principles of "adaptable design."[43] Developed in the mid-1980s by the disability community in conjunction with architects, adaptable design incorporates certain fixed access features but allows others to be added to existing structures as they are needed. Thus, this design enables all people to remain in their homes if their physical conditions change as a consequence of disability or age.[44]

Adaptable design, however, applies only to newly constructed multi-family dwellings with four or more units that were ready for first occupancy on or after March 13, 1991. In addition, Access Living supports city and state legislation mandating "visitability"—basic access to newly-built single-family homes for which owners receive financial or other assistance from city or state government.[45] Known across the nation for its pioneer work in fair housing,[46] Access Living also provides technical assistance on the Fair Housing Amendments Act to over five hundred organizations across the United States.

Characteristics of Independent Living Centers

Certain services are basic to all ILCs, yet they vary in their programs, staffing organization, and funding sources, as well as the consumers they target. Some ILCs are associated with uncommon services; for example, one of the first services offered by the Berkeley CIL was wheelchair repair. Two early ILCs founded in New York City—the Center for Independence of the Disabled in New York in 1978 and the Brooklyn Center for Independence of the Disabled (BCID) in 1979—include personal attendant, deafness and blindness services, as well as housing, benefit, and transportation information. In addition, CIDNY, in partnership with Tisch Hospital (one of the facilities at New York University Medical Center), provides primary care services to people with disabilities. While Bronx Independent Living Services helps crime victims with disabilities, Queens Independent Living Center (QILC) includes the Cork Art Gallery, which displays the work of artists with disabilities. Because people from ethnic and racial minorities were underserved by ILCs, Harlem Hospital—in conjunction with QILC and Sylvia Walker of Howard University—created the Harlem Independent Living Center (HILC) in 1991, the last of six ILCs in New York City, all of which remain in existence today. At the same time

QILC, like many other ILCs, developed minority outreach programs to deal with multicultural disability issues.

An ILC in a state where disability activists are well organized has an increased probability of receiving state funding, allowing it to join with other ILCs from that state to form a network. Some states with effective ILC networks are California, Illinois, Massachusetts, New York, and Pennsylvania. Not only do the ILCs in these states share information and innovative approaches, but they also gain considerable political clout. Despite their efforts, disability rights activists did not succeed in getting federal subsidies for independent living services until the 1978 amendments to the Rehabilitation Act of 1973.[47] Although disability leaders requested funding for a variety of ILC programs, by 1978 ten ILCs received only start-up money. With the passing of the 1986 amendments to the act, additional federal funds were provided for establishment and operation of ILCs as well as legal services.[48]

The 1992 amendments to the Rehabilitation Act of 1973 increased consumer control of ILCs, for with this new legislation federal subsidies were allocated directly to the centers rather than funded through state rehabilitation agencies.[49] These amendments also mandated that each state establish a Statewide Independent Living Council, primarily to prepare and monitor a three-year plan for independent living services.[50] In addition, these amendments were designed to motivate ILC participants to advocate for equal access to health care, housing, public accommodations, communication, and transportation, and for equal opportunity to education and employment. Since enforcement has not kept pace with the existing laws dealing with many of these issues, ILCs are faced with a significant challenge: to educate people with disabilities, as well as businesses, government, and

the general public, regarding disability civil rights legislation.

Independent Living as an Extension of Rehabilitation

Independent living centers were an extension of the concept of rehabilitation in a civilian context. The convalescent project in the military hospital, the forerunner of rehabilitation, originated as a halfway program between the hospital and the battlefield. On the other hand, ILCs complement civilian rehabilitation, offering support to enable people with disabilities to become integrated into the mainstream. Rehabilitation refers to a medical field; independent living denotes people with disabilities relying on their own resourcefulness to acquire the social services they need in order to participate in society. "It [independent living] is deciding one's own pattern of life—schedule, food, entertainment, vices, virtues, leisure, and friends. It is the freedom to take risks and the freedom to make mistakes."[51]

Gerben DeJong succinctly describes the differences between the rehabilitation and the independent living approaches to disability.[52] While the rehabilitation model locates the problem in the person with the disability, emphasizing fixing the individual, the independent living paradigm places the problem in the attitudes of society and stresses changing the environment. The language of rehabilitation uses expressions such as "patient" or "client," connoting dependence on authority, whereas the vocabulary of independent living employs the term "consumer," suggesting control by the user of the service. The purpose of the rehabilitation prototype is to enable the person with the disability to be as physically and economically self-sufficient as possible. The objective of the independent living construct is to fully integrate the person with the disability fully into the social, economic, and political fabric of the community.

Evaluation of the Independent Living Movement

In the late 1970s, Sandra Schnur, a quadriplegic wheelchair user who would become chair of the board of Concepts of Independence in 1980, expressed concern that the ILCs would become another self-perpetuating, bureaucratic layer between the disabled consumer and the provider of services.[53] Suggesting that ILCs encourage preservation of the status quo rather than social change, *Mouth* editor Lucy Guin asserted in the late 1990s: "The ILC movement still hasn't caught up with him [Ed Roberts]. He was a gentle and a patient man. But he would have howled if he heard ILCs say, 'We'd *love* to get people out of institutions, but we aren't *funded* for that.'"[54]

Yet however cautious some ILCs may be, others have engaged in controversial activities. For example, four New York City ILCs provided funding for two buses of disability activists to travel to the demonstration organized on January 8, 1997, by Not Dead Yet, the disability organization protesting against physician-assisted suicide in front of the U.S. Supreme Court. Patricio Figueroa, first director of the CIDNY, pointed out that ILCs were the appropriate resource for people with disabilities because the service providers, themselves disabled, had coped with the same problems and frustrations confronting their clients.[55] Tom Clancy, NYU computer programmer and polio survivor, urged the disability community to protect Ed Roberts's concept of the ILC as an organization of people with disabilities, advocating for and empowering themselves.[56]

Independent Living and the New Disability Activism

The emergence of people with severe disabilities from institutions, in combination with the strategies for independent living that allowed them to participate in the community, was a pivotal force in the evolving disability rights movement. At a previous time, many of the individuals who would become prime movers in the ongoing civil rights struggle for equal rights for people with disabilities might have remained hidden away in institutions or confined in their homes. Edward Roberts, founder of the worldwide Independent Living Movement, had to sleep in an iron lung. Assistant Secretary of Education Judith E. Heumann, who founded Disabled In Action and, with Roberts, established the World Institute on Disability, requires attendant care for activities of daily living. By the late 1990s, Boston Center for Independent Living and American Coalition of Citizens with Disabilities cofounder Fred Fay would be lying on his back "all day, every day in Concord, Massachusetts, operating not only his home but also state and national political campaigns and international [disability] advocacy through an economical combination, which he developed, of personal assistance and three computers."[57] Leading disability advocate Justin Dart added, "Our society [still] puts people like Fred into nursing homes at far more cost than would be required to empower them."

The Independent Living Movement reflected a change in social perceptions about disability as illustrated in the difference between two popular Hollywood films, *The Men* (1950) and *Coming Home* (1978). At the end of *The Men*, the hero, a World War II veteran in a wheelchair, asks his wife for assistance in getting up a step. This scene signals to the audience that the disabled veteran will be all right because he is finally able to ask for help—something he often will have to do to survive in a society with so many obstacles. A fitting finale for a film of that period, this scene would not have been consistent with the 1970s sensibility, a time when architectural and attitudinal barriers were no longer deemed unalterable by the disability community. Unlike his counterpart in *The Men* who deals with the necessity of acceptance and adjustment, the disabled Vietnam veteran hero of *Coming Home* learns the value of protesting social injustice and educating a misinformed public.

The prophetic language of the 1970s disability rights activists, many of whom benefited from deinstitutionalization and independent living, is reminiscent of the rhetorical exhortations of the 1960s civil rights orators inspiring listeners to fight for racial justice. For example, at "The Psychological Impact of Disability," a conference held at the New York University Medical Center in New York City on October 5, 1977, speaker Tom Clancy, a quadriplegic wheelchair user and a former resident at Goldwater Hospital as a chronic care patient, roused the audience with a challenge. Echoing images of Martin Luther King's "dream" and James Baldwin's "rainbow sign" and "fire next time," Clancy invoked a new age that would supplant the Age of Aquarius:

Look out America, because I'm coming. I have always had my dream and my rainbow, but now the picture is clearer and the colors are brighter. I have tried and failed, cried and raged in silence. I have sat and watched because I could not keep in step with you, but I never gave up.

You have not heard the last of me. In fact, you have not yet heard me at all. Until recent times, you kept me out of sight and sound. Now as you begin the search for a moral answer to the materialistic chaos which you now have created, my voice will rise. For I am the living proof that physical and mental perfection are not the answer. It is the inner fire that will not accept the "impossible."

Move over Aquarius! There is a new dawn coming.[58]

Chapter Four

Groundbreaking Disability
Rights Legislation: Section 504

ON OCTOBER 26, 1972, and again on March 27, 1973, President Nixon vetoed early versions of what ultimately became the Rehabilitation Act of 1973—including Sections 501–504—both times asserting that the legislation was too expensive. He also argued that the act "diverted the program from its vocational objective into medical and social welfare policies" and "added a variety of new categorical programs."[1] Throughout the country, disability activists protested these Nixon vetoes. In New York City, Judith E. Heumann and eighty allies organized a sit-in on Madison Avenue in October 1972, bringing traffic to a halt.[2]

At the annual meeting of the President's Committee on Employment of the Handicapped in May 1973, disability activists marched to—and rallied at—the Capitol demanding passage of the act.[3] Following this demonstration, the participants took part in an all-night vigil in the rain at the Lincoln Memorial. A compromise between both houses of Congress and President Nixon resulted in a watered-down version of the proposed legislation, the Rehabilitation Act of 1973, that was signed into law on September 26, 1973. While funding and programs in this enacted rehabilitation act were reduced from the original proposal, neither the disability activists, the legislators, nor the president, at the time of the act's passage, realized what had been wrought.

Although disability rights activists strongly supported the Rehabilitation Act of 1973, they did not play a role in adding the inserted provisions, Sections 501–504, that significantly expanded disability rights. Sections 501 and 503 bar employment discrimination because of disability and mandate the use of affirmative action programs to hire qualified people with disabilities. Section 501 applies to federal agencies while Section 503 applies to recipients of federal contracts. Section 502 created the Architectural and Transportation Barriers Compliance Board, now known as the Access Board, to enforce the Architectural Barriers Act of 1968, disseminate information concerning barriers, and provide technical assistance regarding their removal. Section 504, the provision with the most far-reaching repercussions, provided civil rights for people with disabilities in programs receiving federal financial assistance.

The Cherry Lawsuit for the Section 504 Regulations

As significant as this legislation was, however, its effectiveness would have been severely limited without implementing regulations. James L. Cherry, plaintiff in the lawsuit that ultimately led to the issuing of regulations for Section 504 of the Rehabilitation Act of 1973, asserted that without these regulations "disability rights would still be in the dark ages, and there would be no Americans with Disabilities Act."[4] Steeped in the civil rights milieu of Howard University Law School in 1968, Cherry, a white student with a severe disability, recognized the connection between social accommodation denied because of race and physical accommodation denied because of disability. Although Cherry appreciated the reasons for the unswerving focus on the civil rights issues of African Americans by the Howard students, faculty, and administrators, he was disappointed that his access issues were not addressed by representatives of the university. For example, Cherry's request for a parking space near the building where his classes were held and a key to the elevator was rejected by the law school administrators.

When the Ninety-second Congress failed in 1972 to add a disability provision to the 1964 Civil Rights Act—despite the efforts of Senators Hubert Humphrey and Charles Percy and Representative Charles Vanik—Cherry was frustrated that he had no legal remedy for the discrimination he encountered. Some legislators and members of their staffs, however, conjectured that laws protecting the civil rights of people with disabilities could be tacked onto another federal law. Indeed, in *From Goodwill to Civil Rights*, Richard K. Scotch revealed that staff members of the Senate Committee on Labor and Public Welfare, in putting together the final draft of the Rehabilitation Act of 1973, "adapted and inserted" the language of Title VI of the Civil Rights Act of 1964 at the very end of the bill.[5] When the bill was enacted, this provision became Section 504, the first federal civil rights law for people with disabilities.

Almost immediately after passage of the Rehabilitation Act of 1973, Cherry began to write letters to the Department of Health, Education, and Welfare (HEW) requesting the issuance of Section 504 regulations. Meeting with no success, he sought legal support, as well as the assistance of disability organizations and sympathetic legislators. When Representative Vanik also urged HEW to issue regulations for Section 504, the congressman, like Cherry, received "an unresponsive response"; in fact, Cherry remarked that "in street terms, we were told to go take a hike." Hospitalized at the National Institutes of Health from 1974 to 1976, Cherry spent much of that time telephoning potential allies: "Seeing me talking on the phone constantly," Cherry commented, "some nurses asked if I was making obscene phone calls."

Finally, the Washington, D.C., law firm Arnold and Porter directed Cherry to attorney Victor Kramer of the Institute for Public Interest Representation at Georgetown University Law School. After hearing about Cherry's efforts, Kramer offered this advice: "Don't call anyone else; bundle up your material and send it to me as soon as possible." Kramer then instructed his graduate law students to prepare and file preliminary legal petitions for Section 504 regulations. By late 1975, Kramer determined that the endeavor had resulted in the "exhaustion of administrative procedure," legal terminology indicating that failure of the petition process, despite a sincere attempt, made legal action appropriate.

At this point Kramer asked Cherry, "Would you consider the next step, filing a lawsuit?" After almost two years of unsuccessful efforts at employing administrative remedies to urge HEW to issue Section 504 regulations, Cherry enthusiastically paid the filing fees to initiate the case on February 13, 1976, against HEW Secretary David Mathews. Kramer's argument for summary judgment was that since Section 504 was not self- effecting, the need for regulations was implicit for Section 504 enforcement. HEW filed a cross motion for summary judgment claiming that since there was nothing in the legislative history of the act necessitating the issuance of Section 504 regulations, the law did not require comprehensive guidelines.

Fearing that a decision against Cherry would discourage further disability legislation, Kramer asked the plaintiff if he would be willing to withdraw his lawsuit if he were so advised. Notwithstanding the ultimate decision of Cherry's attorneys to take their chances with a judge whom they perceived as sympathetic to their position, in Cherry's words, "It was no slam dunk." On July 19, 1976, Judge John L. Smith of the U.S. District Court for the District of Columbia issued an order requiring that HEW develop and promulgate Section 504 regulations "with all deliberate speed."[6]

Although Judge Smith had not imposed a specific deadline, his intention was clear. Nonetheless, in an unprecedented act, Secretary Mathews sent the regulations back to the Labor and Public Welfare Committee for further review. On the same day, however, Judge Smith issued a restraining order directing Mathews to issue the regulations. In order to permit the government to state its case, the U.S. Court of Appeals on January 19, 1977, stayed the order. The next day, the Carter administration assumed office and Joseph Califano was designated Secretary of HEW. David Mathews was gone, the legal maneuvering ended, and it was now up to a new administration to deal with the implementation of the act.

Were it not for the Section 504 lawsuit, which resulted in the issuance of specific regulations, Cherry still believes that the history of disability law would be "a litany of cases, a crazy quilt of decisions, narrowly defined, on issue, after issue, after issue." Without precise regulations, Section 504 lawsuits would be based on the succinct, but unelaborated, language of the law itself. Confident about his legal actions, Cherry was skeptical of the value of the nationwide Section 504 protests by disability activists that followed his successful lawsuit: "The demonstrators would have been more effective if they had dealt with my lawyers, coordinated with my case. In fact, the sit-ins may have delayed the signing of the Section 504 regulations."

Questioning the advantages of organized demonstrations, Cherry wondered whether these actions laid the groundwork for backlash against Section 504, as some of those affected feared the cost of implementation. "The impact of an individual is greater than the power of an organization without direction," Cherry asserted, "and even organizations with direction usually get their inspiration from one or two people." Cherry does not choose to engage in social actions such as sit-ins and protests that place him in opposition to the law: "Let people like HEW Secretary Mathews get arrested, not me; they're the lawbreakers."

Section 504 as a Spur to Political Organizing

After Cherry won his Section 504 lawsuit, the struggle of other disability activists to secure the signature of HEW Secretary Joseph Califano on the regulations became the central point of a broad-based movement. This effort was especially concentrated in those cities where the ten regional offices of HEW were located—

Atlanta, Boston, Chicago, Dallas, Denver, Kansas City, New York, Philadelphia, San Francisco, and Seattle—as well as in Washington, D.C. Until this point, the disability rights movement had been local and disparate. With this concerted endeavor to obtain implementation of the Section 504 regulations, the movement became national and focused.

The fact that candidate Carter sought the votes of people with disabilities revealed his awareness of the ballot-box clout of this frequently overlooked population. Aware of the symbolic meaning of the location, Carter made a campaign speech on September 6, 1976, in the place that FDR had made famous, Warm Springs, Georgia:

> Section 504 prohibits discrimination against disabled citizens by recipients of federal financial assistance. These are fine in theory, but they will mean very little until an administration in full accord with their spirit stands behind the law. No administration that really cared about disabled citizens would spend three years trying to avoid enforcing Section 504. No compassionate administration would force disabled consumers to take it to court before it would enforce the law.[7]

Once elected, President Carter was strongly urged to satisfy the interests of two conflicting constituencies: the disability community and the many institutions—including hospitals, colleges and universities, as well as local governments—whose federal funding would soon be affected by the signing of HEW's Section 504 regulations. Fearing costly and burdensome requirements, these institutions lobbied for watered-down regulations. The voice of the national disability movement, the newly-formed Washington, D.C.-based American Coalition of Citizens with Disabilities, however, reminded the president of his commitment to people with disabilities.

ACCD, Propelling Section 504

Cofounded April 30, 1975, by people with a variety of disabilities—Fred Fay, Judith E. Heumann, Ralf D. Hotchkiss, Sharon Mistler, Roger Peterson, Al Pimentel, and Eunice Fiorito—ACCD received a grant from the commissioner of the Rehabilitation Services Agency to serve as a national cross-disability model.[8] Fostering coalition-building among disability groups throughout the country, ACCD played a pivotal role in the signing of the Section 504 regulations. While she maintained her position as first director of the New York City Mayor's Office for the Handicapped (later known as the Mayor's Office for People with Disabilities in New York City) in the administration of Mayor Abraham Beame, Fiorito served as first president of ACCD.

Fiorito, who was the driving force behind ACCD, suggested why Beame may have supported her travels around the country to organize the national disability coalition: "Perhaps the blindness of his father played some part in the mayor's sensitivity to the concerns of people with disabilities. But Beame did warn me that if I was using New York City resources for ACCD," Fiorito continued, "the work should clearly serve people with disabilities in the city." These resources—telephoning, mailings, trips to Washington—though relevant to New York City business, also contributed to the work of ACCD.

Fiorito honed her organizing talents functioning as a staff person on New York Mayor John Lindsay's Committee on the Handicapped. Supported by committee member Dr. Howard Rusk, in 1971 Fiorito developed a plan to set up a city office for people with disabilities, the first of its kind in the country. As Mayor Lindsay directed, Fiorito wrote to twenty disability advocates inviting them to a meeting to discuss the possibility of initiating this new office. Fiorito, however, also called over two hundred disability advocates, many of whom appeared at that meeting. By the time the mayor arrived—surrounded by this throng as well as members of the press—he was forced to announce the *creation* of the New York City Mayor's Office for the Handicapped, Fiorito explains, rather than merely to consider the wisdom of such an undertaking, as he had planned.

As president of ACCD, Fiorito, who was blind, was joined by a brilliant twenty-five-year-old deaf advocate, Frank Bowe, who became executive director of the organization. Consistent with the unifying mission of ACCD, its director, president, and board were people with different disabilities. Fiorito observed, "People with all kinds of disabilities were able to feel, it's okay to be a person with a disability. I have the same rights as anyone else has. We're not just poor people with disabilities; instead, we believe in ourselves. And in politics you have to have self-respect and self-liking in order to show that you mean business."

The Washington, D.C., location of ACCD provided the organization with many advantages, such as the opportunity for its spokespeople to confer with members of Congress, their aides, and other government officials. Besides raising the consciousness of Washington insiders about the determination of the disability community, ACCD developed a rapport with significant individuals in the Carter administration, including Peter Libassi, aide to HEW Secretary Joseph Califano. In fact, on April 28, 1977, when Califano finally agreed to sign the Section 504 regulations, Libassi telephoned Fiorito in New York City at 6:45 in the morning to be certain that she approved of Califano's press release.

Since candidate Carter had backed the goals of the disability community in his campaign for president, the leaders of ACCD expected more of this new Demo-

cratic administration than of the former Republican one. In order to offer their services to expedite the issuing of the Section 504 regulations, over a dozen members of ACCD began meeting with Califano and his staff two days after President Carter took office.[9] About two months later, on March 18, 1977, Bowe wrote a letter on behalf of ACCD to Carter, with a copy to Califano, as a statement of the organization's frustration with the government's delay.[10] Furthermore, the letter included a warning of ACCD's decision to take action if the Section 504 regulations were not signed by April 4, 1977.

The Section 504 Demonstrations

Attempts at last-moment negotiations between disability community leaders and Califano failed because the new HEW secretary requested additional time to study the Section 504 regulations. The leaders feared that Califano wanted this extra time to weaken or evade the original intent of the regulations. Therefore, on April 5, 1977, disability activists demonstrated—and in many locations also sat-in—at most of the HEW offices in the ten federal regions and in the nation's capital. The dramatic events of the D.C. sit-in, and especially the San Francisco sit-in, have been well-documented—for example, in Joseph Shapiro's account in *No Pity*.[11] Despite Califano's refusal to allow the demonstrators food or telephone access, the forty D.C. protesters remained for twenty-eight hours. "Rather than allow them to leave in small groups until they trickled down to nothing," Fiorito decided that they should make a dramatic exit as a group calling attention to the insensitivity of Califano's response to the sit-in. However valuable the determination of all the demonstrators throughout the country, it was in San Francisco that the unyielding resolve of the disability community was most convincingly exhibited.

As the number of days of the San Francisco sit-in began to add up, disability activists across the country were checking their newspapers with mounting astonishment and pride. "They're still there!" they kept saying. Close to half of the more than 120 initial protesters, representing a variety of disabilities, remained for twenty-five days, the longest sit-in at a federal building. Despite the difficulties endured, particularly by the severely disabled demonstrators who were courageous and resourceful enough to manage without their needed devices or attendants, the San Francisco group was well-organized and widely supported. Since a great number of the protesters either were employed by, and/or clients of, the Berkeley Center for Independent Living, they came to the experience with an established sense of community and, where relevant, job security. Whereas demonstrators in other cities had diverse occupations and employers, most of whom would not countenance long-term absences, in a sense many of the employed San Francisco protesters were doing their jobs.

The CIL was an integral part of the small Berkeley community, so the individuals involved in the demonstration and their concerns were familiar in the general Bay Area. Food, mattresses, and shower equipment were provided by sources as diverse as McDonald's, the California Department of Health Services, and the drug program of Delancy Houses.[12] Government officials, such as U.S. Representative Philip Burton, San Francisco Mayor George Moscone, and State Director of Rehabilitation Edward Roberts, offered their encouragement and assistance.

Judith E. Heumann, leader of the San Francisco sit-in and later assistant secretary of the U.S. Department of Education, analyzed the event in 1978:

> The 504 demonstrations last year in California were successful for a number of reasons: because the disabled community was united; because the disabled community absolutely unequivocally believed that 504 was our civil rights provision; because we knew if we did not fight for this civil rights provision, we were in fact going to slide backward instead of making further progress.
>
> But the other factor was that because of the programs evolving in the Bay Area that were controlled by disabled individuals, and because changes were being made (curb cuts, electric wheelchairs, Bay Area Rapid Transit being accessible, etc.), we were more visible in our communities. So we went out into other organizations; we approached, surprisingly, such groups as United Cerebral Palsy and Easter Seal and those kinds of organizations and they came in and worked with us. We received support from the churches and synagogues and from the labor unions. We had support from all over the place. The Black Panthers fed us for four weeks during the sit-in. And we were supplied with food from Safeway stores. It was a totally bizarre event; it really was. People that I could not conceive of being together were living in a building on one floor for four weeks.[13]

Lacking the organization and experience in disability politics of the Berkeley CIL, New York City's disability community was represented by a small group of about eight people who sat in at the HEW office at the federal building in Manhattan. Although approximately fifty disability activists rallied in the rain outside the building, the New York disability rights organizations had decided to have only their leaders participate in the sit-in. Because coalitions of diverse disability groups had not yet become a reality outside of California and Washington, D.C., the New York City contingent was almost entirely mobility impaired. Despite the regional HEW director's effort to convince the protesters to reconsider their tactics, she welcomed these uninvited guests into an office, allowing them to bring in food and other supplies, as well as come and go as they pleased.

Since they had access to the phones, they were able to inform various media outlets of the ongoing sit-in. For example, one protester—who coincidentally had tutored Felipe Luciano, later an NBC television news reporter—used that relationship to persuade Luciano to cover the sit-in. Having been one of the leaders of the Young Lords—a youthful, progressive, Latino political organization in the late 1960s and early 1970s—Luciano revealed his sensitivity to civil rights issues in his broadcast. While the other reporters tended to concentrate on the nature and degree of the protesters' disabilities, Luciano focused on the faces of the demonstrators and on their issues. Because of their individual obligations to jobs and families, the disability leaders sitting in at the New York City HEW office voted to disperse, en masse, after thirty-three hours.

Like many of the reporters, the HEW officials misjudged the demonstration. In New York City, they arranged for a nurse to stay overnight with the protesters. In San Francisco, on the first day, officials served cookies and punch to the demonstrators.[14] These responses reveal commonly assumed, patronizing attitudes toward people with disabilities. Adults with disabilities were treated as if they were "medical models," unable to make reasoned decisions about their capabilities, or as if they were hysterical children to be placated. Surprised by the fervor, persistence, and stamina of the protesters, Califano and his staff could not have predicted the twenty-five-day San Francisco sit-in. On April 28, 1977, Califano signed not only the Section 504 regulations in their original form, but also the regulations for the Education for All Handicapped Children Act, now called the Individuals with Disabilities Education Act. The San Francisco demonstrators did not leave until April 30, 1977, after they had examined the

signed Section 504 regulations in order to be sure that they had not been diluted.

With the signing of the Section 504 regulations, the disability community discovered its muscle. Borrowing the strategy of passive resistance from the 1960s civil rights movement, the disability activists had the advantage of usually having to contend with, at most, condescension and hostility, rather than physical violence. Reminiscent of the 1930s League of the Physically Handicapped, the Section 504 protesters absorbed the social consciousness of a politically active milieu and thus exceeded their own expectations. However, unlike the earlier efforts by the League of the Physically Handicapped, these nationwide Section 504 demonstrations, orchestrated by ACCD, were an initial thrust, generating further actions.

In 1978, Hofstra professor Frank Bowe, then director of ACCD, asked the question, "Why did it [the signing of the Section 504 regulations] happen?"

> For a long time I had trouble answering that question because so many different factors and influences seemed to have combined to make it happen. Then, sometime later in 1977, I happened to be reading a book about the black civil rights movement, and I found the answer to that question.... This advisor [to Martin Luther King] said, "People think that revolutions begin with injustices. They don't. A revolution begins with hope." If you think about that, if you move back to the Spring of 1977, then you will understand that the reason disabled people came together and demonstrated as they did in the Spring of that year was because *they had hope.*
>
> It is a tremendously tragic commentary upon the United States of America that it was only in 1977 that disabled people came to have enough hope to protest. It took two hundred years after this country was formed—*two hundred years*—for these people to begin to have hope. That is what happened. A law had been passed in 1973, the Rehabilitation Act of 1973, and included in it was Section

504, which many people realized was going to become the cornerstone of the civil rights of disabled Americans.... For four years we had fought behind the scenes to try to get the law implemented and enforced. And at the beginning of 1977, for the first time, we had some reason to hope that the law was at last going to become effective.[15]

The Transbus Controversy

Accessible transportation became the major Section 504 local government issue in the 1980s as disability groups in different parts of the country—such as Chicago, Rhode Island, Maine, and Philadelphia—filed lawsuits against transportation agencies. Perhaps because transportation, essential for social participation, is a tangible and easily understood cross-disability issue, many disability activists were drawn to the cause. Also, the precipitous opposition to the mainstreaming provisions in Section 504 by most of the transit agencies throughout the nation provided the disability community with a clear focus.

A 1976 transportation case set the stage for the development of a wheelchair-accessible lift bus that—beginning in the late 1970s in California—eventually became the prototype for the nation. Thus, an appropriate technology was available for the newly-signed Section 504 regulations issued by the Department of Transportation. In *Disabled In Action of Pennsylvania v. Coleman* (E.D., Pa. 1976),[16] known as the Transbus lawsuit, a coalition of thirteen disability and senior citizen organizations[17] sued three federal transportation agencies[18] so that the federal government would mandate the wheelchair accessible Transbus.[19] The plaintiffs claimed that although Transbus—the low-floor, wide-door, ramped bus—was technologically feasible, it would be produced only if it were required by the government. Therefore, they charged that the govern-

ment was in contravention of existing legislation requiring accessible public transportation unless it compelled manufacturers to produce Transbus.[20]

Although the plaintiffs had no success during the Ford administration, President Carter's first Secretary of Transportation, Brock Adams, responded to the Transbus lawsuit. Consistent with Section 504, he decreed on May 19, 1977, that all buses purchased with federal funds on or after September 30, 1979, must have the same wheelchair-accessible design as Transbus.[21] Anticipating an impending congressional decision to delay Transbus, the American Coalition of Citizens with Disabilities, the National Council of Senior Citizens, and Paralyzed Veterans of America sponsored simultaneous July 12, 1978, demonstrations in Chicago, Detroit, New York, Philadelphia, San Francisco, Washington, D.C., and other cities.[22] In New York City, wheelchair users and other people with disabilities blocked the main thoroughfare in front of the United Nations during rush hour.

Despite these protests, Congress, encouraged by pressure from the American Public Transit Association (APTA)—which included General Motors—voted later in July 1978 to reevaluate the Transbus mandate, thus deferring the development of Transbus. In keeping with the spirit—if not the letter—of Section 504, Transbus allowed everybody to get on and off the bus in the same way in contrast to the General Motors lift-equipped bus, which provides a separate means of entering and exiting for people who cannot negotiate steps.[23] Since a device that all can use is more likely to be properly maintained than one used only by a particular population, Transbus, not the lift-equipped bus, was the first choice of the disability community as well as the California transit agencies.

Dennis Cannon, Access Board accessibility specialist and wheelchair user, points out that APTA disseminated misinformation indicating that a low-floor bus was technologically infeasible, especially in snowy areas where, supposedly, inadequate clearance underneath would create insurmountable problems.[24] "Stanford Research Institute revealed that because the primary business of General Motors was producing automobiles, the corporation had a disincentive to develop an attractive easy-to-use accessible bus, such as Transbus," Cannon notes. Moreover, he adds that General Motors, the corporate giant of the industry, had already retooled for a more traditional bus than Transbus.

James Raggio, general counsel for the Access Board, indicates that the increasing numbers of low-floor buses being purchased by transit agencies in the 1990s demonstrates the technological superiority of the Transbus design.[25] He observes that not only are these vehicles easier to board and more comfortable to ride than most other models, but also passengers do not tend to trip as frequently on low-floor buses as they do on lift-equipped buses. Because General Motors had an economic motive in the 1970s for preferring to add lifts to their existing design, rather than produce Transbus, the lift-equipped model became the accessible bus central to the Section 504 controversy.

Accessible Transit and New York City

Soon after the Section 504 regulations were signed in 1977, New York City disability activists pointed to the Seattle accessible bus system as the paradigm for mainstreamed barrier-free transit. Yet the mindset of most directors of transit agencies was revealed by their response to contrasting 1980s accessible bus programs, one in Seattle, the other in St. Louis. Since the Seattle lift-equipped buses, besides being safe and re-

liable, arrived at reasonable and predictable intervals, they enjoyed comparatively high ridership by wheelchair users. On the other hand, wheelchair users, having no confidence in the poorly managed and therefore unreliable St. Louis lift-bus system, did not ride the buses. Cannon observes, "To prove their preconceived notion that wheelchair users would not ride buses in significant numbers, many transit agency 'experts' generalized the St. Louis experience, while labeling the Seattle program an anomaly. Thus, they reversed the adage, 'Success has many fathers; failure is an orphan.'"[26]

Although Seattle and the metropolitan San Francisco area developed effective accessible transportation systems before New York City, the impact of the two smaller sites was limited. With residents and a workforce from other localities dependent on New York City's largest transit system in the country, this system provided the most significant experiment in the feasibility of accessible public transportation. With an activist disability community willing to engage in the contest, New York City would be a major setting for the struggle for accessible public transportation.

A significant 1979 U.S. Supreme Court decision, *Southeastern Community College v. Davis,* ruling against a plaintiff, a deaf nurse, although technically limited in scope to the physical requirements of a professional training program, seemed to have ominous implications for other Section 504 lawsuits. Consequently, Eastern Paralyzed Veterans Association (EPVA) attorney James Weisman chose to file a New York City public transportation wheelchair-accessibility case (*EPVA v. MTA*) under two New York State statutes that same year. He successfully argued that MTA's failure to provide barrier-free subway stations, when they were newly built or extensively renovated, failed to comply with the state's building code. His contention that inaccessible buses discriminated against people with disabilities under the state's Human Rights Law—a nondiscrimination statute—did not succeed, as the court held that the inclusion of bus lifts was "affirmative action" and not required by the Law.[27]

In 1980, Disabled In Action of Metropolitan New York (DIA) filed a Section 504 lawsuit against city, state, and federal transportation agencies for "violating the rights of wheelchair users by operating buses that are inaccessible to them."[28] Unlike the New York State Human Rights Law, Section 504 requires "reasonable accommodation," adaptations providing access that do not incur prohibitive expense or require extensive modifications. DIA's goal was to secure a wheelchair-accessible multi-modal New York City transit system, meaning fully accessible buses, "key" wheelchair accessible subway stations[29] (an issue addressed in *EPVA v. MTA*), and a supplemental paratransit service in the form of door-to-door lift-equipped vans. Once the U.S. District Court (S.D. N.Y.) accepted two similar Section 504 class action lawsuits, *Dopico* emphasizing paratransit and *DIA* stressing lift-equipped buses, the cases were joined under the name of the earlier of the two, *Dopico v. Goldschmidt.*[30]

Although the District Court ruled against the plaintiffs in *Dopico,* the U.S. Court of Appeals (Second Circuit) found in 1982 "that Section 504 does require at least modest, affirmative steps, to accommodate the handicapped in public transportation."[31] Furthermore, the court decided that "a $6 million expenditure for transportation services to the handicapped out of a total federal mass transportation subsidy to [New York] City of $490 million, although a considerable sum, 'was not massive either in absolute terms or relative to the city's total receipt of mass transportation's assistance.'"

The *Dopico* decision mandated that *only*

newly-purchased buses be lift equipped. Because the decision did *not* require retrofitting,[32] one practical effect of *Dopico* was that it increased the acceptability of accessible buses in the courts and initiated the purchase and use of these buses in New York City. In *Rhode Island Handicapped Action Committee v. Rhode Island Public Transit Authority,*[33] the Court of Appeals (First Circuit) determined in 1983, however, that "the benefit of the purchase [of accessible buses] to the handicapped" did not outweigh "the financial expense that would be incurred by the State."[34] Thus the decisions in *Dopico* and *Rhode Island* revealed that interpretation of Section 504 with respect to public transportation was still evolving.

From 1976 until September 1980, disability leaders worked together with the MTA as part of the Tri-State Regional Planning Commission (representing New York, New Jersey, and Connecticut), successfully developing a Section 504 transition plan for accessible transportation. On September 19, 1980, however, the MTA decided *not* to submit the transportation plan. Instead, the MTA asked for "a six-month extension or partial exemption from the [Section 504] requirements, on the grounds that it would cost too much and force the curtailment of service to other riders."[35] Recognizing that the goals of the MTA and the disability community no longer were compatible, a broad coalition of disability groups and individuals concerned with transportation organized Mobility Through Access.[36]

Because of the MTA's Section 504 violation, the first tactic employed by Mobility Through Access was a sit-in at the MTA building in Manhattan on November 21, 1980. Led by DIA, approximately fifty people, some in wheelchairs, some on crutches, and still others accompanied by guide dogs, expressed their outrage by blocking the four elevators that served the first twelve floors of the twenty-four-story MTA building. Not being allowed access to the bathroom, mobility-impaired activists were required to be especially resourceful. The result was a pail of urine left in MTA board member Stephen Berger's office. As one activist recalled, "A small support contingent of some fifteen people carried posters and distributed informational leaflets on the street and in the downstairs lobby. A half dozen of these had gotten up at five o'clock to be shuttled from their homes on Long Island into the City on a lift-equipped van."[37] From 8:30 a.m. to 5:30 p.m., the protesters occupied the main stairwell and the administrative offices of MTA chairman Richard Ravitch and his staff on the seventh floor.

The demonstrators presented Ravitch with four demands:

(1) that the MTA submit by January 2, 1981, the Alternative [Section 504] Transportation Plan developed in conjunction with the disabled community to the Tri-State Regional Planning Commission and the U.S. Department of Transportation; (2) that the MTA withdraw its request for a six-month extension to submit a plan; (3) that the MTA discontinue its fraudulent media misrepresentation of the facts concerning transportation accessibility; and (4) that the MTA address the real needs of mass transit users and act in the best interest of all people, disabled and nondisabled alike.

Characterizing the demonstration as inappropriate, Ravitch offered to negotiate with a small representative group if the members would make an appointment in advance. The protesters refused, indicating that they had been negotiating in good faith to no avail since 1976.

Worried about the bad press that would result from arresting demonstrators with disabilities, the MTA arranged for the removal of the protesters by police supervised by a team of medics. MTA's concern regarding media coverage was well placed, for the major television networks, radio stations, and New York City newspapers treated the nonviolent civil disobedience at the MTA sympathetically. The New York City disability community considered their action successful for three main reasons. First, disability activists believed that they had gotten the "real" facts on Section 504 requirements for accessible mass transit to the public. Second, many people with disabilities who had never before participated in social action were motivated to continue their involvement in disability rights issues. And finally, lift-equipped buses that MTA had recently purchased to comply with Section 504 began to appear on the streets of New York City.

MTA sent written notices to members of the disability community who had attended the Section 504 transportation meetings, informing them that on September 30, 1981, lift-equipped buses would be available on the M104, M14, and B41 routes. On the appointed day, wheelchair user Denise McQuade was accompanied by CBS television news reporter Arnold Diaz and his camera man, who planned to cover one of the first uses of the new lift-equipped New York City buses acquired to conform to the Section 504 mandate. When McQuade attempted to board the M104 bus, however, the driver did not have the key needed to operate the lift. Other wheelchair users, such as Anne Emerman, later director of the Mayor's Office for People with Disabilities from 1990 to 1994, were having the same experience on other routes. Some have speculated that the MTA's contradictory behavior was consistent with the agency's conflicting attitude toward wheelchair accessibility. Whatever the reason, the MTA's motive for apparently reneging on its agreement remains a mystery.

Once McQuade realized that the lift was not going to function, she lifted herself from her wheelchair to one of the front steps of the bus. Diaz, recognizing that this story was better than the one he had come to cover, waited with McQuade for seven hours while the MTA officials deliberated. The MTA's efforts to persuade McQuade to allow herself to be carried onto the bus failed, for she persisted in her demand that, in keeping with Section 504, she be enabled to board the bus by means of the lift. Finally, the MTA capitulated as the bus driver obtained the required key. As McQuade got on the bus using the lift, she flashed the "V" sign for victory. Not only did Diaz present her story on the local CBS news program, but McQuade also appeared the next day on the front page of the *New York Post.* Ironically, but appropriately, ten years later McQuade was employed by the MTA.

On the same day, Anne Emerman met with similar frustration when the driver of the bus she tried to board did not have the lift key.[38] She responded by moving her wheelchair to the front of the vehicle and grabbing onto the windshield wipers. Perhaps, because there were no television cameras recording the event, Emerman was treated more harshly than McQuade. Not only did the police pull her fingers off the windshield wipers, but she also was given a summons for disorderly conduct. In fact, one police officer remarked that she was receiving the same kind of citation given to prostitutes. Accompanied by her husband and daughter, Emerman laughed at the absurd insinuation. Later that day, Emerman filed two complaints, one with the New York City Commission on Human Rights against New York City Transit, and the other with the Civilian Review Board against the New York City Police Department. Since the police had placed her wheelchair on the sidewalk, Emerman never got on the bus that day, unlike McQuade. Nonetheless, McQuade's success, proving that the lifts could work properly, meant that the Section 504 accessible bus program had been launched in New York City. A day later, an overly solicitous bus driver of a lift-equipped bus

was so eager to accommodate Ellen Nuzzi, a scooter user, that he drove her—picking up no other passengers—directly from her home to her place of employment.[39]

Still, many disability activists believed that the MTA was employing tactics to discourage ridership on the buses by wheelchair users. There were only a few routes on which the infrequent accessible buses operated, and even those rare vehicles often did not function consistently. Although the MTA used various media outlets to advertise some of its programs, such as the unsuccessful "Train to the Plane," the agency made no effort to publicize the lift-equipped buses required by Section 504. Outside of those involved with the accessible transportation coalition—Mobility Through Access—few wheelchair users knew about these buses. Therefore, the MTA created a self-fulfilling prophecy when it claimed that the accessible buses were not needed since few people made use of them.

Realizing that outreach was necessary to increase ridership on the accessible buses, Mobility Through Access initiated "Ride the Bus Days" in order to attract media attention to the Section 504 mandate. Furthermore, members of the coalition recommended responses to the common sources of frustration experienced by wheelchair riders. For example, if for any reason the bus driver did not deploy the lift, wheelchair users were encouraged to ask the driver to call a supervisor. Then they were advised to stand in front of the bus to prevent it from proceeding until the supervisor dealt with the problem.

On the first "Ride the Bus Day," April 20, 1982, Michael Imperiale, disabled but not a wheelchair user, accompanied Frieda Zames who was in a motorized scooter waiting for a lift-equipped M14 bus on the corner of East Third Street and Avenue A in Manhattan.[40] When an accessible bus arrived, the driver declared, almost predictably, that the lift was broken. After Imperiale and Zames requested that the driver call his supervisor, they stood in front of the bus. Suddenly three police cars rounded the corner with great urgency. Two police officers jumped out and accosted Imperiale, socking him and using a billy club on various parts of his body.

After this event, James Weisman, attorney for Eastern Paralyzed Veterans Association, met with success in his effort to make the police understand that attempts of wheelchair users to board the buses, in keeping with Section 504, were lawful. When Emerman had been mishandled by the police, Weisman recommended that posters explaining correct police procedure concerning the rights of wheelchair bus riders appear in every police station. Perhaps, after the Imperiale incident, police officials realized that unless officers were appropriately trained with respect to these issues, vulnerable people could be endangered. Rather than treat the wheelchair user as the transgressor, the police, now cognizant of Section 504, began to settle conflicts amicably between bus drivers and riders with disabilities.

Despite the new police sensitivity in dealing with wheelchair bus riders, Imperiale filed a civil lawsuit in U.S. District Court against New York City for police violation of *his* rights. In 1987, five and a half years later, when the case finally came to trial, the pivotal witness was a disinterested bystander, an Off Track Betting employee on her way to work. Although the police officers involved in the action claimed to have been totally unaware of Imperiale's disability, as well as the presence of a person in a motorized scooter, the onlooker recognized the situation immediately. Her choice of language may not have been "politically correct," but her powers of observation were acute. As a result of her cries to the police, "Stop hitting the invalid," she received first a warning to

mind her own business, and then a summons for disorderly conduct. Her convincing and unshakable testimony, in combination with the testimony of Anne Emerman and EPVA attorney Weisman, persuaded the six-person jury to find on behalf of plaintiff Imperiale.

Although Section 504 supported wheelchair users of public transportation, they frequently experienced the frustration of broken lifts and untrained bus drivers. In response, on November 4, 1982, EPVA filed a Section 504 transportation lawsuit, *EPVA v. MTA*, against the MTA and New York City Transit for mismanagement of the accessible bus program.[41] EPVA's argument was that wheelchair riders and nondisabled riders received unequal bus service from the New York City local transit agencies. The suit depended on more than twelve hundred complaints filed by people with disabilities who had attempted to use accessible buses. The specific and inexpensive relief sought by EPVA included daily cycling of bus-lifts for proper maintenance, availability of bus keys for wheelchair riders, and training of bus drivers for improved operation of lifts.

Nonetheless, the cost of replacing two hundred newly-purchased Grumman buses that had unreliable and unsafe lifts did appear to be a stumbling block in EPVA's effort to convince the court to mandate MTA's compliance with Section 504. Because two hundred buses were bought *after* the Section 504 transportation regulations of 1979 were signed, these vehicles had to be accessible. EPVA's concern was that the expenditure involved could be deemed extraordinary, causing the judgment to favor MTA. These two hundred buses were the last shipment out of 837 Grumman buses purchased by MTA, three times the number normally bought in any other single year.

Despite the agency's awareness that the buses were not roadworthy, MTA rushed to sign a contract with Grumman before Section 504 became effective in order to circumvent the regulations necessitating accessible vehicles.[42] In fact, MTA board member Stephen Berger boasted that the intentional timing of the bus purchase would save the city from spending money on accessibility. Because of the consequence of this precipitous acquisition, not only the two hundred accessible buses, but also the other 637 inaccessible buses, all the Grumman buses were so inappropriate for New York City streets that MTA was forced to sell the vehicles at a loss. Thus, nondisabled as well as disabled riders were inconvenienced by being deprived of bus service and burdened by additional taxes.

Moreover, MTA began renovating ten subway stations without including wheelchair accessibility in contravention of the Public Buildings Law requirement that all newly-built or extensively modified subway stations be barrier-free. When Weisman learned in 1982 that the MTA had ignored this law, he sought an injunction preventing further renovations of the ten stations. Perhaps in order to embarrass EPVA, MTA chairman Ravitch stopped modifications, not only at the ten designated stations, but at all subway stations. Although the *New York Times* editorial "There's a Wheelchair on the Tracks" blamed EPVA for impeding subway improvement, the court determined that MTA was at fault.[43]

The 1982 election of New York Governor Mario Cuomo, however, changed the relationship between MTA and wheelchair users of public transportation. Supported by the disability community in his campaign, Cuomo appointed Robert Kiley—a transportation expert sympathetic to consumers of accessible transit—as MTA chairman. At a public forum in Brooklyn Heights shortly after accepting his new position, Kiley indicated that the first question Governor Cuomo asked him was, "What is your view of accessible public transporta-

tion?"[44] EPVA attorney Weisman revealed that Cuomo impressed upon Kiley that the governor's administration supported lift-equipped buses and barrier-free subway stations in compliance with Section 504.

Once a settlement appeared imminent, Mayor Edward Koch suspended transportation negotiations on June 21, 1984, publicly announcing his objection to accessible subways and his support for a paratransit plan instead.[45] Regarding wheelchair accessible transportation as a luxury that New York City could ill afford, Koch was frequently in conflict with the disability community. In *Goodwill to Civil Rights*, Scotch points out, "While a member of the House of Representatives, [Koch] was a leading proponent of civil rights for disabled people. Several years later, following his election as mayor of New York City, he became a prominent critic of the accessibility requirements of the Section 504 regulation."[46]

A resumption of talks called by Kiley on June 28, 1984, between the MTA, EPVA, and DIA, nevertheless, resulted in a compromise, followed by a ceremony on November 19, 1984, at Grand Central Station, acknowledging the signing of the New York State Handicapped Transportation Act.[47] In keeping with the Section 504 mandate, this act established the multi-modal transportation system that EPVA and DIA sought. First, the MTA was required to spend $5 million per year for eight years, 1985 through 1992, to make "key" subway stations wheelchair accessible. Second, although only 65 percent of all New York City buses were mandated to be wheelchair accessible (with equipment properly operated and maintained), the MTA eventually recognized the advantage of providing 100 percent accessible buses, a decision satisfying EPVA and DIA. Finally, the settlement necessitated the formation of an eleven-member committee, the Transportation Disabled Committee, with five members appointed by the governor and six by the mayor, to develop a plan implementing a paratransit system within seven months, known as Access-A-Ride. The ultimate victory of the disability community in the development of an accessible transit system in New York City paved the way for similar systems throughout the country.

Bay Area Rapid Transit (BART)

New York City disability activists were confident that their city's subway system could become accessible in compliance with Section 504 because they knew that in the Berkeley/San Francisco region such a system, the Bay Area Rapid Transit (BART), had been operating successfully since the 1970s. While those in New York City involved in accessible transit were dealing with retrofitting an old subway system built at the beginning of the twentieth century, those in northern California in the 1960s were planning the inclusion of wheelchair accessibility in the development of a new train system. Harold Willson, senior economic analyst for the Kaiser Medical Care Program and a wheelchair user, was the catalyst who successfully appointed himself the guiding spirit behind the creation of a barrier-free train system.[48]

Unlike tenBroek or the Gallaudet demonstrators, Willson had no broad political agenda outside of accessibility. Since he lived near one BART station and worked near another, he wanted to be able to use the system to travel between his home and his place of employment. Yet, because of his laser-beam focus on his particular concern, making BART available to wheelchair users, he got the respect of the BART staff as they responded to the feasibility of his detailed specifications for wheelchair accessibility.

Acquiring data from the American National Standards Institute (ANSI), Willson encouraged applying these barrier-free designs and specifications of buildings and facilities for people with physical disabilities to the BART system. The ANSI standards had resulted from a 1961 conference sponsored by the President's Committee on Employment of the Handicapped and the National Easter Seal Society for Crippled Children and Adults.[49] Originally providing "a mechanism for creating voluntary consensus standards,"[50] ultimately, these ANSI specifications would become the required guidelines for train and subway systems throughout the country. By 1965, after three years of planning for the new BART system, the board of directors determined that plans would be made to accommodate all categories of people with disabilities except nonambulatory passengers. Willson, who did not accept the argument that costs precluded the inclusion of elevators and other requirements for wheelchair users, became a frequent speaker at conventions and meetings of people with disabilities, as well as various social, political, and religious groups. For three years, a stream of letters flowed to the BART board and staff from many of the people who had been influenced by Willson, including doctors, rehabilitation agencies, members of Congress, and the board of supervisors of San Francisco.

On February 29, 1968, the BART board requested an additional $7 million from the California legislature for the inclusion of elevators in the new train system. A colorful illustration of the pressures brought to bear on the California legislature occurred in March 1968:

> An ad hoc committee calling itself the Committee for the Freedom of Mobility of the Disabled called for a demonstration. People in wheelchairs and on crutches and some with white canes, all carrying banners proclaiming the need for elevators in the BART system, converged on the construction

site of the downtown Berkeley BART station. Work was halted by the demonstration. The result was wide press coverage which added to the public's awareness of the issues.[51]

Once the BART board declared itself in favor of the inclusion of elevators, Willson carried his campaign to the state legislature. Willson and the board were joined in Sacramento, the state capital, by representatives of the Architectural Barriers Committee of the Easter Seal Society. After the state legislature agreed in 1968 to guarantee the redesigning of BART to accommodate wheelchair users, Willson and the board continued to lobby Sacramento until the $150 million in additional funding to provide wheelchair accessibility was allocated in March 1969. Perhaps the most far-reaching effect of Willson's relentless, almost quixotic, determination was BART's role as a Section 504 model for a barrier-free train system.[52] Never again would skeptics be able to argue that trains could not be made wheelchair accessible. Furthermore, once wheelchair users were riding the trains, the great distance between the Bay Area stations increased the likelihood of the connecting bus system eventually becoming wheelchair accessible.

California Accessible Buses

Perhaps because wheelchair users and other people with disabilities rode the BART system in northern California alongside nondisabled people by the early 1970s, local transit agencies in California were especially receptive to accessible public transportation. For example, Southern California Rapid Transit, a bus system, joined with two other California transit systems in a 1974 policy resolution that all new bus purchases would be wheelchair accessible.[53] According to California law, every transit agency in the state was required to purchase

accessible buses if at least two manufacturers were willing to produce them. The submission of bids by three manufacturers—General Motors, Flexible (earlier known as Rohr), and American General—triggered a domino effect so that all the California transit agencies sought to purchase accessible buses.

Although the Section 504 regulations were not signed until 1977, Nathanael Gage, deputy director of the Metropolitan Transportation Commission of the Nine County Planning District around and including San Francisco, believed as early as 1975 that the federal government would require all new buses to be accessible within a few years. Demonstrating the forward thinking that characterized the directors of California transit agencies in the 1970s, Gage conducted pilot demonstrations in the late 1970s to test prototype buses with wheelchair lifts.[54]

Unlike the California agencies, many transit agencies throughout the country did not support the creation of accessible buses on fixed routes because they believed that wheelchair users would cause havoc. In order to avoid the cost and the effort involved in developing an accessible transit system, many transit officials sought to have other organizations, such as social service agencies, deal with the problem. People in these agencies, who were not transportation experts, did not always find the most efficient means of transporting their clients from place to place. For example, in many localities, accessible paratransit systems were devised in which people with disabilities were driven in accessible vans from door to door. As a result, public transit expert Dennis Cannon indicated, "The transit industry created a Frankenstein, a paratransit-dependent population, so that the industry then could go to Congress and say, 'Our consumers don't want to use fixed route systems.'"[55]

Beginning in the 1970s, encouraged by the 1977 signing of the Section 504 regulations, disability advocates argued that the number of people requiring barrier-free transportation would justify accessible buses on fixed routes. Except in California, directors of transit agencies tended to underestimate this ridership. These directors soon discovered, however, that the accessible paratransit systems on which the industry relied were not only inadequate to accommodate the disability population they served, but also that the cost of total dependence on this accessible door-to-door transit was impractical. Although accessible paratransit functions well as a primary service in some small localities and as a supplementary service in many other areas, accessible paratransit cannot replace the accessible fixed route transportation (buses and trains).

Mainstreaming Public Transit

In the intervening years between the 1977 signing of the regulations for Section 504 and the 1990 passage of the ADA, disability leaders concentrated on the courts to ensure enforcement of Section 504. The evolution of federal laws and litigation that provided access to transportation for the disability population epitomizes the Section 504 struggle of those who sought integration—as opposed to those who favored continued segregation—of people with disabilities. Section 504 in effect mandated that all recipients of federal funds mainstream people with disabilities. Transcending the particulars of the case, the 1977 Seventh Circuit Court of Appeals decision in *Lloyd v. Illinois Regional Transportation Authority*[56] created a precedent for people with disabilities and their organizations to sue federal agencies and recipients of federal funds to enforce Section 504.

Although *Southeastern Community College v. Davis*[57] was not a transportation case, this 1979 decision had a profound effect on Section 504 transportation lawsuits. Frances Davis, a severely hard-of-hearing licensed practical nurse, was denied entrance to Southeastern Community College's associate degree nursing program because of her disability. Davis contended that the college was unlawfully discriminatory, in violation of Section 504, to insist that functional hearing was essential for acceptance into the nursing program. The college argued that extensive modifications would be necessary for Davis to participate safely in the program or to practice the nursing profession.

The U.S. Supreme Court ruled for the college against Davis, deciding that the accommodation to provide equal opportunity constituted affirmative action, so Section 504—a nondiscrimination, not an affirmative action, statute—was inapplicable. The fact that one hundred and fifty hard-of-hearing and deaf nurses were already working for the federal government according to a 1976 Civil Service Commission survey would have supported Davis's contention that she could work safely as a nurse.[58] Not introduced in the original lawsuit, however, this statistic could not be used by the plaintiff on appeal. *Davis,* the first Section 504 case to reach the U.S. Supreme Court, established a disappointing precedent for disability lawyers because the suit set the stage for the 1981 APTA transportation decision.

Within weeks of the 1979 *Davis* ruling, APTA filed a lawsuit (*APTA v. Lewis*) in the D.C. Circuit contesting the 1979 Section 504 regulations of the U.S. Department of Transportation (USDOT).[59] Modeled on the HEW regulations, these USDOT regulations—clearly a mainstreaming approach—required that not only newly-purchased buses be lift-equipped, but also that existing bus fleets must be retrofitted with lifts. In *APTA v. Lewis,* APTA cited the *Davis* decision, claiming that public transit accessibility would involve excessive expense, burdensome modifications, and technological problems, while affording benefits for few people with disabilities. The administration of newly-elected President Reagan accepted the U.S. Court of Appeals (D.C. Circuit) unanimous *APTA* decision that extended the *Davis* rationale to public transit agencies. The disability community had assumed that Section 504 would advance the cause of integration, promoting equal access to society for people with disabilities, but as a consequence of the 1981 *APTA* decision, the 1979 bus retrofitting requirement was invalidated.

Required to write new Section 504 regulations, USDOT issued the 1981 *interim* regulations until final regulations were developed. Abandoning the 1979 Section 504 mainstreaming regulations, USDOT returned to a less precise concept of "special efforts" and coined a new term, "local option."[60] "Special efforts" made unspecified reference in federal public transportation law to "the planning and design of mass transportation facilities and services" so that they could be utilized by "elderly and handicapped persons."[61] "Local option" allowed local transit agencies to choose to purchase buses with lifts, or to establish a mixed system of some lift-equipped buses and some wheelchair-accessible vans, or to institute *only* a segregated wheelchair-accessible door-to-door (paratransit) system.[62] Local transit agencies could employ one of these "local option" choices to demonstrate their compliance with "special efforts."

In elevating "special efforts" and "local option" over mainstreaming, the 1981 interim regulations appeared to disability activists to have undermined the Section 504 national mandate for integrated accessible public transit. Furthermore, the only criterion used to determine compliance with these interim regulations was the spending by local transit agencies of at least 3½ percent of the federal funds for transportation services for people with disabilities. "Once the spending requirement was met, there would be no federal scrutiny of the extent of the transportation services provided to the handicapped."[63]

By the early 1980s, accessible transit expert Dennis Cannon had devised six "equivalent service criteria" for accessible paratransit based on the concept of "equivalent facilitation" in the building code.[64] The purpose of these criteria was to make paratransit systems, consistent with Section 504, function in a manner roughly equivalent to the transportation service provided to the general public. Cannon soon recognized that accessible paratransit, even with these criteria, could never provide transportation services equal to public transportation. Only accessible public transit could approach the public transportation services offered to the general population. In 1982, in response to a request from Senator Alan Cranston (D-Calif.), Cannon redesigned his equivalent service criteria for accessible paratransit so that these standards also could serve as minimum service criteria for lift-equipped bus systems.

The equivalence of the standards for accessible paratransit and lift-equipped bus systems to standards for public transit systems was determined by the following criteria: the eligibility of the ridership, the response time of the accessible vehicle, the fares, the hours and days of the service, the catchment area of the service, and the restrictions or priorities based on the purpose of the trip. Each locality was responsible for determining specific standards; for example, what might be considered reasonable hours and days of service in one area may be unacceptable in another. The judgment depended on the degree to which there was equivalence between the accessible transportation systems and all forms of public transit in that region with regard to, say, the hours and days of service. To illustrate, New York City's twenty-four-hour, seven days a week availability of public transit would have to be duplicated in the city's accessible paratransit system and lift-equipped bus system.

On December 14, 1982, Senator Cranston referred to accessible bus service as "fast becoming a lost hope in many parts of the country"; in addition, he noted that "paratransit [service] for handicapped persons [is] proving to be unsatisfactory."[65] Thus, he offered a clear explanation of the need to establish these minimum service criteria, in compliance with Section 504, so that people with disabilities would be provided with adequate accessible transportation:

> Just imagine, if you need to use a wheelchair, the enormous barriers you would face in using those services as others use the bus or subway. If you need transportation to get to a new job, you may lose that job because you have been put on a paratransit waiting list. If you need to get to a medical clinic or doctor's office, even if you have given over twenty-four hours' notice, you might be turned down because the paratransit service has insufficient capacity. If you use the paratransit service to get to a government office to conduct business, you may learn upon arrival that despite what you had been told by phone or letter, you need to go to another office a few miles away in addition to or instead of where you had gone. Obviously, in most places, you cannot use the paratransit service to complete your business that day or even the next; you have got to go back home and make a new request with a day or more advanced notice.[66]

On December 20, 1982, Senator Donald Riegle (D-Mich.) responded to a colleague's question about the cost of accessible transportation services:

> What will be the costs of continuing the present state of neglect? What will be the costs of treating disabled and elderly individuals as third-class citizens, the costs of precluding them from getting into the job market, the costs of forcing them to stay on the disability and welfare rolls? These are surely very substantial costs in both human and economic terms. Those are the costs that we should be focusing upon and trying our best to avoid.[67]

Later in December, Congress passed the bill sponsored by both Senators Cranston and Riegle, the Surface Transportation Assistance Act of 1982, mandating that USDOT issue new regulations to establish *national* minimum service criteria for paratransit services and lift-equipped buses for people with disabilities.[68]

In 1985, in the *Alexander v. Choate* Section 504 Supreme Court decision,[69] Justice Thurgood Marshall, representing the majority, pointed out that the use of the term "affirmative action" in the *Davis* decision has been appropriately criticized "for failing to appreciate the difference between affirmative action and reasonable accommodation: the former is said to refer to a remedial policy for the victims of past discrimination, while the latter relates to the elimination of existing obstacles against the handicapped."[70] Thus, more consistent with *Dopico* than with *Rhode Island,* the *Choate* decision determined that accommodations for accessibility, including those for transportation, must be made so long as they are reasonable. Also in 1985 in *Maine Association of Handicapped Persons v. Dole,*[71] a federal district court criticized Secretary of Transportation Elizabeth Dole's "unimaginably leisurely pace," ordering her to promulgate *final* USDOT Section 504 regulations for accessible transportation.[72]

Published on May 20, 1986, the final Section 504 USDOT regulations required "local option" with minimum service criteria for all forms of accessible transportation. Any local transit agency, however, that spent 3 percent of its average annual operating cost on transportation services for people with disabilities was relieved of its obligation to meet minimum service criteria.[73] In *ADAPT et al. v. Dole* (E.D., Pa., 1988), the plaintiff sought to enjoin the implementation of these final Section 504 USDOT regulations. Recognizing that the "local option" provision could result in a denial of accessible public mass transit, ADAPT was concerned that mobility impaired individuals would be solely dependent upon segregated transportation facilities. Consolidated with ADAPT's complaint, the complaint of EPVA challenged the use of the 3 percent spending cap as a means of avoiding compliance with the minimum service criteria. In addition, the plaintiffs contended that "the 3 percent limitation chosen was selected in an arbitrary and capricious manner."[74]

Concluding that Congress had *not* yet legislated mainstreaming, the District Court in *ADAPT v. Dole* determined that USDOT's decision *not* to require that all newly-purchased buses be lift-equipped was lawful.[75] Therefore, the court accepted the "local option" choices allowing segregated transportation for people with disabilities. Yet, finding the 3 percent figure unreasonable, the court decided that USDOT may not use cost considerations to "'abrogate entirely the rights granted by the statutes,'" such as Section 504. Because the District Court upheld "local option," while at the same time denying the 3 percent cap, both the plaintiffs and the defendant appealed.

Although the Third Circuit Court of Appeals in *ADAPT v. Skinner* was divided on whether Congress intended "mainstreaming" in the legislation, the plurality opinion of the court written by Judge Edward R. Becker held that it was reasonable for local transit authorities to use either accessible buses, paratransit, or mixed systems. The court also held that while costs could be considered as one factor in the regulatory process, the use of a 3 percent cost cap as a safe harbor was arbitrary and capricious.

As Richard Treanor notes, however, in citing the concurring opinion of Judge Carol Los Mansmann in the *Skinner* case, "What remains unclear is how there could possibly be a paratransit option as the sole and exclusive means of transportation of disabled people if the regulations also require . . . that all new buses be lift equipped, since inevitably, cities must replace worn-out buses."[76] Proposed new regulations were issued by the Department of Transportation in March 1990 to conform to the *Skinner* decision that all new buses be accessible. In July of that year the Americans with Disabilities Act was signed, providing further accessibility to the pubic transit system.[77]

The *ADAPT v. Skinner* decision was a fitting end to an over twenty-year circuitous course leading to a federal mandate requiring accessibility of public transportation. Emanating from the effort to make the built environment barrier-free, accessible transportation was the logical next step toward integrating people with disabilities into the mainstream. During the disability community's struggle for accessible public transit, seminal conflicts emerged: accommodation versus affirmative action, mainstreaming versus special services for people with disabilities, local versus federal solutions of disability issues, and costs versus benefits of accessibility and mainstreaming.

Eventually, the courts asserted that accommodation, as long as it was reasonable, was necessary though different from affirmative action. Despite the courts' acknowledgment of the need for "special services" in certain situations for some people with a variety of impairments, mainstreaming was the primary goal for most individuals with disabilities. However valuable local experiments may have been in providing responses to disability issues, courts tended to move toward broad federal resolutions. Ultimately, courts came to appreciate that an initial outlay of funds for accessibility and mainstreaming, in keeping with the Section 504 mandate, resulted in economic benefits for people with disabilities as well as for society at large.

The Civil Rights Significance of Accessible Transportation

In his 1980 testimony before the U.S. Commission on Civil Rights, public transit authority Dennis Cannon considered the connection between the integration of people of color and the integration of people with disabilities.[78] He observed that what appears to be a problem unique to the disability population—physical barriers—is in truth a civil rights issue.

> In 1954 with the Supreme Court decision *Brown v. The Board of Education,* many people assumed that full integration of public education was just around the corner.... Again in 1977, when Secretary Califano signed the HEW 504 regulations, disabled people hailed the event as their emancipation and expected doors to open and curbs to fall virtually overnight. Obviously, none of these events has occurred.
>
> Barriers to the participation of black people in society are primarily institutional, educational, and economic. Barriers to the participation of disabled people in society include all of these, plus the additional barriers presented by the physical environment. Because physical barriers appear to be a "natural" part of the environment rather than existing because of overt oppression, and because removing them is perceived as costly, opponents have tended to focus on...barrier removal as the excuse for maintaining the institutional, [educational], and economic barriers....[79]
>
> [But] I maintain that the *only* barrier is an attitudinal barrier. If there were no attitudinal barriers, when we perceive a problem such as transportation, the two parties would sit down and work out a simple engineering solution. The fact that that does not occur even when there is, indeed, a simple engineering solution available is due to the attitudinal barrier, not to the physical barrier.

Cannon pointed out that discrimination against people with disabilities, limiting their mobility, is costly not only to the disability population, but also to the wider society.

> This particular discrimination, of course, has had a profound effect on the lives of disabled people. It has a psychological effect, among other things, but it also prevents [them] from participating in society actively, getting jobs, paying taxes; in effect, paying back some of the cost that is incurred in providing the transportation services in the first place. This lack of mobility in many cases even affects the participation in the fundamental democratic process, the right to vote. Without transportation, in many cases it is impossible even to cast your ballot in an election, something which means that, at least in part, disabled people are excluded far more or just as much from the process as black people were by closed polls and poll taxes.

Thus, relegated to second-class citizenship no less than people of color, people with disabilities, like other minority groups, have required civil rights legislation in order to secure equality of opportunity.

The Section 504 struggle for inclusion of people with disabilities into the mainstream was played out primarily in the transportation arena. It may be more than coincidental that one of the first issues addressed by both African Americans and people with disabilities seeking their civil rights involved buses. Automobiles, especially those with adaptive devices for people with disabilities, are expensive; moreover, not all people with disabilities are able to drive. Varying greatly in size, rapid transit systems—subway, elevated, and commuter trains—were found in only ten localities in the United States in 2000.[80] Buses, however, requiring a modest fare, are the most democratic form of public transportation.

They link people to employment, education, entertainment—all forms of social intercourse.

In addition, the symbolic significance of buses for both African Americans and people with disabilities should be noted. The requirement in the late 1950s that Rosa Parks sit in the back of the bus was emblematic of her second-class legal status. The inability of many people with disabilities to even board buses until the late 1970s and the 1980s was representative of their de facto segregation. The signing of the Section 504 regulations and the subsequent success of the disability activists in many transportation confrontations emboldened them to work toward full participation of people with disabilities in society.

Chapter Five

The Struggle for Change: In the Streets and in the Courts

THE STRUGGLE FOR CIVIL rights for people with disabilities took place with less visibility than, but in the same venues as, the battles fought by African Americans—the streets and the courts. Demonstrations were held; lawsuits were filed; new organizations sprung up. While the names associated with the disability rights movement—leaders such as Judith E. Heumann, Patrisha Wright, Wade Blank, Michael Auberger, and Justin Dart, and attorneys like Sidney Wolinsky and Stephen Gold—do not resonate in the same way as, for example, Medgar Evers and Thurgood Marshall, the victories, large and small, of disability activists brought about a similar revolution.

The organizations that led the way were both local and national. Disabled In Action began as a grass-roots organization in New York City. Disability Rights Education and Defense Fund was formed out of an independent living center in California. ADAPT, which shifted its focus after attaining its original goal, began in Denver. And D.C.-based Justice For All (JFA) was sponsored by a wealthy businessman with a disability who was energized by an army of activists whom he refers to as his mentors. Although most of the organizing, demonstrating, and litigating were triggered by desires to see new laws passed and effective regulations issued and implemented, accomplishing goals—such as the signing of the Section 504 regulations in 1977 and the passage of the ADA in 1990—have not marked the end of the battle.

Disabled In Action

Conceived of as a New York citywide civil rights organization committed to ending discrimination against people with *all* disabilities, Disabled In Action works to eliminate barriers that prevent the disability population from enjoying full equality. DIA was born out of the 1970 lawsuit, brought by Judith E. Heumann—currently U.S. Assistant Secretary of Education and a quadriplegic wheelchair user—against the New York City Board of Education when her application to obtain a teaching license was rejected because of her disability. According to board policy, people with disabilities could not be teachers because they were deemed fire hazards. Nonetheless, Heumann decided in college that she wanted to major in education: "That was both a statement that I wanted to work with children, and it was also a statement that in the New York City school system with seventy thousand people working in it, there were no disabled people who had been accepted as teachers and were disabled at the time they were certified."[1]

Because Heumann took her oral, written, and medical examinations in buildings that were physically inaccessible, she had to be carried up and down the stairs. Although she passed the oral and written portions, she failed the medical. Heumann recollects her experience when she took the board's medical test for teachers:

> This woman and two other doctors (men) were in the room to examine me, so it was three to one. They asked me the most bizarre questions. Then I told them I had not brought my crutches and braces, so they marked me down as insubordinate. Then, out of the clear blue sky the woman said to the other doctors, "She wets her pants." That was such an insulting remark that I could not even react to it. I started to cry; again, I was so angry that I did not know what else to do. Anyway, I failed the medical part of the exam, needless to say. I wrote to ask the reason, and I got the reason—one sentence: "paralysis of both lower extremities, sequelae of poliomyelitis."[2]

Heumann remembers her answer to one of the "bizarre questions"—concerning how she used the bathroom—that she was asked during her medical examination: "She [the doctor] wanted me to show her how I went to the bathroom, and I remember telling her that unless it was going to be a requirement for me to teach elementary school children how to go physically to the bathroom, I

didn't see any relevance in my showing her how I went to the bathroom." Undaunted by failing the board's medical examination, Heumann appealed in the late 1960s to the American Civil Liberties Union (ACLU) to act on her behalf. Heumann recalls:

> The ACLU said there was no reason for me to come down for an interview because it was not a case of discrimination that they felt they could win in court. It was purely a medical decision, and no judge was going to rule in my favor on an issue like that. I remember those scenes so vividly; I remember trying to talk to this person on the phone between crying. It was like saying, "You've got to let me into your office; at least let me talk to you. How can you tell me that I am such an invalid person that you're not even going to let me sit down and talk to you?" But at any rate, they did not let me sit down and talk to them, and I dropped them.

Still unintimidated, Heumann not only publicized her struggle in the New York City press, but also continued pursuing her dispute with the board. Perhaps the most succinct headline appeared in the New York *Daily News:* "You Can Be President, Not Teacher, with Polio."[3] Two attorneys, having read about her quarrel with the board in the local newspapers, offered to represent her pro bono. One, formerly an attorney for the Scottsboro boys, was a customer at the Heumann family butcher shop.[4] Heumann explains, "I was fortunate enough to get Constance Baker Motley as the judge on the case, who was the first black woman judge appointed to the federal district court, and she basically made it clear that she was going to keep the case and that it looked like she was going to rule in our favor. So they settled out of court."

Although no class action suit had been filed, the case established a precedent for other people with disabilities seeking certification as public school teachers. Despite her success in court, Heumann still had to contend with discrimination, before she eventually acquired a teaching job, as well as with hostility while on the job:

> I couldn't get a placement. Finally, I was placed in a school that I had been a student in, and that was a very interesting experience because it really brought home to me the problems that were going on in special education.... The goals of many of the special education teachers were not the same goals that they had for nondisabled children.... There was a much lower expectation that disabled children, in fact, were going to be able to achieve. So, consequently, the quality of education was really substandard. Now, when I went into the system—during my court battle, I had been getting a lot of publicity and had been speaking out a lot on the problems—a number of teachers in the school had considered me rather a pariah because of my statements about what I felt were the problems in special education.

Before Heumann, a great number of capable individuals with disabilities were discouraged from the teaching profession by the Board of Education's prohibition. The board's logic—which appeared irrefutable to many would-be educators with disabilities—was that leading pupils out of a building in case of fire was part of a teacher's job description. As a result, Heumann, like numerous applicants with disabilities before her, failed the medical portion of the required examination. Rather than accept this decision, however, Heumann responded by aggressively challenging it, realizing that its real purpose was to legitimatize discrimination. She understood that a teacher's primary task is not to guide students in the event of fire since others can provide this service.

Relevant questions emerge from Heumann's experience. What made this penetrating insight available to her at that particular time? What allowed her to perceive the issues in a political context? Contributing to her incisive analysis was her supportive family, the liberal political atmosphere of

the university she attended—Long Island University (LIU) in Brooklyn, the spirit of the times, as well as LIU professor Theodore Childs. Heumann describes her relationship with Childs:

> He [Ted Childs] is black, and he had been very active in black political activities. I would consider him, in a certain respect, to be my mentor because he really put me in touch with a lot of discrimination issues—the problems of the minority group he was part of, the problems he had encountered and the political activities with which he had been involved. He was an inspiration to me.

Heumann's conceptual breakthrough was that successful use of the media and legal system by the civil rights movement of the 1960s had potential pertinence to disability. Including discrimination against people with "physical handicaps" (referred to as "handicapism" or "ableism") in his catalogue of prejudices, Andrew Hacker has observed, "Racism has much in common with other 'isms.'"[5] The observations of disability advocate and Hofstra professor Frank Bowe, who is deaf, regarding prejudice are applicable to race, ethnicity, and gender, as well as to disability:

> What we are aiming for, what the hope is all about... is to make people in this country see beyond that hearing aid, beyond that cane, beyond that guide dog, beyond those crutches or that wheelchair—to the *person*. That is something that most people cannot do. They see the disability and they stop. It is very difficult for many people to perceive that a disabled person can contribute to limits that are defined by his or her abilities, intelligence, or potential, rather than by his or her disability. But that is what we hope to do—get people to see beyond the disability.[6]

Because LIU was threatened with serious economic problems in the 1960s, school officials made its Brooklyn campus accessible to people with disabilities in order to take advantage of the potential enrollment that this population provided. Soon the university served as a propitious breeding ground to nurture disability activists, generated by their physical proximity in one educational institution and an activist milieu. For the many mobility-impaired students attending LIU and living in the university's dormitories, travel had been extremely limited in the inaccessible environment of the time. The energy unleashed by the gathering together in one place of a heretofore often disenfranchised group of people, coupled with the political upheaval of the 1960s, opened up new possibilities. Heumann was inspired by, and fostered, the new militancy. The publicity resulting from her lawsuit against the New York City Board of Education, as well as the hundreds of supportive letters she received, served as an impetus for her founding Disabled In Action in 1970 at the age of only twenty-two.[7]

Encouraged by Ed Roberts, Heumann moved from New York City to the more accessible and politically-active Berkeley, California, in September 1973. Nevertheless, DIA continued to establish its identity, developing new leaders as well as increasing and diversifying its membership. In order to counteract traditional negative stereotypes of people with disabilities, DIA initiated consciousness-raising sessions, a practice borrowed from the women's movement. Recognizing its need, as a civil rights organization, to publicize its mission to foster integration of individuals with disabilities into the mainstream, DIA began using advocacy methods it still employs. By testifying at public hearings—in addition to participating in public forums, conferences, and advisory committees—DIA educates not only government officials and leaders of established institutions, but also the general public.[8]

DIA achieves further outreach by means of a quarterly newspaper, the *DIA Activist*; a column in a monthly publication, *New York*

Able; and through standard media sources. DIA even has a singing group, the DIA Singers, encouraged by the venerable Pete Seeger and led by a gifted musician, Eric Levine—when he is not engaged in his other professional or political activities or on dialysis. The DIA Singers, who perform at the Clearwater Folk Festival and other events mainly in the New York Metropolitan area, have a repertoire that includes provocative lyrics, such as the following:

> Oh yes, I am disabled, but I'm able to say this:
> "When you see me come, see a whole human
> Not the parts that I might miss
> And I won't hide all my shortcomings
> If yours you'll also wear
> For humanity, not ability, is the handicap we share."
> (From "Two Good Legs," words and music by singer-songwriter Patricia Shih)[9]

To focus public attention on and galvanize support for significant issues, DIA plans and participates in public demonstrations. DIA demonstrated in Washington, D.C., joining other disability organizations from all over the nation, to gain passage of the Rehabilitation Act of 1973. In 1976 and 1977, DIA organized protests against the United Cerebral Palsy telethon and, in 1993 and 1994, against the Muscular Dystrophy Association—Jerry Lewis—telethon, for their paternalistic and demeaning attitude toward people with disabilities. In the 1980s, DIA members blocked accessible New York City buses when wheelchair users were refused access. In 1997, DIA joined in a national disability demonstration against the Greyhound Bus Company for its failure to provide wheelchair accessibility. From its inception, DIA has organized protests at inaccessible business establishments, post offices, other government offices, and polling sites, as well as demonstrated against federal, state, and city budget cuts to programs that are vital to the disability population.

Although DIA has received grants from government and private foundations, its viability does not depend on such grants since the organization relies on the efforts of the members themselves. Operating without an office or paid staff, DIA has maintained this luxury of independence by utilizing different members' residences for various organizational activities. Taking its cue from Heumann, DIA plays the role of David to the Goliath of city, state, and federal government, as well as private businesses, large and small. For example, DIA has won lawsuits against the New York Metropolitan Transportation Authority, the New York City Board of Elections, and the Empire State Building. Like many people with disabilities, most members of DIA are unemployed, living on government benefits. Hence, the organization is eligible to secure attorneys provided for people of limited means from the federally-funded Legal Services Corporation.[10] In addition, DIA has benefited from public interest law centers and the pro bono services of private law firms. Contrary to Philip K. Howard's contention in *The Death of Common Sense,*[11] public interest lawyers are unlikely to accept frivolous lawsuits. These lawyers are compensated by fixed salaries, so their only incentive in the lawsuits they pursue is success in winning noteworthy cases. As a result, DIA wins most of its cases.

DIA's mission involves not only the passage of new laws that affirm and defend the rights of people with disabilities, but also the enforcement of existing legislation. Recognizing that without visibility at voting booths people with disabilities would never be perceived as a voting bloc, DIA demonstrated its tenacity in its ten-year effort to ultimately win its wheelchair accessible polling site lawsuit, *Hill v. New York City Board of Elections,* finally settled in 1994.[12] Despite the passage of a 1980 amendment—which DIA supported—to the New York State Election Law, requiring that all polling places have at least one wheelchair-accessible entrance by 1990, voting sites were still inaccessible in the mid 1980s. With no effort being made by the administration of New York City Mayor Edward Koch to locate accessible sites or renovate inaccessible ones as late as June 1984, DIA realized the law was being ignored. Consequently, Brooklyn Legal Services filed a New York State class action lawsuit on behalf of DIA of Metropolitan New York and several individual plaintiffs, naming the New York City and the New York State Boards of Elections as defendants.

The experience of DIA member Betsy Gimbel, a wheelchair user, demonstrated the effects of Koch's noncompliance with the law. Arriving at her supposedly accessible polling site at 6:30 in the morning in November 1985, Gimbel found that all three entrances had flights of steps. Following instructions from the Board of Elections, she traveled around the city the entire day, from Brooklyn to City Hall to the Board of Elections and back to Brooklyn. Finally, she voted at 6:30 in the evening at a polling site less accessible than her own. Ironically, several years earlier, at a 1981 conference celebrating the International Year of Disabled Persons (IYDP), Koch challenged the disability community to vote in great numbers in order to become as politically effective as the older community. In response, DIA member Olga Hill asked the mayor if he knew that less than a third of polling sites, 419 out of 1,337, were wheelchair accessible.[13]

Despite his apparent evasion of the New York State Election Law, Koch gave DIA lawyers verbal assurances during the 1985 mayoral campaign that he would settle the polling site lawsuit. Although the upstate New York Boards of Elections of Oneida County and the City of Utica agreed to settle a similar lawsuit based on the same election law, lawyers representing Mayor Koch would not sign a settlement agreement. Since Koch had reneged on his promise to the DIA lawyers, Jane Greengold Stevens—the lead attorney representing the plaintiffs—announced that she was going to proceed with the suit within the month. In 1986, Judge Herbert Kramer ruled in favor of the plaintiffs, but the city continued to procrastinate until Stevens, on behalf of DIA and the individual litigants, filed a contempt motion in 1988. Judge Kramer, who took an active interest in the case, required that many polling sites be barrier-free by 1990. Nonetheless, the lawsuit was not settled until December 1994 when only five voting locations were still inaccessible.

Furthermore, in order to ensure that voting places would remain available to people with disabilities and older citizens, "The City Board of Elections [was] enjoined from relocating polling sites to nonaccessible sites without prior written permission of the court and after a statutory fair hearing by the Board of Elections."[14] Judge Kramer was especially concerned with the issue of whether distance or steps was the main barrier for older voters with disabilities. As a result of the intervention of Legal Services for the Elderly, the court was convinced that the primary hindrance for voters with disabilities regardless of age was steps. This experience revealed the natural political affinity between people with disabilities and older people, since their interests frequently intersect.

New York Lawyers for the Public Interest

In two pivotal DIA cases, the 1982 *Dopico v. Goldschmidt* transportation lawsuit[15] and the *Hill v. New York City Board of Elections* polling site lawsuit, New York Lawyers for the Public Interest (NYLPI) played a vital role. Appreciating the limits of testifying at government hearings and demonstrating for the

civil rights of people with disabilities, DIA sought attorneys from legal services agencies to litigate disability rights cases. Having emerged from Heumann's successful lawsuit against the New York City Board of Education, DIA considered litigation as one of the most effective ways of implementing social change. When Brooklyn Legal Services attorney Jane Greengold Stevens served as principal lawyer in both *Dopico* and *Hill,* she sought legal assistance from NYLPI. In the transportation suit, she called upon the pro bono services of a private law firm—Winthrop, Stimson, Putnam & Roberts, a member of NYLPI—while in the polling site case, she worked with an attorney from NYLPI, Herbert Semmel.

Forming a central plank in the Office of Economic Opportunity national war on poverty, legal services programs funded by the federal government began their steady decline in the 1970s. Furthermore, during this period of retrenchment even private foundations began to withdraw support for public interest law. Although racial equality and economic opportunity (not disability rights) was considered the crucial issue in the late 1970s, the fact that so many people with disabilities were living below the poverty level made this population eligible for public interest legal services. A March 1976 Ford Foundation report observed, "If public interest practice is to remain and grow, it must be seen as an enlargement of the scope and responsibility of the legal profession."[16]

Combining the pro bono activities of major law firms and corporate law departments with a public interest law office, NYLPI was established in January 1976 to provide private legal support for poor and under-represented communities, including the disability population.[17] Private law firms and corporate law departments become members of NYLPI both by volunteering their expertise and by financially supporting pro bono projects. As a reaction to continuing cutbacks in legal services programs, membership in NYLPI has increased from the original nine participants in 1976 to seventy-eight in 1999.[18] Once a body of laws and legal precedents had been established regarding civil rights for people with disabilities, NYLPI founded the Disability Law Center in 1991 within its public interest law office.

Recognizing Disability as a Civil Rights Issue

Founder in 1977 of an early disability law center known as the Handicapped Persons Legal Support Unit (HPLSU), Paul Hearne made disability litigation his mission until his untimely death on May 3, 1998, at the age of forty-eight.[19] Hearne, a severely disabled wheelchair user, described an incident that caused him to work in disability law: "I had originally planned to work in poverty law, but I discovered I was a person with a disability that had a political dimension and that became my life's work." In 1976, when an office of the Legal Services Corporation, Hearne's employer for two years, relocated to a new office up two flights of stairs, the civil rights lawyers Hearne worked alongside and admired showed no awareness of his needs. Forced to acknowledge Hearne's access problem, the Legal Services attorneys maintained that Section 504, prohibiting disability discrimination by recipients of federal funds, did not apply to this federally-funded government agency. They argued that since the Legal Services Corporation was not a recipient of a federal grant, but rather an agency of the government, the corporation was exempt from Section 504.

Nonetheless, under the auspices of New York Senator Jacob Javits, the Legal Services Corporation established a fully accessible office, HPLSU, with Hearne as director in May 1977, a month after the regulations for Section 504 were signed. HPLSU was terminated within three years as other Legal Services Corporation offices became accessible. Over time, some Legal Services Corporation offices became barrier-free while others moved to wheelchair-accessible sites. Hearne's recognition of the insensitivity to disability issues of even these "defenders of justice," as he ironically referred to his legal colleagues, clarified his own purpose: to play a part in the expansion of civil rights for people with disabilities. Hearne's experience, similar to the experiences of many other people with disabilities, reveals that even well-informed and politically sophisticated people often do not appreciate the relationship between disability rights and other forms of civil rights.

Disability Rights Education and Defense Fund

The leaders of the Berkeley Center for Independent Living founded the Disability Rights Education and Defense Fund (DREDF) in 1979 after receiving a one hundred thousand dollar federal grant. Because New York City's Legal Services Corporation lost a portion of its federal funding as a consequence of its noncompliance with Section 504, this same one hundred thousand dollars was transferred to the Berkeley Center.[20] DREDF's mission is to promote the integration and civil rights of people with disabilities, and "to establish disability rights as the recognized equivalent of race and gender-based civil rights."[21] Led by people with disabilities and the parents of children with disabilities, DREDF is a national law and policy center with offices in Berkeley, California, and Washington, D.C.

Besides continuing to receive government grants and contracts, DREDF—a nonprofit organization—also secures financial support from foundations and corporations, as well as attorneys' fees resulting from successful disability litigation.[22] Because of DREDF's involvement with disability issues on a grass-roots level, the organization has been a key player since its inception in drafting, negotiating, and passing major federal disability civil rights legislation such as the Americans with Disabilities Act. For example, in 1981 when the Reagan administration attempted to weaken the regulations implementing Section 504, the White House received forty thousand letters as a result of a nationwide DREDF alert.

DREDF offered leadership in educating Congress before the passage of two major national laws, the Fair Housing Amendments Act of 1988 and the Handicapped Children's Protection Act of 1986. The former law renders housing discrimination against people with disabilities a federal offense. The second law provides that government or business defendants who lose lawsuits pay attorney's fees to plaintiffs in special education or disability discrimination cases related to the Individuals with Disabilities Education Act. Although generally plaintiffs pay their own lawyers' fees, Congress deemed the Handicapped Children's Protection Act necessary in order to offer parents, regardless of their income, a means of protecting their children with disabilities from the potential bias of educational institutions.

Committing one-third of its services to issues concerning the education of children with disabilities, DREDF pursues cases in which parents participate in planning their child's individualized educational plan (IEP).[23] In fact, DREDF encourages parents, as advocates for their children with disabilities, to secure *all* the educational and related services mandated by state and federal laws. Grants and contracts received from the U.S. Department of Education and the Equal Employment Opportunity Commission (EEOC) enable DREDF to provide training sessions not only for parents of children with disabilities but also for adults with disabilities to monitor compliance with disability legislation.

In order to foster integration of adults as well as children with disabilities into the mainstream, DREDF litigates cases enforcing access to housing, transportation, benefits, education, employment, and public accommodation of the disability population. DREDF also serves as a resource for information, referral, and technical assistance on disability rights laws and policies. Through the Disability Clinical Legal Education Program, DREDF, along with a consortium of five law schools, trains law students by offering a course in disability rights law, as well as a clinic for students to work on DREDF cases.[24] A DREDF leader, Patrisha Wright, who played a prominent role in rewriting the ADA so that it would gain broad legislative acceptance, reflects on the ADA: "You can't legislate attitudes. But you can level the playing field, and that's what the ADA is all about. It signifies the end of second-class citizenship for people with disabilities in this country."[25]

One of DREDF's most notable achievements was its role in the 1988 Civil Rights Restoration Act, which in effect overturned the U.S. Supreme Court's 1984 *Grove City v. Bell* decision.[26] According to *Grove City,* if a court ruled against any division of an institution in a civil rights lawsuit, only that particular division, not the entire institution, was required to comply with Section 504. Besides prejudice based on race, national origin, sex, and age, the *Grove City* ruling applied to bias on account of disability. In order to urge Congress to overturn *Grove City* by passing the 1988 Civil Rights Restoration Act, DREDF provided materials and information to, and testified before, congressional committees. Once the act was passed, it was applied to civil rights legislation enacted since 1964, thus restoring those laws to the original intent. Before the passage of the 1988 Civil Rights Restoration Act, DREDF brought the issues of people with disabilities to the rest of the civil rights community by its "rigorous participation" in the ongoing Leadership Conference on Civil Rights, organized in 1980 to unite leaders from the various civil rights movements.[27] Thus, DREDF was instrumental in presenting disability discrimination as akin to racial, ethnic, and gender discrimination.

The Need for Disability Rights Attorneys

Because of a continuing increase in local, state, and federal disability legislation—especially since Section 504 of the Rehabilitation Act of 1973, the 1975 Individuals with Disabilities Education Act, and the 1990 ADA—the need for attorneys specializing in disability law has expanded considerably. Impressed by the activist approach toward civil rights for people with disabilities of Berkeley's Center for Independent Living (especially evident in the charismatic leadership of its director, Ed Roberts), one prominent lawyer, Sidney Wolinsky, chose to become a disability rights attorney in the mid-1970s.[28] Wolinsky, now director of Litigation of Disability Rights Advocates of Oakland, California, described his first major disability lawsuit, the mid-1970s Post Street, San Francisco, nursing home case (*Bracco v. Lackner*).[29] This successful litigation prevented the residents of the nursing home, older people with disabilities, from being forcibly transferred from one facility to another. To win his case, he used the concept of "transfer trauma," the probability that his frail elderly clients would suffer serious injuries if they were moved against their will. Originally specializing in elder law and problems of older people, Wolinsky increasingly focused on disability law.

In the late 1970s, he averted the dispersal of roughly 150 people with Hanson's disease, more commonly known as leprosy, who lived together in a community on the Hawaiian island of Molokai. Because their disease was contagious before the availability in the early 1970s of a category of drugs known as sulphones,[30] these individuals—who had been ripped from their families—had established an emotional attachment to one another and their home. When land developers realized the value of the property on which these people with Hanson's disease lived, their community was jeopardized. The dispute was tied up in litigation sufficiently long, however, so that the issue ultimately was settled by federal legislation decreeing the area on which this community resided a national preserve under Federal Park supervision. Once there are no Hanson's disease survivors left on the property, the area will become a permanent memorial, a testament to the experience endured by those who had this condition.

During the late 1980s and early 1990s, Wolinsky dealt with a number of significant architectural barrier cases. In an attempt to save about fifteen thousand dollars, the owner of Specialty Restaurant failed to make the entrance accessible when the establishment was undergoing major remodeling. As a consequence of the 1989 lawsuit *Weissman v. Specialty,* based on California state law, an Alameda County Superior Court jury awarded the plaintiff $670,000, perhaps the largest verdict for a single individual ever in an architectural barrier decision. Before his successful ADA class action lawsuit representing DREDF against United Artists Theatres for its lack of accessibility, *Arnold v. United Artists Theatre Circuit* (1996), Wolinsky won a landmark pre-ADA judgment in an architectural barrier lawsuit, *Henry v. Squaw Valley Ski Resort.* The court decided in favor of the plaintiffs because the resort neither allowed wheelchair users on lifts nor provided accessibility on the mountain.

Wolinsky also discusses his lawsuits dealing with psychiatric and learning disabilities (LDs). He is especially pleased with a decision in a 1993 case (*Putnam v. Pacific Gas and Electric*) he brought involving a lawyer with a psychiatric disability—major depression—who worked for Pacific Gas and Electric. "These kinds of cases are not being won. They either get thrown out of court before they get to trial or receive a small recovery," Wolinsky observes. Yet, after Wolinsky's client, who was working under "a harsh supervisor," was refused an ADA accommodation and then fired, an arbiter awarded the plaintiff $1.1 million. Wolinsky followed his victory in a much publicized class action lawsuit against Boston University, *Elizabeth Guckenberger v. Boston University* (1997), for its systemic refusal to accommodate students with learning disabilities, with a similar class action lawsuit against the California Bar Association for failing to provide accommodation for students with learning disabilities. "Although it had been previously good, the Bar had decided in its great wisdom in 1997 to crack down on LD students," Wolinsky notes sarcastically:

We started receiving floods of complaints from candidates taking the bar exams, whose LD accommodations were dramatically cut or turned down totally. This California Bar case, that's still in litigation, is a sign of what's happening and what's to come. Fifteen years ago, if you were seriously dyslexic, you were going to end up a janitor even if you had an I.Q. of 150. Now a considerable number of people with learning disabilities are going to college, and so you get cases like Boston University. And some, who self-identify as LD, have even worked further along the system to law school, so we have the California Bar case (*Mueller v. Committee of Bar Examiners of the State of California*).

Wolinsky compares the kinds of cases he dealt with when he began practicing

disability law to the suits he has recently litigated. Many of his early cases involved airline carrier access, "a primitive pre-ADA law," according to the attorney, "that did not offer much protection." By the late 1990s, he noticed that he had been seeing many fewer of these cases. In order to get appropriate settlements in his early architectural barrier cases, he would have to go to trial. "The good news is now defendants know how difficult it is to justify steps, and they also know," he observes, "we get better settlements." Still, he emphasizes the significance of geographical areas:

If we get enough architectural barrier cases in a particular area, soon building departments in that locality begin to get educated, and we don't have to bring lawsuits. Because people with disabilities in Oakland are aware of their rights, I can't remember the last time I had to bring a lawsuit in Oakland. The Oakland Building Department has become knowledgeable about and sensitive to access issues. But the bad news is that forty-five minutes north in the Napa Valley, the Building Department doesn't get it yet. From my experience sometimes the periphery of the country is the slowest to get it. Consider, for example, Hawaii and south Florida. And the point is that it doesn't seem to relate to need. There are lots of elderly and lots of people with disabilities in south Florida. Still there aren't enough activist organizations in some areas, so people are timid; they don't know the law, and they don't assert their rights.

Wolinsky acknowledges that his cases are getting "more difficult" as the other side has gotten increasingly sophisticated. "They're cleverer at job discrimination now. They don't say we're not hiring you because you're disabled; they say they've found somebody more qualified." Also, he remembers that in the past his cases revolved around "core issues" while now he has moved into "somewhat fuzzier territory." He explains, "Nobody now refuses to settle cases with us about inaccessible front entrances, but they argue about width of aisles in stores and their right to crowd aisles with display racks." He is referring to the Disability Rights Advocates lawsuit against Federated Department Stores, which includes Macy's and Bloomingdale's.

Another issue with which Wolinsky has become recently involved concerns insurance for people with disabilities. "Insurance companies routinely turn down people with disabilities or charge them premiums that are too high," he contends. He describes a summary judgment that he won against United of Omaha (*Chabner v. United of Omaha*), which charged double the normal premium to a person because he was in a wheelchair: "We sued and sure enough they had no hard evidence to go on to justify their unreasonable premium. They were just stereotyping. They figured, 'Oh well, he's in a chair; he's not going to live too long; we'll charge twice the regular rate.'" Wolinsky regrets that because of their history and their isolation from the rest of the disability community, deaf people have neither taken advantage of the laws that could serve them nor developed an adequate number of attorneys from their own community. "Although someone on our staff is hard of hearing," Wolinsky indicates, "there are not enough good deaf lawyers. In my view there are a lot more cases to be brought than have been brought. There don't seem to be a sufficient number of hard-hitting advocacy firms that focus on the deaf community." Wolinsky is especially concerned about the lack of sign language interpreters in public facilities such as hospitals, courts, and schools.

As he prepares for new disability cases, he reveals how much he would like to see people who are deaf and hard of hearing become more aggressive than they have been in pursuing their legitimate rights. Looking forward to a continuation of lawsuits in the employment context, Wolinsky anticipates that "they will get so fact-specific that prior

cases may not be very helpful. We'll bring the suits and hope we can settle them if not win them," he says. While he asserts that future cases will clarify the interpretation of terminology relating to disability law, he emphasizes the importance of the growing degree to which people with disabilities are becoming cognizant of "what they are entitled to."

Another major litigator, a private Philadelphia attorney, Stephen Gold, recollects that about 50 percent of his caseload prior to 1992 involved disability litigation. With the passage of the ADA, however, he was able to make a decent salary practicing only disability law. Gold states, "I have no interest in pursuing bad disability lawsuits. We had too many bad ones following Section 504, and that does not serve the cause of disability rights. Also, of course, I am only entitled to attorney's fees when my plaintiffs prevail; when I lose, I get no money. But I get more winning cases than I can handle. So we need more good disability lawyers."[31] James Raggio, general counsel to the Access Board, agrees with Gold: "There are not enough resources for the meaningful ADA lawsuits that should be litigated."[32]

Gold describes how, quite by accident, he became a disability rights attorney:

In the late 1980s, I was asked to litigate a case for a school bus driver who wore a hearing aid. Soon after I won this suit in the Third Circuit using Section 504, I won another disability employment case that was based on a myth that perpetuates disability discrimination. Several blind people working in the Social Security Administration, who were providing information by telephone, were refused a promotion to a job that required them to furnish the same information in person. The supervisor was concerned that clients would not have confidence in information given by blind people.

Another disability case that I won in the Third Circuit led to several wheelchair-accessible subway and elevator train stations in Philadelphia. When I noticed that the newly-renovated subway station, which I used to get to the Temple University Law School course that I was teaching, did not have an elevator, I brought a Section 504 lawsuit. Also, I had the good fortune by 1990 to co-counsel disability cases with Tim Cook, a highly-respected disabled disability lawyer who died young, at the peak of his career.

Although Gold refers to himself as merely "playing second fiddle" to Tim Cook in ADAPT's significant 1989 Section 504 transportation federal lawsuit, *ADAPT v. Skinner*, now Gold is known as the ADAPT lawyer. Commenting on ADAPT's mission, Gold maintains that it is important for disability activists to keep the pressing disability issues—vital to such a surprisingly high percentage of Americans—in the eye of the public and the lawmakers.

ADAPT

Despite the fact that ADAPT has been the plaintiff in successful disability lawsuits, the organization—according to one of its leaders, Michael Auberger—stresses "the tactics of street fighters."[33] A student of the 1960s and 1970s civil rights and antiwar movements, Auberger refers to the nonauthoritarian structure of ADAPT as it eschews incorporation, officers, and board development, relying instead upon leadership and consensus. The acronym "ADAPT" has had two different meanings: from June 1983 to August 1990, it meant American Disabled for Accessible Public Transit; since August 1990, it has stood for American Disabled for Attendant Programs Today.

When ADAPT in its early phase, 1983 to 1990, required a victory to become a credible force in the disability rights struggle, the organization chose accessible transportation

as a more attainable objective than personal assistance services. With the 1990 passage of the ADA, ADAPT had made much progress toward its first goal, accessible public transit, so the organization moved on to its current and principal concern: community-based personal assistance services. Emerging out of Wade Blank's relocation of sixteen adults with severe disabilities from a nursing home into apartments in 1975, ADAPT, from its inception, focused on independent living. Blank, founder of ADAPT, describes how his recruitment by the nursing home industry in 1971 introduced him to radical disability politics:

> The nursing home industry in Denver recruited its nursing home administrators from the ranks of ex-ministers [like me]. The industry had built too many nursing homes in Denver. There weren't enough old people, and the state institutions were dumping disabled people out, so the nursing home industry decided they would get them. A nursing home executive called. He said, "You're young. You're hip. Could you start a youth wing for us?" So I started a youth wing.... I had sixty young people recruited.... They wanted coed living. They wanted to have pets. They wanted to have rock 'n' roll bands. So three years into this experiment, this nursing home is just like a college dorm on a crazy weekend all the time.... We [moved] a few of them out into apartments [in 1975], and we let the aides and orderlies punch in at the nursing home, then go to the apartment and give them service. The nursing home saw where I was going and they couldn't let me go in that direction.[34]

Because of his "experiment," Blank was fired; the nursing home—removing all stereos, televisions, and animals—wiped out all of the improvements that he implemented over a period of four years. Not fully cognizant of the enormous responsibility he was undertaking, Blank decided to begin to move his young recruits out of "this hell" and care for them himself: "You think marriage is a serious commitment; you try moving eight people who are severely disabled out into their own apartments and be responsible for dressing them, feeding them, bowel programs, bathing them. But within the first six months, I'd moved eighteen severely disabled people out, so now I was wed to the concept. You know, I couldn't walk away from it."

Pointing out that Section 504 and the ADA do not prevent people with disabilities from being locked up in institutions, Blank notes the limitations of what he considers the social and economic elitism of the mainstream disability movement: "The Ed Robertses and the Judy Heumanns don't deal with nursing homes. They've never been in one. They don't understand them.... You go around to the independent living centers, and you'll see a lot of post-polios and a lot of spinal cord injuries. But you won't see a lot of people who slobber and can't speak clearly like you do here [Atlantis and ADAPT]." Learning how to challenge authority from his successful efforts in the 1960s civil rights movement, Blank encouraged people with severe disabilities to achieve their goals using confrontational tactics. By 1980, funded by the U.S. Rehabilitation Services Administration, the Atlantis Community, with 120 clients—including Blank's former nursing home recruits—had become an independent living center providing housing and home health services. Auberger describes Blank, who died on February 15, 1993, while attempting to rescue his eight-year-old son from drowning, as "a teacher, inspiring left-out people, people with significant disabilities, to advocate for themselves."[35]

Although ADAPT was officially established in Denver in June 1983 by Blank and the Atlantis Community, the successful Denver 1982 demonstration for lift-equipped buses propelled these disability advocates toward activism. In 1981, when the U.S. Court of Appeals for the District of Columbia decided in favor of the American Public Transit Association in its lawsuit against the U.S. Department of Transportation concerning the Section 504 regulations,[36] the Denver Transit Authority—like many transit authorities across the nation—considered the decision a signal to cease efforts to make public transportation accessible. In order to advance the cause of accessible public transit, ADAPT protested against APTA at its regional conferences in localities throughout the country. ADAPT positioned itself as the courageous "enfant terrible" facing the bully—APTA—or, in Auberger's words, "the bad guy." ADAPT used nationwide demonstrations to rally the disability community in these localities to fight for buses with lifts.

Auberger argues, "We don't appear to public opinion to be reasonable, but we are."[37] ADAPT's effort to get businesses to install ramps, as required by the ADA, begins with letter writing, followed by demonstrations, and lawsuits only as a last resort. "It's a hell of a lot easier to do it in a meeting.... It takes a hell of a lot of energy to do the demonstrations, to do the lawsuits," Auberger observes. "We'll do that if that's what it takes. But my preference is, let's do it nice and resolve it as amicably as possible."

When the contractor and owner of an elegant Denver restaurant violated city accessibility laws, the ADAPT protest demonstrated its usual flamboyance and wit. Setting up tables in front of the restaurant where they ate cans of Chef Boy Ardee and drank cheap wine, ADAPT members displayed a sign that read "accessible seating." Although ADAPT sometimes acts locally pursuing disability activities in Denver, with its existing affiliate network throughout the country, it always thinks nationally.

Transferring this successful strategy to the personal assistance services issue, ADAPT, in its second incarnation since

1990, identifies the $90 billion per year nursing home industry, represented by the American Health Care Association (AHCA), as "the bad guy." Continuing to use confrontational techniques, ADAPT surrounded buildings such as the Chicago regional office of the Department of Health and Human Services, the American Medical Association (AMA) National Headquarters, and the San Francisco convention site of AHCA. In each case, ADAPT, declaring the location a nursing home, required that people receive ADAPT's permission to leave or enter the premises. Thus, these people were given a taste of the nursing home life against which ADAPT was protesting.

A 1992 ADAPT flyer succinctly expressed the organization's position on nursing homes:

Q. & A.

Q. What's the difference between a nursing home and a jail?

A. The uniforms are different. The weapons are different, in jail it's a gun, in a nursing home it's pills.

The parole is different. In jail, you serve your sentence and get paroled. In nursing homes there's no parole. You're in for life!

Referring to the nursing home industry as "a beast that nobody likes," Auberger indicates that government agencies and health maintenance organizations both realize that it is cheaper to provide services for people with disabilities in the community than in nursing homes.[38] Many people are in nursing homes, Auberger continues, because there is no support system available for them to live in their own homes; were they given a choice, however, "more and more would move out." Auberger's solution is to create models, such as those in Colorado, Kansas, Vermont, and more recently

Missouri, to demonstrate that "elderly people and younger people with disabilities can live in the community more economically, more productively, and more happily than in nursing homes." ADAPT has been urging that 25 percent of federal nursing home dollars be redirected to a national attendant services program to be available, as a basic civil right, to anyone needing such services. Auberger contends that "this issue strikes a responsive chord in most Americans since they fear aging and ending up in a nursing home."

In the summer of 1997, ADAPT focused on both the nursing home issue—Medicaid Community Attendant Services Act (MiCasa)—and transportation—the Greyhound controversy. As a result of occupying the office of then Speaker of the House Newt Gingrich on several occasions from 1995 to 1997, ADAPT pressured Gingrich to introduce the MiCasa bill.[39] Instead of being sent to nursing homes, people under MiCasa would be permitted to remain in their own homes with attendant services. "On the eve of the last election [1996], Gingrich had promised, in a hand-written agreement with ADAPT, to 'seek final passage and enactment [of MiCasa] into law prior to the end of the first session of the 105th Congress.'"[40] When Gingrich commented in a June 5, 1997, conference with ADAPT that "you know the institutional providers [nursing homes] are going to go berserk," Auberger responded, "We're willing to take on the fight with them."

In addition to its efforts regarding MiCasa, on August 8, 1997, ADAPT organized about forty demonstrations throughout the nation protesting the refusal of Greyhound to provide wheelchair accessibility on its buses. The New York City protesters chanted, "'At least Rosa Parks could get on the bus'—a reference to the Alabama woman whose refusal to sit in the back of the bus sparked the civil rights movement."[41] A member of the New York City contingent, Thomas K. Small, observed, "Buses are widely used by the disabled because they are cheaper than trains and planes, and 75 percent of people with disabilities in the United States have low incomes." Philadelphia disability rights attorney, Stephen Gold, added:

> Greyhound has already bought eighty or ninety inaccessible buses. For many people, in many parts of the country, these buses provide the only means of inexpensive long-distance transportation. If the company's allowed to go ahead with their plan to purchase another two hundred of those buses, it will be twenty-five years before people in wheelchairs will be able to ride Greyhound buses. This is clearly discrimination in violation of the ADA. Technology for accessible over-the-road buses—with storage space for luggage—such as Greyhound buses, is available as demonstrated by the accessible Canadian buses of this type.[42]

In 1999 the Department of Justice reached an out-of-court settlement with Greyhound in which the bus company agreed to phase in lift-equipped buses over the following two years.

Whether ADAPT members are sliding out of their wheelchairs to crawl up the steps of the Capitol as Congress deliberates over the 1990 ADA, or disrupting the speech of President Bush's Health and Human Services Secretary, Louis Sullivan, at the 1992 University of Illinois graduation ceremony, they employ theatrical maneuvers though their purposes are utterly serious. ADAPT considers its confrontational tactics most successful when police are so provoked that they are placed in the embarrassing position of arresting these ADAPT demonstrators with severe disabilities. Representing many people with serious disabilities, ADAPT sometimes uses members with speech problems—such as individuals

with cerebral palsy—as spokespeople. As a result, listeners who are intent upon getting the message are forced to concentrate on the content of the speech regardless of the speaker's clarity of diction. Despite some disability activist's discomfort with ADAPT when it flaunts old images of disability, the organization, as Auberger puts it, "is willing to take flak for its actions since it works for people with the least who need the most and intend to get what they want."[43]

Auberger draws a parallel between the American Revolution and the "Disability Revolution." He likens the ineffective entities in the system, such as APTA and the nursing home industry, to the powerful British army, the Redcoats, who did not know how to fight in the new environment. Comparing ADAPT members to the army of the American Revolution, he calls them "guerrilla fighters taking shots at the system where it's vulnerable." Auberger explains, "The stuff ADAPT does in the streets makes Justin Dart, who works through the system, seem sane when he talks about our rights in the halls of Congress."

Justice For All

Founded in 1995 by Justin and Yoshiko Dart, Becky Ogle, Fred Fay, and Mark Smith, Justice For All adopted a platform, Solidarity 2000, committed to establishing a consensus in the disability community on the major disability rights issues.[44] By means of action alerts, information updates, meetings, and conference calls, JFA created a nationwide disability rights network. Considering listening crucial to building consensus, Justin Dart, post-polio wheelchair user, toured all fifty states in 1996 in order to consult with disability groups in each state.

Dart, who contracted polio in 1948 at the age of eighteen, was born into wealth and the corporate life. However, an experience at a 1966 media event at a Saigon facility for children with polio changed his life:

> The floor of the place was covered with children ages four to ten, with bloated stomachs and matchstick limbs. They were starving to death and lying in their own urine and feces. A little girl reached up to me and looked into my eyes. I automatically took her hand and my photographer took pictures. She had the most serene look I have ever seen—and it penetrated to the deepest part of my consciousness. I thought, here is a person almost dead, and she knows it. She's reaching out for God and has found a counterfeit saint doing a photo op. . . . I told [my fiancée] Yoshiko, "We cannot go on as we have been. Our lives have got to mean something. We have got to get into this fight and stop this evil."[45]

After cofounding an independent living center in Texas in 1978—holding five gubernatorial, one congressional, and five presidential appointments associated with disability policy—as well as helping to shape the ADA, Dart used his own funds to support JFA, "a communication base for grassroots organizers and a lobbying force in Washington."

Dart's wife, Yoshiko, her three foster daughters, and a small band of other volunteers throughout the nation perform the day-to-day tasks of the organization. Congressional and White House watchdog and wheelchair user Becky Ogle attends numerous meetings enabling her to report "up-to-the-minute information to the JFA headquarters at the Dart home."[46] Organizing conference calls, mailings, and meetings, Mark Smith coordinates the JFA network, known as the Truth Team, from the organization's Mississippi office. Fred Fay, who has been in bed since 1981 with a progressive disability (a spinal cord cyst), is JFA's telecommunication network chair, communicating with disability leaders nationwide while monitoring the latest events by means of the Internet.

Fay describes his work: "When I first realized I'd be in bed for the rest of my life, I thought, 'Wow. I'm going to get awfully bored reading books.' But I continued my advocacy work, thanks to the phone, fax, and modem."[47] Lying flat on his back in the motorized wheelbed that he designed, Fay uses a joystick to drive up "to a customized electronic work station [in his home] and reads material displayed on either of two computer monitors resting on pull-out glass shelves suspended a foot from his head."[48] Using this technology, Fay says, "I conduct meetings [by means of video conferencing], write articles, . . . lobby Congress, execute grass-roots campaigns, and reach thousands of people with disabilities every day."

While Fay was winner of the 1997 Betts Award for outstanding contributions to people with disabilities, Dart was a recipient of a 1998 Presidential Medal of Freedom, America's highest civilian honor. In accepting the award, Dart thanked members of the disability rights movement by saying, "This is your medal. I am so proud to be one of you. I will fight at your side until the last breath."[49] Dart has always credited those who preceded him and those who have joined him in the movement with educating and energizing him: "I think of Ed Roberts dreaming up a revolution of independence in his iron lung, and I think of many others on my list of empowering people." In 1995, when the 104th Congress threatened to roll back existing federal legislation (such as ADA and the Individuals with Disabilities Education Act) providing opportunities to people with disabilities, Justin Dart recognized the need for a national, unified voice of the disability community:

The war for the survival of the disability rights movement had begun. Our independence and rights were being debated in Congress.... We [JFA] realized that we would have to do some hard-hitting advocacy. We needed to be an independent entity, free from government contracts and other limitations.... Empowerment is the issue of the age.... Nobody is going to give it to us [the disability community]. We have to empower ourselves.[50]

Chapter Six

The Americans with Disabilities Act

AT AN APRIL 18, 1997, conference of disability advocates in Uniondale, New York, Joseph Shapiro, author of *No Pity: People with Disabilities Forging a New Civil Rights Movement*,[1] indicated that because the ADA had so much support, its passage was not a daunting task. In a meeting with New York City disability rights advocates on the following day, Justin Dart, who has been called the "father of the ADA," disagreed, pointing to the concerted effort to prevent the passage of, or weaken, the ADA by such powerful forces as, for example, the five hundred thousand-member National Federation of Independent Business.[2] Having given top priority to defeating the ADA, National Federation of Independent Business was the subject of a *Washington Post* front-page article entitled "The Organization That Never Loses." In addition, the U.S. Chamber of Commerce, the *New York Times,* the *Wall Street Journal,* the Restaurant Association, Greyhound Buses, and the entire public transportation community, as well as conservative elements of the Republican party represented by people like Pat Buchanan and Representative Dick Armey (R-Tex.), joined in opposition to the ADA.

Lex Frieden, the first permanent executive director of the National Council on Disability[3]—an independent federal agency appointed by the president—who served from December 1984 to April 1988, indicates that, in a sense, both Dart and Shapiro were right:

> But Shapiro's focus may have been too narrow; he didn't open up his lens. He was just taking a snapshot. He was concentrating on a specific point in time—once the bill was before Congress, while Dart participated in the years of hard work, the struggle that paved the way for the passage of the ADA. An Olympic gold medal swimmer makes getting from one end of the pool to the other look easy. What you don't see is the years of preparation and sweat that were necessary for success.[4]

Dart's work on legislation that culminated in the ADA had begun in the early 1980s when he was chair of Texas Governor William Clements's Task Force for Long-Range Policy for People with Disabilities.[5] Dart points out that disability rights advocates recognized that the very real threat of weakening the provisions of the ADA, in effect creating legislation legitimizing the segregation of people with disabilities, would be worse than no law at all:

If you don't have a watered-down ADA law, the Bill of Rights and civil rights laws apply to you. But you can be exempt from these laws if you have a Jim Crow law called a civil rights law. The ADA advocates participating in framing the legislation were willing to be flexible with regard to time limits, remedies, and undue hardship. However, they were determined to prevent permanent exemption of coverage from any group of people with disabilities, such as people with AIDS or psychological disabilities, or any separate but equal provisions in the law.

Enacting the ADA

In 1982, President Reagan dismissed all President Carter's appointees on the National Council on Disability (NCD), including Judith E. Heumann and Elizabeth Boggs—one of the founders in 1950, and later first woman president in 1958, of the National Association of Retarded Children.[6] Mother of a child with a developmental disability, Boggs was "perhaps the nation's greatest authority on programs that affect the mentally retarded, . . . a woman of encyclopedic knowledge and enormous energy."[7] Boggs—a Ph.D. in theoretical chemistry and mathematics, and a well-trained scientist—changed careers when she and her group organized classes for her son and other developmentally delayed children, in order to enable them to register at public schools.[8]

When President Reagan replaced these appointees with Republican disability leaders, he may not have realized that disability issues often transcend liberal-conservative ideology. Recognizing the limitations of Section 504, holding meetings with disability leaders in every state, the new council appointed by President Reagan—with South Carolina Commissioner of Rehabilitation, Joseph Dusenbury, as chair, and Dart and Sandra Parrino as vice-chairs—published the "National Policy for Persons with Disabilities" in 1982.[9] Maintaining a unity of purpose with the former members of the council, vice-chair Dart conferred frequently with the Carter appointees. In fact, he refers to Heumann, a woman about twenty years his junior, as his mentor.

One of the NCD's recommendations approved by President Reagan was that "Congress should act forthwith to include persons with disabilities in the Civil Rights Act of 1964 and other civil and voting rights legislation and regulations."[10] Later the council resolved, however, that "disability discrimination is distinctive," substantially different from other kinds of prejudice, and thus "a separate civil rights law" was necessary to address disability bias. Paul Hearne—Frieden's successor as NCD executive director, serving from July 1988 to September 1989—suggested that "unlike the women's lobby, the disability lobby was not strong enough to assert itself so that people with disabilities would be included in the Civil Rights Act of 1964."[11] Acknowledging the advantages of the ADA, some disability advocates still believe that inclusion of people with disabilities in the Civil Rights Act of 1964 would have underscored the requirement by the disability population for the same civil rights protection as racial and ethnic minorities as well as women.

Frieden describes the change of the NCD from a governmental advisory body in 1978 to an independent federal agency under the 1984 Amendments to the Rehabilitation Act:

Originally an advisory body under the Department of Education, the NCD was housed in a small office in the basement of the Mary Switzer building.[12] Lacking visibility, authority, and independence, the council didn't have much congressional support. During the 1983 review of the Rehabilitation Act, it was probably Senator Weicker who recommended raising the status of the NCD to make it independent of the

Department of Education. Once the council became independent, the president [Reagan] picked the members, and the Department of Education could no longer edit or censor NCD reports.[13]

Under the leadership of Parrino, Frieden, and disability rights attorney Bob Burgdorf, NCD proposed an ADA[14] that would require accessible public transportation and removal of employment disincentives from social security.[15] Its February 1, 1986, report, *Toward Independence: An Assessment of Federal Laws and Programs Affecting Persons with Disabilities—With Legislative Recommendations,* suggested that "Congress should enact a comprehensive law requiring equal opportunity for individuals with disabilities, with broad coverage and setting clear, consistent, and enforceable standards prohibiting discrimination on the basis of handicap."[16] Both Parrino and Frieden credit Alvis Kent Waldrep Jr., the only member of the Council who remained in the NCD during Parrino's entire tenure as chairperson, with naming the ADA.[17]

Toward Independence formed the basis of an early version of the ADA introduced in 1988 by Senator Lowell Weicker (R-Conn.) and Representative Tony Coelho (D-Calif.). In the 1980s, many disability rights leaders believed that chances of passing comprehensive disability legislation were slim.[18] The best that was achievable, these leaders presumed, were laws providing "services and partial rights in incremental steps." Concerned about enforcement of Section 504, as well as continued funding for disability services, disability rights advocates feared backlash resulting from further disability civil rights legislation.[19] Dart characterizes the mindset of a large segment of the disability community at that time: "We can't even enforce 504. Why waste our time talking about more? The day of civil rights is gone; there will never be another civil rights law passed." In *From Good Will to Civil Rights: Transforming*

Federal Disability Policy, written in the early 1980s, Richard K. Scotch concludes that "the effectiveness of the disability rights movement appears to have peaked in 1978."[20]

Dart refers to the 1988 version of the ADA, proposed primarily to gain endorsements during an election year as "the regulatory version" of the act.[21] For example, the original version included a mandate to make all buildings accessible in two years, "an unrealistic demand" according to Dart. Hearne calls what he considered this infeasible mandate for precipitous universal accessibility "the flat earth rule. The whole world had to be wheelchair accessible by being flat in two years," Hearne notes sarcastically, "but this nonsense was wisely replaced by the reasonable modification rules in the ADA."[22] While Frieden describes the 1988 proposed legislation as having "a broader definition of disability and stricter provisions" than the enacted legislation, he views the 1988 bill somewhat differently from Hearne: "The thirteen-page 1988 version was introductory, an outline for the more specific fifty-two-page 1990 enacted bill. But if you ask me which one I prefer, I would have to say that although the 1988 bill was the stronger of the two, I'd choose the 1990 ADA because it passed."[23]

The 1990 enacted ADA, which Dart labels "the empowerment version," requires that people with disabilities and their advocates file complaints and lawsuits, when appropriate, as a means of monitoring compliance.[24] Unlike Dart, Hearne considers the enacted legislation as both regulatory and empowering:

This law is very regulatory. It regulates states, municipalities, agencies, behavior, and they all have to comply with the Access Board. But the law also empowers people with disabilities to recognize that they have a role in society. And there are two other major differences between the proposed and the enacted ADA. The first one defined disability by giving a laundry list of disabilities, an inefficient and anachronistic way of doing it. Ultimately the ADA went back to what I supported, the well-crafted Section 504 definition of disability. Also, the legislation includes some essentials the original version didn't—the right to sue, attorney's fees for successful plaintiffs, and the right to collect punitive damages.[25]

The disability community was aware of and fought for the ADA unlike its initial response to the Rehabilitation Act of 1973, which includes Section 504. As Edward D. Berkowitz in *Disabled Policy: America's Programs for the Handicapped* notes, "In 1974, for example, when President Ford met with a group of handicapped individuals, they talked about the need for a barrier-free society, the desirability of a spokesman for the handicapped in the White House, and the importance of making Washington's Metro accessible to the handicapped. No one mentioned Section 504 of the Rehabilitation Act of 1973."[26] Not until the 504 regulations were at risk was the disability community galvanized into action. By the time a small group of disability advocates launched efforts leading to the ADA, the consciousness of people with disabilities had been raised nationwide.

Established in 1988 by Brooklyn Congressman Major Owens (D-N.Y.), the Task Force on the Rights and Empowerment of Americans with Disabilities was created to make recommendations to Congress on the ADA. In his role as co-chair of the task force, Justin Dart brought together a distinguished panel to gather information, develop ideas, and unite disparate elements of the disability community behind the ADA. Present were representatives of often overlooked disability groups, such as people with psychiatric and developmental disabilities.[27]

To the surprise of many disability advocates, some members of the disability community expressed doubt about the inclu-sion of people with learning disabilities and AIDS in the ADA. Persuasion by individuals like Dale Brown, founding member of the National Network of Learning Disabled Adults, was required to include people with learning disabilities on the task force.[28] Because the assumption has prevailed that people grow out of learning disabilities, this impairment in adults frequently has been unrecognized or treated with skepticism by schools, vocational rehabilitation, and even—Brown suggests—the task force itself. Furthermore, as Fred Fay recalls, "There were objections to having members with AIDS—we should not have representatives of people with AIDS; people with AIDS will die,' [some disability advocates insisted]. Dart bristled. 'Of course they will die; so will you and I. We are not into perpetuating paternalism,' [Dart responded]. He appointed two people with AIDS."[29]

Some legislators unsuccessfully attempted to include language in the ADA that would have prevented people who have or are "regarded as" having AIDS, or individuals who are HIV-positive, from working in jobs involving food handling. Rather than accepting this addition to the law, the disability community assented to the inclusion of language in the ADA requiring the publication of a list of infectious diseases transmittable through food handling. If reasonable accommodation cannot reduce or eliminate the risk of transmission, the law allows the employer to refuse to assign food handling duties to the infected individual. Many disability advocates perceived the failed attempt as an effort to discriminate against people who are HIV-positive or have AIDS.

Justin Dart reveals how the community had organized and coalesced across disabilities in its support of the ADA:

> During the mid-months of 1989, virtually every disability rights organization and leader

in the country—more than eight thousand five hundred of them—signed and paid for a full page ad in the *Washington Post* urging Congress to pass the ADA and to reject "weakening amendments that would legalize intolerable discrimination." For strategic reasons the ad was held for publication until February 7, 1990. It was hand-delivered to every office in Congress and to the President and was distributed throughout the nation.

During the same period, the Epilepsy Foundation printed and all of us [the disability community] distributed more than one million New Year's postcards for Congress: "Don't weaken a law that will strengthen America." Congress received hundreds of thousands of messages—cards, letters, calls, "No weakening amendments!" This became the battle cry and the required symbol of membership in our movement. Communication to the President and the members of Congress was clear: "a vote for one weakening amendment is a vote against forty three million people with disabilities."[30]

Guided through Congress by Senator Tom Harkin (D-Iowa) and Representative Steny H. Hoyer (D-Md.), the ADA overwhelmingly passed the Senate by 76 to 8 and the House by 377 to 28. Hearne recounts an experience that may have heightened the awareness of two elected officials:

> In 1987 as a way of explaining the constitutionality of the Individuals with Disabilities Education Act, I spoke as a lawyer for a child with a disability on one of the discussion shows Fred Friendly ran on PBS, "The Constitution: A Delicate Balance." A gala honoring the participants on the show was held up a huge flight of stairs at the Philadelphia Hall of Man and Science. Soon after I arrived, two tall men appeared. One took the front of my motorized scooter and the other the back, and they carried me up the steps. One of them was Arizona Governor Bruce Babbitt; the other, Utah Senator Orrin Hatch, who had turned blue by this time, said, "Now I know what you disability people are talking about." At that point it occurred to me that maybe every elected official should

have this experience. When people doubted Hatch's vote on the ADA, I predicted correctly that he would vote for it.[31]

Dart characterizes the ADA victory in Congress: "A ragtag hodgepodge of advocates with disabilities, families, and service providers, who had never completely agreed on anything before, joined together with a few farsighted members of the older civil rights movement, business, the Congress, and the Administration to defeat the richest, most powerful lobbies in the nation."[32] The fact that President Bush, who signed the ADA into law, as well as the legislators leading the effort for congressional approval of the ADA were either themselves disabled or closely related to people with disabilities supports Representative Coelho's observation: "The disability movement boasts 'a hidden army.' Since a sixth of the nation's population has some form of disability, 'disability impacts practically every family.'"[33]

Besides having spent his formative years with an uncle, his mother's brother John, who used a wheelchair as a result of polio,[34] President Bush had three children with disabilities. His daughter died of leukemia when she was three years old; one of his sons had a colostomy after part of his colon was removed in 1986, while another son is dyslexic.[35] Parrino recalls Representative Coelho's comment: "George Bush does not get enough credit for the ADA. If he hadn't wanted it, we wouldn't have had it. He made it very clear that he wanted that bill on his desk at some point in time, and he wanted to sign it."[36] Like President Bush, Representative Coelho (who has epilepsy), Senators Weicker (R-Conn.) and Harkin, and Representative Hoyer (who have family members with disabilities), are examples of political figures with intimate knowledge of disability who played an active role in the passage of the ADA.

Despite the overwhelmingly enthusiastic support for the ADA from all segments of the disability population, the National Federation of the Blind—an organization that contends that blindness is an inconvenience rather than a disability—asserts that a person with a disability has the right to refuse an ADA accommodation. A complaint expressed by blind-from-birth NFB member Arthur Wohl, who was experienced at walking without assistance using a white cane, explains NFB's position. Wohl frequently felt provoked by airline policy: "Often as I was getting off the plane, the flight attendant would first tell me to wait for all the other passengers to leave the plane, and then say get into a wheelchair. I was annoyed that I had to wait, but I absolutely refused to get into a wheelchair. I said, 'I'm blind, but I can walk as fast and as well as anyone else.'"[37]

Justin Dart tells a similar story: "After landing in England, I was informed that as a wheelchair user, I had a right to ambulance service. When I declined, I was told you can use the service or you can stay on the plane and go back to America."[38] Dart points out that this attitude is antithetical to the spirit of the ADA, for the purpose of the law is to serve people with disabilities, *not* limit their choices.

The ADA and Section 504

Although many individual states had statutes protecting people with disabilities from discrimination, the character and degree of these laws varied from state to state. Incorporating policies and language from the Civil Rights Act of 1964 and the 1977 regulations of Section 504, as well as previous laws pertaining to equality for the disability population, the ADA federalized the legal rights of people with disabilities.

The ADA defines disability as "a physical or mental impairment that substantially limits a major life activity, such as walking, seeing, hearing, learning, breathing, caring for oneself, or working."[39] It protects "those who have a disability, those who have a record of such an impairment," and those who are "regarded as having such an impairment."[40] The law protects a blind or deaf person, or a person with a spinal cord injury, but the ADA also applies to a person who has recovered from cancer or mental illness since such people have a record of having a disability. Because a qualified individual with a severe facial disfigurement is regarded as having a disability, the ADA protects such a person from being denied employment because an employer fears the negative reactions of customers or coworkers. As in Section 504, the definition of individuals with disabilities in the ADA includes people with psychiatric disabilities, alcoholics, and recovered drug addicts.[41] Yet the ADA specifically excludes current drug addicts because drug addiction is illegal.[42]

In *Disability Watch: The Status of People with Disabilities in the United States*, H. Stephen Kaye notes: "Although people often associate disability with its more visible manifestations—such as wheelchairs, the canes used by blind people, and sign language—the vast majority of people with disabilities do not require them."[43] As indicated by data provided by the 1992 National Health Interview Survey, the most frequent causes of disability in order of prevalence were back problems, heart disease, arthritis, asthma, leg or foot problems, psychiatric disorders, learning or developmental disabilities, diabetes, cancer, and cerebral vascular disease.[44] By 1997, psychiatric disability claims increased so significantly that they comprised the greatest number of disability discrimination complaints.[45] As these statistics reveal, "invisible" disabilities account for the overwhelming percentage of the fifty-four million whose conditions are included in the ADA definition of disability. On the other hand, the conditions usually thought of as disabling—mobility, visual, and hearing impairments—are less prevalent than is commonly assumed.

Section 504 was used primarily to address what disability advocates have referred to as the comparatively "easy" issues—for example, architectural and transportation accessibility. The major argument put forth by disability advocates for the 1990 ADA was to increase employment of people with disabilities.[46] Since employment discrimination—often difficult to prove—is relevant to people with all types of disabilities, visible and invisible, individuals with a greater variety of disabilities filed complaints and lawsuits under the ADA than those filing under Section 504. In some cases, the ADA has resulted in thornier legal questions than Section 504. Whether or not a building is physically accessible is generally readily apparent; however, whether a job applicant is rejected because of lack of qualifications or because of disability bias frequently is not so clear.

Unlike other civil rights legislation, laws ensuring federal civil rights for people with disabilities occurred in two stages: first, Section 504 applying to entities receiving federal financial assistance; second, the 1990 ADA dealing with both the public and the private sector. Inasmuch as 80 percent of American jobs was in the private—rather than the public—sector, the ADA was required as a supplement to Section 504 in order to increase occupational opportunities for the 75 percent of unemployed people with disabilities who can and want to work.[47] "In signing the ADA, President Bush estimated that federal, state, and local governments spent almost $200 billion to support people with disabilities."[48] A 1990 to 1993 study determined that "the ADA has played a significant role in enhancing labor force participation of persons with disabilities and in reducing dependence on government entitlement programs."[49]

Title I of the ADA, enforced by the Equal Employment Opportunity Commission, bars employers from discriminating against a qualified individual with a disability because of the "disability of such individual in regard to job application procedures, the hiring, advancement, or discharge of employees, employee compensation, job training, and other terms, conditions, and privileges of employment."[50] Just as the ADA definition of an individual with a disability is identical to the Section 504 term, "handicapped person," the ADA meaning of a qualified individual with a disability is similar to the Section 504 designation, "qualified handicapped person." In order to prevent employment discrimination against qualified persons with disabilities, employers are barred from asking perspective job applicants if they have a disability. Title I went into effect on July 26, 1992, for employers with twenty-five or more employees; since July 26, 1994, however, Title I requires employers with fifteen or more employees to comply.

"Reasonable accommodation" for a qualified employee with a disability is mandated unless that provision causes the employer "undue hardship," which refers to significant difficulty or expense.[51] "Reasonable accommodation" may include, but is not limited to, the following: making existing facilities used by employees readily accessible to and usable by persons with disabilities; restructuring jobs, modifying work schedules, or reassigning employees to vacant positions; acquiring or altering equipment or devices; adjusting or revising examinations, training materials, or policies; and providing qualified readers or interpreters.

While a qualified individual presently using alcohol may be covered by the ADA, a current illegal user of drugs who can perform the essential functions of the job is not protected by the law because alcohol use is legal while illegal drug use is criminal. Yet the ADA covers a person "erroneously regarded" as using drugs or an individual who has "successfully completed" or is "participating in a supervised rehabilitation program" and is no longer engaging in the use of drugs. Nonetheless, the ADA provides employers with the authority to hold all employees, regardless of disability, who abuse legal drugs or alcohol to the same job performance criteria as other employees.[52]

Title I: Employment

Two 1995 cases demonstrate how appellate courts have interpreted three terms fundamental to Title I of the ADA, the "essential function of a job," "reasonable accommodations," and "undue hardship." In *Riley v. Weyerhaeuser Paper Company*,[53] the court determined that the employers did not discriminate on the basis of disability because the company could not provide an alternate position for the employee who was unable to perform the essential function of the job. Defendant Weyerhaeuser Paper Company successfully argued that plaintiff Riley could no longer be employed in the firm. Since all the jobs in the plant involved working around machinery and Riley's disability—multiple sclerosis—prevented him from performing any of them, there was no position in the firm appropriate for him. Thus, Weyerhaeuser Paper Company was unable to provide "a reasonable accommodation" for Riley.

In *Benson v. Northwest Airlines*,[54] the Eighth Circuit Court of Appeals reversed the district court's decision that the plaintiff, diagnosed with a repetitive motion injury, failed to establish his ability to perform the essential function of his job. The appeals court offered these reasons for its determination that under Title I of the ADA, the district court should have shifted the burden of proof from Benson to Northwest.

The defendant neither offered evidence of the essential functions of the job at issue nor indicated which of these functions Benson could not perform with a "reasonable accommodation." In addition, Northwest failed to show that either restructuring or transfer would cause the airline "undue hardship."

EPVA attorney James Weisman points out that many ADA cases are avoided because the opposing parties settle their differences out of court. At a 1998 conference of social work professionals,[55] he described his role in settling an employment discrimination dispute:

> A woman called me to ask for my help because she claimed that she was just fired because she recently had a mastectomy. When I called the chic Fifth Avenue department store [in New York City] where she worked, I said to the manager, "I have a woman here who says you let her go because she had a mastectomy." He could have given a legitimate reason for firing her. But no, he said, "it wasn't the mastectomy; it was the cancer. It depressed the other workers, so I thought it was best to get rid of her." Of course, when I informed the department store that this was an ADA violation, she was immediately reinstated.

If there were no ADA, would this woman have felt that she had the right to demand her job back? If there were no ADA, would the department store have given her the job back?

Title III: Public Accommodation

Like Title I covering employment, Title III of the ADA concerning public accommodation derives from the Civil Rights Act of 1964. Effective since January 26, 1992, the public accommodation provisions, regulated by the Department of Justice, bar discrimination based on disability in any public business or service operated by private entities.[56] Moreover, goods, services, and accommodations must be offered in the "most integrated setting appropriate to the needs of the individual."[57] Places of "public accommodation" includes stores and shopping centers, restaurants, offices, banks, theaters, museums, stadiums, and hotels and motels, as well as any site open to the public operated privately such as schools, day care or senior citizen centers, and recreational establishments.[58]

Title III requires that new, or newly altered, facilities constructed after January 26, 1993, be wheelchair accessible.[59] Buildings less than three stories or less than three thousand square feet per story do not require elevators, except for shopping centers and offices of professional health care providers.[60] In addition, the law mandates that if "readily achievable," architectural and communications barriers must be removed in existing structures. The term "readily achievable" is defined in the statute as "easily accomplishable and able to be carried out without much difficulty or expense."[61] Factors to be considered include the nature and the cost of the structural modification, as well as the size, financial resources, and type of business. If removal of the barrier is not "readily achievable," the ADA decrees that goods or services must be made available through alternative methods if such methods are "readily achievable."[62]

On January 27, 1992, the day following the effective date of Title III, Disabled In Action of Metropolitan New York and Barrier Free Living, an agency providing transitional housing for people with disabilities, demonstrated for accessibility to the observation tower on the eighty-sixth floor of the Empire State Building. The protest at a national symbol, one of the first Title III legal actions, called nationwide attention to DIA's Title III complaint against the Empire State Building Company. By March 3, 1994, the Department of Justice announced that the parties involved had reached a settlement whereby the observation tower of the Empire State Building would become available to people with disabilities, including wheelchair users, by June 6, 1994. The concept of "readily achievable" when applied to the observation tower of the Empire State Building—which in 1994 attracted 2.5 million visitors a year, each paying a $3.50 entrance fee—has a very different meaning when applied to, say, a small neighborhood grocery store.

The modifications by architect Peter Hanrahan—including the ramp leading from the eighty-sixth floor to the observation tower surrounding the edifice—were designed in Art Deco style, the same style as the Empire State Building. Furthermore, the railings of the outside deck were gracefully constructed, allowing wheelchair users an unobstructed view from four different locations: north, south, east, and west. Playfully spoofing the access to the observation tower of the Empire State Building, the satirical television show *Saturday Night Live* presented a cartoon of an absurd mile-long ramp extending from the eighty-sixth floor to Central Park. Seven years after the lawsuit was filed, artist Janet Koenig's poster celebrating *Disabled In Action v. Empire State Building* was chosen by the *Fordham Urban Law Journal* as representing the collaboration of community activism and law "to move the most rooted of institutions and structures."[63]

A similar Title III complaint filed by DIA at the same time as the Empire State Building case involved the Inter-Continental Hotel, the New York City headquarters for the Clinton entourage during the 1992 Democratic Convention. Managers of the Clinton campaign were troubled when they learned that an ADA complaint had been initiated against the inaccessible hotel. Expeditiously, the hotel erected a temporary ramp at the entrance during the weekend so that the parties could meet at the hotel a few days later to reach an agreement. A year later, after all the modifications were completed, the hotel held a press conference, together with the U.S. Justice Department, in order to exhibit the excellence of its ADA compliance.

Despite the apparent success of the Title III complaint filed against the United Artists Theatre Circuit by the Disability Rights Education and Defense Fund, the organization's goal—accessible movie theaters—has not yet been fully realized. United Artists agreed to make more than four hundred of its movie theaters across the country accessible by the year 2001.[64] Although all the theaters built before January 26, 1993, were required to be barrier-free, newly constructed theaters built after that date were to be held to a higher standard of accessibility. The May 1996 resolution sent what seemed at the time to be an unambiguous message to all large movie chains regarding Title III compliance.[65] After the resolution, however, a wheelchair inaccessible movie theater design, known as "stadium seating," began to be used increasingly in theater architecture.[66] Consequently, people with mobility impairments are still frequently unable to get appropriate seating at the movies.

The February 1996 suit by the Justice Department against Days Inn, the biggest economy hotel chain in the country with seventeen thousand hotels in forty-nine states, reveals the potential scope of the ADA. Twenty-eight hotels in seventeen states that were built since January 26, 1993, were sued under Title III of the ADA for failing to comply with the public accommodation law.[67] The cases also illustrate, however, the vulnerability of small business people. The attorney for Richard and Karla Hauk, the owners of one of the charged motels, characterized the litigation as one in which individual entrepreneurs are caught in the struggle "between two heavyweights, the Justice Department and Days Inn":

> "The Hauks constructed their hotel in accordance with Days Inn standards," [the attorney] continued, "had their building plans reviewed and approved by Days Inn prior to construction, and obtained Days Inn approval before opening." [The attorney] reported that Mr. Hauk said: "We believe in making buildings accessible to the disabled and we thought that we had done just that. Our expectation was that Days Inn, when it set forth standards for the building we could construct and approved of our building, was watching out for whether our hotel was in compliance with Federal laws."
>
> "The Hauks were trying to work out modifications with the Justice Department that may cost well into six figures," the lawyer said.
>
> Mr. Hauk said, again through his lawyer: "We feel betrayed and abandoned by both Days Inn, which so far has washed its hands of the matter, and the Justice Department, which seems to be using us to prove a point."

The proprietors of twenty-three of the twenty-eight newly-built Days Inns agreed to negotiate with the Justice Department. The defendants were the owners of the five remaining Days Inns, the individual architects and general contractors of the hotels, as well as Days Inn of America, Inc., and its parent company, HFS, Inc. Days Inn of America and HFS argued that although they fully support the ADA, they only franchise hotels, so they bear no responsibility in this controversy. Yet, John Wodatch of the Justice Department contended that the failure of HFS to design and construct places that accommodate everyone was an act of discrimination.

Wodatch pointed out that owners and architects must be alerted to follow the law in the planning and building of *new* structures. In fact, he observed that the Days Inn cases—stemming from the complaints of several dozen travelers—concern the least burdensome type of compliance:

"New construction is the easiest part," he said. "We [the Justice Department] want them [owners and architects] to take a look when they build and then they won't have to worry." A bathroom doorway to accommodate a wheelchair, for example, would need a clear width of 32 inches. This is a no-cost item in the design stage, he said, but widening a doorway in a cinder-block construction is another matter.

Building according to the ADA specifications is uncomplicated and cost effective; problems arise when new structures not in compliance with the ADA have to be retrofitted. By late 1999, Days Inn of America and its new parent company, Cedant Corporation, settled their lawsuit with the Justice Department by providing interest-free loans to newly-built franchises of the hotel chain for renovations necessary for ADA compliance.[68] Wodatch noted that the settlement reveals "an industry-wide problem" and that "we [the Justice Department] intend to follow up with other hotels and hotel chains in the United States to ensure that this problem doesn't exist."

In addition to a movie theater chain and a hotel chain, the Justice Department dealt with an ADA issue involving a restaurant chain, Friendly's family restaurants.[69] In the May 19, 1997, settlement with the Justice Department, under Title III, the Friendly Ice Cream Corporation agreed to a six-year program that would increase the accessibility of 704 of its restaurants in fifteen states. The accommodations that will be provided include redesigned dining areas to suit wheelchair users, accessible parking areas and curb cuts, modified existing restrooms or newly-constructed accessible restrooms, and provision of menu readers or audio versions of the menu for blind customers.

Although Title II covers *public* transportation, Title III regulates two types of *private* transportation, both overseen by the Department of Transportation.[70] The first involves carriers in the business of transporting people, such as private bus lines, taxicabs, and limousines. With regard to newly-purchased buses on fixed route systems, all *intracity* buses are required to be accessible, while *intercity* buses must be accessible beginning October 2000.[71] Taxicabs using sedan-type automobiles do not have to be accessible, while taxicabs using vans must be accessible.

The second type of private transportation covered by Title III deals with services *incidental* to the primary purpose of the business, such as hotel vans transporting people to and from airports. Depending on the seating capacity of the vehicle, the second type requires either wheelchair accessibility or "equivalent service."[72] "Equivalent service" in this context means that although all hotel vans do not have to be accessible, a sufficient number of vehicles must be available to serve wheelchair users.

Title II: Public Services (State and Local Government)

Title II of the ADA, dealing with public service[73] and public transportation, is based on Section 504. Like Title III, two different agencies implement and enforce Title II: the Justice Department covers public service, and the Department of Transportation monitors public transportation. Effective January 26, 1992, no qualified individual with a disability may be excluded because of that disability from "participation in or denied the benefits of the services, programs or activities of a public entity."[74]

Moreover, Title II requires "program accessibility," meaning that all public programs and services, when viewed as a whole, must be accessible to and usable by individuals with disabilities, "in the most integrated setting possible." For example, if the setting is not accessible to a wheelchair user, the government is required to move the site or offer an alternative that allows the wheelchair user to participate "in the most integrated setting possible." Structural changes required for "program accessibility" must be made as quickly and efficiently as possible, but no later than January 26, 1995. A public entity employing fifty or more people must have devised a transition plan by July 26, 1992, indicating the steps needed to implement changes.

An example of such structural changes, curb cuts—sloped areas at street intersections[75]—are required by people using wheelchairs and scooters. Because the Pennsylvania Department of Transportation and the Philadelphia Streets Department were constructing and altering streets without building curb cuts at intersections, Disabled In Action of Pennsylvania (together with twelve individual plaintiffs) and Eastern Paralyzed Veterans Association filed a Title II class action lawsuit in July 1992.[76] The decision in this suit mandated that not only the defendants, but also ultimately all localities nationwide, were compelled to provide curb cuts whenever streets were repaired or newly constructed. Compliance with this ruling has been required since Title II went into effect on January 26, 1995.

Soon after, the plaintiffs sued the defendants again, this time for the installation of curb cuts on *every* street intersection in Philadelphia, not just on those altered or newly built. The settlement, favoring the plaintiff, necessitated curb cuts on every corner in the downtown business district of Philadelphia by December 31, 1996, and in the rest of the city by December 31, 2001. Since Title II had required these curb cuts by January 26, 1995, this agreement represented a compromise.

Noting that New York City had not prepared the required schedule for constructing curb cuts at all sidewalk corners mandated by Title II of the ADA by July 26,

1992, EPVA filed suit against the New York City Department of Transportation in 1994. EPVA observed that with neither a plan nor preparation for curb cuts in place, New York City clearly would be unable to meet the ADA effective date, January 26, 1995. Since curb cuts are relevant to any locality with sidewalks, most of the nation is impacted by decisions in these cases. Despite complaints by many localities that implementing the law requiring curb cuts is an undue financial burden, the Justice Department did *not* extend the ADA compliance date.[77]

Disability advocates argued that if localities had acted in accordance with the 1977 regulations of Section 504 (which later became the flexible federal ADA mandate), most curb cuts would already be completed. In 1995, when many members of Congress were criticizing unfunded federal mandates, the ADA was inappropriately targeted as a law to be suspended or limited to voluntarily compliance in a manner that takes into account the needs of state and local governments. First, as civil rights legislation, the ADA was mischaracterized as an unfunded federal mandate. Second, laws are ineffective when compliance is not required. The fact that this mischaracterization of the ADA as an unfunded federal mandate lingers suggests that many policymakers and social critics do not recognize that people with disabilities are covered by civil rights legislation.[78]

In another Title II case, a deaf attorney, Michael Chatoff, sued the New York City Police Department under the Public Services section of the ADA, on behalf of more than two hundred thousand deaf and hard-of-hearing residents of New York City, for failing to make the 911 emergency system directly accessible to teletypewriter users. On January 27, 1992, the effective date of Title II, Chatoff filed the lawsuit in U.S. District Court (S.D.), arguing that the issue was "a matter of life and death."[79] Because of this lawsuit, the New York City Police Department's Communication Division 911 Emergency Call Center became fully accessible by December 1, 1992, to persons utilizing teletypewriters. As a means of implementing this accessibility, members of the center participated in a training program that included teletypewriter operation, disability awareness sessions, and protocol in American Sign Language for communicating with people who are deaf, hard of hearing, or speech impaired.

A 1996 class action Title II lawsuit on behalf of the New York City Civic Association of the Deaf involved a similar issue: elimination of many New York City lever-activated fireboxes and conversion of the remaining fireboxes to intercoms. The court decided that the two-way voice system did not provide deaf people, who cannot use ordinary telephones or intercoms, with equal access to a vital public service. A solution offered by the New York City administration, utilizing tapping codes so that deaf people could indicate different types of emergencies, left many questions unanswered. For example, will the city provide a training program for the deaf population as well as the dispatchers handling these problems? The newspaper accounts dealt only with the issue of bias against poor communities where fireboxes are often essential because telephones are not readily available.[80] Discrimination against deaf people was not mentioned.

On December 8, 1995, the Disability Law Center of New York Lawyers for the Public Interest initiated Title II complaints against fifteen courthouses in New York City because they were not accessible to people with all types of impairments. Filing on behalf of Disabled In Action of Metropolitan New York, Cary LaCheen, senior staff attorney at the Disability Law Center, argued that these courts lack important features for people with disabilities, such as accessible front entrances, elevators, courtrooms, public seating, jury boxes, restrooms, and parking facilities, as well as assistive listening devices, teletypewriters, and signage. Consequently, LaCheen continued, people with disabilities are prevented from fully participating in the legal system in New York City as litigants, lawyers, witnesses, jurors, court personnel, and spectators. Although the case was still pending in 2000, courts that failed to make modifications necessary to accommodate people with disabilities by January 26, 1995, were in violation of Title II of the ADA.

Decided on January 31, 1995, by the U.S. Court of Appeals, Third Circuit, *Helen L. v. Didario* was a Title II lawsuit that may have far-reaching consequences for people with disabilities who are institutionalized in nursing homes although they wish to remain in their own communities and in their own homes.[81] The appeals court reversed the ruling of the U.S. District Court for the Eastern District of Pennsylvania that Didario (the nursing home administrator) was in compliance with the ADA because he was not discriminating against Helen L. Rather than accepting Didario's argument that shifting attendant care services from the nursing home to the home of Helen L. involved "fundamental alterations," the appeals court determined that the modifications constituted "reasonable accommodations."

Because the ADA decrees that home attendant services be provided in the "most integrated setting appropriate," the appeals court supported the plaintiff's claim that the services she received in the nursing home could be given in a setting she preferred, her own home.[82] The appeals court considered the nursing home a "segregated" environment, not consistent with the ADA mandate requiring "the least restrictive environment," because in the institution Helen L. had "no contacts with nondisabled persons other than the staff of the nursing home and visits from her two children."

Without demanding proof of "intentional or overt discrimination," the appeals court determined that "unnecessary segregation of individuals with disabilities in provision of public services is itself a form of 'discrimination'" according to both the ADA and the Rehabilitation Act. The Supreme Court's denial of certiorari in 1995 in the *Helen L.* case sustains the Third Circuit court's decision.[83] Furthermore, as indicated by the 1995 statistics, the average annual cost of caring for a person in a nursing home is $45,000, while the average annual cost of caring for a person in the attendant care program in his or her own home is $10,500.[84]

Title II: Public Transportation

Title II also mandates that people with disabilities, including wheelchair users, have access to public transportation, which refers to transportation within and between cities, such as bus and train systems, provided by state or local governments. All newly-constructed public transportation facilities and portions of existing facilities being altered, such as train stations or bus depots, must be barrier-free. Fixed-route systems, meaning commuter rail systems,[85] subways, trolleys, and buses, must ensure that people with disabilities, including wheelchair users, can access and use the vehicles. All rail systems must have at least one accessible car per train. Furthermore, public entities that operate fixed-route systems must provide paratransit service, which is comparable in service level and response time to service typically available to fixed-route customers, unless so doing would impose an undue financial hardship.

Effective dates for required accessibility of rail stations were extended because they are more difficult and expensive to modify than vehicles such as trains, trolleys, and buses. The effective date that all "key" rail stations, except for commuter rail stations, were required to be barrier-free was July 26, 1993. If renovations involve extraordinarily expensive structural changes, however, this date may be extended to July 26, 2020, provided at least two-thirds of the key stations are accessible by July 26, 2010.

Title IV: National Telephone Relay Service

Unlike Titles I and III based on the Civil Rights Act of 1964, and Title II modeled after Section 504, Title IV mandating nationwide, daily, twenty-four-hour intrastate and interstate relay services originated with the ADA.[86] To ensure equal access to telephone services, Title IV enables people with hearing and speech impairments who use teletypewriters to communicate with people who use voice phones. Relay operators cannot change the content of conversations, limit the length of calls, maintain records, or disclose to others the contents of relayed conversations. Rates for relay users cannot exceed rates charged for voice calls of equivalent duration, time of day, and distance called. Title IV also requires television stations to include close-captioning of public service announcements that are federally funded, in whole or in part. The Federal Communications Commission serves as the implementing and enforcement agency.

Title V: Miscellaneous

Title V consists of some key clarifications, exclusions, and add-ons to the ADA.[87] First, the ADA cannot be employed as a means of decreasing the standards established by Title V of the Rehabilitation Act of 1973, which consists of Sections 501 through 504 and additions to Title V. Second, states are subject to the ADA, but the ADA does not nullify state or local laws that provide protections equal to or greater than those of the ADA. Third, the winning party in an ADA action, other than the U.S. government, may be awarded reasonable attorneys' fees, including litigation expenses and costs. Other significant provisions involve the following: explanations of the definition of disability according to the ADA; protection of people who have filed claims or participated in investigations, proceedings, or hearings under the ADA; and the role of agencies in offering technical assistance to entities covered by the ADA.

The Supreme Court and the ADA

On March 30, 1998, the U.S. Supreme Court heard oral arguments on its first ADA case, *Bragdon v. Abbott*, a lawsuit to determine whether or not the ADA definition of disability includes asymptomatic HIV.[88] The case involved the appeal of a Maine dentist who was found to have discriminated against a woman—infected with the HIV virus—by refusing to treat her in his office.[89] Interestingly enough, her case was supported by both the American Medical Association and the American Dental Association.[90] Before the case reached the U.S. Supreme Court, the U.S. Court of Appeals for the First Circuit accepted the argument that the woman's HIV status substantially limited a major life activity, reproduction, and thus she was covered by the ADA. Consequently, the appeals court did not accept the weaker argument that because of her HIV status, she was regarded as having a disability and therefore covered by the ADA.

A week before the Supreme Court heard the arguments in the case, the *New York Times* reported in a front-page article that "discrimination against people who carry the virus that causes AIDS offers the Justices a surprisingly blank slate on which to write an opinion with major implications not only for the law on the disease itself but also for disability rights law in general."[91] On April 7, 1998, "Gay Men's Health Crisis in Brief," a weekly newsletter, noted that "no matter what legal niceties are displayed to convince the highest court in the land on this matter, we who deal with the HIV-positive virus every day on legal matters recognize the following painful reality. An HIV-diagnosis casts a long shadow of discrimination over the person who lives with it whether or not that person is symptomatic." This lawsuit was especially compelling for two reasons: "After seventeen years, the [U.S. Supreme] Court [had] its first case involving AIDS,"[92] and lower courts had been split on the applicability of the ADA to invisible disabilities such as HIV.

On June 25, 1998, in a five to four ruling, the Supreme Court held that the woman's decision not to have children because of her HIV-positive status brought her within the ADA's definition of disability: an impairment that substantially limits one or more major life activities.[93] The *New York Times* reported, "Millions of Americans with conditions like diabetes, epilepsy, and even infertility and alcohol addiction appear to have won important new protection against discrimination as a result of [this] Supreme Court ruling, . . . advocates say.[94] Subsequent ADA decisions by the Supreme Court, however, countered this impression.[95]

As with the *Bragdon* case, lower courts were divided on the basic issue underlying the second ADA lawsuit considered by the Supreme Court, *Pennsylvania Department of Corrections v. Yeskey:* Does the ADA cover state prisons?[96] When Ronald Yeskey, because of his disability—hypertension—was denied the opportunity to shorten his state prison sentence by spending six months in a youthful offender "boot camp," the district court dismissed his complaint, finding the

ADA inapplicable to state prisons. Ruling that the ADA *does* cover state prisons, however, the Supreme Court on June 15, 1998, unanimously upheld the 1997 decision of the Court of Appeals for the Third Circuit that had reversed the district court.[97] Arguing for Yeskey, the U.S. Solicitor General said that "the law applied to state prisons, [citing] the Rehabilitation Act's twenty-five years of application to federal prisons."[98] The ADA, "a logical extension" of the Rehabilitation Act, "could work without undue difficulty," he added.[99]

On May 24, 1999, the Supreme Court decided *Carolyn C. Cleveland v. Policy Management Systems Corp., et al.,* a case dealing with the differing definitions of disability in the ADA and in the Social Security Disability Insurance (SSDI) provision of the Social Security Act.[100] Delivering the opinion of the Court, Justice Stephen Breyer stated:

> The Social Security Act and the ADA both help individuals with disabilities, but in different ways. The Social Security Act provides monetary benefits to every insured individual who "is under a disability".... The ADA seeks to eliminate unwarranted discrimination against disabled individuals.... In our view, however, despite the appearance of conflict that arises from the language of the two statutes, the two claims do not inherently conflict to the point where courts should apply a special negative presumption.... That is because there are too many situations in which an SSDI claim and an ADA claim can comfortably exist side by side.
>
> Cleveland explains the discrepancy between her SSDI statements that she was "totally disabled" and her ADA claim that she could "perform the essential functions" of her job. The first statements, she says, "were made in a forum which does not consider the effect that reasonable accommodations would have on the ability to work."

The unanimous Supreme Court decision vacating the summary judgment against Cleveland offered both parties "the opportunity... to present, or to contest, these explanations." The impact of the decision will make it possible for millions of adults who receive Social Security disability benefits to be protected against discrimination under the ADA if and when they are able to return to the work force.

On June 22, 1999, the Supreme Court ruled on four cases involving two ADA issues: First, in *Olmstead v. L.C. and E.W.,*[101] the Court upheld the "integration regulation" of the ADA, which ordains that individuals with disabilities must be offered services in the "most integrated setting." The Court further stated, "Undue institutionalization qualifies as discrimination 'by reason of... disability.'" Second, in three employment cases, *Sutton et al. v. United Air Lines, Inc.,*[102] *Murphy v. United Parcel Service, Inc.,*[103] and *Albertsons, Inc. v. Kirkingburg,*[104] the Court determined that individuals whose conditions do not substantially limit any life activity and/or are easily correctable are not disabled according to the ADA.

William Stothers, deputy director of The Center for an Accessible Society, describes the *Olmstead* decision: "The high court upheld... that Georgia's Department of Human Resources could not segregate two women with mental disabilities in a state psychiatric hospital long after the agency's own treatment professionals had recommended their transfer to community care."[105] This ruling, Stothers adds, "is consistent with research that demonstrates the social and economic value of having individuals with disabilities live in their community with the appropriate services." *Olmstead,* in which seven states—down from twenty-six—filed an amicus curiae brief with the Court supporting the State of Georgia, is characterized by disability attorney Stephen Gold as a defining moment for the ADA.[106] If the Supreme Court had ruled in favor of Georgia, he observes, the ADA would have become a mere shell of what it was intended to be, stripping away its major civil rights provision—integration.[107]

Each of the three employment cases had a different twist: In *Sutton*, two pilots were turned down for jobs because they did not meet the airline's minimum requirement of uncorrected visual acuity at 20/100 or better, a condition that was correctable. In *Murphy*, a mechanic/driver was fired for high blood pressure, a condition correctable with medication. Finally, in *Albertsons*, a truck driver was dismissed because of a serious vision impairment causing him to fall below the Department of Transportation standards of visual acuity. In all three decisions, the majority of the Supreme Court supported the employer. Justice Sandra Day O'Connor delivered the opinions of the Court in both the *Sutton* and *Murphy* cases. In the *Sutton* opinion she wrote, "A 'disability' means only where an impairment 'substantially limits' a major life activity, not where it 'might,' 'could,' or 'would' be substantially limiting if mitigating measures were not taken. A person whose physical or mental impairment is corrected by medication or other measures does not have an impairment that presently 'substantially limits' a major life activity."[108] She continued:

> Congress did not intend to bring under the [ADA] statute's protection all those whose uncorrected conditions amount to disabilities.... Had Congress intended to include all persons with corrected physical limitations among those covered by the Act, it undoubtedly would have cited a much higher number [than forty-three million] of disabled persons in the findings. That it did not is evidence that the ADA's coverage is restricted to only those whose impairments are not mitigated by corrective measures.

Disability advocates concur with Justice John Paul Stevens in his strong dissents in *Sutton* and *Murphy*. In *Sutton*, Stevens stated that the question "whether an individual is 'disabled' within the meaning of the Act—

and, therefore, is entitled to the basic assurances that the Act affords—focuses on her past or present physical condition *without regard to mitigation that has resulted from rehabilitation, self-improvement, prosthetic devices, or medication*."[109] Stevens noted that the case asks whether the ADA allows people to claim its protections "in the same way as Title VII of the Civil Rights Act of 1964 does for every single individual in the work force." Continuing the analogy to race, he stated, "Congress . . . focused almost entirely on the problem of discrimination against African-Americans when it enacted Title VII. . . . But that narrow focus could not possibly justify a construction of the statute that excluded Hispanic-Americans or Asian-Americans or, as we later decided (ironically enough . . .) Caucasians."[110] Moreover, he added, "The Court was cowed by respondent's [United Airlines] persistent argument that viewing all individuals in their unmitigated state would lead to a tidal wave of lawsuits. . . . The Court's approach would seem to allow an employer to refuse to hire every person who has epilepsy or diabetes that is controlled by medication . . . or every person who functions efficiently with a prosthetic limb." Both *Sutton* and *Murphy* were about whether people were "disabled" as the ADA defined the term, Stevens argued in *Sutton*, instead of about whether people had encountered disability discrimination.[111]

Disability rights attorney Chai Feldblum, who helped draft the ADA, explains how the decision will militate against the intention of the Congress when it passed the ADA—keeping people with disabilities in the work force: "These decisions create the absurd result of a person being disabled enough to be fired from a job, but not disabled enough to challenge the firing."[112] While disability activist and scholar Nadina LaSpina, a wheelchair user, attributes the success in *Olmstead* to the mobilization of the disability community by American Disabled for Attendant Programs Today (ADAPT), she holds disability activists responsible for loss of the three Supreme Court employment cases:

> Busy organizing to fight the Olmstead threat, our community did not pay very much attention to the three employment cases being reviewed by the Supreme Court. And that was a *big* mistake. The Justices didn't hear from us, but you can bet they heard from the business community. In the papers, the op-eds and letters to the editors were all from business interests hellbent on undermining the ADA....
>
> And while the ADA's enemies wailed and raved, our community kept quiet. Why? Because we thought we had more urgent matters to address, more important battles to fight? Because we couldn't really identify with nearsighted pilots the way we could with two women locked up in an institution? Because secretly or not so secretly many of our own people feel annoyed when those who are not "truly disabled" try to reap the fruits of our hard work? Whatever the reason, the damage is done.[113]

Disability attorney Peter Thompson describes the damage. As Justice Stevens predicted, Thompson says that his clients with diabetes, epilepsy, or severe arthritis will no longer automatically be considered disabled.[114] Consequently, the time-consuming, expensive effort to determine "the extent to which the person is impaired," he points out, will discourage lawyers from bringing claims. For example, Thompson indicates that one of his clients who received a disciplinary memo after experiencing an epileptic seizure at work is not only unable to sue as a result of the Supreme Court decision but also cannot invoke the law to prevent further harassment.

Just as the Court failed to appreciate the real disability issues inherent in *Davis* (1979) and *Rowley* (1982), the Court has misinterpreted these three employment cases.[115] In decisions following *Davis* and *Rowley*, the Court's position was more consistent with that of the disability community's. With the passage of time, the Court may revisit the issues in the employment cases, ultimately recognizing that the disability discrimination—not the definition of disability—should be the primary focus. Perhaps, had there been a national cross-disability organization, such as the American Coalition of Citizens with Disabilities (1974–1983), the disability community would have been galvanized to carefully examine the implications of—and effectively assert its position on—these pivotal employment cases.

The Myth of "The Disability Lobby"

Echoing many ADA critics, Philip K. Howard's statement in *The Death of Common Sense*, "The disabled lobby is waging war against every other citizen,"[116] assumes a clear adversarial relationship between nondisabled and disabled people. Apparently, the author has not accepted disability as a universal possibility, or even probability, for most of humankind. Furthermore, he ignores the great number of nondisabled people intimately connected with loved ones with disabilities, for whom they care and advocate. Although Howard presents the "disability lobby" as a potent adversary, another critic of the ADA, Brian Doherty, asserts in the *American Spectator* that "no grass-roots movement campaigned for the bill."[117] At the same time, Doherty imagines a well-orchestrated, well-financed campaign in which "a disabled person from every member's district *was sent* to lobby for the ADA."[118] Doherty never indicates *who sent* these lobbyists. The truth was that many individuals with disabilities, and members of grass-roots organizations such as independent living centers, ADAPT, DIA, and the American Council of the Blind, as well as Gallaudet students, used their own limited financial and physical resources to advocate in Washington for a bill that they considered essential for their own achievement of equality.

Besides organizing a celebration on the day of the signing of the ADA, disability activists coordinated two earlier ADA marches in Washington in order to rally support for the legislation. People with varying degrees of disability traveled from all parts of the country, some from as far as California, many at their own expense. Harry Wieder, a New York City demonstrator with a disability, describes his experience at the second of the two marches:

> We took the Amtrak train at 5:30 in the morning from Pennsylvania Station to Union Station in Washington, D.C. We joined the march to the Capitol and stayed there while the Senate was debating the ADA. At the last demonstration, some people in wheelchairs climbed up the Capitol steps, which some of us thought really made a point, and others thought fit the negative stereotypes too much, so we all don't think alike. This time, even though they told us to go, we stayed in the Capitol for hours, all kinds of people, blind people, deaf people, people in chairs, people with developmental impairments, all kinds. Then when we got word that the Senate passed the bill, we cheered and hugged and went home. It would have been nice to sleep over at a hotel because we could have used the rest, but the hotels were too expensive, so we went home the same day even though we were very tired.[119]

Except for the planning these crusades required, the disability community by and large formed an ad hoc, loosely-organized army committed to the passage of the ADA.

Backlash

Like other civil rights legislation pertaining to discrimination because of race or gender, the ADA has been the recipient of backlash. Justin Dart has suggested that all movements that allow a formerly powerless people to determine their own destiny engender hostility in individuals comfortable with the status quo. Dart explains, "Many of these journalists and media personalities antagonistic to the ADA expect oppressed people to stay in their place."[120]

The anticipated backlash has been surprisingly pernicious, however, spreading confusion and misinformation about the legislation. For example, in his *Reason* article "Unreasonable Accommodation: The Case against the Americans with Disabilities Act," Doherty reveals a lack of understanding of the meaning of significant terms essential for comprehension of the law. In fact, Doherty argues that an ADA complaint involving the ramping of four steps to a diner will contribute to establishing "the specific meaning" of "ambiguous phrases" such as "undue burden" and "reasonable accommodation," two terms applicable *only* to Title I and Title II, not to Title III public accommodation cases. The appropriate term for this Title III case that Doherty described is "readily achievable." The law is simple; the complication is caused by Doherty's lack of understanding of the legislation he is criticizing. For the $5 million business cited in Doherty's example, a ramp to remove the barrier of four steps is indeed "readily achievable," meaning the owner can comply with little difficulty or expense. Furthermore, the carefully crafted language of the legislation, characterized by Doherty as ambiguous, is clear-cut though flexible enough, in fact, to suit the great variety of situations to which it is applied, from a multinational corporation to a small business.

James Bovard, in his *American Spectator* piece "The Lame Game," denigrates the ADA by referring to a litany of preposterous employment lawsuits, often without indicating their final disposition.[121] Many of these cases, such as the one involving a guidance counselor arrested for cocaine possession who claimed ADA protection,[122] were probably dismissed forthwith. These unlikely suits, reiterated by ADA antagonists, "aren't typical, however, and in most of them the plaintiff loses." Ironically, the quote is from Doherty, one of the ADA's severest critics, who offers his own list of ridiculous ADA employment cases.

Early in his July 19, 1996, ADA segment on ABC's "20/20" television program, John Stossel resurrected the inventory of foolish ADA employment complaints. Stossel's failure to air any portion of a half-hour videotaped interview with a prominent disability rights attorney, James Weisman, on a March 12, 1993, "20/20" segment involving an ADA issue lends credence to Dart's doubts about Stossel's evenhandedness regarding the ADA debate. Dart questioned Stossel's impartiality when the television commentator turned down offers to have disability advocates appear on the July 19 program."[123]

Claiming that the ADA has "employers running scared," Stossel offered his reason for the supposed failure of the employment title, Title I, of the ADA:

> They [employers] fear any disabled person could tie them into knots, that if they hire disabled people, they might never be able to fire them. As a result, we're told many employers are now so fearful they simply avoid the disabled. After interviewing for the job, a disabled person's simply told, "Sorry, someone else was better qualified." Lawyers like [Julie] Janofsky who represents many companies say it goes on all the time.[124]

Rather than an argument against the ADA, Stossel's explanation could be used to make the case for increased enforcement of the legislation or, as some disability advocates contend, for affirmative action to ensure that people with disabilities are treated equitably in employment.[125]

Demonstrating how employers evade the ADA, Janofsky revealed the persistence of disability discrimination and the resourcefulness of those who practice it. The poor employment statistics for people with disabilities prior to the ADA provide ample evidence that bias in hiring for these underemployed workers was not initiated by the ADA. On the contrary, unfair employment procedures, such as the one described by Janofsky, were the reasons an ADA was required.

Stossel also criticized the ADA because "most of the complaints are not coming from the blind or people who are paralyzed. They're coming from people with sore backs or stress-related complaints." Stossel's analysis fails to consider the difference between visible and invisible disabilities. Since people with visible disabilities are much more likely to be rejected when seeking employment than people with invisible disabilities, the workforce includes many more individuals with sore backs or stress problems than with visual or motor impairments. Employees with disabilities can file ADA complaints much more easily than unsuccessful job applicants with disabilities, as Janofsky's depiction of employers' circumvention of the law so effectively illustrates.

Furthermore, Stossel reveals the commonly held misconception that the ADA was specifically designed only for people with ostensible disabilities, when in fact the definition of disability includes hidden as well as obvious disabilities. For example, is an individual with a severe, though not immediately discernible, heart condition or psychiatric disability less disabled than a person who is clearly blind? Yet as Stossel demonstrates, too often only disabilities that are observable are deemed legitimate while conditions that are not overtly evident are considered spurious. As noted in an EEOC report, "Given that there are many more people with hidden disabilities than there are people with visible disabilities," it is not surprising that so many ADA employment cases involve these often imperceptible disabilities.[126]

Using one specific anecdote as evidence, Stossel suggests that the "reasonable accommodations" required by the ADA to enable people with disabilities to be employed often cost "a fortune." Janet Reno, Attorney General in the Clinton administration, and Dick Thornburgh, Attorney General in the Bush administration, however, disagree. Reflecting the population at large, both attorneys general have had intimate experience with disability; Reno has Parkinson's disease, and Thornburgh has a child with a developmental disability. Unequivocally, Reno and Thornburgh jointly dispute those they label "journalistic naysayers" who have charged that "the law imposes unreasonable burdens":

> They [these journalists] mischaracterize the ADA by implying that it requires businesses to spend outrageous sums removing barriers almost overnight. These criticisms miss the mark. The ADA's requirements provide flexibility to business and government. The ADA strikes a carefully calibrated balance between the rights of people with disabilities and the legitimate concerns of business and government, including costs. It merely codifies common sense.[127]

In fact, in *Transcending Compliance: 1996 Follow-up Report on Sears, Roebuck and Company* (hereafter *Sears Report*), Peter Blanck states that the average cost of providing workplace accommodations at Sears between 1993 and 1995 was $45, less than half of the $121-dollar average cost from 1978 to 1992, as reported in the 1994 study.[128] The *Sears Report*, sponsored by the Annenberg Washington program where economist Blanck is a senior fellow, notes that of more than seventy "reasonable accommo-

dations" provided by Sears, 99 percent required little or no cost. As Reno and Thornburgh agree, "Most people in the business community understand that the ADA has been good for business; it has expanded the markets served by most establishments and opened the doors to productive people with disabilities, all at a minimal cost." Major industries have been especially receptive to the disability population; in fact, the probability of people with disabilities being hired increases with the size of the company.[129]

The impression given by commentators such as Doherty, Bovard, and Stossel—and in books like Philip K. Howard's *The Death of Common Sense*, and Walter Olson's *The Excuse Factory: How Employment Law Is Paralyzing the American Workplace*[130]—is that the ADA generates a deluge of frivolous ADA lawsuits. Yet, Reno and Thornburgh agree that "one thing is clear: The ADA has not resulted in a flood of litigation." The Justice Department reported in 1995 that "litigation under the [ADA] Act has been rare. The Justice Department and the Equal Employment Opportunity Commission together have averaged fewer than twenty-five suits during each of the past five years."[131] James Raggio, general counsel of the Access Board, observed, "Of course you can point to cases stretching the limits of the ADA. Lawsuits on the fringes are to be expected. That's the way the system works. But the overwhelming majority of the cases are valid. They concern a legitimate issue, and they deserve to be aired."[132] Bernadette B. Wilson, EEOC supervising program analyst, responds to criticism of the ADA:

> And contrary to some widely circulated misinformation that this agency [EEOC] is overrun with frivolous ADA charges, no-cause findings are rendered in far fewer instances with ADA cases than they are with our other statutes. And while monetary awards for cases resolved under the Civil Rights Act and our

other statutes declined between 1994 and 1995, monetary awards increased for those who file ADA charges. This hardly represents the profile of a frivolous case load.[133]

In his introductory remarks to the March 12, 1996, Commissioners' Meeting of the EEOC, chairman Gilbert F. Casellas relates the story of a *Rapid City Journal* columnist, Richard Kahler, who gained an understanding of the reality of the ADA after first being swayed by the myths. In his April 1995 article, Kahler attacked the ADA as "a recurring nightmare that just keeps getting worse." After receiving information from people with disabilities and their advocates, however, he admitted that he "blew it." In a September 1995 piece, he quoted Justin Dart of Justice For All: "It's a fallacy that the ADA costs too much. It's discrimination that costs too much. We can't afford not to get the disabled into the work force so they can lead independent and productive lives."[134]

Although American business has been presented as viewing the ADA unfavorably by news commentators, on television and in print,[135] a July 2, 1995, Harris Poll offers a different picture. The poll reported that 80 percent of executives of small, medium, and large corporations indicated that the cost of accommodating people with disabilities has either not increased or increased only a little since the passage of the ADA. Moreover, 66 percent stated that litigation has not increased since the ADA while 14 percent said that litigation has increased only a little. Overall, 82 percent of these executives concluded that the ADA is worth the cost of implementation.

Every American's Insurance Policy

Too frequently, the public conceives of the ADA as a law serving a special minority whose concerns are separate and distinct from the interests of the general population. People in the disability community describe nondisabled individuals as "temporarily able bodied" or "TABs" as a means of fostering the recognition that, rather than an anomaly, disability is a natural aspect of the human condition. As people age, they are likely to experience increasing degrees of disability, first in their parents and then in themselves.

Clay Haughton, director for Civilian Equal Opportunity for the Defense Department, addressed this issue:

> No one is immune to developing a disability, and almost no one, regardless of race, gender, religion, or economic status, will go through life without suffering from some form of physical or mental impairment. It's truly the equal opportunity situation, and those of us who are disabled are a constant visual reminder of the frailty of each member of the human race. And so accepting this possibility and adjusting to disabilities, those are matters that must concern all of us.[136]

Becky Ogle, chairperson for Justice For All, observes that "the ADA can be viewed as an insurance policy against discrimination that every American in this society should cherish and protect as a matter of enlightened self interest."[137]

Chapter Seven

Access to Jobs and Health Care

UNLIKE OTHER TARGETS OF job discrimination, people with disabilities have an obstacle embedded in the language that defines them. The term "disability" has varying meaning in at least three different contexts: In the Workers' Compensation program "disability means the damages that one person collects from another as a result of an insult or injury. In the Social Security Disability Insurance program, disability refers to a condition that links ill health and unemployment."[1] And in the context of civil rights laws, "disability" is linked to discrimination. Disability advocates believe that the Supreme Court misinterpreted the application of the Americans with Disabilities Act in three 1999 employment cases, treating them as if they pertained to benefits—the first two definitions—rather than, more appropriately, relating the claims to the third definition—discrimination.[2] Since disability is commonly associated with disability benefits—implying the inability to work—employment for people with disabilities appears to be a contradiction.

On the contrary, with modern technology such as computers, motorized wheelchairs, teletypewriters, and Kurzweil readers, an increasing number of people with disabilities will be employable. The growing disability and aging population—a consequence of advances in medicine—presents a compelling economic argument for encouraging these people to become job holders. This rationale played a significant role in the enactment of the 1990 ADA, a law focusing heavily on employment. Eleven years before the ADA was passed, disability advocate Frank Bowe stated that it is better for people with disabilities, as well as for the nation, if they are working, supporting their families, and contributing to the community rather than being dependent; it is better if they are taxpayers rather than tax users.[3]

Employment Discrimination

The 1998 study by Louis Harris and Associates for the National Organization on Disability (NOD) reveals that 79 percent of the nondisabled population of working age are employed, compared to only 29 percent of people with disabilities, a difference of 50 percentage points.[4] NOD president Alan Reich comments, "At a time when the U.S. unemployment rate is at an historic low and there is a crying need for workers, it is astounding to learn that the employment gap remains so wide." Although the primary intention of the ADA was to increase employment opportunities for people with disabilities, "at least 85 percent of the charges are filed by those who are already employed."[5] The difficulty in proving employment discrimination is compounded by the inability of rejected applicants with disabilities to compare their qualifications with those of people who are hired.

Despite being a highly regarded graduate with a master's of science in social work from Columbia University, Caren Potoker— who uses a scooter because of rheumatoid arthritis—required almost two years and nearly fifty interviews to get a job appropriate for her qualifications.[6] Although her fluency in Spanish should have made her especially employable in New York City, she "faced blatant discrimination" in her interviews as she was asked insulting questions, such as "Why are you in that thing?" and "What is wrong with you?" Potoker still believes that she was "lucky" to finally get a position: "It just happened that the agency that hired me was opened to employing people with disabilities."

Most Americans with disabilities who are employed hold only marginal jobs, and many of those who are unemployed are so discouraged that they are not even looking for work.[7] The experience of wheelchair user Raphael Nisan—a forty-three-year-old immigrant from Baku, Azerbaijan, who is seeking American citizenship and employment—illustrates how the system sometimes places impediments in the path of even the most ambitious and determined job-seeker with a disability:

> I interviewed at at least a dozen places. I had my accounting certificate, plus all the years of work experience in Baku. But nobody would hire me. One place was willing to give me a shot, but I couldn't get Access-A-Ride to give me a subscription for van service to and from

work. So I couldn't even get there for the tryout. And without a job, I couldn't buy a car. And without a car, I couldn't work.[8]

Moreover, women as well as racial and ethnic minorities with disabilities confront dual employment discrimination. Rebecca Ogle of Justice For All notes that "it's a ceiling for all women; it's a double ceiling for women with disabilities."[9] While Commissioner Joyce E. Tucker of the EEOC refers to the need for her agency to focus its outreach efforts on minorities with disabilities seeking jobs,[10] EEOC Commissioner Paul S. Miller compares racial prejudice to disability discrimination:

> In my mind, there is no difference between being asked to be sent to segregated schools because you are black or being sent to colonies because you have mental retardation and society believes that you will be better off with your own kind. There's no difference between being asked to leave a restaurant because you are black or because you use a wheelchair and you're considered a fire hazard. There's no difference between being denied the right to vote because you are black or because of an inaccessible polling place. And yes, there's no difference between being denied the right to a job or to a promotion because you are black or because you are blind or deaf. All of it's discrimination. No such thing as separate but equal.[11]

Affirmative Action

While the Rehabilitation Act of 1973 *requires* affirmative action in federal employment and federal contracts, the ADA's *omission* of an affirmative action requirement has resulted in the failure of the private sector to seriously pursue qualified workers with disabilities. Eastern Paralyzed Veterans Association attorney James Weisman asserts that although preferences were awarded to veterans with disabilities for service to the nation, preferences given to civilians with disabilities have been tainted:

For example, the newsdealer concessions in federal buildings granted to people with disabilities was patronizing, protectionist, and separatist, confirming rather than countering the negative stereotypes concerning disability. This kind of employment focused the public's attention on the disability rather than on the capability of the worker. In the old days, people with disabilities did not have access to education or employment. The 1990s generation has the qualifications to be competitive with the nondisabled population. Society's consciousness is changing. The expectation of the disability population is also changing. Then too, if the general public has encountered people with disabilities in classrooms, in public transportation, in restaurants and shops, in theaters and stadiums, in factories and offices, the anti-disability bias will fade away.[12]

"If you build it *accessible,* they will come," comments Terence Moakley, associate executive director of Eastern Paralyzed Veterans Association.[13] Moakley's point is that if public places are barrier-free, people with disabilities will participate in every aspect of social life as employees and employers, students, consumers, spectators, and travelers. Moakley, who unlike Weisman, is both a veteran and a wheelchair user, is skeptical, however, of accessibility and integration, *alone,* serving as the solution to disability discrimination, especially with regard to employment:

> For people with disabilities, there are other disincentives to getting a job besides physical barriers. When they get jobs, they often lose health systems supports such as Medicaid, Medicare, and personal attendant services. And people who own small businesses are so misinformed that they are afraid they'll go out of business because of the cost of providing accommodations and health insurance for disabled workers. Besides, without some kind of pressure, it'll be hard to persuade corporate America that people with disabilities should be hired because they can do the job.

John Wingate, former director of the International Center for the Disabled, argues that members of a group that have been discriminated against have never obtained their fair share of employment by using nondiscrimination laws only.[14] These laws, he observes, are effective in addressing discrimination against people already employed, not against job seekers. Anne Emerman, a quadriplegic wheelchair user and former director of the Mayor's Office for People with Disabilities, is unequivocal about the pressure required to prod business to employ qualified people with disabilities: "What is needed is affirmative action that includes goals and timetables,[15] as well as a vigorous search for competent people with disabilities to fill positions for which they are appropriate. More than three-quarters of the disability population between the ages of sixteen and sixty-four, able and eager to work, are unemployed."[16]

Disability Employment in Corporate America

The 1994 *Sears Report* of the Annenberg Washington program examining the employment practices of Sears Roebuck and Company, before and after the passage of the ADA, determined that the impact of the law on American business is "evolutionary, not revolutionary."[17] The appraisal of the effectiveness of the ADA by Sears employees who participated in the *Sears Report* varied greatly. Blind computer programmer Don Mott comments, "I don't think [the ADA] had any impact on Sears. The company was doing these things for people with disabilities before the ADA." Another blind computer programmer, Alan Sprecher, observes, "Most people don't know the requirements or implication of the law until someone makes an issue of it."

Yet another blind Sears employee, import manager Brad Shorser, has a different perspective on the ADA's influence: "The ADA has helped raise the consciousness of hiring managers, who now seem more willing to accept people with disabilities. But it's not just the ADA. It's everything that led up to it, including the civil rights legislation of the 1960s. Combined with Sears's policies, the ADA is helping to break down psychological barriers about people with disabilities." An administrative assistant who is visually impaired agrees: "The ADA is helping people get information. Now we're not as afraid. There's somewhere to go." Tony Norris, a quadriplegic footwear department executive, expresses a similar view: "The ADA has been good in awakening the public to people with disabilities."

The *Sears Report* refers, however, to impediments to the employment of qualified people with disabilities such as the "Lingering prejudices [by employers] about hidden cognitive and mental disabilities." Furthermore, "even among people with disabilities who have achieved integration into the work force, a perceived glass ceiling limits their career advancement, and [their] sense of separateness is difficult [for them] to overcome." Sprecher reveals, "I don't know if I've ever been or ever will be part of the gang." Echoing this feeling, Shorser remarks, "I don't expect we'll ever get to the point where prejudice against people with disabilities disappears completely."

Employment of People with Developmental Disabilities

Inspired by the 1960s civil rights struggle and the 1970s Independent Living Movement, self-advocacy fostered independent living and employment for people with developmental disabilities. A demographic study of self-advocacy groups in the United States cites the federal definition of "developmental disability" as

any severe chronic disability attributable to a mental or physical impairment, or combination thereof, that is manifested before the age of twenty-two years, is likely to continue indefinitely, and will result in substantial limitation in function in three or more of the following areas: 1) self-care, 2) receptive and expressive language, 3) learning, 4) mobility, 5) self-direction, 6) capacity for independent language, 7) economic self-sufficiency, and 8) necessity for special services that are of extended duration.[18]

Although in most localities the self-advocacy group for people with developmental disabilities is called People First, the national group is called Self Advocates Becoming Empowered (SABE). SABE defines "self-advocacy" as "teaching people with a disability how to advocate for themselves and to learn how to speak out for what they believe in. It teaches us [people with developmental disabilities] how to make decisions and choices that affect our lives so that we can become more independent. It also teaches us about our rights, but along with learning our rights, we learn our responsibilities."

Evolving in the 1970s out of community recreation clubs, the self-advocacy movement was supported by nondisabled staff but organized and run by people with developmental disabilities. Beginning as a local grass-roots movement, by 1990 there were 380 groups of people with developmental disabilities in the United States and British Columbia. Groups such as these and their advocates have been pressuring the Justice Department to use the 1980 Civil Rights of Institutionalized Persons Act more effectively to protect the rights of people with cognitive disabilities in institutions.[19]

The movement has been encouraged by the growing number of those with developmental disabilities living in group homes, an alternative to institutional care. During the period from 1977 to 1992, the number of people in group homes increased dramatically from 14 to 52 percent.[20] The national quarterly magazine *Community Advocacy Press: People with Developmental Disabilities Speak Out for What They Believe* helps unify self-advocacy groups and supports members in their efforts to live independently in the community. For example, the Fall 1997 issue was devoted to the skills necessary for people with developmental disabilities to secure and maintain jobs, as well as the self-esteem that emanates from work.

Harvey Pacht—who serves as both director of public education and group support for the Self-Advocacy Association of New York State and as New York City regional grass-roots organizer—describes how he and his wife have worked to achieve independence:

> My wife, Ethel, was born brain-damaged because her birth mother, who died during the delivery, was not getting enough oxygen. Several years after we were married, we adopted a one-month-old Down syndrome baby girl, Samantha Jean. Now that she's in a special education class in public school, an aide comes in the morning to prepare her for school and get her on the bus and in the afternoon to take her off the bus and care for her until we get home. We both work; I do my advocacy work, and my wife works in a sheltered workshop. So we're able to support ourselves in our own condominium.[21]

Pacht points out that the Self-Advocacy Association of New York State was founded and named by Bernard Carabello, a former "inmate," who in 1972 left Willowbrook, the institution closed in 1987 as a result of the Geraldo Rivera exposé.[22] Pacht continues:

> My job is to encourage the formation of self-advocacy groups all over New York State so that consumers of services for people with developmental disabilities, themselves, determine what programs and services they

really need. They are often supported by family and friends, and when necessary, even a fiscal intermediary. I also work to get these consumers to be on boards of directors of agencies that serve people with developmental disabilities so that they have some say in the policies and procedures that affect them. People with developmental disabilities may learn in different ways than others, or they may be slower than others, but they have capabilities, and many can work.

Supporting Pacht's assertion, the employment of people with developmental disabilities (who are consumers of services of state agencies assisting this population) increased over 300 percent from 1988 to 1996.[23]

Employment of People with Psychiatric Disabilities

On April 29, 1997, EEOC released the *EEOC Enforcement Guidance: The Americans with Disabilities Act and Psychiatric Disabilities,* explaining the ADA as it pertains to employees with psychiatric disabilities.[24] EEOC chairman Gilbert F. Casellas describes the document: "It provides practical instruction to employers and persons with psychiatric disabilities on their respective rights and responsibilities."[25] The *EEOC Enforcement Guidance* indicates that employers may not discriminate against qualified workers with psychiatric disabilities, even those who are taking medication to control their impairments.[26] Although mandated to make reasonable accommodations for employees with psychiatric disabilities, employers are restricted from asking job applicants if they have a history of psychiatric disabilities. Yet for workers with psychiatric disabilities, as for employees with physical impairments, employers are not required to diminish workplace performance standards in order to comply with the ADA. According to the

EEOC Enforcement Guidance, however, "rules of conduct that are not 'job-related and consistent with business necessity'" may not be enforced.

The *EEOC Enforcement Guidance* seeks to dispel "myths, fears and stereotypes" about psychiatric disabilities such as "anxiety disorders, depression, bipolar disorder (manic depression), [and] schizophrenia."[27] Plaintiffs' lawyers observe that "many people with emotional problems are winning important concessions from their employers in out-of-court settlements, including unpaid leaves, modified hours, job transfers, and in some cases, five- and six-figure cash payments. But when negotiations fail, litigation is risky."[28] Although the *EEOC Enforcement Guidance* indicates that people are disabled even if their symptoms disappear when they take medication, trial courts have determined that people did not have a psychiatric disability if medication relieved their symptoms. Caught in a Catch-22 situation, employees with psychiatric disabilities have limited recourse under the employment discrimination laws because if their impairment is treated successfully, they are considered nondisabled under the ADA; yet if their symptoms persist, they may be considered unable to perform the essential function of the job.

While companies have won 92 percent of all final court decisions from 1992 through 1997 under the ADA, companies have won even more often for psychiatric disability cases.[29] The *Mental and Physical Disability Law Reporter* found that by June 1998, although "it has been employers who have complained most of unfair treatment under the ADA, the facts strongly suggest the opposite: employees are treated unfairly under the Act."[30] The EEOC recommends new legislation addressing the Catch-22 problem in order to "eliminate some of the more procedural and substantial roadblocks [to employees winning ADA cases], such as show-ing that the claimant has a 'substantially limiting impairment.'"

According to the *EEOC Enforcement Guidance,* "Between July 26, 1992, and September 30, 1996, approximately 12.7 percent of ADA charges filed with the EEOC were based on emotional or psychiatric impairment."[31] Of all 72,687 complaints filed with the EEOC under the ADA in these four years, 9,216 have alleged discrimination resulting from a psychiatric disability, the largest source of complaints after back problems.[32] By 1997 the number of psychiatric disability claims increased to 15.3 percent, the largest single category of all disability claims, outnumbering those pertaining to HIV, cancer, substance abuse, vision, hearing, and diabetes-related disabilities combined.[33] "The National Institute of Mental Health says one in ten Americans experiences some disability from a diagnosable mental illness in the course of a year."

Two U.S. senators who acknowledge that they have family members who have had psychiatric disabilities, Pete Domenici (R-N.M.) and Paul Wellstone (D-Minn.), successfully sponsored legislation designed to establish parity between psychiatric and physical disabilities.[34] Effective January 1, 1998, this law requires "that insurers set the lifetime and annual reimbursement caps as high for psychiatric disability as for physical illness." Alphonso V. Guida, Jr., vice president of the National Mental Health Association and an advocate for people with psychiatric disorders, asserts, however, that "many insurers and employers are taking steps to bypass the federal law, changing the structure of their benefits to impose discriminatory inpatient and outpatient visit limits in place of previous spending caps."[35] Ronald E. Bachman, actuary at the accounting firm PricewaterhouseCoopers, observes that "the net impact [of day and visit limits] in these cases is to have less mental health coverage."

Contrary to comments of Dr. Sally L. Satel, psychiatrist and lecturer at Yale's School of Medicine, the *EEOC Enforcement Guidance* is not "sending dysfunctional people the message that the world—or in this case the workplace—revolves around them."[36] In fact, Satel's misrepresentation of the *EEOC Enforcement Guidance* reveals that she does not recognize the essence of Title I, the employment section of the ADA that protects only a qualified individual with a disability who is capable of performing the essential function of the job. Instead, Satel treats the *EEOC Enforcement Guidance* as if it interfered with the appropriate demands of the workplace that provide limits for potentially unruly workers with psychiatric disabilities.

Psychiatric disabilities are not confined to the prototype of the undisciplined employee she refers to in her article. Moreover, the purpose of the law is not rehabilitation of people with psychiatric disabilities. Rather, the law is intended to protect these people from discrimination based solely on the stigma associated with their disabilities.[37] Ostensibly supporting workers with psychiatric disabilities, Satel fears that "we can expect waves of backlash discrimination as employers become skittish about hiring a class of people they'll never be able to fire. Co-workers' resentment will build as the stereotypical behaviors of the mentally ill go unchecked." Satel's concern for the consequences of the *EEOC Enforcement Guidance* for people with psychiatric disabilities could have been expressed for the extension of civil rights to any demographic group—racial minorities, women, as well as people with physical disabilities.

Although psychiatrists Satel and Dr. Peter D. Kramer agree that work is vital for the well-being of people with psychiatric disabilities, they disagree, however, about the future medical and social effects of the *EEOC Enforcement Guidance*. Kramer notes that "the stigma attached to psychiatric disabilities" precludes those with such disabilities from using the *EEOC Enforcement Guidance* as an excuse for absenteeism: "I don't see people lining up to say, 'I have a mental illness. I need a day off from work.'"[38] Adhering to the *EEOC Enforcement Guidance* serves not only employees with psychiatric disabilities, Kramer points out, but also employers: "Some of my sicker patients are workers of extraordinary dedication, who, for reasons related to their illness—compulsiveness and obsessional guilt—work scrupulously at tasks others avoid; smart employers do accommodate their needs."[39] Commenting on the value of diverse perspectives in the gene pool, Kramer indicates that obsessive people are thorough, depressed people make good prognosticators, and artists have a tendency to mania. Referring to Abraham Lincoln, who was "recurrently depressed," Kramer observes that "those who suffer mental illness included the most productive members of society."

People with invisible disabilities, including psychiatric impairments, do not have to inform employers of their conditions unless they are seeking reasonable accommodations.[40] A person requesting an accommodation, however, may be asked to submit documentation—which can be a letter from a physician, psychologist, or other specialist—verifying the disability and outlining the necessary accommodations. The employer is permitted to choose the specific accommodation so long as it is effective for accessing the job. The *EEOC Enforcement Guidance* mandates that "Employers must keep all information [even when offered voluntarily] concerning the medical condition or history of applicants or employees, including information about psychiatric disability, confidential under the ADA. . . . Employers must collect and maintain such information on separate forms and in separate medical files, apart from the usual personnel files."[41]

Claudia Center, attorney for the San Francisco Employment Law Center, asserts that "the same job-based analysis that governs the application of the [ADA] statute to physical disabilities must apply to psychiatric disabilities. The appropriate test [for employability] is whether the conduct caused by a psychiatric disability renders that person unqualified to perform the essential job functions of a particular position."[42] Unlike the forms of "reasonable accommodations" for people with physical disabilities, however, Center indicates that people with psychiatric disabilities may need different accommodations such as "tailored shifts and schedules, leaves of absence, and adjustments to job duties and the working environment," as well as employer education regarding these requirements.

The Criminalization of People with Psychiatric Disabilities

As a result of the mass closing of public hospitals for people with psychiatric disabilities beginning in the 1960s—in part fostered by the development of new antipsychotic drugs—jails and prisons became the nation's new hospitals for people with psychiatric disabilities. Laurie M. Flynn, executive director of the National Alliance for the Mentally Ill—an advocacy group of relatives and friends of people with psychiatric disabilities—emphasizes, "Part of mental illness in America now is that you are going to get arrested. What experts call the criminalization of the mentally ill has grown as an issue as the nation's inmate population has exploded and as corrections officials and families of the emotionally disturbed have become alarmed by the problems posed by having the mentally ill behind bars."[43]

Although in Fall 1997 the U.S. Justice Department described this incarceration of people with psychiatric disabilities as unconstitutional, this trend has been increasing: "On any day, almost two hundred thousand people behind bars—more than one in ten of the total—are known to suffer from schizophrenia, manic depression, or major depression, the three most severe mental illnesses. The rate is four times that in the general population. And there is evidence, particularly with juveniles, that the numbers in jail are growing." Sheldon Greenberg, director of Johns Hopkins University's Police Executive Leadership Program in Baltimore, says that it is unconscionable that police get hours of executive training for situations they seldom encounter involving hostages, terrorists, and riots, and only a few hours of technical training on handling people they come across often—people with psychiatric disabilities.[44]

Advocates for people with psychiatric disabilities compare the criminalization of this population since the 1960s to the dehumanizing treatment of people with this disability in the nineteenth century. As noted in the *New York Times,* "Mental hospitals, or asylums, grew out of a crusade in the 1840s by Dorothea Dix, the Boston reformer, who warned that 'insane persons' were being confined in 'cages, closets, cellars, stalls, pens: chained, naked, beaten with rods, and lashed into obedience.'"[45] One of the main reasons that the discharge of people with psychiatric disabilities from hospitals has resulted in such disaster is that the plan was not carried out as designed. Dr. Richard Lamb, one of the originators of the 1960s plan, remembers that local governments were expected to provide community-based settings where discharged patients could continue their treatment, including medication and therapy. "But," Lamb notes, "largely for economic reasons, this was never done." Ironically, community clinics and group homes with live-in counselors, rather than hospitals or prisons, are the most effective and economical way of providing services for people with psychiatric disabilities.[46]

When two Capitol police officers were fatally shot in Washington, D.C., on July 24, 1998, by an individual who had been diagnosed as paranoid schizophrenic, *New York Times* op-ed page columnist Frank Rich stated that "no one said the obvious: It is the gaping cracks in American mental-health care ... that most clearly delivered Russell Weston Jr. [the gunman] to his rendezvous with history."[47] Rich added, "A comprehensive system of mental-health services, including support for parents with sick adult children who refuse treatment, doesn't exist. If it had, the Westons might have had more success in rescuing their son—as might the equally loving family of Michael Lauder, the Yale Law School prodigy charged [June 1998] with murdering his fiancée." While the nation spent one-third less for those with serious psychiatric disabilities in 1998 than it did in the 1950s, and well over three times as many people with these disabilities are in jails and prisons than in psychiatric facilities,[48] "we have the science to treat mental illness at a success rate comparable to physical illness."[49]

Although the public usually hears about schizophrenia, which affects about 2.7 million Americans, "in the context of lurid headlines," like those that followed Andrew Goldstein's arrest and later conviction for pushing Kendra Webdale off a subway platform to her death,[50] most people with psychiatric disabilities are not violent. Even for Goldstein, whose actions seemed to support the arguments for reinstitutionalization and involuntary treatment of people with serious psychiatric disabilities, the real problem was that the treatment he repeatedly begged for was in such short supply that he was unable to get the help he des-

perately sought.[51] Moreover, many of the bizarre symptoms of the Capitol gunman, Russell Weston Jr., "also characterize the paranoid schizophrenia of John Nash, the brilliant, nonviolent Princeton mathematician,"[52] the subject of Sylvia Naser's book, *A Beautiful Mind*, about the winner of the 1994 Nobel Prize in Economics.

Different Approaches to Psychiatric Disabilities

The consumer mental health movement originated as early as 1908 with the establishment of the Connecticut Society for Mental Hygiene (renamed in 1909 the National Committee for Mental Hygiene) by Clifford W. Beers, author of *Mind That Found Itself: An Autobiography* (1908), a memoir chronicling his harrowing personal experiences in a succession of mental institutions.[53] The federal Census Bureau requested in 1923 that Beers and his associates gather data concerning various state mental institutions. Besides developing "model commitment laws" that were adopted by several states in the 1920s, the National Committee for Mental Hygiene administered studies that altered the treatment of people with psychiatric disabilities.

In 1950, the National Association of Mental Health (by 1979 known as the National Mental Health Association) was established, combining three organizations: the National Committee for Mental Hygiene, the National Mental Health Foundation, and the Psychiatric Foundation (a fund-raising organization). The National Mental Health Foundation was formed in the early 1940s by conscientious objectors to World War II—working in psychiatric hospitals in place of military service—who were appalled by the conditions in these hospitals. The National Mental Health Association (NMHA) was instrumental in the passage of the 1980 Mental Health Systems Act—encouraging the development of America's Community Mental Health Centers—as well as the 1990 Americans with Disabilities Act and the 1996 Mental Health Parity Act. The NMHA argues that improved access to and quality of mental health services will markedly decrease the cost to society of medical care, welfare, homelessness, prison, and reduced human potential in school and the workplace.[54]

In the early 1970s, about the same time as the rights movement of people with physical disabilities was emerging, the rights movement of people with psychiatric disabilities expanded as consumers organized in such cities as New York, Boston, and Vancouver.[55] The mental health system was slow to respond to the lack of recourse for many consumers forced into compliance without due process of law—one result of the closing of mental hospitals and the development and use of psychotropic medications.[56] Too often isolated from the wider society and ignored even by the disability rights movement, former psychiatric patients organized around issues of patients rights,[57] stressing consumers using their experience with the health care system to help other consumers with issues of daily life and empowerment through mutual support and self-help.[58] While the New York City group became known in the 1970s as the Mental Patients Liberation Project, similar organizations in other cities, independent of each other, were also demanding that their members have a voice in their own psychiatric treatment as they struggled against what they considered "a helping system that did things against their will, things like forced institutionalization, drugging, and electric shock."

Because of the negative stereotypes, the stigmatizing and discrimination, former psychiatric patients frequently hide their impairments, thus depriving themselves of peer support and reasonable accommodations. Judi Chamberlin, a former psychiatric patient who refers to people like herself as "psychiatric survivors," insists, "The stereotypes, of course, have little to do with the facts. Most people with psychiatric disabilities are living successfully in the community, raising families, working, going to school and, in general, leading essentially 'normal' lives."[59] A study published in 1998 in the *Archives of General Psychiatry* finds that most patients discharged from psychiatric hospitals pose no greater threat of violence to the community than similar people without psychiatric disabilities.[60] The study, which includes those with psychiatric disabilities such as depression, schizophrenia, and bipolar illness, reveals that the significant factor in predicting whether or not individuals are at risk for committing violence to others is if these individuals are alcoholics or drug abusers, not if they have psychiatric disabilities.

Although some "psychiatric survivors" are unaware of the ADA or the law's application to them, others were heartened by the firm stand of disability activists who refused to weaken the legislation by excluding people with psychiatric disabilities. By the late 1990s, however, "psychiatric survivors" were expressing concern about the meaning of "parity," with respect to insurance, between people with psychiatric disabilities and people with physical disabilities. As Chamberlin asserts, "Without parity in terms of rights, parity in terms of [insurance] payment can result in people being coerced into treatment that they find totally unacceptable. If people with psychiatric disabilities get their rights, everything else they are struggling for will follow."

Yet Richard Greer, president of the Virginia Alliance for the Mentally Ill and an advocate who describes his son as "mentally ill," not only uses language different from Chamberlin's, but also approaches this disability from a perspective different from those who refer to themselves as "psychiatric survivors." The fledgling National Alliance for the Mentally Ill opened its first office in the District of Columbia in 1979.[61] In the 1990s the National Alliance nurtured and supported chapters in each state in the country. Whereas "psychiatric survivors" believe that the National Alliance for the Mentally Ill overemphasizes the biological basis for psychiatric disabilities, Greer notes that his organization takes pride in having encouraged research on the brain that is useful in dealing with "mental illness."[62] On the other hand, the NMHA deals with psychiatric disabilities using a bio-psycho-social approach, thus fostering a combination of "consumer-focused" strategies appropriate to the particular needs of the individual.[63]

While the National Alliance for the Mentally Ill generally supports "involuntary outpatient commitment" legislation enacted by a majority of states, both the NMHA and "psychiatric survivors" fervently oppose these laws.[64] Perhaps the major reason for the differences in the underlying assumptions of these three camps stems from the membership: the National Alliance for the Mentally Ill is primarily made up of relatives, often parents, and friends of people with "mental illness"; "psychiatric survivors" are people who themselves have experienced, or episodically experience, a psychiatric disability; and the NMHA is an umbrella organization linking advocates (including parents of young children with psychiatric disabilities), consumers, and providers.

Joseph Rogers, a leader in mental health for over fifteen years, notes that self-help—consumer-run programs in the community in which people are engaged in their own treatment—in combination with life supports, such as housing and employment, have proven most effective for people with psychiatric disabilities.[65] One consumer-

run program, the Mental Health Voter Empowerment Project, was founded in 1994 by Ken Steele, who, after controlling his schizophrenia with medication, devised his own treatment—advocacy.[66] By 1999, Steele's Project with seventy volunteers had registered thirty-five thousand "mental health consumers" in the New York Metropolitan area. A major aim of the project—to turn the forty-four million people who have experienced "some form of mental illness" into a significant voting bloc—is supported by the NMHA, which by 1999 sought to replicate Steele's effort nationwide.[67]

Nonetheless, there are significant issues on which the three camps agree. The NMHA, "psychiatric survivors," and the National Alliance for the Mentally Ill all strive to remove the stigma—what Chamberlin prefers to call discrimination—associated with psychiatric disabilities. All are working toward deinstitutionalization with resources redirected so that services can be provided in local communities. As Greer indicates, some states, such as New Hampshire, are better than others in moving toward this model. All fear that threats to the 1988 Fair Housing Amendments Act jeopardize group homes, a way that the three groups strongly support for some people with psychiatric disabilities to live in the community.[68] Yet these three advocacy groups are concerned that although many people with developmental disabilities have been successfully moved out of institutional settings into group homes of fifteen or fewer residents (or into their own homes), the result of deinstitutionalizing people with psychiatric disabilities remains controversial. Seeking to eliminate the disincentives to employment, members of all three camps approve of Social Security laws that have been rewritten so that people with disabilities, including those with psychiatric disabilities, are able to maintain benefits while earning reasonable incomes. Finally, the NMHA, "psychiatric survivors," and the National Alliance for the Mentally Ill vigorously assert that managed care companies generally deal ineffectively with people with psychiatric disabilities.

Mangled Care

With more than 140 million Americans covered by some form of managed care in the event of psychiatric disability, Dr. Harold Eist, president of the American Psychiatric Association, recalls his troubling conversation with an insurance company executive:

> I said, "Why are you [the executive] doing this [taking advantage of] the mentally ill?" He said to me, "Because they're vulnerable." It's known that if you put impediments in the way of the mentally ill, it will be more difficult for them to fight through them. . . . I hear hundreds and hundreds of heartbreaking cases on a regular basis. And every time I hear of one of these cases, I vow that I will fight this scourge of managed care harder and harder because it's not care; it's managed cost, and as somebody said, "mangled care". . . . They delay access to care. They don't provide sufficient care. They throw people out of the hospital too soon, people who are still very, very ill. So how can they possibly get people better quicker [as they claim]? What they try to do is put a Band-Aid on and get rid of people quicker.[69]

Although Keith Dixon, CEO of the Vista Behavioral Health Plans, argues that private managed care companies are bringing needed capital and expertise to the "shambles" of a nonmanaged, "publicly tax-supported mental health system," he concedes that "there's something inherently disturbing about Wall Street investors investing in companies whose responsibility is for one of the most vulnerable sectors of our population." James Wrich, a consultant who evaluates "mental health plans" for businesses, points out that from 1992 to 1997 managed care companies have made enormous profits from "mental health care," much more than from physical health care. Moreover, Wrich reveals that people in severe psychiatric distress, such as acute depression, not only have not gotten the immediate treatment they require, but even the delayed treatment they finally do receive is questionable: "Anywhere from 20 percent of the time to 30 percent of the time it either was not the right level of care, or if it was the right level of care, the lengths of treatment were not sufficient to take care of the problem."

A Two-Tier Health Care System

Managed care organizations often operate in a manner that is inconsistent with the needs of people with disabilities, a population with lower income and greater care needs than the average person. Tending to use health services more frequently and requiring greater use of specialty and long-term care, people with disabilities generally do not fit within most "capitation payment" structures,[70] which are designed for average patients. The *Journal of the American Medical Association* reports that older people and chronically ill poor people "were more than twice as likely to decline in health in an HMO as in a fee-for-service plan,"[71] such as Medicare.

Starting in Fall 1998, people with disabilities and older people who receive health care through Medicare were asked to choose from a variety of new options, including traditional Medicare, HMOs, Medical Savings Accounts (MSAs), and other types of health plans.[72] A study by older people and their supporters noted that "beneficiaries with chronic illnesses, requiring many expensive health care services, would be hurt by the

MSA program because the money in the MSA would not cover their medical costs under the deductible."[73] Because the variety of other types of health plans—lumped under the rubric Medicare Plus Choice—are private, they include many financial incentives to reduce care, provisions that do not serve the needs of people with disabilities.[74]

Although the revised system was designed to reduce federal spending on Medicare and to save consumers money, the program began precariously as insurance companies decided whether or not to participate, and the government attempted to accomplish a formidable task—to educate Medicare's thirty-nine million beneficiaries about the complicated choices available.[75] Rather than reducing federal spending, the proliferating varieties of Medicare plans increased federal spending and presented recipients with confusing choices to comprehend; moreover, in 1998 over four hundred thousand Medicare beneficiaries were dropped by HMOs. At a 1998 meeting of the National Bipartisan Commission on the Future of Medicare, the concern of older people about threats to the traditional Medicare system was demonstrated by the protest of dozens of members of the Gray Panthers.[76] Demanding that the commission hold public hearings, they held up signs saying, "No more Medicare cuts!"

Disability activists have raised serious questions about the real possibility of formally establishing a two-tier health care system in the country based on the economic level of the recipients of services. For example, the 1997 Kyl Amendment permits doctors to charge more than the Medicare rate, whatever the market will bear. The only consequence for these physicians would be their inability to treat Medicare patients for two years. Before the Kyl Amendment, if physicians did not accept Medicare fees, they were not allowed to treat Medicare patients—a population that doctors were

not willing to risk losing, as indicated by the fact that roughly 96 percent of physicians participated in the Medicare program. Since those paying the higher fees may receive better services than Medicare patients, a two-tier system may be established. "In a two-tier system," Lani Sanjek, associate executive director of New York StateWide Senior Action Council, asks, "Would those with special needs, people with disabilities, many of whom have very limited resources, receive the benefits of improved technology and care obtainable by the general public?"

Often, people with disabilities have requirements—such as durable medical equipment, assistive technology, and personal assistance—not covered by many health insurance plans, certainly not the managed care models that were driving medical practice in the United States in the 1990s. Since this health care system was set up to deal with acute, rather than chronic, health problems, the long-term services and supports essential to people with disabilities are seldom provided.[77] For example, other states learned from the hastily executed 1993 experiment when Tennessee placed all its Medicaid recipients, all at once—including those with special needs—into managed care.[78] Although the plan resulted in a major expansion of coverage to people previously uninsured, care was disruptive for those who required the coordination of several doctors and services—people with disabilities and older people.

Since HMOs tend to avoid accepting people with disabilities because they fear they may be frequent users of expensive medical services, examples of people who sought payment for significant medical treatments most often involve those who were in apparently good health, but became seriously ill or disabled *after* joining an HMO. As Sanjek points out, "If we look at 1995 to 1996 Medicare data, we see that 10 percent of the recipients used 70 percent of the medical cost. Of course, HMOs have been selecting their members from the 90 percent that use only 30 percent of the cost." Sanjek offers an example of the recruitment strategies often used by HMOs to "cherry pick" those they deem to be the least costly Medicare clients, people without visible disabilities:

> An HMO invites prospective clients to a hotel breakfast. After the HMO representative makes a pitch to encourage the Medicare recipients to join the HMO, those who wish to become members are invited to walk up the steps to the mezzanine to sign up. In this way the HMO has ruled out people who have difficulty leaving their homes, traveling, or climbing steps. According to the HMO's assumptions, they've eliminated a large percentage of potentially expensive clients.

HMOs advise people to join a plan that suits their present medical requirements; yet destined to change with age, medical necessities are really unpredictable at any age. Therefore, a plan that initially may seem appropriate may be totally inadequate after the consumer experiences a catastrophic illness or an accident. Everyone needs lifetime benefits that cover a broad spectrum of unforeseen medical circumstances. Dr. Linda Peeno, an HMO medical director from 1987 to 1991, describes the industry's rationale for tending to deny doctors' requests for assistive devices such as a computerized voice machine for a young woman who was struggling to deal with a rare, catastrophic brain stem stroke that prevented her from speaking.[79] According to HMO logic, "She purchased a Volkswagen plan and wants Cadillac care—she will have to live with [what the HMO labeled] her choices."

Moreover, given the myriad disabilities and the potential cutting-edge treatments, a particular managed care organization is unlikely to include within its network of providers all the needed services. The "gatekeeper," usually a general practitioner or internist who determines access to specialty care, may not have the expertise to deal with a specific disability nor to make judgments regarding appropriate specialists. Dr. Stuart Jamieson of the University of California San Diego Medical Center observes that even when a patient is assigned to a specialist, an HMO, in its effort to be cost-effective, "doesn't recognize that one doctor has a special skill over another doctor."[80]

People with Special Needs in Managed Care

Susan Scheer of the New York City Public Advocate's office describes how working people with disabilities—who were in managed care because of the health plan at their places of employment—experienced difficulty when they tried to obtain the durable medical equipment they required.[81]

> Three cases involved wheelchairs, two manual and one power. All of them were in the Oxford HMO, and in each case the individual was told that the plan didn't cover wheelchairs. When they complained and appealed, each was given some money to cover the cost of the wheelchair. But the one who complained the loudest, the longest, and the best got ten times as much as the person who did the least complaining. This is arbitrary and capricious.

Scheer refers to other durable equipment that people with disabilities had to fight for, such as a commode for a quadriplegic and a voice synthesizer for a person who had a stroke. Scheer's point is that the services people receive are dependent on the degree to which they were capable of contending with the HMO. To illustrate, Scheer describes the case of an Oxford client who had a stroke:

> While the man was rehabilitating in a Staten Island facility, Oxford refused to

continue to pay although there was no plan in place for him to go home. After the family put up a fuss, Oxford allowed him a little more rehab time. At the discharge meeting, Oxford promised speech therapy, occupational therapy, and home care. But they didn't give anywhere near the number of hours they promised. They claimed it was the family's responsibility to give home care. In this case, as in many others, that was almost impossible. The man was about six feet two inches, 240 pounds, and hemiplegic. His wife was about five feet tall, and she had multiple sclerosis. His daughter-in-law, who was about the same size as his wife, had two small children.

His son, a cop who was running his father's business at night, was very good at fighting Oxford and got the Public Advocate [office] involved. But since the man who had the stroke didn't have the home care he needed, he fell when he tried to get to the bathroom himself. So he landed back in the hospital in rehab, and his story appeared in the New York *Daily News*. Then Oxford paid the maximum amount for his care. After the publicity, I received many similar complaints at my office.

Alexander Wood, a paraplegic wheelchair user with Big Apple Greeters—a nonprofit company geared toward boosting tourism in New York City—also was refused a wheelchair by Oxford.[82] "Up to now, I've been pretty successful with Oxford," Wood points out, "but I've had a strategy. I tell the truth. When they turned down my request for a pillow to prevent pressure sores, I told them, 'If I get pressure sores, I may need an operation and end up in the hospital. That would cost a lot more than a pillow.' Within ten minutes I got a phone call from Oxford approving my pillow."

Wood's struggle with Oxford to get an appropriate wheelchair was described on the nightly local NBC-TV news program for the greater New York City area. With his lightweight, easy-to-maneuver wheelchair, Wood explains, "I can get anywhere I need to; I can compete with anyone I want; I

rarely notice my disability in New York City, believe it or not. I'm actually faster on these wheels. What I always like to say is 'rubber on wheels is faster than rubber on heels.'" Determined to keep on working after his 1992 spinal cord injury, Wood travels around the city welcoming tourists with disabilities, among his other responsibilities with Big Apple Greeters.

Because these activities have taken such a toll on his wheelchairs, Wood has requested a thirty-two hundred dollar titanium wheelchair, stronger and more expensive than the two thousand dollar aluminum wheelchair for which Oxford has provided most of the cost in the past. Having no wheelchair policy until 1995, Oxford paid for wheelchairs on a case-by-case basis. With its new wheelchair policy, Oxford claims that "in the spirit of human care," the HMO "will cover wheelchairs with a contribution of five hundred dollars." Wood points out, however, that five hundred dollars would not allow him to purchase the kind of chair he requires: "I wouldn't be able to take the wheels off and put the chair in back of my car. I wouldn't be able to propel myself. I wouldn't be able to be independent the way I am now." According to the HMO Council of New York, insurance coverage of wheelchairs is not mandatory in New York, New Jersey, or Connecticut.

An Arbitrary Patchwork

Disability groups, older people, and doctors have begun to influence legislators and the general public regarding HMOs. This shift in public opinion may have been reflected in the $1.1 million awarded to Joyce Ramey—in a binding arbitration with her Medicare HMO—because as a dialysis patient, she was denied access to an HMO-approved kidney specialist for two years.[83] In 1997, twenty-one states passed comprehensive consumer rights bills dealing with HMO issues, such as mandates especially beneficial to people with disabilities. These mandates included nondiscrimination based on genetic information, disability, or preexisting condition; "point of service" (which means permission to go outside the HMO if the organization cannot provide a needed service); and acceptance of a specialist as the primary care physician when appropriate.[84] Responding to the outrage of constituents (people with disabilities—denied essential treatment by HMOs—and their families), the House of Representatives overwhelmingly voted by late 1999 to expand the rights of patients in managed care programs, including the right to sue their insurance companies for punitive damages.[85] Yet as of July 2000, Congress had not enacted a patients' bill of rights.

The health care system in the United States, still an arbitrary patchwork in flux in the 1990s, has had devastating effects on too many people with severe illnesses. As former New York Lieutenant Governor Betsy McCaughey Ross observes:

> For many people with serious illnesses, including some forms of cancer, experimental treatments like bone marrow transplants are often the only hope. But insurance companies often deny coverage of these expensive treatments. They are not required to cover experimental therapies, even when no conventional remedy exists. . . . Thousands of patients in nationally known health plans have opened letters [in which they are refused vital medical care], suddenly finding out how uninsured they actually are.[86]

Moreover, Dr. Jonathan Finley of New York City's Memorial Sloan-Kettering Cancer Center indicates that potentially lifesaving plans of treatment (such as "high dose chemotherapy with stem cell rescue"), supported by peer-review data, are inaccurately labeled "experimental" by insurance companies and routinely denied.[87]

If people with life-threatening illnesses—who were turned down for treatment by their health plan—lived in California rather than, say, New York in 1996, their doctors could have appealed to "a panel of independent physicians with no financial stake in the decision."[88] Had Robert Fasano been a resident of Oregon rather than New York while an early version of the Oregon Medicaid plan rationing health care—ultimately struck down as an ADA violation—was in effect, the favorable outcome of his liver transplant might have been tragically altered.[89] Disabled because of a liver ailment, Fasano became a recipient of Medicare, a federal health insurance system that *does not* cover drugs. Since Medicare would not pay for the expensive medication that he would require following his upcoming liver transplant, Fasano had to "spend down"[90] and then wait for last minute acceptance by Medicaid, which *does* cover medication. Experiencing one medical crisis after another, including end-stage liver disease in which toxins distort brain functioning, Fasano fortunately received a liver transplant at New York City's Mount Sinai Hospital in 1990, in time to save his life.

Although in the 1990s, for many people like Fasano or those with AIDS on protease inhibitors, pharmaceuticals are essential to survival, the 1965 decision to exclude drugs from Medicare benefits seemed appropriate to prevent costly red tape and fraud when it was made in the pre-computer age.[91] Frequently costing no more than one or two dollars, medications were not only inexpensive at that time, but they were also not nearly as significant a factor in health care as they would later become with advances in technology. Because Medicare has not caught up with current medical realities, many people with disabilities requiring expensive pharmaceuticals are forced to become Medicaid recipients or to join managed care plans that—except for covering drugs—do not adequately serve their needs.

Described in an April 1998 brief filed by Legal Aid on behalf of the Connecticut Union of Disability Action Groups as an "abrupt, unprecedented break with over twenty years of federal court jurisprudence in the Medicaid arena," *Desario v. Thomas*[92] galvanized the disability community. A temporary setback for disability advocates, this February 1998 decision by the U.S. Court of Appeals of the Second Circuit upheld a federal law that permitted New York, Connecticut, and Vermont to deny some Medicaid funds to poor people with severe disabilities.[93] As Justice For All notes, "In reversing the district court's injunction, the Court of Appeals authorized states to ration health care by providing only the type of treatment needed by 'most' Medicaid recipients."[94] The threat to access of Medicaid services was so great that a broad coalition of eighty-one state and national disability, disease, provider, religious, and labor organizations filed an amicus curiae brief in support of the plaintiff's position.

After disability advocates persuaded the Clinton administration to review this ruling, federal policy was changed. The federal Health Care Financing Administration noted in a September 1998 letter to Medicaid directors that a state "'may not impose arbitrary limits' like those apparently endorsed by the Appeals Court, on necessary equipment." Consequently, in January 1999 the U.S. Supreme Court in *Slekis v. Thomas* vacated the ruling, returning the case to the Court of Appeals for the Second Circuit for further consideration in light of this new federal directive concerning the scope of Medicaid coverage. *Slekis* demonstrates what disability activists vigorously assert: the necessity for vigilance in a time of volatility in health care policy.

Falling through the Cracks: Children with Special Health Needs

Melinda Dutton, senior health policy specialist for the New York State Children's Defense Fund, notes that by early 1999, nationwide, "progress has been made on behalf of children with disabilities generally."[95] Peggy McManus, codirector of the Maternal and Child Care Health Policy Research Center, describes the effect of the 1996 welfare overhaul on children with disabilities: "The infrastructure that has been created as a safety net for kids with special needs is crumbling."[96] In the same year, the *New York Times* reported that "the number of children on the disability rolls...tripled [since 1989], and costs...quadrupled, to more than five billion dollars a year."[97] This number grew not because of welfare fraud, as had been incorrectly reported,[98] but rather as a result of the swelling childhood poverty rate, a loosening of eligibility rules that provided benefits to children with "mental impairments," as well as court decisions—especially the 1990 Supreme Court's *Zebley* ruling, that resulted in increased accuracy in government assessment of children with disabilities.[99] Dutton continues, "With the changes included in the Balanced Budget Act of 1997, the safety net is better than ever, but many children with special health needs are still falling through the cracks."

Dutton is referring to the block grants to the states included in this act—resulting in the expansion of Medicaid as well as the new federal Child Health Insurance Program (CHIP)—that benefit children with disabilities. With states receiving increased Medicaid funding, "more children who meet certain qualifications related to their medical condition or disability are able to participate in Medicaid without regard to their parents' financial resources," Dutton states. While an existing Medicaid waiver program[100] provides health insurance for many children with severe disabilities or illnesses, the program has significant limitations: only children with specific diagnoses are eligible; unlike in other Medicaid programs, the dollar amount of services is capped per year; and historically, there have been waiting lists for eligible children.

CHIP covers children whose parents earn too much for Medicaid, but too little to afford private health insurance. Although many children with disabilities are included in CHIP, the provisions of the new program are not nearly as comprehensive as those of the thirty-year-old Medicaid program.[101] For example, the Early Periodic Screening, Diagnosis and Testing (EPSDT) provision in Medicaid requires that if treatment, service, or equipment—such as an organ transplant, a wheelchair, or an air conditioner (for an asthmatic child)—is medically necessary for a child's health, welfare, growth, and well-being, it must be granted. Efforts by advocates of children with special health needs to get provisions in CHIP equivalent to Medicaid's EPSDT failed, for there was no political will—even among the most liberal legislators—to have that broad Medicaid package included in the new program. With caps similar to those in private insurance and with each state defining its own benefit package, too often CHIP does not adequately serve children with the most serious disabilities and illnesses.

Dutton points out that "despite the improvements, we've got a long way to go to get all children with special health needs access to all the health services they require." Many uninsured children, a significant number with disabilities, who are eligible for Medicaid or CHIP are not enrolled "because their parents don't know what their children are entitled to."[102] While children with special health needs who are covered through their parents' private health insurance may be eligible for routine medical care, Dutton asserts that "they may not be able to get the machine they need to breathe, or the home care they require, or the wheelchair inserts that they grow out of every year. If we just look at children with special health needs who are uninsured, we would grossly underestimate the challenge. These private insurance products were not written with children with disabilities in mind." Dutton observes that in order to craft a big-picture solution that would eliminate the cracks in the system, families of and advocates for children across various disabilities, illnesses, and programs must be provided with the resources they require to organize. Such coalition building, she adds, would facilitate communication among—and provide a sense of empowerment to—these families and advocates, as well as create a mobilizing political force that would increase public awareness of these issues.

Long-Term Care in the Community

The National Council on Disability, an organization that played a pivotal role in the enactment of the ADA, indicates that long-term home health care (including "effective rehabilitation, prevention of secondary disabilities and complications, and independent living"), which is vital to many people with disabilities, is excluded from most managed care programs.[103] Some people with physical, psychiatric, or developmental disabilities need personal assistance services in order to live independently in the community. Yet, as Melvin R. Tansman, director of health policy at Eastern Paralyzed Veterans Association, states, "There is no comprehensive federal policy that addresses the need for long-term care."[104] Many disability advocates indicate that independent living is usually not only less expensive than institutionalization, but also that many people with disabilities prefer participation in the community to what they perceive as "incarceration" in a nursing home. The nature of independent living is determined by the home care needs of the particular individual served. Some require as much as twenty-four-hour services; for others an hour in the morning and an hour in the evening would suffice.

Moreover, NCD observes that "escalating restrictions from private [health care] insurers have increasingly pushed high-risk, high-utilization people with disabilities into public sector programs"—Medicare and Medicaid.[105] Since "hospitals have strong financial incentives to discharge Medicare patients as soon as possible," growing numbers of people—younger than sixty-five—with disabilities, as well as many older people with chronic conditions, are being served by home health care.[106] Many Medicaid beneficiaries also depend on home health care. "Because of advances in medical science and technology, people living at home can receive complex services that were once available only in nursing homes or hospitals. An example is infusion therapy, which supplies medication and nutrition to patients with cancer, AIDS or other serious illnesses." Other complicated treatments possible in the home that were once provided only by doctors and nurses include dialysis, chemotherapy—even suctioning the excess mucus from the trachea of a two-year-old "whose brain does not emit the signals for him to breathe properly while he sleeps."[107] Yet political pressure to reduce mounting Medicare and Medicaid spending threatens to limit the provision of this crucial long-term home health care.[108]

In part as a response to fraudulent providers, the Balanced Budget Act of 1997 froze home health care at 1994 funding levels, resulting in a 30 percent cut in services.[109] Noting that the act punished the consumers of services rather than the perpetrators of fraud, disability advocates argue that the 1997 funding levels were more reasonable than the 1994 levels. Furthermore, they point out that the cuts are fiscally ill-advised because, for example, if a person who needs home care is denied Medicare services amounting to twenty thousand dollars annually, then that individual will be placed in a nursing home costing Medicaid fifty thousand dollars a year. A series of studies conducted from the mid- to late 1990s by New York City comptroller, Alan Hevesi, "Net Loss I, II, and III," demonstrates the economic advantage of home health care for people with chronic conditions. Hevesi states, "If you do harm—cut home care services and put people in nursing homes—and you save money, you have a debate. But if you do harm by institutionalizing people and you lose money, as our studies have revealed, how can you argue against long term health care in the community?"[110]

Health Policy Reforms

In *Achieving Independence* (1996), the NCD provided to the president, the Congress, and the nation with an analysis of federal laws and programs affecting the disability population, including an assessment of trends in the health care system. In order to ensure that private and public entities providing health care services do not discriminate against people with disabilities, NCD offered to establish an advisory committee to work with the Department of Justice.[111] The NCD suggested special consideration of issues and promulgation of regulations "clarifying the application of Titles II and III of the ADA and Sections 503 and 504 of the Rehabilitation Act of 1973 to private health insurance companies and health plans," including those that service Medicare and Medicaid recipients.[112]

Although Medicaid was specifically created for people with limited incomes, many of whom are disabled or older, Medicare originally was established to deal with the acute health care requirements of older people who contributed to Social Security. The 1972 amendments to the Social Security Act, however, allowed recipients of disability benefits under the age of sixty-five to qualify for Medicare.[113] Yet by 1999, the expanded Medicare program was not adequately serving the needs of the roughly five million Medicare beneficiaries under the age of sixty-five with disabilities,[114] the fastest growing group of Medicare recipients.[115]

In order to update Medicare, the NCD urged Congress to periodically review the benefit package so that services, such as medical treatment and therapy, as well as assistive technologies, reflect current health care and medical practices.[116] "A [1998] National Organization on Disability/Harris survey of Americans with disabilities noted that 69 percent of adults with disabilities who are not employed gave the need for continued medical treatment or therapy as a reason for not returning to work. These services are rarely covered by employer-sponsored health insurance."[117] The NCD advised that Medicare recipients with disabilities should be encouraged to return to the workforce by allowing them to retain their Medicare benefits when they acquire jobs. Both workers with disabilities and the general public would benefit from such a provision since these gainfully-employed individuals with disabilities would no longer be receiving Social Security payments.

Inasmuch as Medicaid payments are essential to many people with severe disabilities, the NCD recommended the continuation of appropriate funding levels, establishment of a federal definition of disability, and the maintenance of a "federal private right of action." With projected increased state control over Medicaid, a "federal private right of action" would enable Medicaid recipients to petition federal courts as

"an incentive [for government] to meet the health needs and long-term services needs of people with disabilities."[118] As the NCD pointed out, mechanisms for the presentation of suitable appeals and grievances to entities—such as ombudsmen—not connected to health plans would enable people with disabilities and other consumers to challenge health insurance decisions. The NCD also endorsed the transformation of "Medicaid's institutional bias" into a presumption that "long-term services and supports should be provided in the home and community, with congregate-care settings as a last resort."

Recognizing the increasing numbers of people with disabilities dependent upon Medicaid-sponsored managed care health plans, and the potential for these plans to incorporate Medicare recipients, the NCD emphasized the importance of significant federal control in establishing standards and monitoring compliance.[119] Contending that segmentation of the health insurance market based on risk militates against access to coverage by many people in the disability population, the NCD favors a health care system by the year 2006 that spreads risk by including everyone; thus, public and private insurers would compete on the basis of price and quality, not price and risk.[120]

The Nexus between Jobs and Health Care

The disincentives resulting from the nexus between jobs and health care for people with disabilities have presented a major obstacle to the employment of potential workers with disabilities who can and want to work. Since Medicaid—the sole source of reimbursement for long-term services and supports—has been available only to people who are not working, many people with disabilities have been forced to remain unemployed. In order to remain on Medicare by 1999, recipients of Social Security Disability Insurance were precluded from earning more than seven hundred dollars a month.[121] In addition, because of "preexisting condition exclusions, limits on benefits, and caps on payments," most health insurance companies do not adequately cover people with disabilities.[122] Consequently, many workers with disabling conditions, no longer covered by health insurance companies, have been forced to become Social Security beneficiaries on Medicare or Medicaid rather than employees.

"Because there is no well-established or well-funded system to provide supports to maximize employment, and there is a well-established system for providing cash compensation, people with disabilities may have no choice except to leave the workforce and accept the cash."[123] In order to get potential workers with disabilities out of government subsidized income-maintenance programs and into the workforce, Rebecca Ogle of Justice For All maintains that the nation would be best served by "a national non-means tested program for home and community-based services and supports."[124] A growing bipartisan effort in the Congress to counter the disincentives to employment for beneficiaries with disabilities who have the ability and desire to work was demonstrated by the 1999 unanimous Senate vote, as well as the 412 to 9 House vote, for the Work Incentives Improvement Act (WIIA).[125] The conference version of WIIA, approved in November 1999 and signed by President Clinton in December 1999, would permit states to set up buy-in programs to extend Medicaid coverage to Supplemental Security Income (SSI) and SSDI recipients who work.

Paul Longmore, historian and director of the Institute on Disability, San Francisco State University, is a polio survivor who requires the in-home support services provided by MediCal.[126] MediCal is California Medicaid, the California health care system for those on SSI,[127] a federal benefit program for people with disabilities and older people living at the poverty level. Since even with a well-paying job he could not afford to pay for his in-home services, he doubted that he would be able to accept employment after he completed his Ph.D.

When Longmore was offered a fellowship, he discovered that—according to the rules of SSI—he was neither allowed to accept the fellowship nor royalties from the book he had published, a biography of George Washington. A few months after a story appeared in the *Los Angeles Times* about Longmore burning his book in front of the Social Security offices to demonstrate against the injustice he was forced to endure, an amendment to a congressional bill corrected some of the inequities against which he had protested. Yet income maintenance programs for people with disabilities such as Workers' Compensation, SSDI, and SSI have continued to keep many qualified people out of the labor force.

On a more optimistic note, President Clinton quotes President Franklin Roosevelt: "No country, no matter how rich, can afford to waste its human resource."[128] EEOC vice chair Paul M. Igasaki elaborates on this point:

Corporate America is beginning to realize that a diverse work force makes economic sense and is critical to its success. A 1993 Standard and Poor's study showed that those companies that achieved some threshold level of diversity had stock market records that were almost two and one-half times better than similarly situated companies. That diverse work force includes individuals with disabilities.[129]

Employment laws applicable to the federal government—but not to the private sector where over 85 percent of the jobs are found—require affirmative action for people with disabilities. Consequently, the vocational talents of people with severe impairments who require home care services, such as Judy Gilliam, are seldom realized outside of the federal government.[130] Claiborne Haughton Jr., director for Civilian Equal Employment Opportunity, described Gilliam, his GS-15 manager for people with disabilities at the Defense Department: "She's a quadriplegic, Phi Beta Kappa, and she says it this way. 'I can't dress myself. I can't walk. I can't drive. I can't pick up a glass of water. But I can work.' And her work, I'm here to tell you, is consistently characterized by superior quality and productivity."[131]

Chapter Eight

"Not Dead Yet" and Physician-Assisted Suicide

WITH INCREASINGLY SOPHISTICATED technology for life-sustaining treatment, doctors frequently are given the awesome responsibility of determining when a life should end. Anthropologist Margaret Mead observed that "society is always attempting to make the physician into a killer—for instance, to kill the defective child at birth. . . . It is the duty of society to protect the physician from such requests."[1] People with disabilities are particularly vulnerable to judgments that their lives are not worth living.[2]

Opposition to "the Death Train"

On January 8, 1997, while the U.S. Supreme Court was hearing *Vacco v. Quill*—a case involving the constitutionality of state laws prohibiting physician-assisted suicide—people from many parts of the nation demonstrated in front of the Court. Many of the demonstrators, people with severe disabilities—blind people, deaf people, people in motorized wheelchairs—displayed signs proclaiming the sardonic name of their organization, Not Dead Yet, in "spooky-shaped" letters evoking the spirit of Halloween.

The organization was founded in Spring 1996 in reaction to public support for legalization of assisted death that had been promoted by the well-publicized suicides aided by Jack Kevorkian.[3] Mark O'Brien— journalist, poet, and member of Not Dead Yet, as well as the subject of the 1997 Academy Award-winning documentary "Breathing Lessons"—responds to the Kevorkian ethic:

It is tempting to pity a man in an iron lung. But pity has become a lethal weapon. On January 8 [1997], the Supreme Court heard arguments in favor of killing people like me— out of pity—to end our suffering. An iron lung has been my second skin since the 1955 polio epidemic. For forty years, people have said, "That poor thing—how he must suffer! He's terminally ill, you know." I'm not "suffering," "terminal," or even "ill." Don't waste your pity on me. I want to live. Every year, the practitioners of mercy death kill thousands of people against our will—out of pity. If the Supreme Court declares mercy death legal, that's like declaring open season on people with disabilities. We are not contagious or dangerous. And we aren't affiliated with any political party. We are people who hear the death train. We will not board that train willingly.[4]

In the amicus curiae briefs submitted by Not Dead Yet and American Disabled for Attendant Programs Today (ADAPT), attorneys Diane Coleman and Stephen Gold—supporting former New York State attorney general Dennis Vacco's effort to uphold the constitutionality of the state's ban on physician-assisted suicide—contended that "the creation of a right to assisted suicide for a class of individuals based on health status or disability is a lethal form of discrimination that violates the ADA."[5] The disability community was concerned about the potentially ominous consequences of physician-assisted suicide for those people whose quality of life may be considered unacceptable by members of the medical profession.

Responding to the much publicized November 22, 1998, "60 Minutes" spectacle of Kevorkian injecting Thomas Youk—a man with amyotrophic lateral sclerosis (ALS)—with lethal chemicals,[6] Coleman, founder and president of Not Dead Yet, asserted: "Reporters ignore the fact that most of Kevorkian's victims have been disabled, not terminal, ignore the discrimination and oppression that drove each of them to despair—ignore the injustice in a society that helps people die, *but refuses to help us* [people with disabilities] *live with the basic respect and the simple supports we deserve.*"[7] Kevorkian, who claims he has helped more than 130 people commit suicide, was found guilty of second-degree murder in the Youk case, after prosecutors had unsuccessfully attempted to convict him in five former cases.[8]

Michael Betzold explains in his 1997 exposé of journalist Jack Lessenberry, "The Selling of Dr. Death," how Kevorkian became a national hero.[9] A personal friend of Kevorkian and his attorney Geoffrey Fieger, Lessenberry reported on Kevorkian for the *New York Times* from 1993 until publication of the Betzold exposé, thus playing a major

role in shaping that newspaper's approach to assisted suicide.[10] Betzold reveals that "in his writings and statements, Kevorkian advocates a society that allows euthanasia for the dying, the disabled, the mentally ill, infants with birth defects, and comatose adults; and he sanctions experiments prior to their death and organ harvesting. He envisions a global system of death on demand run by doctors who operate without oversight from government or ethicists."[11]

Critic of physician-assisted suicide Nat Hentoff of New York City's *Village Voice* notes:

> It's a bitter irony [that a] quintessentially liberal judge [Ninth Circuit Court Judge Stephen Reinhardt] has opened the door wide not only to assisted suicide but also to euthanasia, because the majority of the resultant dead will be the poor, the disabled, and other vulnerable people. Many of them will persuade themselves to die because they feel nobody thinks their lives are worth preserving. Or that keeping themselves alive will cost too much, thereby burdening their families and companions.[12]

The Supreme Court

Reversing the 1996 rulings in the Second Circuit Court of Appeals in *Vacco v. Quill* and in the Ninth Circuit Court of Appeals in *Washington v. Glucksberg* the U.S. Supreme Court on June 26, 1997, unanimously upheld state criminal laws against physician-assisted suicide.[13] Prior to *Quill*, competent adults in New York State had the right to refuse medical treatment, and physicians were allowed to honor the requests of such patients to withhold or terminate life support. At the same time, intentionally assisting another person to commit or attempt suicide was a felony according to New York State law.

The Second Circuit Court of Appeals recognized that the right to refuse life-sustaining treatment gives those patients who become dependent on life support the opportunity to have some control over the timing of their death. Finding no rational basis for the state allowing patients to end life by requesting cessation of life support while, simultaneously, denying patients similar control when life support is not involved, the court ruled in favor of Dr. Quill. This difference, the court held, violates the Equal Protection Clause of the U.S. Constitution. Attorney General Vacco, appealing the court's decision, argued before the U.S. Supreme Court in 1997 to uphold New York State's ban on physician-assisted suicide.

While the appeals court decisions in both *Quill* and *Glucksberg* supported physician-assisted suicide, Judge Reinhardt's definition of "terminal" in the latter case as any "medical condition that is incurable and irreversible" seemed threatening to many people with disabilities and chronic illnesses.[14] As early as 1958, law professor Yale Kamisar warned of courts and physicians, even clerics, allowing family members to remove feeding tubes and respirators from people who were supposedly terminal.[15] Anticipating a movement towards active euthanasia for the socially vulnerable, Kamisar cautioned that some of those patients' lives could have been extended considerably. In his essay "Against Assisted Suicide—Even in a Very Limited Form," Kamisar quoted his former colleague, Robert Burt: "It would be ironic if [at a time when millions of Americans lack adequate health care] the judiciary selected physician-assisted suicide as the one health care right that deserves constitutional status."[16]

Strongly influenced by Kamisar's analysis, Ninth Circuit Judge Robert Beezer, in his dissenting opinion in *Glucksberg*, quoted from a 1994 report by the New York State Task Force on Life and the Law: "It must

be recognized that assisted suicide and euthanasia will be practiced through the prism of social inequality and prejudice that characterizes the delivery of services in all segments of society, including health care." He noted that even if they are not dying, "persons requiring dialysis, respirators, insulin or long-term nursing care would all be candidates for euthanasia."[17]

Yet allegiances on this issue are unpredictable, as illustrated by the court challenges by the National Right-to-Life Committee to the Oregon aid-in-dying measure, an initiative approved by the voters in 1994, preventing physician-assisted suicide from taking effect until a later Oregon vote in 1997. On the other hand, three New York law firms—Arnold & Porter; Cravath, Swaine & Moore; Debevoise & Plimpton— each with a history of pro bono legal contributions to disability causes and organizations, *supported* physician-assisted suicide.[18] Also, liberal Harvard law professor Laurence H. Tribe argued before the U.S. Supreme Court in 1997 for physician-assisted suicide.

In his majority opinion in *Vacco v. Quill* validating the state prohibition on physician-assisted suicide, Chief Justice William H. Rehnquist noted that this issue is properly within the jurisdiction of the states:

> The state has an interest in protecting vulnerable groups including the poor, the elderly, and disabled persons from abuse, neglect and mistakes. The court of appeals dismissed the state's concern that disadvantaged persons might be pressured into physician-assisted suicide as "ludicrous on its face." We have recognized, however, the real risk of subtle coercion and undue influence in end-of-life situations.[19]

AIDS Activists

Most AIDS activists take a position sanctioning physician-assisted suicide, contrary to the majority of other disability rights activists. Three terminally-ill patients, one with cancer and two with AIDS, as well as Dr. Timothy Quill and two other doctors, initiated the case in support of physician-assisted suicide. An amicus curiae brief supporting the patients and doctors included not only the well-known gay rights organization, Lambda Legal Defense and Education Fund, and some religious groups, but also the National Association of People with AIDS.

Larry Kramer, a vocal activist in the AIDS movement, indicates that "since the start of the epidemic, there have always been doctors one could talk to. . . . All of us who have been on the front line have experiences—plural—with people who didn't want to suffer anymore."[20] Although he knew many desperately ill people who had procured lethal medication, he was profoundly affected by the death of Brad Davis, the star of Kramer's AIDS play, *The Normal Heart*: "The medicine was very painful, and it wasn't working, and he just saw no sunshine ahead or anything. He was just going to get sicker and sicker, and he didn't want to put his family through that. And he did not want to suffer the pain himself." Stirred by this incident, Kramer allied with a Seattle group, Compassion In Dying, that was pursuing "a constitutional right to 'self-deliverance.'" Revealing that he felt like "the casting director," Kramer recruited two other physicians—his own psychiatrist, Dr. Samuel Klagsbrun, and an old friend, Dr. Howard Grossman—to affiliate with Quill in the lawsuit.

On October 30, 1996, for the first time a small group of medical practitioners, four physicians and a psychologist, publicly endorsed the campaign of Jack Kevorkian, initiated in 1990, for physician-assisted suicide.[21] In 1991, Quill, a mainstream physician, wrote his unprecedented public confession regarding his prescribing a fatal overdose of sleeping pills for a patient with end-stage leukemia, a woman who was seeking his assistance in dying.[22] Quill defended his action with a question: "Are we going to, as a culture, override a person's deathbed request, a person who is dying who says, 'I need some help here?'"

Supporting Quill's position, Dr. Lonnie Shavelson argued for the establishment of protocols for physician-assisted suicide: "It [physician-assisted suicide] is happening anyway, whether it's legal or not. . . . I see a tremendous amount of hidden, underground practice [of such suicides] in which nobody knows if there are abuses. I see potential disasters." Confirming Shavelson's assertion, a survey published in 1997 of 118 members of the Bay Area Community Consortium, an association of local AIDS doctors, revealed that 53 percent of the respondents reported helping at least one of their patients to commit suicide.[23]

Pain Management

Other medical practitioners argue that the technology to manage pain is available. Pediatric AIDS nurse Sheila Diamond states that "there is really no such thing as intractable pain, but only pain which is under-recognized, under-treated."[24] Reinforcing Diamond's assertion, hospice doctor Ira Byock explains:

Not only do we know that people's pain of their terminal illness often goes inadequately treated, it's often not even addressed. Beyond that, as if that weren't bad enough, our current non-system of health care routinely pauperizes people simply for being chronically ill and not dying quickly enough. . . . When you look at the curriculum of medical training, there is very, very little attention to caring for people at the end of life. Even pain control occupies no more than a handful of hours in a four-year course of study.

Dr. Kathleen Foley, palliative care specialist at New York's Memorial Sloan-Kettering Cancer Center and a pioneer since the mid-1970s in the field of palliative care and pain management, points out that "even oncology residents and fellows are poorly trained. It's a well-documented fact that those asking for assisted suicide almost always change their mind once we have their pain under control."[25]

Both proponents and opponents of physician-assisted suicide agree that pain management is a preferable option to state-sanctioned suicide. Dr. Daniel Carr (internist and anesthesiologist at the New England Medical Center in Boston, who has helped craft two sets of pain management guidelines issued by the federal government) and Dr. Nelson Hendler (clinical director of the Mensana Clinic near Baltimore, who has written extensively on pain management) support the medical profession's movement of the 1990s from a disease-centered to a patient-centered approach.[26] For example, formerly doctors were so concerned with the cancer patient's tumor or the AIDS patient's white blood cell count that they often neglected attending to the patient's experience of the illness. Carr refers to the federal guidelines for pain control, a graded step-wise progress from less to more invasive as the medical situation requires. Hendler criticizes the multiple disincentives to pain management: insurance companies that refuse to pay for pain medication prescribed by physicians, medical societies and medical schools that remain insufficiently involved in pain management, and the Drug Enforcement Agency that aggressively pursues doctors dispensing pharmaceuticals for pain control.

Both Carr and Hendler agree that pain is frequently undiagnosed or misdiagnosed and, as a result, undertreated or even mistreated. Carr points out that for too long doctors accepted myths such as that third-degree burns do not hurt, or that children—because of their undeveloped nervous systems—do not feel pain, or that cancer pain can never be alleviated. In fact, Carr indicates that although 90 percent of instances of cancer pain can be managed successfully, at least 30 to 40 percent of these cases are undertreated. Furthermore, 30 to 40 percent of cancer patients experience clinical depression, which Carr insists can be treated and reversed. Carr and Hendler maintain that with the treatment of depression—a major cause of suicide among patients with acute physical illnesses—in combination with proper palliative care, physician-assisted suicide could well be rendered unnecessary.

Carr is concerned that managed care "threatens to take away all the hard-fought-for advances [achieved] over the last couple of decades" in pain control. While the physiology of pain requires aggressive and early treatment, managed care organizations tend, in Carr's words, to "delay, defer, and deny." Thus, he adds, appropriate pain management and managed care are "at loggerheads with what we [pain management experts] know should be done." Although in 1996 Congress required health plans to cover at least forty-eight hours of hospital care for mothers and newborns, and in 1997 President Clinton recommended similar safeguards for mastectomy patients,[27] many critics of the current health care system are skeptical about the outlook for pain management procedures. Because "a drive-by mastectomy"—breast surgery for which managed care organizations formerly covered only one day in the hospital—is a dramatic denial of an essential service, such practices received much public condemnation. Since pain management is such a complex issue, however, the mishandling of this vital service by these organizations may continue to be neglected for a long time.[28]

Focus on Cure:
A Pernicious Message

Campaigning for research into a cure for spinal cord injuries, *Superman* star Christopher Reeve, who uses a ventilator and a motorized wheelchair, provokes disability advocates who believe that he is inadvertently sending a pernicious message: disabled people are not whole unless cured. Reeve notes that "until five years ago, it was believed that spinal cord could not regenerate. Now it's proved that it can. Research deserves our support, though there's a long way to go."[29] Many in the disability community, however, argue that this costly research, whose practical application may not be apparent for many years, "could drain resources from the more realistic [and in some cases even desperate] needs of the present."[30]

Speaking in neither of her official roles—as chair of the National Council on Disability nor as president and CEO of Access Living, the Chicago independent living center—Marca Bristo does not object to Reeve's desire to encourage research or even to seek a cure for spinal cord injuries.[31] The increased survival rate of spinal cord injured people has resulted from research, she observes. Yet, uncomfortable with Reeve soliciting from the private rather than the public sector, she considers "the hype" that he uses to generate donations detrimental to the disability rights movement. Frustrated by the mass media's general inability to perceive disability in a civil rights context, many disability advocates view Reeve's March 1, 1998, two-hour television special, *Christopher Reeve: A Celebration of Hope,* as a sophisticated version of a Jerry Lewis telethon, employing pity to elicit contributions.[32]

Other disability advocates point out that although Reeve is articulate, well-informed, and socially conscious, he is new to disability culture and issues. They commend his efforts to improve funding and legislation for people with disabilities, as well as to encourage equipment suppliers to decrease costs.[33] More to the point has been Reeve's ability to resume working in his field. He directed a well-received HBO special, *In the Gloaming,* in late 1996, and in 1998 he directed and starred in a remake of Alfred Hitchcock's 1954 classic film *Rear Window,* with the protagonist in the new version using the modern technology available in the late 1990s. Yet the fact that Reeve has been able to continue his involvement in so many activities—his autobiography, *Still Me,* was published in 1998[34]—does not preclude the possibility that he may still be in the "mourning phase" for his paralysis resulting from his 1995 horseback-riding accident. Regardless of Reeve's focus on cure in his discourse, in his life he demonstrates his determination as a person with a disability to participate in the world utilizing his unique intelligence, talents, and visibility.

In his book *Moving Violations,* journalist John Hockenberry, who also has a spinal cord injury, writes: "There is much more effort put into curing spinal cord injuries or discussing the legal issues involved in suicide for the severely disabled than there is integrating disabled folks into society at large. Pray to be normal no matter how impossible it seems is the sentimental message. The alternative is too horrible to contemplate."[35] Disability activist and quadriplegic motorized wheelchair user Daniel Robert describes the quandary in which people with disabilities find themselves: "And there we are, between a rock and a hard place, between waiting for a 'Cure' (read Miracle) and waiting to be 'offed.' The sum total of all the media attention given to Christopher

Reeve and Jack Kevorkian . . . boils down to this simple formula. If they can't fix us *we're better off dead*. It's our civic duty."[36]

The Eugenics Movement and Euthanasia

Medical historian Martin S. Pernick documents the sensational story of Dr. Harry Haiselden, a prominent Chicago surgeon, who in 1916 was as well known to Americans as Jack Kevorkian is in the 1990s.[37] As Pernick explains, when Haiselden decided in November 1915 to allow a newborn baby with an impairment to die, he told a reporter for Hearst's *Chicago-American* that although he had permitted other newborns to die quietly, he wanted to make this case a public issue:

> Haiselden and his supporters were torn between passionate expressions of sympathy and love, versus, in the next breath, expressing contempt, hatred, fear and loathing for those born with disabilities. . . . The disabled were a menace, an evil stalking beast, that was going to devour society. Haiselden was investigated three times by different legal authorities, for allowing impaired newborns to die, and each time he was upheld, but he was expelled from the Chicago Medical Society for writing newspaper articles and making a movie, [*The Black Stork*].[38]

Working with "muckraking" Hearst journalist Jack Lait, Haiselden was both writer and star of *The Black Stork,* a film whose storyline resembled a widely publicized incident involving a newborn girl with spina bifida:

> The main plot of this remarkable film begins with Claude, who has an unnamed inherited disease. Despite repeated graphic warnings from Dr. Dickey (played by Haiselden himself), Claude marries his sweetheart, Anne. Their baby is born so severely disabled that it needs immediate surgery to save its

life, but Dr. Dickey refuses to perform the operation. Anne is torn by uncertainty until God reveals a lengthy vision of the child's future, filled with pain, madness, and crime. Her doubts resolved, she accepts Dr. Dickey's judgment, and the baby's soul leaps into the arms of a waiting Jesus.[39]

Pernick reveals why Haiselden was not only supported by so many prominent early twentieth-century Americans, but also won editorial endorsements from some of the country's most prestigious publications, including the *New York Times* and the *New Republic:*[40] "The common progressive belief that science provided objective means for distinguishing good lives from bad ones hid the subjectivity of the values people actually used to make such judgments. And because they believed their values to be objectively proven, they could dismiss ethical or political criticisms as biased, unscientific, and therefore irrelevant."[41]

One of the most egregious examples of the perversion of medicine was the mass killing of people viewed as mentally or physically inadequate by the Nazi doctors. Robert J. Lifton links this so-called "biomedical vision" practiced by leading physicians in Nazi Germany with the eugenics movement that continued to be deemed respectable in the United States and England in the 1920s and even beyond.[42] In 1923, Fritz Lenz, a German physician-geneticist, complained that "Germany had nothing to match the eugenics research institutions in England and the United States."[43]

Lenz rebuked the German people because of "their backwardness in the domain of sterilization as compared to the United States [for] Germany had no equivalent to the American laws prohibiting marriage . . . for people suffering from such conditions as epilepsy or mental retardation." Virginia Kallianes and Phyllis Rubenfeld discuss the impact, especially on women with disabilities, of the reoccurrence of the eugenics movement in the late twentieth century:

> Given the repression of sexuality and social proscription of mothering among disabled women, it is not surprising that they look suspiciously upon selective abortion or genetic technologies that are used to prevent reproduction by disabled women or the birth of disabled babies. Some of this concern arises from the legacy of sterilization abuse among disabled women, particularly in the early 20th century United States eugenics movement.... Many see in advancing reproductive technologies, such as genetic screening combined with abortion, the return of eugenics practices and claim society is reverting to attitudes such as those embodied in the 1927 United States Supreme Court case upholding compulsory sterilization in the state of Virginia which came from Oliver Wendell Holmes's often quoted statement: "Society can prevent those who are manifestly unfit from continuing their kind."[44]

J. P. Landman, in his 1932 study of the sterilization movement in the United States, refers to "overzealous and overardent eugenicists" who "regard . . . the feebleminded, the epileptics, the mentally diseased, the blind, the deformed, and the criminals as inimical to the human race . . . [because] these people perpetuate their deficiencies and thus threaten the quality of the ensuing generations."[45] Because they contended "a nation must defend itself against national degeneration as much as against the external foreign enemy," these eugenicists believed, according to Lenz, that the nation should endeavor "to exterminate these undesirables."

In their 1996 testimony delivered before Congress, Diane Coleman and Carol Gill succinctly articulated the strong objections to physician-assisted suicide by many members of the disability community.[46] Having experienced discrimination and persecution, people with disabilities and incurable chronic diseases fear a reemergence of

the 1930s euthanasia movements in England and the United States. These movements inspired execution by Nazi doctors of two hundred thousand people judged deficient because of their physical and mental impairments.[47] Although Hitler rescinded this euthanasia policy on August 24, 1941, the only official order reversed in his twelve years of power,[48] the killing of people with disabilities continued by means that were not always obvious, such as withholding of treatment, medication, or food.[49] Yet the Nuremberg court did not require that reparations be paid to the families of those with disabilities who were killed, nor that their murderers be punished.

In this context, Coleman and Gill's reference to Kevorkian's admission that his suicide device was designed as an answer for quadriplegics is a chilling harbinger to many people with disabilities of "the right to die" becoming "the duty to die."[50] Echoes of Nazi rhetoric are evident in Kevorkian's defense of "medicide": "The voluntary self-elimination of individual and mortally diseased or crippled lives taken collectively can only enhance the preservation of public health and welfare."[51] Women's roles as nurturers and caretakers make them especially vulnerable when they become dependent:

> If anyone doubts that women will be exploited and endangered by assisted suicide, the doubters should study Kevorkian's "clients." The first eight were all middle-aged or elderly women with chronic illnesses and disabilities. Many said they feared being a burden on others. An autopsy on one of them revealed no evidence of any physical illness. Women with disabilities are going to be the first to feel a "duty to die."[52]

Despite the current prosperity, opponents of disability rights always claim that resources are scarce; therefore, people with disabilities are apprehensive about being perceived as costly, unproductive expendables.[53] Campaigners for a right-to-die movement in the 1990s Derek Humphry and Mary Clement state that "in the final analysis, economics, not the quest for broadened individual liberties or increased autonomy, will drive assisted suicide to the plateau of accepted practice."[54] More radically, John Hardwig asserts, "In fact, there may be a fairly common responsibility to end one's life in the absence of any terminal illness at all. Finally, there can be a *duty to die* when one would prefer to live."[55] In reaction to this mindset, Coleman and Gill warn that assisted-suicide proponents have been feeding public misconceptions regarding the social expense of disability in their characterization of services, devices, and technology for people with disabilities as resulting in an inherently undignified lifestyle.

The Politics of Physician-Assisted Suicide

As former director of the New York City Mayor's Office for People with Disabilities, Anne Emerman and law professor Yale Kamisar predicted, the decision regarding the "Pandora's box" of physician-assisted suicide is being determined in state legislatures rather than in the Supreme Court.[56] Ezekiel and Linda Emanuel chronicle the national experience with efforts to legalize assisted suicide: "Since 1995, nearly fifty bills have been introduced in more than twenty states concerning assisted suicide, but none of the bills [until the Oregon 1994 referendum] calling for legalization have passed.... Today [July 24, 1997] thirty-five states have laws that explicitly criminalize euthanasia and doctor-assisted suicide."[57]

Although Oregon voters had approved legalizing physician-assisted suicide in 1994 by a 51 percent to a 49 percent margin, the referendum was held up by legal challenges

for three years.[58] The Emanuels note the "historical precedent for blocking efforts to sanction euthanasia": Despite much public debate in the United States from 1890 to 1906 regarding legalization of physician-assisted suicide, in 1907 the Ohio legislature failed to support the measure and, as a result, "euthanasia all but disappeared from the public agenda until the last few years."[59]

While the Emanuels believe that "legislators understand that deep down the public is ambivalent about euthanasia," Emerman is profoundly concerned about this controversy. Given the common public misunderstandings about disability and assisted suicide, as well as the complexity of this contentious issue, those in the disability community who are fervently opposed have their work cut out for them, she maintains. They must embark on "a crusade to educate the public." She was referring to the Gallup survey revealing that 75 percent of Americans believe doctors should be legally permitted to "end a patient's life by painless means," as well as the poll of the American Society of Internal Medicine indicating that 40 percent of all doctors had provided assistance to their patients who sought a means to end their lives.[60]

A 60 to 40 percent vote by Oregon citizens on November 4, 1997, on a new referendum not to repeal the 1994 referendum permitting physician-assisted suicide,[61] as well as Attorney General Janet Reno's June 5, 1998, ruling removing "the last legal obstacle to the full operation of Oregon's landmark assisted-suicide law," added to Emerman's apprehension.[62] "It is ironic," Emerman says, "that at a time when technology permits people who are very disabled to be independent and productive members of society, they have to contend with this movement for assisted suicide."[63] Confirming Emerman's fears, Reno's decision signified that other states may pass comparable legislation sanctioning physician-assisted suicide without federal restriction. Though the front-page *New York Times* article describing Reno's Oregon judgment noted the strong opposition of the Roman Catholic Church to authorized assisted suicide, no reference was made to the intense and vocal objection of most of the disability community.[64]

Netherlands "Slippery Slope" vs. U.S. "Political Strategy"

Characterizing the policy of the Netherlands as a "slippery slope," psychiatrist and psychoanalyst Herbert Hendin issued a warning to the United States: "The Netherlands has moved from assisted suicide to euthanasia, from euthanasia for people who are terminally ill to euthanasia for people who are chronically ill, from euthanasia for physical illness to euthanasia for psychological distress, and from voluntary euthanasia to involuntary euthanasia (called 'termination of the patient without explicit request')."[65] In their 1996 congressional testimony, Coleman and Gill offered several illustrations of the relaxation of laws and policies protecting the lives of people with disabilities in the United States: Oregon's endeavor to ration health care based on "quality of life" judgments made by nondisabled people reveals the vulnerability of people with costly conditions; lifesaving organ transplants regularly are denied to people with rather mild disabilities; assisted breathing frequently is not presented as an option to people with disabilities who need ventilators; and many using ventilators indicate that they are increasingly requested to contemplate "do-not-resuscitate (DNR)" orders and withdrawal of life support.

Coleman pointed out that bioethicists have asked if American society is willing to allocate scarce resources to people with disabilities: "Whether it's a 'voluntary' DNR order, a surrogate decision by a family member, an involuntary 'futility guideline,' or health insurance denials, we [people with disabilities] are being eliminated through the withholding of medical treatment."[66] Futility guidelines, developed by the AMA and many individual hospitals, allow doctors to withhold medical treatment against the expressed wishes of a patient or the patient's family.[67] Referring to a statement in the December 1997 fund-raising letter of the pro-euthanasia organization Compassion In Dying, Coleman revealed that "pro-euthanasia advocates are now raising funds for expansion of their advocacy efforts to openly include people with nonterminal conditions."

Unlike in the Netherlands where the assisted suicide movement was accurately described as a slippery slope, the United States right-to-die campaign is a "political strategy," asserted Coleman,[68] "as people with disabilities are regularly bombarded with messages that [they] cost too much to be allowed to live."[69] She referred to the vision embodied in a statement by the founder of the right-to-die organization, the Hemlock Society, Derek Humphry: "Like it or not, the connection between the right-to-die and the cost, value, and allocation of health care resources are part of the political debate, albeit frequently unspoken."[70] Citing well-documented physician biases about quality of life for people with impairments and chronic illnesses, Coleman fears further justifications for refusing to provide appropriate health care for the disability population: "People with disabilities have no confidence that either the civil or criminal justice system will value [their] lives enough to protect [them] equally in a society which is more and more open in its certainty that everyone would be better off without [them]."[71]

First-Year Report on Physician-Assisted Suicide in Oregon

In 1999, the *New York Times* compared two reports on assisted suicide, one in the *Journal of Medical Ethics* on the fifteen-year practice in the Netherlands, the other by the State Health Division on the one-year experience in Oregon.[72] The *New York Times* reported that the *Journal of Medical Ethics* found a "fatal confusion" in the Netherlands because assisted suicide is technically illegal but widely practiced: "In one in five cases surveyed there, euthanasia was performed on patients who had not requested it, and on patients for whom other untried treatments for their illnesses were still available." In contrast, the *New York Times* indicated that the Oregon report found no confusion or abuses resulting from the law: "Only 15 people, 8 men and 7 women, were helped to die in 1998. Thirteen were cancer patients, and many, their doctors said, were decisive personalities, or people acting on long-held principles."

Dr. Kathleen Foley and other specialists in terminal care are skeptical about Oregon's positive judgment regarding the effect of the legislation.[73] Not only was the state's report based on twenty-minute telephone interviews with the doctors who prescribed the lethal drugs, but the 40 percent of the doctors in the Oregon cases who refused to give the drugs because of their misgivings in assisting in a suicide were not represented. As Foley observes, perspectives essential to comprehending people's motives in seeking assisted suicide were omitted: "We lost the voices of the patients; we lost the voices of the families."

Although the report indicated that only one person specified fear of pain as a reason for seeking assisted suicide, Joseph Shapiro refers to others with similar objectives. Since those who opted for suicide were "several times more likely" than the norm to be divorced or never married, Shapiro wonders whether a care-giving spouse would have altered the patients' decisions. Finally, while the report underplayed the significance of fear of financial consequences in the patient's choice of assisted suicide, others disagree. As Shapiro notes, "At a recent public meeting in Oregon, Ric Burger, a diabetic who uses a wheelchair, complained that the state's Medicaid program now pays for assisted suicide [supposed "death with dignity"] but not for enough hours for in-home aids necessary for many elderly and disabled to live—in dignity—in their own homes."

Legalizing Disability Discrimination

In her 1998 testimony before Congress, Diane Coleman maintained that the Oregon assisted-suicide law not only "violates the Americans with Disabilities Act, [but] under a disparate impact analysis, may also violate the Civil Rights Act of 1964."[74] She added, "People with terminal illnesses generally qualify as people with disabilities, yet policymakers have completely ignored the ADA violations inherent in assisted-suicide laws. Unfortunately, discrimination based on health status is still fundamentally acceptable in this culture, still so deeply ingrained that it's hard for people to recognize it when it stares them in the face."

In fact, Coleman pointed out that Congress included language in the ADA stating that disability discrimination may warrant more "judicial and legislative scrutiny" than it has frequently been given: "Individuals with disabilities are *a discrete and insular minority* who have been faced with restrictions and limitations, subjected to a history of purposeful unequal treatment, relegated to a position of political powerlessness in our society."[75] She cited a dramatic example of such "unequal treatment," an experiment that occurred at Children's Hospital of Oklahoma between 1977 and 1982. Twenty-four babies with spina bifida died because their parents did not know they were being used in a study testing whether parents would accept "do-not-treat" recommendations from doctors.

Explaining that the Oregon law cannot be understood outside its social context, Coleman described the first widely reported case involving an eighty-year-old woman with breast cancer whose doctors denied her request for assisted suicide because they diagnosed her as depressed. Once Compassion In Dying found a doctor who would grant her suicidal request, her case met the explicit requirements of the law. As Coleman observed, "Nothing in the law says the individual has to be informed about independent living or social service options, nothing says that an individual has to actually be provided any medical or service alternatives he or she might prefer, and nothing says people can't shop around until they find a doctor who will do it." In addition, Coleman notes that "since there's no enforcement mechanism, there are no legal consequences for failure to report assisted suicides."[76]

Coleman described this type of discriminatory law to hasten death as tantamount to "a denial of equal protection of the law under the Fourteenth Amendment." Although she noted that courts have so far not granted "'suspect class' status to people with disabilities," the landmark U.S. Supreme Court assisted suicide ruling recognized disability discrimination: "The State's interest goes beyond protecting the vulnerable from coercion; it extends to protecting disabled and terminally ill people from prejudice, negative and inaccurate stereotypes, and 'societal indifference.'... [A] seriously disabled person's suicidal impulses should be interpreted and treated the same way as anyone else's."

Dangers of an Inflexible Law

In his article "Whose Right To Die?" oncologist Dr. Ezekiel Emanuel reveals that interest in euthanasia—which dates back to 1870—was generated not by new technologies that extend life, but rather by the discovery of pain-relieving drugs such as morphine that could also result in painless death.[77] Although drugs administered aggressively—not to hasten death but to relieve pain—may ultimately induce death, this practice, both ethically and legally sanctioned, is not physician-assisted suicide. Since depression, not pain, primarily motivates patients to request physician-assisted suicide, Emanuel notes that our usual approach to people in psychological distress is "psychiatric intervention—not... a syringe and life-ending drugs." Moreover, patients kept alive by technology who no longer wish to live do not require new legislation permitting physician-assisted suicide since they already have the constitutional right to discontinue medical interventions.

Fearing legalization of physician-assisted suicide, Emanuel predicts that the most vulnerable will be "children, the demented, the mentally ill, the old, and others." No doubt paramount among "the others" would be people with disabilities, for frequently presumptions made by healthy people about those who are suffering, or those assumed to be suffering, would not be countenanced by the objects of those presumptions. Many people with visible impairments are concerned that the same kind of presumptions often are made by nondisabled people about the quality of life of people with disabilities.

According to a 1996 *Washington Post* poll, marginalized demographic groups, other than people with disabilities, also tend to feel threatened by legalization of physician-assisted suicide: African Americans opposed legalization 70 percent to 20 percent; people over seventy opposed it 58 percent to 35 percent.[78] Lacking the universal and comprehensive health care of the Netherlands, patients and doctors in the United States could be making decisions about physician-assisted suicide while encouraged to cut costs. The significance of this factor will be amplified "in the context of demographic and budgetary pressures on Social Security and Medicare as the Baby Boom generation begins to retire, around 2010."[79]

Believing, like Emanuel, that ethical ambiguities regarding physician-assisted suicide are better addressed on a case-by-case basis than by an inflexible rule, ethics professor emeritus Lewis Smedes maintains that "sometimes it is better just to leave things murky."[80] Harvard's Michael J. Sandel explains why even laws that are disregarded from time-to-time serve a purpose: "It [physician-assisted suicide] should be burdened morally by the sense that we are taking a life, something that isn't entirely ours to take. Preserving the laws on the books is a way of keeping this sense of burden." Similarly, Emanuel asserts that physician-assisted suicide should remain illegal and exceptional so that those who make "moral judgments" will be "accountable before the law."

Rather than providing the technology and services that would allow people with disabilities to live productive lives in the mainstream, the health care system too frequently supports—sometimes even elicits—misguided suicidal impulses in vulnerable people. Given the many people with disabilities who may be included among the "marginalized," the warning of psychiatrist Herbert Hendin threatens the disability population in the United States: "The Netherlands? With a homogenous, pretty much law abiding citizenry, almost all of whom have medical coverage? And America, with many different cultures represented, many marginalized people, tens of millions without health care insurance? As bad as it was *there,* in other words, it could be much, much worse *here.*"[81]

"A Better Solution"

Describing the popular support for physician-assisted suicide as "neither strong nor deep," Emanuel observes that answers to questions on the subject are dependent on how these queries are crafted. "For the majority of people with disabilities, whose only information about living with disability comes from health care providers, today's trends do not bode well," cautions Diane Coleman: "In those critical early hours, weeks, and months after injury, people could easily be swayed to make a so-called 'choice' for death."[82] In his article "Americans Want a Right to Die. Or So They Think," David E. Rosenbaum refers to "the opinion surveys [that] have not addressed the wrenching specifics . . . that for many people first have meaning when they face them personally."[83]

Nancy Rolnick, a C1–2 quadriplegic—paralyzed from the neck down as a result of an automobile accident and unable to breathe without a respirator (or the phrenic nerve pacer she now uses)—describes her fundamental difficulty with the "right to die" movement:

> Before my accident, I saw Brian Clark's play *Whose Life Is It Anyway?* about a young man paralyzed in an accident, struggling for the right to cease living. Along with my husband and friends, I sided with the protagonist, never questioning his decision. After my accident, I saw the movie made from the play, and while I still identified with the young man, I thought, "Gee, this guy is making his move much too soon. He's not giving himself the chance to find out what it's like to live outside the hospital." In other words, as a disabled person, my perspective changed. I no longer automatically accepted suicide as a good solution to disability.

So what is a better solution? I can only answer for myself. First of all, I've been surrounded by people who fully expected me to come home from the hospital and pick up my life—my husband, my children and their spouses, a few good friends, and my nurses. Their attitude has been—do it. At crucial moments I met disabled people who inspired and guided me—a paraplegic woman when I first entered the rehabilitation hospital, and as I left the hospital, a young woman quadriplegic who became my mentor, for she had created a fantastically independent life for herself. Other disabled people along the way have been important to me, and of course working with disability advocacy groups has given a new focus to my life.[84]

Recognizing the significance of her accessible living quarters, as well as her private insurance—which provides her with care and equipment to achieve maximum independence—Rolnick continues, "Given the tools and the proper support, most people with disabilities want to continue laughing, loving, and living."

The Distinction between Severe Disability and Terminal Illness

The following examples reveal how the difference between severe disability and terminal illness easily may become obscured by the courts. In making judgments, do courts value the life of a person with a disability as much as the life of a nondisabled person? American disability rights advocates have seized upon the case of Tracy Latimer, a twelve-year-old Canadian child with cerebral palsy who was killed by her father, Robert Latimer, in 1993 by means of a lethal dose of carbon monoxide.[85] Although Tracy's father was convicted of second degree murder—a verdict usually carrying a mandatory life sentence without a chance of parole for ten years—the jury recommended parole after one year.

Not only did the jury consider Robert Latimer's deed a mercy killing, but there also was an outpouring of public support for Tracy's father. Disability advocates asked, however, why does the killing of a nondisabled child evoke outrage while the killing of a child with a disability is accepted? Another question they posed concerned the necessity for the medical procedures that Tracy was forced to undergo to improve her condition. "News accounts...suggest the girl was relatively stable and happy before doctors started operating on her to 'correct things.'" Was it these surgeries rather than the cerebral palsy that caused Tracy's reported suffering? Disability advocates fear that the notion that killing a person with a disability is different from killing anyone else encourages courts to condone physician-assisted suicide.

Utilizing the joystick on a motorized wheelchair, twenty-six-year-old Elizabeth Bouvia, a college graduate studying for a master's degree in social work, lived independently in her own apartment with her husband until, over a short period of time, everything she sought to accomplish seemed to unravel:

> The dean of the program where she had planned to get her master's degree in social work told her that no matter how well she might do, there was not going to be a job at the end of her efforts. In despair, she dropped out of school, and the state then took away the van it had made available for her transportation to and from school.
>
> Her little family fell apart as her husband left her, and she suffered a miscarriage. She retreated back to her father's house, but together they decided this arrangement would not be convenient for him. With her world out of control, she decided to take her own life. She checked into Riverside Hospital in California and made the demand that she be kept comfortable as she starved herself to death. Within a very short time, the psychiatric staff of that medical facility had officially designated her as mentally

competent, and the American Civil Liberties Union was in court pleading her right to this bizarre form of suicide.[86]

Although her disability, cerebral palsy, was not progressive, the California Supreme Court judged her 1983 bout with depression as an acceptable reason for allowing the hospital to assist in her suicide. Bouvia's subsequent change of heart—her decision to go on with her life—underscored the fact that the court would be highly unlikely to accept depression of a nondisabled person as suitable grounds for physician-assisted suicide.[87]

In 1984, Mary Jane Owen, blind disability activist, editor, writer, and former faculty member of the graduate program in social work at San Francisco State College, made this observation about the Bouvia case: "What we keep telling each other about Bouvia illustrates more about how *we* feel about disability than it does about how this young woman is dealing with her depression. She is trapped by the snare of our terror and prejudices. She has come to personify our horror of vulnerability, frailty and all the 'imperfections' of disability."[88]

The highly publicized requests for physician-assisted suicide by two other quadriplegics also were sanctioned by the courts. Without having ever met Kenneth Bergstedt, a highly intelligent quadriplegic, Las Vegas District Court Judge Donald Mosley ruled in June 1990 that a physician could sedate Bergstedt and then remove the respirator upon which he depended for breathing.[89] Using peculiar logic, Mosley determined that Bergstedt's death in this manner would not be suicide; rather, Bergstedt would be regulating his medical care. Neither a newspaper reporter who covered the case, nor Mary Johnson in her capacity as editor of the *Disability Rag*, nor any disability activist was able to speak to Bergstedt directly. After Bergstedt, assisted by a physi-

cian, had committed suicide with court approval, Johnson—in the September/October 1990 issue of the *Disability Rag*—revealed her impression that Bergstedt, himself, was never consulted regarding his life or death decision.

Founder of the Independent Living Movement and winner of a MacArthur "genius" fellowship, Edward Roberts, who like Bergstedt relied on a respirator, expressed his feelings about the case:

> The whole thing is outrageous. I am getting angrier and angrier about these cases. They feed on each other. The attorneys, the courts, the judges, they don't know anything. They see somebody like Bergstedt, and they say, "Of course he wants to die." What's happening is we're killing disabled people in this country and then act like we're doing them a favor. It's outrageous. I've been on a respirator for twenty-six years, and I watch these people's cases. They're just as dependent on a respirator as I am. The major difference is that they know they're going to be forced to live in a nursing home—or they're already there—and I'm leading a quality life. That's the only difference. It's not the respirator. It's the money.

Lacking the technology that would make it possible for him to live and work independently, thirty-four-year-old Larry McAfee, a quadriplegic, clearly planned to commit suicide in 1989, a decision supported by the court, the clergy, and his family. "McAfee, who became disabled in 1985, won court approval to hook up a switch to his motorized chair to allow him to turn off his own respirator and kill himself. Disability activists got involved, fought for other options for him, and showed McAfee the possibility of community living arrangements [that] no one else (including those that [were] helping him win his death) had told him about."[90] Once he acquired the opportunity to function in the community (using a puff-and-sip motorized wheelchair) and to work in the professional world (employing a voice-activated computer), McAfee changed his mind, for he found new meaning in his increasingly self-directed life. The 1992 made-for-television film dramatizing McAfee's plight made no reference to the role of disability advocates, who showed McAfee how to live rather than how to die.

Like McAfee, who could utilize his professional training and skills as an engineer when he was provided with the proper tools, many people with severe disabilities are living fulfilling and productive lives employing appropriate technologies. In 1992, a coalition of six independent living centers of New York City gave its annual award for outstanding achievement by a student with a disability to an African-American teenager with cerebral palsy. Although he was originally labeled as "retarded," once he was given the chance to use computers to operate a power wheelchair, a voice synthesizer, and a word processor, he was upgraded to very intelligent. While still profoundly disabled, the youngster was no longer handicapped in revealing his talents.[91] Disability rights advocate Professor Frank Bowe, who is deaf, draws a distinction between the words "disability" and "handicapped":

> Our disabilities are not going to disappear, but what we can work on are the handicaps. In this room today I am not handicapped. I can talk to anyone here and you can talk to me because I have an interpreter. I am still disabled; I am as deaf as I ever was—as I was this morning, as I will be when I go to bed tonight. But I am not handicapped in this room. And because this room is accessible, people, whatever their disability, can get into it. So the people in this room are not handicapped. They are still disabled, but they are not handicapped. This means that the people in this room can do whatever their intellect, their knowledge, their training, their ability enable them to do.[92]

Technology has allowed Stephen Hawking, the world renowned British physicist with a severe disability, to continue to pierce "the mysteries of the universe with the mind of a latter-day Einstein."[93] In 1963, Hawking, just twenty-one years old, working in Cambridge on his Ph.D. in physics, was told that he had two and a half years to live as a result of ALS, a degenerative motor neuron disease that causes atrophy of muscles throughout the body. Inexplicably, however, Hawking continues to thrive beyond any reasonable expectation. With a voice synthesizer, provided after his 1985 tracheotomy resulting from his bout with pneumonia, and a small personal computer mounted on his wheelchair, his ability to lecture and to collaborate with other physicists, as well as to publish books and articles, has not been compromised.

For Hawking, the knowledge that he had a severe disability seemed to act as a spur, focusing his intellect and his energy on his study of cosmology: "Before my condition had been diagnosed, I had been very bored with life. There had not seemed to be anything worth doing. But shortly after I came out of hospital, I dreamt that I was going to be executed. I suddenly realized that there were a lot of worthwhile things I could do if I were reprieved."[94] In fact, a colleague suggested that Hawking's illness may have made new creative possibilities available to him:

> As he gradually lost the use of his hands, he had to start carefully choosing research projects that could be tackled and solved through geometrical arguments that he could do pictorially in his head, and he developed a powerful set of tools that nobody else really had. So in some sense, when you lose one set of tools, you may develop other tools, but the new tools are amenable to different kinds of problems than the old tools. That means certain kinds of problems you can solve, and nobody else can.

As Intel vice president Stephen Nachtheim observes, "Wherever Hawking rolls along the Gothic splendor of Cambridge or anywhere throughout the world, he has constant access to the Internet, a faster voice synthesizer and infrared remote control of doors, lights and his personal entertainment center."[95] Nachtheim characterizes Hawking as "a man who does what he wants and tries to be minimally inconvenienced by his disability, so he uses all the technology he can to overcome a problem." Making only passing reference to Hawking's very apparent and well-known disability, a 1997 *New York Times* front-page article described the visit of "the brilliant theorist" to the California Institute of Technology.[96] Hawking explains:

> I regard my disability like color blindness— something that is an inconvenience but which one can live with and get 'round. Obviously, my disability is more severe than color blindness, but to me it is incidental and does not shape my world view. The way for disabled people to be appreciated is to be successful. For the physically disabled, this means being smarter than the next guy. No one is going to be impressed if you are a Paralympic champion. You have to be outstanding in absolute terms.[97]

Can the value of a life be judged by the degree of a disability? Can these lives of people with serious disabilities be described as unworthy to be lived? Too commonly, policy decisions reflect a confusion between terminal illness and disability, as well as an arrogance and complacency in judging the value of a life, even for those who have not made world-shaking contributions. As Not Dead Yet attorney Diane Coleman stated in the conclusion of her 1998 congressional testimony, "Our society is wrestling with what is perhaps the most pivotal issue of our time: whether a cost-benefit analysis will determine the value of a human life, whether people with disabilities, including terminal illnesses, belong in our society as a part of humanity's diversity, or whether we [people with disabilities] will be pushed, subtly and not-so-subtly, toward the Final Exit solution."[98]

Chapter Nine

Disability and Technology

THE DISABILITY RIGHTS MOVEMENT "is a by-product of the technological revolution," in the words of one commentator.[1] "Breakthroughs in medicine, the development of computers that allow the hearing and speech impaired to use telephones, and advancements in motorized wheelchairs have meant that more people with severe handicaps can live longer, can do more for themselves and have the potential for enjoying fuller lives." Without political activism, however, technological advances do not automatically translate into gains for people with disabilities.

Universal Design

"Growing up in a world full of barriers," the design pioneer Ronald L. Mace, a polio survivor and a wheelchair user, had a clear incentive for creating his visionary concept of universal design.[2] Not only did he have to be carried up and down stairs so he could attend classes at North Carolina State—from which he graduated in 1966—but also he could not fit his wheelchair into the men's room. Universal design is "the holistic approach" to accessible environments "that goes beyond minimum codes and standards to create designs that serve the broadest public [including people with disabilities] throughout their life spans."[3] Wheelchair designer Ralf Hotchkiss describes the evolving "revolution in human interaction," a consequence of inventors, artists, and architects who are redesigning the infrastructure and creating a new aesthetic for the changing environment: "Without changes in how things are laid out physically, the changes of mind [allowing for inclusion of people with disabilities] will be slower to come."[4]

Often involving subtle design changes and adaptations to already existing products and environments, universal design is more practicable and cost-effective than many people realize.[5] For example, it is neither difficult nor expensive to provide counters at a level that accommodates children and people in wheelchairs or to include labels with large type, readable by partially sighted and older people.[6] Yet too frequently lack of technical feasibility is one of the first arguments offered against universal design, observes disability rights advocate Professor Frank Bowe.[7]

When universal design is disparaged despite the compelling arguments for the concept, the real problem may be a lack of will to be inclusive, or more insidiously, the profit motive masquerading as an effort to protect the public. One glaring example involved the 1992 decision to set up an experiment putting pay toilets, inaccessible to wheelchair users, on the streets of New York City. The manufacturer, JCDecaux, wanted to impose the same unit on the United States that he had sold in Paris and other cities in Europe, where there is no ADA. The fallacious explanation given by JCDecaux for not providing a single model for a street toilet in compliance with ADA and "universal design" was accepted in a *New York Times* editorial: "Units large enough for wheelchair users will inevitably accommodate unsavory activity like prostitution and drug abuse.... The company therefore insists that their [the accessible toilets'] use be restricted to disabled patrons who gain access with key cards."[8]

Six months later, in an article "Toilet Wars," subtitled "How a battle over handicapped rights is keeping those spotless wonders off the street," *New York* magazine appeared to have been persuaded by JCDecaux's public relations campaign.[9] The same can be said for the American Broadcasting Company's television magazine "20/20" in its segment aired three months earlier, "There Goes Another Good Idea."[10] Like the *New York Times*, *New York* magazine and "20/20" erroneously assumed that it was the disability community who was selfishly thwarting technological improvement. Philip K. Howard, in *The Death of Common Sense* (1994), continued to assert the misleading notion that "in New York, the unintended consequence of giving the disabled the 'right' to do everything in the same way was the imposition of a de facto prohibition of sidewalk toilets."[11] The spurious case JCDecaux made was that technology did not exist to deal with the social problems that

would be created by the size of the accessible unit.

JCDecaux's way of dealing with this supposed dilemma was to create two separate and unequal units, an "elegant kiosk" for the general public and an accessible toilet for wheelchair users. The accessible unit necessitated inconvenient special cards, as well as a full-time attendant, for—unlike the kiosk—it was not self-flushing and self-cleaning. Howard misunderstood the implication of the facts he offered: "The regular units averaged over three thousand flushes per month, or 50 percent more than the average in Paris. The larger units reserved for the disabled were basically unused, the cost of the full-time attendant wasted."

Rather than proving that the disabled advocates were, as Howard referred to them, "unreasonable zealots" demanding a technology for which they had no real use, the disability community's refusal to participate in the four-month street toilet experiment was a political gesture. On the contrary, accessible street toilets would be very useful for wheelchair users, especially women, who have great difficulty finding appropriate facilities. In fact, disability activists were demonstrating that they would not accept second-class status. Moreover, consistent with the concept of universal design, these "larger units" would have been accessible not only to individuals who use wheelchairs and other mobility devices, but also to people with small children, baby strollers, luggage carriers, large packages, and countless other things.

After New York City had just completed the JCDecaux experiment, San Francisco issued a Request for Proposals (RFP) for a street toilet, requiring compliance with the ADA. It should be noted that in San Francisco disability activists had more political clout than in a megacity such as New York. Also, unlike in New York City, public officials in San Francisco were open to man-ufacturers of street toilets other than the well-known and well-connected JCDecaux. Proposals came from places as far away as Germany and Israel. These manufacturers offered designs for single units, complying with the ADA, that incorporated technol-ogy that solved the potential social prob-lems connected with the size of the acces-sible units. At this point, JCDecaux sud-denly revealed that it, too, had the tech-nology to manufacture a single accessible unit that would be safe on the streets of New York City. Even when solutions to technological problems are not immedi-ately evident, the will to find answers of-ten serves as a spur to creativity, just as a lack of determination precludes the solving of problems.

Many people still blame the disability community for New York City's failure to provide street toilets after the four-month experiment.[12] Yet the reason for this fail-ure was that the community boards, indi-vidually, voted against the JCDecaux plan, which included, with each public toilet, two or three obtrusive advertising kiosks. Al-though JCDecaux intended these kiosks to add considerable profit to its operating ex-penses, the community boards objected to having their neighborhoods cluttered with advertising.

The *New York Times* misinterpretation of the accessible street toilet issue is no sur-prise considering the frequent failures of even the medical profession to be sensi-tive to the concerns of people with dis-abilities. Until the 1990s, entrances to—and bathrooms in—many hospitals were built without consideration for wheelchair acces-sibility; in fact, bathrooms in many doc-tors' offices are still inaccessible. In order for examining tables to meet the demands of "universal design," thus becoming usable by people with mobility impairments as well as others—such as older people and small

children—the tables require a relatively sim-ple technological device enabling them to be lowered and raised. These kinds of tables, however, are rarely found in medical facili-ties. Physicians infrequently take advantage of the easy enlargement of typed material, using computers or copying machines, to offer written instructions in large print for people who are partially sighted. Nor do medical practitioners tend to utilize the tape recorder to give written information to blind people.

To allow for communication between medical personnel and people who are hard of hearing, assistive listening devices, such as the kind employed in theaters, are needed but rarely provided in medical facilities. Al-though required by the ADA, sign language interpreters are seldom available for deaf people during their medical procedures, as demonstrated by the refusal of Mount Sinai Medical Center to provide a sign language interpreter for Jeffrey Bravin, the deaf hus-band of a hearing pregnant woman attend-ing Lamaze classes.[13] The center had ille-gally discriminated against the husband, violating state and federal laws requiring accommodations for people with disabil-ities. Alan J. Rich, lawyer for the couple, said that "the birth...was like a 'Marx Brothers movie,' with Mrs. Bravin 'trying to interpret between contractions,' to ex-plain what Mr. Bravin was supposed to be doing."

As with the installation of lifts on buses, accessibility in medical facilities requires a new approach, relating rather common-place technology to the needs of people with disabilities. In 1990, the Center for Indepen-dence of the Disabled in New York received a major grant from the Robert Wood John-son Foundation to establish a primary care facility, open to all members of the commu-nity, but totally accessible to people with disabilities.[14] The Downtown Family Care Center, opened in August 1995, marked the first time that a disability service and advocacy group, such as an independent living center, received funding to provide medical care in an environment consistent with universal design. The fact that this center was an anomaly when it was conceived underscores the inaccessibility of many medical facilities, even in the 1990s.

Accessible Taxis

Although wheelchair-accessible taxis are found in a variety of locations throughout the world, some major cities have resisted this much-needed technology. Most minivans that have been converted into accessible taxis have, at the rear of the vehicle, a lowered floor, a manual ramp, and a hydraulic "kneeling" suspension. Wheelchair users who drive this type of modified minivan clearly demonstrate that this vehicle is technically viable as an accessible taxi. Nonetheless, until as late as 2000 technological infeasibility continued to be the explanation given for the unavailability of accessible taxis in many cities such as New York, the site of the largest taxi fleet in the country.[15]

The mechanical concepts for wheelchair accessible taxis, similar to the techniques used in accessible buses, have been available for many years. As a result of prodding by disability advocates, technology—similar to hydraulic lifts used to move goods on and off trucks—was applied to buses by the late 1970s. Employing either this technology or low-floor ramps, wheelchair-accessible taxis have proven to be a financial success, despite doubts about their profitability. As with accessible taxis, however, too often both business and government cling to rigidly-held, preconceived notions about the limits of technology despite evidence to the contrary.

Teletypewriters and Relay Systems

The Communications Act of 1934 ostensibly made the telephone accessible to everyone. In reality, however, people with hearing disabilities were excluded from utilizing this technology because modern methods of telephone amplification, as well as the teletypewriter (TTY), were as yet not invented. Considering the numbers of people who are deaf or hard of hearing at birth (or at an early age)—combined with those whose hearing diminishes with advancing years—a large segment of the population could not take advantage of the telephone without additional technology. Not until the 1964 invention of the TTY could the 1934 law be universally applied.[16] The use of the TTY became increasingly widespread after 1971 when a smaller, more compact, and more affordable model was developed.

Because of lack of consultation with those being served by the TTY, a problem arose regarding the naming of this new technology. Though in 1979 the TTY was renamed the telecommunication device for the deaf (TDD), the designation was changed again in 1990 to text telephone (TT) when the TDD proved useful not only for deaf people, but also for others, such as people with speech impairments. Since the sign for TT in American Sign Language is similar to the sign for toilet, the deaf community insisted on returning to the TTY designation.

A flashing light signals the "ringing" of the TTY, a "telephone" comprised of a typewriter and a narrow screen. The TTY allows deaf people—by typing messages to each other—to communicate on the telephone. The relay system combined the technologies of the TTY and the telephone, enabling a deaf person and a hearing person to communicate. Either the deaf person or the hearing person can initiate a phone call by dialing a special 800 number. Then, the operator acts as an intermediary between the two parties, typing to the deaf person and speaking to the hearing one. California was the first of only a few states with statewide relay systems until Title IV of the ADA required that one relay system function throughout the country by July 26, 1993. Whereas the law necessitating lifts on buses was a catalyst for employing available technology, the TTY created the possibility for real implementation of an existing 1934 law.

A Clash of Cultures

When Mother Teresa, reflecting her ascetic religious vision, refused to include modern appliances such as dishwashers and washing machines in her planned New York City homeless shelter in 1989, she discovered that the city building code required one of the mechanical devices she had rejected, the elevator. Not recognizing the danger—as well as the humiliation—to mobility-impaired people, Mother Teresa intended to have them carried up and down the stairs. Deriding the regulation mandating elevators, Philip K. Howard failed to grasp the significance of this traditional technology for a great number of homeless individuals: "No person decided to spite Mother Teresa. It [an elevator] was the law. And what it [the law] required offends common sense."[17] For many low-income people with disabilities for whom stairs are a formidable barrier, the elevator is a necessity, not, as Howard contended, a frivolous means of satisfying "middle-class standards."

Furthermore, Howard's indication that Mother Teresa's Missionaries of Charity abandoned their intention to build a homeless shelter in New York City because of their problem with the elevator is inaccurate.[18] In fact, they did not leave New York City because of the elevator controversy, but rather because they decided that their funds would

go further in a developing country than in the United States. Yet the determination of the disability community to refuse to compromise about the elevator had been appropriate. Not merely a gratuitous time or labor-saving convenience, the elevator for a person unable to climb stairs means independence, dignity, and equality.

The One-Step Campaign

Another illustration of an effort to employ a commonplace technology that would serve people with disabilities, as well as older people and others, is the One-Step Campaign that began in New York City in 1993. Because of an architectural tradition in the city, many apartment buildings, stores, and restaurants were built with a single step in front of their entrances. For most people who walk, a single step is hardly noticeable; for most wheelchair users, however, that step is insurmountable without the burden and indignity of securing help. Generally, building a ramp as a level-changing device is "readily achievable" under the ADA as well as an improvement to business, for an accessible establishment is available to an increased number of customers, including those with baby carriages and shopping carts.

Since constructing a ramp in place of a single step can be easily accomplished with little difficulty or expense, in most cases this modification is required by the ADA as well as many local laws. The reason the One-Step Campaign has been a greater problem than disability activists had assumed is not related to the alterations required. Rather, the difficulty stems from the inability of too many business people to alter their thinking and appreciate the benefits that would accrue—not only to the general public, but to their own financial interests—by replacing single steps with ramps.[19]

Wheelchair Ingenuity

People with motor impairments not only required changes in the built environment, but also ingenuity in wheelchair design. Although the 1937 Everest & Jennings (E&J) wheelchair patent was an improvement over the former model, further modifications were stifled by E&J's monopolistic control of the wheelchair market.[20] A combination of the 1977 United States Justice Department antitrust lawsuit and the newly-emerging wheelchair industry terminated E&J's national and international stranglehold on the production and distribution of wheelchairs. Moreover, between the 1940s and the 1980s, the lack of rehabilitation engineers with disabilities played a significant role in the failure of wheelchair modernization. Competition did not serve wheelchair users until the early 1980s.[21] With the dramatic increase in the number of wheelchair-using rehabilitation engineers, as well as the variety of innovations springing forth from diverse parts of the world, wheelchair design has been revolutionized.

Because of the devastating effects of violent conflict, disease, and inadequate medical care, developing countries—often plagued by rough terrain and limited materials—have been a source of creativity in the construction and maintenance of wheelchairs. As Ralf D. Hotchkiss explains:

> There's a level of hands-on understanding that a lot of Third World bike builders and blacksmiths have that can inform the application of our new mathematical optimization [wheelchair] models. You need to mix the new with the old. . . . With rougher roads and fewer cars, they [wheelchair users in developing countries] have far more use for all-terrain wheelchairs. With far less money to buy new chairs, many more riders repair, modify and improve their own chairs. By helping them network and share their developments, we have tapped into a gold mine of new wheelchair designs.[22]

The foremost U.S. wheelchair inventor and designer, as well as the leading disseminator of information on wheelchair technology worldwide, Ralf D. Hotchkiss received the prestigious 1989 MacArthur Award and the 1994 Henry B. Betts Award. Setting an example for originators of assistive technologies for people with disabilities, Hotchkiss eschews patenting his mobility devices. Instead, he leaves them in the public domain in order to encourage the continuity of the creative process, thus endeavoring to prevent a reoccurrence of the E&J fiasco.

Not beguiled by high-tech glamour, Hotchkiss prefers practical solutions that benefit the greatest number of people at the least cost. For example, he indicates that more people will be served by inexpensive, easily repairable, customized wheelchairs and barrier-free environments than by extravagant technologies such as computerized walking stimulators for people with spinal cord injuries.[23] In addition, he has realized that increasing the mobility of wheelchair users enhances the employment opportunities of people with disabilities, a demographic group dramatically underrepresented in the workforce of every country. Echoing Roberts's and Heumann's accomplishments in the World Institute on Disability and appreciating the common concerns of wheelchair riders, Hotchkiss's focus on disability issues is international.

In 1989 at San Francisco State, Hotchkiss established the Wheeled Mobility Center, from which his International Wheelchair Program emanates, serving both students on campus as well as in the developing countries to which he travels. Although Hotchkiss fears that the task exceeds human ingenuity, he seeks to devise a wheelchair that can traverse unpaved rural areas and yet maneuver easily in a home. Because wheelchair users understand the requirements of other wheelchair users like themselves, Hotchkiss encourages the inclusion of people with disabilities in rehabilitation technologies. Furthermore, he has observed in his travels all over the world that people tend to trust the technical expertise of others living with similar impairments. Recognizing that there are twenty million people—predominantly in developing countries—in need of wheelchairs, Hotchkiss's ultimate goal is to set in motion the education of an army of sixty thousand professional technicians building and repairing wheelchairs. Hotchkiss's creativity is in direct contrast to the early wheelchair manufacturers, whose closed minds were reflected in the inflexibility of their wheelchairs.

Before the new approach to wheelchair technology that Hotchkiss embodies, models were not adapted to the needs of the individual user as is, for example, the fluid aerodynamic prototype employed by the modern wheelchair athlete or wheelchair dancer. Not only do modern motorized and computerized wheelchairs and scooters suit the technology to the consumer, but they also serve people with different kinds and degrees of disability. Unable to propel the chair by themselves until the invention of these assistive devices, many quadriplegics were indeed "bound" by and "confined" to their wheelchairs because the chairs did not offer freedom of independent mobility. With older people's increasing acceptance—and society's decreasing stigmatizing—of motorized scooters, advancing age no longer deters many people's participation in the social mainstream. Moreover, increasingly manufacturers are employing modular design, which refers to detachable units or components of mechanisms. With modular design, wheelchairs and scooters may become reasonably priced and easily repaired so that users may have control of their assistive devices. Folding and modular motorized wheelchairs, how-ever, are rarely produced although the technology is available. Modular design is a significant engineering technique because modular and folding wheelchairs and scooters usually fit in automobiles, adding greatly to the mobility of the user.

In Andrew Wyeth's famous 1942 painting "Christina's World," a young woman disabled by polio is sitting on the ground looking out on her limited vista.[24] John Hockenberry, in his 1995 memoir *Moving Violations: War Zones, Wheelchairs, and Declarations of Independence,* and in his 1996 one-man performance *Spoke Man,* described his experiences as a wheelchair-riding journalist, traversing the world.[25] The circumscribed view of the subject of Wyeth's painting is being supplanted by the free-wheeling and liberating vision of Hockenberry's work.

Accessible Classrooms and Laboratories

Exhibiting a resourcefulness reminiscent of Hotchkiss's ingenuity, mechanical engineer Ira Cochin of the New Jersey Institute of Technology and biologist Ben Van Wagner of Fresno Pacific College created innovative classrooms and laboratories.[26] In 1977 Cochin, who was blind and later became deaf, devised instruments—in what he called the Macrolab—so that people with sensory and speech impairments could be integrated with nondisabled people in schools and industry. For example, Cochin connected an oscilloscope to a microphone so that deaf (as well as hearing) students literally could see how frequencies changed by viewing sound waves on a screen. With Cochin's instruments, blind people—by interpreting sound—were able to determine the chemical constituents of a product, using a modified spectrometer, and to accurately measure weights up to a milligram, using a precision balance scale. Referring to

the "designing" of an early speech synthesizer at the lab, William Skawinski, blind
chemist at the New Jersey Institute of Technology who directed the Macrolab, indicated that the key to the program was that
the students served were involved in the
development of all of these instruments.

After his own careful research and much
medical consultation, Ben Van Wagner created an environment that no longer precip-
itated "sick-building syndrome." Van Wagner, a professor of science education, describes how he felt when he was diagnosed
with multiple chemical sensitivity: "The toxins of the synthetic 1990s had finally weak-
ened my immune system," Van Wagner observes, for "I was suffering from extreme
fatigue, lightheadedness, and arthritis so
bad that I could barely walk." Van Wagner
feared that since he had become allergic to
formaldehyde, he might not be able to go
on teaching.

Still undaunted, Van Wagner persisted in
his probing and ultimately discovered the
solutions that he was seeking:

> I have adapted my zoology courses so as to use
> alternative dissection materials from the local
> fish market, non-formaldehyde substitute
> specimens and computer technology....
> My college has ... allowed me to establish
> a new "toxin-free" classroom outside of the
> official science building and has provided me
> with an excellent office with a window that
> opens, which frees me from my ... air-tight
> office.... As I continue to research the issue
> of Environmental Illness, it is apparent that
> it is a significant problem for many students
> and adults.

People with disabilities, including those
with sensory and speech impairments and
multiple chemical sensitivity, can be successful students and employees when they
are afforded appropriate, reasonable accommodations.

The Computer as an Accommodation

The computer serves not only those with
multiple chemical sensitivity and motor impairments, but also many others with a variety of disabilities. Better than the TTY
and the relay system, the new "information superhighway" will allow deaf people to
use a telephone that includes an interactive
television monitor. Consequently, they will
be able to employ the language they generally consider most natural, sign language.
Just as this new technology can serve as
ears for deaf people, the Kurzweil reader
and computer add-ons, such as the voice
synthesizer and Braille keyboard, can provide eyes for blind people.[27] For example,
although totally blind, Dr. Peter Torpey—
who has not required eyesight to pursue
the ideal color-printer in seventeen years of
creating software—types with a Braille computer keyboard at the Xerox Corporation.[28]

Computers also accommodate many people with cognitive and learning disabilities,
as well as those with autism: "for many
autistics, the internet is Braille."[29] Temple
Grandin, author of *Thinking in Pictures: And
Other Reports from My Life with Autism,*[30] seizes
on the internet and the web as "the best
possible metaphors for her own brand of
thinking." In response to one critic's observation that *Thinking in Pictures* has "occa-
sional signs of autism, abrupt transitions,
sudden leaps of thought not easy for the
reader to follow," Grandin says, "I'm going
to write another book in which I try to
explain how associative thinking [leaps of
thought] works like links on the internet."

People who are unable to use their hands
because of, for example, paralysis or severe
repetitive strain injury are still capable of using voice-activated computers by means of
software such as IBM's Dragon Dictate.[31] In
the early 1990s, veteran *New York Newsday* reporter Susan Harrigan developed a serious
case of carpal tunnel syndrome resulting

from her typing on a computer keyboard.[32] She credits her use of a voice activated computer, in combination with the ADA's "reasonable accommodation" requirement, for the opportunity to resume her career. After Christopher Reeve became a quadriplegic because of a horse-riding accident, Dragon Dictate enabled him to continue using a computer. Brian Dickenson, who has ALS—"which has stripped him of the power to speak, swallow, move his legs or arms, wiggle his fingers or turn his head"—is still able to work as a columnist for the *Rhode Island Providence Journal-Bulletin,* using his eye movements to write on a computer employing the Eyegaze system.[33]

Furthermore, advances in telecommunications have ushered in choices heretofore unavailable to people with disabilities, such as the option of bringing the workplace or classroom into the home by means of computer technology. Computers function interactively so that students with disabilities can use distance learning to participate in the classroom and employees with disabilities can take part in workplace activities, even though they are not physically present. Moreover, virtual reality technology is being used as a tool, preparing people with disabilities for real-life situations.[34] Judy Brewer—director of the Web Accessibility Initiative International Program at the World Wide Web Cambridge Consortium—points out that not only is it incumbent on people with disabilities to learn new technologies, but they must also claim them as they are evolving, as illustrated by the interaction between the disability population and individuals developing technical guidelines for writing accessible web pages.[35]

Evidence that computers tend to level the playing field, thus minimizing the limiting effects of disability, was presented at the May 1998 New Orleans conference of the President's Council of Employment of People with Disabilities. The researchers began by examining one easy-to-track disability, spinal cord injury. Consistent with the employment statistics for the general disability population, only one-third of those with spinal cord injuries were employed. Yet those who were already computer literate before their injury found jobs faster than those who did not have computer skills. Of those employees with spinal cord injuries, two-thirds used computers on the job. There was no salary gap between employees with spinal cord injuries and nondisabled employees when both groups were computer users. Those employees with spinal cord injuries who were not computer users had an income 36 percent lower than their nondisabled counterparts.

Although Brewer observes that a partnership was developing between industry, government, research organizations, and the disability community regarding web access, she finds no such industrywide interest in working with the disability community in the development of computers themselves. For example, accessibility and costs still are significant deterrents to getting computers to people with disabilities. Paul Schrader, director of the National Technological Program at the American Foundation for the Blind in Chicago, notes that despite the later improvement in the system for people with visual disabilities, when Windows—the visually-based operating system for Microsoft—opened, the door was closed for blind people.[36]

While computer costs have decreased, the prices are too often out of reach for people with disabilities, many of whom are unemployed or dependent on limited benefits. Disability advocates suggest that since computers become obsolete so quickly in corporate America, procedures could be implemented to make these no longer state-of-the-art computers available to people with disabilities. Given the multiplicity of web sites particularly geared to people with specific disabilities, the internet is an especially valuable resource for this population. Having diminished less quickly than the cost of computers, the cost of add-on technology—necessary to make computers accessible for those with a variety of impairments—doubles the price of computers for many people with disabilities. Just as including access into the original plan of a building is simpler and less expensive than renovation, designing access into new computer technology is easier and less costly than add-ons. Besides, consistent with the concept of universal design, much of the computer technology developed to accommodate people with disabilities ultimately serves the general population.

Psychopharmacology

Just as computers have opened new possibilities for many people with physical impairments, the development of new pharmaceuticals has removed barriers for many of those with severe psychiatric problems. Such people no longer feel as restricted by their disabilities—in their professional as well as their personal lives—as they did before the advent of these drug therapies. Yet psychopharmacology is a double-edged sword, requiring those who employ this new technology to confront critical issues.

According to Dr. Peter Kramer, author of *Listening to Prozac,* new medications serve many people with psychiatric disabilities who would never be open to psychoanalytic approaches.[37] Yet even about his patients on psychotherapeutic drugs, Kramer observes, "When medication altered their temperament, as occasionally it appeared to do, my response was ambivalent. Yes, the men and women attained relief, but perhaps something precious was lost in the process."[38] Peter R. Breggin, author of *Toxic Psychiatry,* adds that the trend in psy-

chopharmacology may be resulting in cosmetic drugs devised to produce specific personality changes or to induce docility or, even worse, pharmaceuticals that impair brain activity much like amphetamines or cocaine.[39] Moreover, the specter of rising health expenditures has elevated cost-effectiveness to such a premium that the quick-fix of chemical treatment appears to be the present-day panacea, replacing more time-consuming, personal, and expensive psychoanalytic procedures.

Cognizant of the pharmaceutical industry's search for expanded markets, advocates for children with psychiatric disabilities are apprehensive about the speed with which antidepressant drugs—never approved by the Food and Drug Administration for children or adolescents—have flowed into the children's market: "Critics worry... that not enough is known about how antidepressants work on the growing brain and that cost-conscious insurance companies will turn too quickly to drugs instead of costly psychotherapy."[40] Although roughly three million children have severe depression and over two thousand between the ages of five and nineteen commit suicide every year, most of the antidepressant medicines prescribed for children have been based solely on medications for adults.[41] Without denying the possible value of the appropriate use of drug therapy in specific instances, Dr. Leon Eisenberg, professor of social medicine at Harvard Medical School, is concerned about the effect on youngsters of the change in the practice of medicine. "Managed care and psychotropic drugs are a Satanic mix," Eisenberg warns.

In addition, disability advocacy groups—such as Citizens for Responsible Care in Psychiatry and Research—and bioethicists, as well as federal and state agencies, question the ethical appropriateness of experimentation in which researchers either use drugs that provoke psychotic symptoms in psychiatric patients or deprive these patients of the medications they require:

> Federal ethics officials estimate that there have been one hundred to three hundred experiments in which patients were taken off their medicines when no new medicines were being tried; rather, they were taken off their medicines to observe the patients as they relapsed in order to study the illnesses. Among those experiments were some in which potentially toxic drugs like PCP, a hallucinogen known as "angel dust," and ketamine, an anesthetic related [to] it, were given to provoke patients into relapses.[42]

Dr. John K. Hsiao, a psychiatrist representing the National Institute of Mental Health in Bethesda, Maryland, indicates that although nothing should be done that could permanently harm patients, "We can ask patients to put up with an exacerbation of symptoms. They should be given a chance to contribute to science. . . . We don't have animal models to study, so we have to do what work we can in humans."

On the other hand, Dr. Adil Shamoo—a biomedical ethicist at the University of Maryland at Baltimore County—who for years has studied the use of vulnerable people as subjects in experimentation, notes, "Many of these experiments . . . give no medical benefits to the subjects. . . . There have been several attempted and successful suicides among the subjects of the experiments. There are no other kinds of medical experiments in which you induce the disease in humans to study it." In Fall 1997, *The Journal of Neuropsychopharmacology* reported on controversial experiments: In one, "thirteen men and women with schizophrenia were not only taken off their medicines, but then injected with ketamine to provoke psychotic symptoms in the subjects . . . so the symptoms could be studied"; in another, "thirty-eight patients were given a drug called methylphenidate, which quickly threw 60 percent of them into severe psy-

chotic episodes." Describing himself as being used as a "guinea pig," Andrew Brownstein, a person with severe manic-depression and a subject of a study at the National Institute of Mental Health, comments, "I don't know how doctors can watch you be in that kind of pain and not do anything."

In *Conquering Schizophrenia: A Father, His Son, and a Medical Breakthrough,* Peter Weiden describes the remarkably beneficial effects that new pharmaceuticals have had on his schizophrenic son.[43] Not available until 1997, these drug therapies significantly improve the functioning of schizophrenics without side effects, Weiden states. In addition, he points out that although psychoanalysis may work with neurotics, even Freud acknowledged that talking therapy is not as effective for schizophrenics. Marvin Spieler, who refers to himself as "a mentally ill consumer," says, "My illness will be with me until I die. I take my 'pink beauties' as I call lithium carbonate to maintain my sanity. For I know without them the gates of Riker's Island [a New York City prison] or worse will open for me."[44] Despite the dangers these pharmaceuticals pose, experiences such as Weiden's and Spieler's will encourage the continued development of such technology.

Bioethical Dilemmas

Decisions regarding the appropriate uses of technology require reference to real human beings in specific circumstances. Given the new procreative alternatives with which people are presented by biological and genetic engineering, who could criticize the desire of prospective parents to use this technology to prevent their baby from being born with sickle cell anemia or cystic fibrosis? Yet the capacity to create designer offspring—with predetermined physical characteristics, intelligence quotients, or personality traits—is too reminiscent of the distorted vision of the eugenicist. Even the technology that allows expectant parents to acquire increasingly detailed information about the fetus creates new ethical and pragmatic problems. The practice, in some parts of China, of aborting female fetuses in order to produce sons rather than daughters has become prevalent because of the "one child per couple" dictum, employed to reduce the population. We may agree that the moral issue, as well as the resulting gender imbalance, necessitates education and perhaps stronger measures to discourage this misguided and potentially dangerous use of new reproductive technology.

How do we deal, however, with a response by some deaf couples to a new option? Learning they could choose to abort if the fetus had inherited their predisposition to deafness, they indicate, on the contrary, that they would choose to abort if the fetus did *not* inherit their deafness. Do we accuse them of limiting their child's horizons? Or do we accept the argument that the deaf community's isolation from the mainstream has resulted in a unique culture and language that this couple might seek to protect as a cherished legacy?

Although the surgical procedure known as a "cochlear implant" tends not to be controversial for postlingually profoundly deaf adults, do we recommend cochlear implants for children who are prelingually profoundly deaf? While these devices that provide electrical stimulation to the auditory nerve have been used successfully since about 1980, language acquisition was considered more difficult when *first* exposure to sound came from a cochlear implant, rather than from the exquisite natural hearing of an infant.[45] Yet by the late 1990s, prelingually deaf children with profound hearing loss were able to develop understanding and speech by means of cochlear implants

in conjunction with intensive therapy by skilled professionals.[46] Dr. Randolph Mallory, director of the Deafness Rehabilitation master's program at New York University, questions the value of procedures such as this one, suggesting that perhaps we should accept being deaf as "another way of being in the world and involvement with Deaf culture as a reasonable alternative" to mainstream society.[47] On the other hand, critics of this view argue that the focus on Deaf culture has been excessive, given the great number of Americans who have sufficient hearing loss to affect communication, approximately twenty-eight million, and the relatively small number of this population who use American Sign Language, roughly one-half million.[48]

Commenting on the ethical issues concerning conjoined (Siamese) twins, Dr. Alice D. Dreger, a historian of anatomy, notes that the implications of this condition go beyond its rare occurrence of one in fifty thousand to one hundred thousand:

> Dr. Dreger and others who share her views see parallels between medical attitudes toward conjoined twins, and toward those children born with other anomalies, including ambiguous genitals, dwarfism, congenital deafness, and the like. Such conditions have invited aggressive attempts at fixing often through a long series of operations, medications and rehabilitations; and most have required that the therapies be performed on children too young to have a say in whether they want to be treated or not.... [Dreger] argues that decisions about who is in pain and who should be fixed— whatever their purported abnormality— must go beyond mechanical, economic or even philosophic considerations, to include the voices of those who know best [people who live with the condition and who are capable of commenting on it.][49]

Bioethicist Dr. Alan Fleischman observes the tension in the dominant culture—increasing accommodation of the disabilities in adults with simultaneous decreasing tolerance of abnormality in children: "We'll blame families if they knew there would be an abnormal child but chose not to abort," Fleischman fears.

Since parents usually function as the advocate for their disabled child, how do we judge the 1983 case of Baby Jane Doe, a newborn with spina bifida?[50] Given a negative prognosis, the baby's parents refused the shunt operation that could have drained the fluid from their infant's brain, and probably would have improved her medical condition. Based on a more optimistic medical judgment, the government sued the baby's hospital, arguing that she was entitled to the surgery as a civil right according to Section 504 of the Rehabilitation Act of 1973. When, as in the Baby Jane Doe case, different physicians offer diametrically opposite prognoses about complex technical procedures, what criteria can parents use to make a serious medical decision?

How reliable can we consider medical research initiated not by scientists and physicians, but by parent advocates of children with disabilities? If the impairment, as in Down syndrome, is progressive, and the promising parent-directed therapy is at worst harmless, some parent advocates contend that they cannot wait for well-controlled, large, randomized, double-blind studies. With only a high school education, self-taught Dixie Lawrence, who formerly ran an adoption agency for severely disabled children, challenged the medical establishment after she adopted a one-year-old baby girl with Down syndrome.[51] The results of the nutritional formula Lawrence devised, now taken by over fifteen hundred children with Down syndrome, including her own daughter, is deemed hopeful by physicians and scientists, such as pediatrician Dr. Peter Wallstein, Down syndrome researcher Dr. Lawrence Becker, and nutritional scientist professor Jim Crow. Nevertheless, Dr. Allen Crocker, scientific advisor to the National Down Syndrome Congress, is skeptical of what he considers a still scientifically unproved formulation, supported only by anecdotal evidence.

Dr. Lawrence Leichman, however, found what he calls "scientifically significant" differences between those of his many patients with Down syndrome who were taking Lawrence's formula and those who were not. Leichman describes Lawrence's approach—dealing with Down syndrome as a treatable genetic problem—as "revolutionary because this is something parent-led, not physician-led, not scientist-led. Instead, there's a group of parents, and it's now become a very large group of parents, who said, 'We want to do something more for our children. Will you help us? If not help us, will you not stand in our way? If not stand in our way, will you at least follow us?' And that is revolutionary in medicine."

Upon what criteria should those making life or death determinations regarding who gets a donated organ—surgeons, nurses, psychiatrists, and social workers—base their decisions? Without interviewing the patient, the medical centers at Stanford University and the University of California at San Diego rejected Dr. Philip Bach's effort to sign up Sandra Jensen, a woman with Down syndrome, for a heart-lung transplant.[52] Because the doctors thought she would not be able to follow the complex schedule of post-transplant drugs, they considered her a poor risk for scarce organs. As the *New York Times* indicated:

> They picked the wrong woman to reject. Ms. Jensen, a lifelong advocate for the mentally disabled, was on hand when President George Bush signed the Americans with Disabilities Act in 1990. She and her friends raised a ruckus. Both medical centers eventually relented and she got her transplant at

Stanford in 1996, although she died six months later of complications unrelated to her mental disability.

In order to reconsider ethical dilemmas and standardize procedures pertaining to the process by which candidates for transplants are selected, new federal regulations were published in late March 1998.

Rather than regulations, however, many bioethical dilemmas require case-by-case judgments. Should we encourage the woman with multiple sclerosis, who has difficulty walking, to use a motorized scooter if the stigma she experiences outweighs the advantage of her increased mobility? How do we reply to the student in a wheelchair, who could easily attend school employing distance learning, but instead chooses not to take advantage of the technology because he prefers the socialization inherent in being physically present in school, even if it may require arduous and costly travel? People are best served by solutions provided not for categories or types, but tailor-made for a particular person in a specific situation.

The Internet and a Miracle Baby

Susan Scheer, a brilliant Yale graduate with spina bifida,[53] who had held several significant positions in New York City government, received the individualized care appropriate for her unusual medical needs.[54] After learning that she was going to have a baby, Scheer discovered, using the internet and email, "a wonderful network of people" who helped her with her pregnancy and delivery, as well as with caring for her infant daughter, Melissa, who doctors referred to as "a miracle baby":

> Because it was assumed that babies with spina bifida would not have a good quality of life, doctors did not close the spine, so the babies were allowed to get infections and die in the hospital. With improved antibiotics—and shunts to relieve the pressure of hydrocephalus—by 1960 doctors did close the spine, and these babies did not have to die or be developmentally delayed. But since there still weren't that many women around with spina bifida who had given birth to babies, doctors had neither experience nor literature to help these expectant mothers.

On the internet, Scheer fortunately found an especially knowledgeable and creative obstetrician in California who consulted with her team of doctors in New York City. Working together on many of her difficult medical issues, they developed a rotating schedule of antibiotics for Scheer. She describes one Memorial Day when she was experiencing very debilitating symptoms:

> My gastrointestinal specialist spent his entire vacation day searching the internet and faxing me a stack of articles that we could use to deal with my condition. This doctor had already figured out a way to stop my contractions, which had occurred dangerously early in my pregnancy. He halted the labor by using a pump that administered medication continuously, and with a monitor I could mark the contractions twice a day. When I stuck the monitor into the computer, it could be read in Atlanta, and they could readjust the medication when necessary.

She also received a great deal of support from people she met on the internet through "Disabled Mommies," one of the chat rooms of America Online. With some, she extended the relationship using email. In this way she got to know thirty-two mothers or pregnant women with disabilities, a few even with spina bifida, who told her about their experiences with pregnancy and motherhood.

Medical and Genetic Information

Because she orchestrated the use of the internet herself, Scheer could be certain that the technology would be used to serve her own purposes. Yet when institutions determine how computers store, retrieve, and process medical information, people may have cause for apprehension. Inasmuch as computers are altering diagnostic procedures dramatically, many medical professionals, especially in the mental health field, are concerned that the uniqueness of the individual is being disregarded. In fact, instead of being dealt with as individuals requiring appropriate treatment specifically designed for them, too often patients are being lumped into categories for short-term cost-effectiveness.

This approach is driving the prevailing trend in health care delivery in the United States. For example, in an effort to curb costs, an increasing number of companies are employing new computer technology to measure treatment of workers with psychiatric disabilities as therapists compare the symptoms of their patients with "a data base of hundreds of similar cases."[55] Maryland psychiatrist Dr. Harold Eist responds, "It is astonishing that someone could even produce outcomes studies. The doctor-patient relationship is as much ruled by art as by science. Medicine is too complex, individuals and their experiences differ so much, and there is so much chaos in biology that looking at outcomes studies can never direct you to what the appropriate treatment for any individual would be."

Moreover, A. G. Greitenstein, director of the Justice Resource Institute, warns that with computers there is less security than with paper charts: "We don't have someone policing the gates. So you have a huge opportunity for folks that are not supposed to be looking at people's records within institutions, accessing people's medical records without their consent, often without their knowledge."[56] Dr. Francis Collins, director of the National Center for Human Genome Research, refers to the impediments imposed on patients and physicians to ensure the privacy of medical records: "The system forces people to take drastic steps to protect themselves. It is putting a terrible burden on patients. [Doctors] are forced sometimes to have interactions with insurance agents or with other physicians or with HMOs where [doctors] have to pretend [they] don't have the information. It's a very strange dilemma—to choose between patient confidentiality and telling the truth."[57]

On the other hand, Larry Gostin, Georgetown University law professor, makes a cogent argument for sharing medical information: "We have a huge amount of data about a whole range of diseases—cancer, heart disease, schizophrenia. But all this information is kept by an individual doctor . . . or managed care organizations. If we could have systematic, retrospective studies to look back at diseases, . . . there would be a great deal of information we could find out." Information privacy consultant Robert Gelman refers to the capacity to track down the names of women who took the anti-nausea drug DES while they were pregnant. As a result of collecting this information requiring access to many medical records, health researchers were able to make the link between the drug and certain cancers in the children of these women.

Genetic testing has been introduced into clinical practice at a time of decreasing privacy and confidentiality resulting from computerization. The *New York Times* reports that "it has become increasingly clear that the Human Genome Project, the plan [initiated in 1990] to sequence human DNA and map the position of human genes, would have to turn into a project in computer science."[58] Thus two technologies, computer and genetic, have fused: "the computer is the management vehicle, the language to decipher, download, organize, and manipulate genes," explains Jeremy Rifkin, author of *The Biotech Century*.[59] Despite the potential medical value, computerized DNA sequencing and genetic mapping raise unprecedented questions.

How do we determine what bioethicist Adrienne Asch refers to as "the fair use of genetic information for both medical and non-medical purposes, such as employment or insurance?"[60] How do we ascertain the social repercussions of providing individuals and families with information regarding their genetic predisposition to illnesses and disabilities? Patient advocate Mary Jo Ellis Kahn points out the conflict between the promise of a breast cancer cure that the Human Genome Project provides and the legal and ethical problems that lag far behind the scientific breakthroughs: "I am a breast cancer patient with a family history, and I have two daughters, and although finding out our genetic status may be very useful to the family to learn who needs to be followed more carefully and what medical care we should receive, it's too dangerous at this point because my daughters could lose their health insurance based on just testing."[61]

Reiterating Kahn's concern about health insurance, Patricia King of Georgetown Law School notes other problems—such as privacy of information and accessibility of medical care, as well as discrimination based on an individual's genetic traits:

> Not only do you have a problem getting health insurance; you may have a problem getting employment because, remember, most health insurance in this country is provided for by employers. Health insurance is expensive. So you not only have to worry about your coverage; you have to worry about your employment. And you have to worry

about what to tell your children or, indeed, whether to have children. So the information is quite powerful. And this information feeds on existing inequities in our system. We can't currently protect persons who know they are at risk for certain diseases or, in fact, have certain diseases, with respect to health insurance or employment.... We can't yet assure you that the information, should we get it, would be protected and kept confidential.

When a patient informed her insurance company that she had a mutated gene that significantly predisposed her to breast cancer, her request for coverage for removal of both breasts was denied on the grounds that she already had a preexisting condition, a genetic defect, when she took out her health policy.[62] Twenty states have passed laws prohibiting health maintenance organizations and health insurance companies from increasing the cost of insurance for people who have a gene mutation. Yet many people belonging to support groups of families with different genetic disorders believe that they have encountered not only insurance discrimination but also employment bias because of their condition.

In late 1996, companies marketing tests to determine whether or not women have the gene mutations that significantly increase their risks for breast or ovarian cancer informed physicians of the potential for insurance and job discrimination. In addition, physicians were advised that the Equal Employment Opportunity Commission's interpretation of the language in the ADA indicates that discrimination based on the results of genetic tests is unlawful. However, the EEOC's associate legal counsel, Peggy Mastroianni, warned that this opinion has not yet been tested in the courts. Apprehension regarding discrimination resulting from genetic testing has broad implications, for tests have been—and are being—developed for other diseases, such as cystic fibrosis, Huntington's disease, and an inherited form of ALS.[63]

Other issues involving the value of these tests remain unresolved. First, the fact that a person tests positive for a specific gene mutation does not mean that the individual will contract the related disease. Second, information about an individual's probability of contracting a disease does not ensure that appropriate treatment exists for that condition, as in the case of breast cancer. Finally, it is often difficult to weigh the medical benefits of presenting an individual or a family with information concerning predisposition to disease against the psychological toll.

Furthermore, how can we discourage the patenting of DNA sequences, the raw genetic data? Instead of publishing the results of new research, biotech firms tend to keep "intellectual property" secret, even though 90 percent of them are associated with universities.[64] When discoveries about the human genome are not shared in the scientific community, the probability of detecting flaws or achieving new insights decreases considerably. For example, a biotech company has patented the genetic sequence for toxic shock syndrome although the firm has not developed an appropriate drug for this dangerous disease. The director of the National Center for Genome Research believes that only newly-designed drugs should be patented, for he fears that biotech companies—from which the infusion of funds for genetic research flows—employ business rather than science ethics.

"Slash, Burn, and Poison"

Yet genetically-based therapies, as for example in the treatment of breast cancer, are indeed promising. This new approach one day may allow for "manipulations far more subtle and specific" than what Dr. Susan Love—surgeon, researcher, fund-raiser, and breast cancer activist—calls surgery, radiation, and chemotherapy: "slash, burn, and poison."[65] To illustrate, if a woman got breast cancer because of a specific mutation on a particular gene causing uncontrolled growth—as opposed to modulated growth, which occurs in normal cells—scientists would figure out an injection to turn the mutated gene off.[66] This potential paradigm shift, more likely to be available to the next generation than this one, is comparable to the 1960s conversion from radical mastectomy to present surgical techniques, radiation, and chemotherapy. Because the medical community has not kept up with the research, Love, despite her skepticism, still uses current traditional procedures, for nothing else has proven effective at all. Yet she looks forward to the future. Karen Stabiner, author of *To Dance with the Devil: The New War on Breast Cancer*, observes: "Change, [Love] would argue, will come only if we start looking at breast cancer in a totally different way. Imagine breast cancer cells as rehabilitatable criminals, she would suggest; we need to change the environment in order to change them."[67]

Contrary to the increasingly common recommendations of the pharmaceutical industry[68] and the American College of Obstetrics and Gynecology,[69] Love argues that long-term—more than ten years—use of replacement hormones for postmenopausal women significantly adds to their risk of developing breast cancer. In fact, Love criticizes both the pharmaceutical industry and the medical profession for redefining menopause as an illness, "just as the baby boomers hit middle age," thus creating a disability out of a natural condition: "A woman's ovaries don't shut down at menopause. They continue to produce low levels of hormones well into a woman's eighties. Synthetic hormones don't replace something that is missing when women reach menopause. They add something that is not naturally there," Love asserts.[70]

Supporting Love, Dr. Christiane Northrup—cofounder of the Women to Women Clinic in Yarmouth, Maine, and a leading women's health advocate—asks, "Why would the female body be designed to go into planned obsolescence at age forty-two?"[71] Like Love, Northrup publicizes her concern that women may be risking overdoses of estrogen because of misinformed doctors and greedy pharmaceutical companies. Northrup states that "there are mechanisms in the body to take over what might be changing during menopause." Finding fault with what Northrup refers to as "the same one-size-fits-all" hormone therapy for all women, both Northrup and Love claim that women can control their health as they mature by eating properly, staying fit, and maintaining emotional vitality rather than by accepting the standardized regimen of hormone replacement.[72]

Like Love and Northrup, the National Breast Cancer Coalition—mainly women with breast cancer and members of their families—works to bring visibility to breast cancer and funding to research of the disease.[73] Founded in 1991 by Fran Visco, the organization has demonstrated on the steps of the Capitol and lobbied members of Congress. Visco observes that "before we began, the federal government spent less than $90 million on breast cancer research. This year [1997] we're spending $530 million on breast cancer research." Having learned from the AIDS activists who began in the early 1980s to procure funds where there seemed to be none, breast cancer activists are promoting research and pressuring the medical community for new kinds of treatments.[74]

Transforming Scientific Orthodoxy: AIDS Activism

Steven Epstein in *Impure Science*[75] recounts how AIDS activists, transforming themselves into self-educated analysts of drug regulations, "have mastered the science of their disease in a manner that changed the history of medicine."[76] They denounced what they saw as the unnecessarily sluggish pace of the drug approval process and self-indulgently elegant guidelines of scientific bodies, such as the Food and Drug Administration (FDA) and the National Institutes of Health (NIH).[77] Reaffirming the 1970s feminist health movement's skepticism of traditional medical protocols, Gay Men's Health Crisis—in concert with other AIDS groups, especially Act-Up (AIDS Coalition To Unleash Power)—pressured the FDA into relaxing standards used to determine a drug's efficacy.[78] Rather than precipitating confusion, this increased freedom produced new drugs, created and tested with the guidance of AIDS activists.

Time magazine "Man of the Year" for 1996, Dr. David Ho, played a major role in the paradigm shift in scientists' picture of AIDS development. When scientists believed that the AIDS virus lay dormant during the early and middle years of infection, doctors delayed treatment until the virus appeared to emerge from its hibernation; however, the experiments of Dr. Ho and University of Alabama AIDS researcher Dr. George Shaw presents a different model of AIDS:

> The results showed that in every day of every year, in every infected person, HIV produced not thousands, not millions, but *billions* of copies of itself. And every day the body launched billions of immune cells to counter the threat. The wonder was not that the immune system eventually crashed. Given such intense fighting and heavy casualties, the wonder was that it lasted so long.[79]

Consequently, instead of waiting until the reemergence of the illness, oncologists began using combinations of the newly-formulated drugs from the very start of the infection, thus changing AIDS from a fatal disease into a chronic one similar to diabetes or hypertension.

Noting the increasingly remarkable pace of AIDS research, Dr. Jerome Groopman, Harvard Medical School professor, is concerned about those people infected with the AIDS virus who may not have access to the expensive drugs required for their survival.[80] Besides battling their disease, many of those who are insured are forced to cope with bottom-line oriented HMOs reluctant to pay for so-called experimental new therapies. Certainly, many of the AIDS patients included among the forty million uninsured Americans are unlikely to be able to afford the approximately fifteen thousand dollars a year for medication necessary to sustain their lives. "Though Dr. Groopman says that 'time is of the essence' in treating the HIV-positive now, he is frustrated by a deficient health care system that can't move remotely 'as quickly as science is moving.'"

Ultimately, most scientists are convinced that only a vaccine will put an end to the worldwide AIDS epidemic.[81] Echoing the AIDS activists' successful assault on the FDA focus on pure, rather than practical, science, Bruce G. Weniger, a member of the Presidential Advisory Council on HIV and AIDS, and Max Essex, professor of virology at Harvard and chairman of the Harvard AIDS Institute, call for the NIH to move beyond the "scientific orthodoxy" that is impeding the promising development of an AIDS vaccine.[82] Weniger and Essex criticize "the NIH culture" for minimizing the value of applied research, the empirical rather than theoretical science that could result in a vaccine that would "work to prevent HIV infection, or to forestall AIDS, or just to reduce contagiousness."

Referring to Salk's struggle to develop a polio vaccine in the early 1950s, Weniger and Essex note that "history teaches" that an organization different from the NIH "should run an expedited vaccine program in the face of a public health emergency." Although by 1949 John Enders and colleagues received a Nobel Prize for growing polio virus in test tubes, Salk "applied this discovery in developing a vaccine." Weniger and Essex extend the analogy between the Salk vaccine and a potential AIDs vaccine:

> But Enders, along with Albert Sabin and other eminent polio researchers, fought to stop trials of the Salk vaccine.... Calling Salk's vaccine "quackery" and "kitchen chemistry," they favored waiting for an ideal vaccine. The independent March of Dimes, whose principal mission was to stop polio, courageously put the Salk vaccine to the test anyway.
>
> On April 12, 1955, the headlines announced to an expectant world, "It Works!" The Sabin oral polio vaccine came into use around 1962. But the availability of the Salk vaccine seven years earlier saved tens of thousands of lives.

In 1997, scientists discovered that even when the AIDS virus could not be detected in the blood, it was still hiding in certain cells producing a reservoir of HIV.[83] At the 1998 Twelfth World AIDS Conference in Geneva, Dr. Ho and other researchers indicated that "they had gone back to the drawing board to map new strategies to eliminate the latent reservoir."[84] The day before the conference Dr. Ho declared, "Every nation must overcome denial and address this [AIDS] pandemic for what it really is—an international emergency in which sixteen thousand people are sentenced each day to a slow and miserable death."[85]

Less euphoric than the 1996 Eleventh World AIDS Conference in Vancouver, the Geneva conference emphasized the disappointments and problems: the failure of a promising AIDS vaccine; the lack of aggressive, preventative, worldwide programs promoting sex education, use of male and female condoms, and needle exchange; and the patients for whom drug therapy was not successful.[86] Many of the benefits from the protease inhibitors and drug combinations seemed to have been achieved by 1998 as the mortality rate appeared to be reaching a plateau.[87]

Even for the vast majority of those who potentially could be helped by the new drugs, thirty-four million people affected with AIDS, the cost per year of the medication is far beyond their reach. Although pharmaceutical companies are working to produce drugs that are increasingly effective and easy to take, Gabriel Rotello, author of *Sexual Ecology: AIDS and the Destiny of Gay Men,* insists, "Activists will have to fight to make them cheaper."[88] Moreover, because in the United States AIDS cases shifted demographically by 1988 from the white gay community (about one-third of all AIDS cases) to racial and ethnic minority communities (more than one-half of all AIDS cases), some African-American community leaders suggest it is time for this new AIDS population, like earlier AIDS activists, to "Act-Up."[89]

Unlike disability or gay rights activists, who focused on civil rights, AIDS activists were single-minded, fixed on issues connected with survival, health, and cure. They separated themselves even from the gay and lesbian community, for AIDS activists felt that they did not have the luxury of concentrating on long-term concerns such as discrimination or access. Their sense of urgency was sparked by what appeared to be the sudden decimation of a whole population, frequently young men at the prime of their lives.[90] Like no other disability group, AIDS activists have had the inspiration to elevate their calamity almost to an art form, as evidenced by the three-day Key West conference in early January 1997 on Literature in the Days of AIDS.[91] One woman participating in the conference—which featured the works of well-known authors such as Larry Kramer, Tony Kushner, and Edmund White—commented on the social and political impact of AIDS activists like those writers: "'The most important thing any writer can do is remember that he is part of history,' [she] said, adding that it was partly because of AIDS writing and advocacy that a cure was now possible. 'You did it,' the woman told the panel of artists."

Toward a New Vision: Three Queries

Basic questions concerning disability and technology need to be addressed. First, why is it that modern technology cannot meet challenges consistent with the principles of universal design, to make universally accessible dentist chairs, mammogram machines,[92] and medical facilities available to people with disabilities and older people? And instead of expecting people to adapt to equipment, why can equipment not be adapted to people, including office furniture that prevents computer users from developing repetitive strain injuries or computers that conform to the needs of people with various disabilities? Second, how can we assert the primacy of the individuals served over the "business ethics" of biotech and pharmaceutical companies or "a deficient health care system"? Finally, what can be done to assure that technological innovation, rather than producing new constraints, will expand the potential for choice and for inclusion for all people, including those with disabilities and chronic illnesses?

To deal with these questions, a new consciousness is required that transcends solutions to discrete technological problems. Barriers to access may recede, and a new vision may emerge, if designers of environments and inventors of new technologies bring all those involved into the creative process. This receptiveness may inspire an imaginative leap that fosters the capacity to experience the world from alternative perspectives—from the vantage point of people with differences that stem from disabilities, or age, or the variety of possibilities that shape the human condition.

Chapter Ten

Disabled Veterans
Claim Their Rights

THE ACTIVISM OF DISABLED veterans from World War I to the Gulf War seeking medical services, benefits, education, and jobs impacted the disability rights movement. Because the general public accepted rehabilitation and inclusion into the mainstream for disabled veterans of the two world wars more readily than for civilians with disabilities, disabled veterans were the first to make progress in social integration. A question became self-evident. If veterans could be successful as students, employers and employees, husbands and fathers, community leaders and neighbors, why couldn't civilians? In addition, a few disabled veterans organizations, breaking with many of their colleagues, recognized that their political influence would be enhanced if they joined with civilians with similar disabilities. All people—veterans and civilians—with spinal cord injuries resulting from battle, accident, or illness share the need for accessible transportation and a barrier-free environment. Disabled veterans, though more readily included in the mainstream, also discovered that they were not immune from the same kind of discrimination as civilians with disabilities.

The story of Herb Klinefeld, a highly re-

garded Harvard junior before he became paraplegic as a result of an injury sustained during World War II, illustrates this pervasive discrimination.[1] Despite Klinefeld's ability to walk with crutches, negotiate stairs, and drive a car, Harvard was "convinced that a paraplegic simply couldn't do the work," according to Dr. Howard Rusk, a pioneer in rehabilitation. Thanks to Rusk's pressure on his friend, Dr. Arlie Bock, the head of health services at Harvard, Klinefeld went on to earn his Ph.D. at Harvard. Although he eventually secured the college teaching job he sought, Klinefeld once again had to struggle, this time against the false assumption that his disability made him unemployable. Innumerable experiences such as Klinefeld's confirmed the need for disabled veterans, like their civilian counterparts, to contend with unresponsive bureaucracies and defy attitudinal barriers, often more resistant than physical ones.

Legislation and Self-Advocacy

As a result of the assumption that society owes a debt of gratitude to its disabled veterans, they have been generally given preferential treatment over civilians with disabilities. For example, although members of the League of the Physically Handicapped were labeled unemployable in the mid-1930s, the government had been attempting to assist disabled veterans in their efforts to secure jobs since World War I. Yet immediately after this war, however, the U.S. government was overwhelmed, unprepared to deal with hundreds of thousands of returning disabled veterans who were coping with conditions such as blindness, tuberculosis, and amputation, as well as the effects of poison gas on their respiratory systems.[2] Veterans faced many obstacles: no single government agency was responsible for veterans' issues; bureaucratic paperwork was difficult to negotiate; hospitals were overcrowded; available rehabilitation and training programs were inadequate; jobs were scarce; and there was no protection from discrimination against people with disabilities.

Two new concepts were initiated with the War Risk Insurance Act, which became federal law in 1914 and was amended in 1917.[3] First, the amount of payment received by a disabled veteran was determined by the degree of disability incurred as a result of military service; military rank was no longer a consideration as it had been in the past. Second, Congress funded vocational training and rehabilitation in order to help disabled veterans become employable. The original legislation was replaced by two later acts, the 1917 Smith-Hughes Vocational Education Act and the 1918 Smith-Sears Veterans Rehabilitation Act.[4] However advantageous this legislation was in theory in providing training, jobs, and follow-up services for disabled veterans until they became independent, disabled veterans encountered frustration when they sought the actual benefits and services, for they had to deal with overlapping laws and government agencies. In 1921, the United States Veterans Bureau was established, combining many government activities for disabled veterans under one administrative unit.

The Disabled American Veterans of the World War (DAVWW) evolved out of two groups: the Ohio Mechanics Institute for Disabled Soldiers, a self-help organization formed from a Cincinnati training school for disabled veterans, and a group of disabled veterans from the University of Cincinnati.[5] The DAVWW, organized as a national body on September 25, 1920, developed a network of local chapters throughout the country, as a consequence, initially, of the efforts of Robert Marx, the DAVWW's first national commander. Acting as an advocacy group for disabled veterans, DAVWW joined the American Legion and other veterans' groups in securing legislation that resulted in the creation of the Veterans Bureau. Formally chartered by Congress in 1932, DAVWW membership increased dramatically in such times of crisis as the Great Depression, World War II (when the name was changed to Disabled American Veterans [DAV]), and the Korean War.[6] After World War II, the DAV developed a program to train national service officers to lend support to other disabled veterans through counseling and assistance in filing claims.[7]

In order to take full advantage of their political clout, veterans' groups frequently sought to disassociate themselves from civilians with disabilities. Although FDR tried to introduce "a unified rehabilitation program for civilians and veterans," veterans' groups successfully lobbied for "a special program for those injured in military service."[8] Ultimately, the law increasing benefits and services for disabled veterans was enacted in March 1943.[9] A separate law, the Barden-LaFollette Act, expanding the 1920 Smith-Fess Vocational Rehabilitation Act, was passed in June 1943 for civilians with disabilities.[10]

Rehabilitation: The Man, Not the Wound

Although vocational rehabilitation began in the 1920s, focusing only on employment of people with disabilities, Dr. Henry Kessler and, later, Dr. Howard Rusk expanded the meaning of the term "rehabilitation." Rehabilitation evolved out of the need to find a means of dealing with disabled soldiers neither ill enough to remain in the hospital, nor well enough to return to battle. Kessler, an orthopedic surgeon who served in World War I, referred to as "the 'Pied Piper of rehabilitation' and 'one of the great pioneers in the field,'" appreciated the requirement for rehabilitative medicine before World War II."[11]

While he initiated surgical techniques in 1923 that allow muscular control of artificial limbs,[12] by World War II he developed an innovative rehabilitation program for more than three thousand amputees. When Kessler realized that insufficient attention was being paid to permanently disabled servicemen after their wounds had healed, he wrote, "The Navy treated the wound, not the man."[13] Although Kessler's superiors did not understand his comprehensive approach, he was successful in training limb-makers, encouraging patients to become informed consumers, and making the medical profession and recently disabled servicemen aware of the concept of rehabilitation.

Sensitive to the problems of the wounded airmen he was treating, Rusk slowly and painstakingly discovered from his patients that "the whole man" required more than occupational counseling.[14] He needed emotional, social, and educational support, as well as training for his family and his friends to accept him in his new condition. In order to provide recuperating airmen with an atmosphere more congenial than a hospital environment, he established the first Air Force Rehabilitation Center at Pawling,

New York, in early 1944.[15] He described this facility as "a combination of a hospital, a country club, a school, a farm, a vocational training center, a resort, and a little bit of home as well." Although dubious about the psychiatric aspect of rehabilitation, philanthropist Bernard Baruch would become Rusk's most supportive benefactor.[16]

Yet Rusk also had to overcome the resistance of his medical peers to his new conception of rehabilitation. As he explained:

> These weren't strangers to whom I was talking. These were my old friends and colleagues, fine men and excellent doctors, but the kind of rehabilitation I wanted to do had never been done. And they didn't see any need to start it.... They seemed to think I was trying to push some kind of "social service boondoggle." It got back to me later that some of them even referred to the idea as Rusk's Folly.[17]

Rusk enlisted the services of Dr. George G. Deaver, medical director of the Institute for the Crippled and Disabled (ICD)[18] in New York City, to train air force personnel in his techniques for teaching paraplegics how to walk on braced legs.[19] At this time, before a barrier-free restructuring of the built environment was a consideration, and before lift-equipped buses and modern wheelchairs were invented, walking was essential in order for paraplegics to participate in many life activities. Using this "total care" approach,[20] Rusk made it possible for disabled veterans to achieve increasing degrees of independence as they gained the skills and self-assurance to participate in society. Some attended institutions of higher learning, while others became entrepreneurs or employees. Kessler's and Rusk's vision of rehabilitation of disabled veterans fostered the movement for rehabilitation and deinstitutionalization of civilians with disabilities, which ultimately developed into the consumer-directed Independent Living Movement.

Paralyzed Veterans of America

More than other major veterans organizations, Paralyzed Veterans of America (PVA) recognized the affinity between its members' issues and those of civilian paraplegics and quadriplegics. Perhaps because these veterans shared a particular disability, most often requiring the use of a wheelchair, they tended to acknowledge their link to civilians with similar disabilities. Articles in *Paraplegia News,* a monthly newspaper that began publication in July 1946, revealed these veterans' discomfort with the disparity between the treatment of disabled veterans and that of disabled civilians. References were made to "civilian paraplegics" who have not had the advantages available to veterans, and more specifically to "techniques of medicine, surgery, and rehabilitation" unattainable by "most non-veteran paraplegics."[21]

Perhaps this receptive vision made possible the unanimous resolution of September 1947 at the second PVA convention, ten months before President Harry S. Truman desegregated the armed services in July 1948.[22] This resolution protested the segregation policy of a southern hotel with a succinct statement sent not only to the hotel but also to the press: "A spinal cord knows no bias." As a result, African Americans were served, without distinction as to race, for the first time in a Richmond, Virginia, hotel.

Beginning with the Van Nuys California Veterans Hospital in early 1945, paraplegics and quadriplegics in similar hospitals throughout the country formed individual groups that eventually merged in 1947 into a national organization, Paralyzed Veterans of America.[23] The disabled veterans in the hospitals created such groups in order to advocate for continuing medical research and rehabilitation programs, as well as for vocational and driver training programs; to publicize disabled veterans' needs for appropriate housing, automobiles, and jobs; and to foster the development of PVA nationwide.[24] In addition, PVA urged legislators to enable the Veterans Administration (VA) to provide attendants for those veterans who were so disabled that they could not otherwise live in the community.

By World War II, advances in medical science such as "the advent of antibiotics and newer and better medical and surgical techniques" made it possible for paraplegics and quadriplegics to survive, for the first time, in significant numbers.[25] Prior to World War II, such patients rarely lived beyond a year because of bedsores and acute kidney and bladder problems.[26] Rusk noted that "of the four hundred men who became paraplegic in World War I, a third died in France, another third died within six weeks thereafter, and of the remaining third, 90 percent were dead within a year."[27] In contrast, three-fourths of the twenty-five hundred surviving paraplegics of World War II were alive twenty years later, and of those fourteen hundred were still working.

The concerted national effort to rehabilitate disabled veterans led to surprising breakthroughs for all people with disabilities. Quadriplegics, formerly approached with hopelessness and futility by the medical profession, were not only surviving but working, attending college, driving cars, initiating and managing businesses, and living independently in accessible homes.[28] Although the term "wheelchair accessibility" was not commonly used until more than a decade later, references to the need that mobility-impaired veterans had for "houses fitted with special equipment"[29] or "remodeling conventional dwellings to wheelchair living"[30] appeared in *Paraplegia News* in the late 1940s. Disabled veterans contended that "for every dollar . . . spent on their rehabilitation, the federal government is securing a return of ten dollars by way of income tax, to say nothing of the immense gain in the men's morale and productive capacity."[31] Allan R. Cullimore, president emeritus of Newark College of Engineering (now New Jersey Institute of Technology), made a clear case for employing people with disabilities:

> The fact—the real fact, the realistic and practical side of the employment problem—is that everybody is handicapped.... The normal person is a pure figment of the imagination.... Different kinds of people must do different kinds of things, for in any particular job all people do not fit. We try to put the right persons in the right jobs picking them not for what they lack, but what they have, what they need, to do the job.[32]

Automobiles: Opening "New Vistas"

With the enactment of Public Law 663 in 1946, members of the armed forces who had become amputees or paraplegics in World War II were granted free automobiles.[33] According to *Paraplegia News,* "When a man who has been limited to wheelchair existence can own and operate a car, new vistas are open to him. The incentive provided carries over to all phases of his life."[34] The inaccessibility of public transportation also provided a compelling argument for granting automobiles to veterans with mobility impairments.

Beginning in the late 1940s, along with the advent of automatic transmissions on a large scale,[35] hand controls—a technologically simple device—became available. Many of these mechanisms included an arm attached to the steering column with a brake and dimmer switch built into the device. Accelerating was achieved by squeezing the hand lever while braking was accomplished by pushing the lever away from the body toward the floor. Costing between thirty and sixty-five dollars, the various models of

hand controls generally worked on the same principle.[36]

The April 1949 *Paraplegia News* described a "driving device for the quadriplegic patient," an apparatus appropriate for people with limited but not total paralysis of their upper extremities. (The use of the term "patient" in a publication encouraging independence for veterans was a vestige of the "medical model" at a time when all people with disabilities were considered sick or hospitalized whether or not they were in a medical facility.) The appliance included a heavy band that held the driver in a secure upright position and an apparatus that attached the right arm and hand to the steering wheel while the left hand was strapped to the accelerator and brake. Thus, quadriplegic drivers able to use the mechanism could steer with the arm and hand as well as start, increase speed, and stop with the left upper hand.

Information about many of the devices developed for the veterans of World War II reached the civilian disability population. For example, a Canadian woman wrote a letter to *Paraplegia News* requesting a copy of the article that described the equipment designed for quadriplegic drivers:

> I was born... with a quadruple handicap—legs off just below the knees and arms just below the elbows. I have grown up on two pair of artificial limbs, which I am able to manage quite well, and get around without aid of a cane, or anything. I am an artist by profession and able to do, with my two arms together, almost everything the average normal person can do—but have not driven a car.... I would love to drive a car and just in the last month I have been giving it serious thought and trying to learn what controls are available that would help me most. Your quadriplegic controls sound like just the thing![37]

Wheelchair users who could not transfer from their wheelchairs to the car seat were unable to drive until the invention of devices enabling them—in their wheelchairs—to maneuver in and out of automobiles. Advertisements appeared in *Paraplegia News* from 1959 to 1964 for such transfer apparatuses as a custom-made hydraulic lift for elevating a wheelchair user seated in his or her chair, a portable ramp, and a device known as the Hoyer Kartop-Lift.[38] Mounted on top of the car, the Hoyer Kartop-Lift transferred the wheelchair user from the chair to the driver's seat, utilizing hydraulic lifting action. Although Hoyer lifts continue to be useful for transferring quadriplegic wheelchair users to and from beds, bathtubs, and toilets, the concept of hoisting an individual out of a wheelchair into a car never became widely accepted by mobility-impaired drivers.

Yet hydraulic lifts did become popular as a means of raising wheelchair users, seated in their wheelchairs, into vehicles. Most wheelchair users who could not transfer independently from their wheelchairs to their car seats preferred to remain in their wheelchairs while driving. This preference was not surprising considering that, unlike the driver's seat, these wheelchairs were designed to provide the specific support many of these mobility-impaired drivers required. Although more often employed to provide wheelchair users access to buildings than automobiles or vans, portable ramps did become a commonly-used device, beginning in the 1980s, for allowing wheelchair users to enter accessible taxis.

An advertisement for a fully hand-controlled motorized vehicle, custom-built on a golf cart chassis, appeared in *Paraplegia News* in the early 1960s.[39] The description of the self-loading, power-elevating platform suggested that the wheelchair user enter the cart in his chair and drive the ambulation device on streets and sidewalks. This model of a motorized vehicle did not gain popularity probably because, unlike the motorized wheelchairs of the late 1960s and the motorized scooters of the late 1970s, this converted golf chassis was appropriate neither for indoor use nor for loading into an automobile or a van.

An advocate for disabled veterans, Henry Viscardi—who at twenty-seven learned to walk with artificial legs—instructed amputee veterans not only in the art of walking with prosthetic limbs but also in driving.[40] Focusing on the high unemployment rate of disabled veterans after World War II, Viscardi joined other prominent business leaders in 1949 to form Just One Break (JOB), an organization in New York City that found jobs for thousands of disabled veterans, and later even for civilians with disabilities. The ability to drive was a significant factor in allowing many of these disabled veterans, especially those who were mobility impaired, to work.

Once paraplegic, triplegic, and quadriplegic veterans owned automobiles and operated them, some using hand controls, many civilians with disabilities recognized that they too were capable of becoming drivers. Although special parking privileges had been extended to disabled veterans shortly after World War II, the definition of disability and the specific privileges varied from state to state. Requiring such privileges as much as the disabled veterans, civilians with motor impairments organized on a local level to obtain special parking permits. Even after securing permits for drivers with disabilities, these organizations were engaged in ongoing struggles to maintain such hard-sought privileges.[41] Originally focused on parking privileges for all those with motor impairments, civilians as well as veterans with disabilities began dealing with broader concerns, such as removing architectural barriers, coping with employment discrimination, achieving political influence, and enabling people with serious disabilities to participate in the wider society.

The Pattern of Denial

While earlier veterans' organizations helped to ignite the disability rights movement, later veterans—reflecting the rights movements of the 1960s and 1970s, including the growing assertiveness of people with disabilities — countered unresponsive bureaucracies and government cover-ups. If civilians with disabilities were gaining services and independence, what did a nation owe those who had acquired their disabilities by serving their country? Many Vietnam veterans—inspired by civil rights activism—learned to oppose an existing veterans bureaucracy that denied the validity of their illnesses,[42] especially conditions resulting from exposure to Agent Orange and from post-traumatic stress disorder.[43]

These concerns were considered "totally alien to the members of the traditional lobby,"[44] organizations such as Veterans of Foreign Wars, the American Legion, and the Marine Corps League. Of course, all issues of Vietnam veterans were complicated by these traditional organizations confusing their own anger about the failure of military policy—and their disappointment in some Vietnam veterans who were skeptical about the war—with the loyalty and courage of those who served in Southeast Asia. Even by the late 1970s and early 1980s, Vietnam veterans with war-related disabilities were still struggling to attain "visibility and subsequently a legitimate voice in veterans' affairs."

Although awareness of the illnesses resulting from the use of Agent Orange dated back to 1969, references to this ailment did not appear in newspapers until roughly *ten years* later.[45] Less than *five years* after the 1991 Gulf War, however, newspaper accounts of

congressional hearings revealed that military personnel were exposed to dangerous levels of chemical and biological agents. The veterans coping with Gulf War syndrome faced a bureaucracy tempered by the struggle of the Vietnam veterans. Yet, similar to Vietnam veterans with Agent Orange syndrome or post-traumatic stress disorder, veterans with Gulf War syndrome had to deal with serious doubts about their condition that frequently—unlike paralysis or amputation—was not immediately discernible nor apparently relevant to the civilian population. As Gulf War veteran and American Legion lobbyist Steve Robertson asserted, "The one thing that stands out in my mind is that I don't want to be in the same position as the Vietnam veterans that had to fight and fight and fight and fight to get the medical attention that they needed and they deserved."[46]

Despite the Pentagon's portrayal of the 1991 Gulf War as surgical, clean, and high tech, in reality this military operation had unhealthy consequences for service personnel and perhaps even their families. Robertson was healthy when he was deployed to the Middle East, but he has been ill since his return to the United States: "I had a chronic cough, diarrhea, aching joints, fatigue. I would sweat profusely, even when I was in an area where I should be cool. . . . I just don't feel like I have the physical strength to do the things I was doing before." General Ronald R. Blanck, commander of Walter Reade Army Medical Center, reported seeing veterans of this conflict with the series of inexplicable ailments of Gulf War syndrome: tiredness, weight loss, joint and muscle aches and pains, hair loss, and sore gums.

Two years after the conflict, Tod Ensign—an attorney specializing in military law and director of Citizen Soldier,[47] a nonprofit organization devoted to defending and expanding the full civil, constitutional, and disability rights of active military personnel and veterans—discussed the synergistic effect that may have caused these health problems. Among these causes Ensign cited massive oilfield fires that burned for months, pollutant fumes from kerosene lamps and heaters that were used in tenting areas, and depleted uranium shells that are radioactive at low levels.

Those on active duty would be hesitant to reveal their symptoms, Ensign noted in 1993, "because today, with the pressure to get rid of people, a person might well be putting his career on the line." Robertson concurred with Ensign's assessment: "Every active duty person that I've talked to, and this is an absolute statement—everyone that I've talked to—says, 'I know other guys that are sick, but they don't want to come forward.'" Cure, not compensation, Robertson emphasized, is the real goal of the very sick and disabled veterans of this conflict.

Two government studies contrast the chronic health problems of military personnel deployed in the Persian Gulf region between 1990 to 1991, with troops that did not serve in the Gulf War.[48] The results reveal that Gulf War troops reported more than three times, and as much as five times, the rate of illnesses such as fatigue, memory loss, joint stiffness and/or pain, rashes, diarrhea, and depression, as troops who were not deployed in the Gulf. In 1997, eighty thousand Gulf War veterans "sought special medical checkups from the government."[49] By 1999, more than one hundred thousand Gulf War veterans filed claims for benefits with the VA for service-related illness.[50] Contradicting earlier studies by a presidential commission and the Institute of Medicine, a scientific survey endorsed by the Pentagon determined in late 1999 that an experimental drug distributed to roughly 40 percent of the nearly seven hundred thousand American troops who served in the Persian Gulf may be a cause of Gulf War syndrome.[51]

"Their cases are much more complex than other vets because they involve so many more toxins than have ever been dumped on people: experimental shots and pills, massive amounts of oil-well fire pollution, radioactive depleted uranium, and low levels of multiple types of chemical warfare agents," notes Paul Sullivan, currently executive director of the National Gulf War Resource Center.[52] "Included in this toxic soup are pesticides and insecticides," Sullivan adds, "so we're dealing with overlapping illnesses resulting from the combination effects of overlapping toxins."[53] Sullivan describes the long-term, potentially lethal consequences of these kinds of toxins: in the course of battle, Gulf War military personnel often were exposed to "a very fine respirable, depleted uranium oxide dust that settles in the lungs and the bones and is known for causing cancer, birth defects, as well as brain and kidney damage."

Veterans' groups have indicated that the Pentagon's denials regarding Gulf War exposure adversely affected the treatment received by returning Desert Storm troops at hospitals run by the Department of Veterans Affairs: "Because doctors were told that chemicals had not been used, many veterans were sent straight to the psychiatric department," reported Sullivan in 1997 when he was spokesperson for Gulf War Veterans of Georgia.[54] Veteran Steve Robertson points out that the Departments of Defense and Veterans Affairs "in just about every case" claimed that the constellation of symptoms known as Gulf War syndrome is stress-related: "The psychiatrist at Walter Reade Hospital told me that I had a lot of pent-up angers, frustrations, and hostilities, about being deployed and spending time in the Persian Gulf."[55]

Although by 1999 the Department of Veterans Affairs refused to grant 60 percent of the disability claims of Gulf War veterans,[56] Sullivan cited the 95 percent denial rate in 1997: "The doctors believed that the soldiers must be faking it."[57] Insisting that he had returned home from the Vietnam War in perfect health, although that conflict was much more stressful and frightening than the Gulf War, Marine gunnery sergeant Wayne Godfrey—who developed severe joint aches and a chronic bleeding skin rash after his service in Desert Storm—was appalled by the notion of some scientists that stress was the main cause of the health problems of veterans of the more recent war.[58]

Post-traumatic stress disorder was a significant psychological ailment for perhaps as many as 450,000 Americans who served in Vietnam, 15 percent of the three million U.S. troops deployed in that war zone.[59] In addition, since American military planes sprayed over twelve million gallons of Agent Orange over jungles and crops in Vietnam between 1962 and 1971, veterans of this conflict also have been concerned about their exposure to that herbicide. The health of twelve hundred veterans who took part in an operation known as "Ranch Hand" was especially scrutinized because they had "the most extensive exposures to herbicides of any group of Americans who served in Southeast Asia."[60] Because a chemical in Agent Orange, dioxin, is known to cause cancer and birth defects in laboratory animals, many members of the armed forces who were stationed in Vietnam blamed this toxin for the diverse physical problems affecting them and their families.

Ensign observes that "the general consensus of scientists who were independent was that anyone who was in a forward zone, where spraying was done in the south, was at risk."[61] Twenty to thirty years after these soldiers' exposure, Congress mandated in 1991 that limited compensation be awarded for ailments caused by Agent Orange. By April 1993, only 486 veterans had been granted compensation although the Department

of Veterans Affairs had received disability claims from 39,419 soldiers who had been exposed to Agent Orange during their service in Vietnam.

Chief of the Division of Epidemiology at the American Health Foundation in New York City, Dr. Steven Stellman, emphasizes the greater potential toxic exposure of Vietnam veterans as compared to Gulf War veterans: "Approximately seven hundred thousand soldiers participated in the Gulf War while 2.3 to 3 million troops served in Vietnam. In the Gulf War, exposures occurred over a period of forty days while a typical tour of duty for a Vietnam combatant was thirteen months, and some even had two tours. Also, the Vietnam War lasted from 1964 to 1975."[62] Yet Stellman points out that there is a significant similarity between the two wars. "As with Gulf War veterans, the early complaints of Vietnam veterans, individually, appeared vague. These symptoms didn't tell much: fainting, memory loss, difficulty sleeping, fatigue, skin conditions, and aches and pains. But as a grouping of symptoms, a pattern emerged. In the Vietnam War, the spectrum of symptoms was related to combat and Agent Orange." This correlation may be attributed to the fact that combatants were far more likely than noncombatants to be exposed to Agent Orange.

The Institute of Medicine of the Congressionally-chartered National Academy of Sciences produced a comprehensive report in 1993, updated in 1996 and again in 1998, on the health effects of Agent Orange. Stellman indicates that the study found evidence of association between exposure to Agent Orange and various types of cancers, such as Hodgkin's disease, lymphoma, and lung and prostate cancers. "The government clearly participated in a major coverup of the Agent Orange issue," Stellman notes.[63]

Atomic and Chemical Guinea Pigs

Unlike troops in the Gulf War and the Vietnam War whose health was compromised in battle-related activities, the approximately 180,000 soldiers exposed to radioactive fallout between 1946 and 1962 were engaged in the more than two hundred U.S. government atmospheric tests of nuclear bombs.[64] Tod Ensign refers to this exposure of military personnel as deliberate, "in the sense that they were put in the area where fallout was likely.... A few of them were actually put right into the bomb shelters right at the site, right near, within a mile or two of ground zero."

One of these was Anthony Guarisco, a sailor stationed in 1946 on Bikini Atoll, where he saw "the first postwar atomic test"—the explosion of two atomic bombs near ninety unoccupied warships.[65] When Guarisco and other sailors were ordered "to check radiation levels and attempt decontamination by scrubbing the decks," they did not realize that they were really involved in an experiment to determine how much radiation a man can endure. Diagnosed with "a degenerative disease of the spine" twenty years after the bomb test, Guarisco experiences intermittent pain and difficulty walking.

Like Guarisco, two to three thousand servicemen "unknowingly participated in classified medical experiments—including tests of flash-blindedness and the psychological effects of radiation—between 1946 and 1963."[66] Guarisco referred to a letter that he found in 1982, written by a deceased army scientist who encouraged "the use of human subjects in radiation research" while acknowledging a potential public relations problem: "Evoking Nazi experiments, the scientist warned [that] 'Those concerned in the Atomic Energy Commission would be subject to considerable criticism, as admittedly this would have a little of the Buchenwald touch.'"

Although by the end of the 1970s atomic veterans obviously were experiencing disproportionately high rates of cancer and leukemia, not until 1990 did Congress finally order the Department of Veterans Affairs to provide limited compensation. Sandra Marlow, the daughter of an air force colonel who observed nuclear weapons tests from the front trenches of Camp Desert Rock, Nevada, in 1955,[67] describes why she became an atomic veterans activist:

My father died [from leukemia] in December of 1977. Three years later I became academic and scientific chairperson of the National Association of Atomic Veterans [NAAV]. I am no longer alone in seeking the truth about the effects of nuclear radiation. NAAV now has over seventy-five hundred members and is growing every day. The members are veterans and their wives, widows and children. They include those who worked on *Trinity,* the first atomic test, as well as the servicemen who cleaned up the contaminated rubble of Hiroshima and Nagasaki. Many have developed cancers and other debilitating illnesses; all share deep personal anxieties about the medical effects of exposure to radiation.... The atomic veterans were neither informed of the dangers nor were they volunteers.[68]

In 1997, the Disabled American Veterans attempted to locate veterans who took part in Operation Castle, a series of nuclear weapons tests in the northwestern Marshall Islands in the central Pacific conducted from March 1 through May 14, 1954.[69] David W. Gorman, DAV Washington Headquarters executive director, said:

Of particular interest is information on the levels of radiation exposure among Operation Castle participants so the DAV can assist those veterans in obtaining adequate medical care and compensation for service-connected disabilities related to exposure to ionizing radiation. The DAV is concerned that many of these atomic veterans were exposed to dangerously high levels of radiation that could have serious health consequences, even decades after their initial exposure.

Dr. Martin Gensler, aide to Senator Paul Wellstone (D-Minn.), observes, "If an atomic veteran who was at ground zero and never smoked in his life gets lung cancer, he has no real chance of getting compensation. Yet even if a Vietnam veteran spent all his time in a café in Danang—nowhere near dioxin—and smoked two packs of cigarettes a day, if he gets lung cancer," he *will* be compensated.[70] Since the Veterans Health Care Eligibility Reform Act went into effect on October 9, 1996, certain diseases are presumptively service-related, according to the VA, if military personnel were in the Southeast Asia theater between specific years in which Agent Orange was used in Vietnam. For atomic vets, on the other hand, the exposure is always determined to have been under five rads—which excludes them from compensation—even though there is no way to reconstruct the dose since the records are so poor.

Though no scientist at the April 21, 1998, Senate Veterans Affairs Committee, chaired by Senator Tim Hutchinson (R-Ark.), would defend this determination regarding the exposure of atomic vets, they continued to be denied compensation. Gensler explains why they are not receiving the benefits to which they are entitled: "They are doing so badly because they have no clout. Many are dead, so the only ones left are their widows and children." Though Gensler calls the situation tragic, he adds that Senator Wellstone is trying to correct this injustice.

By April 1993, only 1,166 of these atomic veterans had been granted compensation of the 13,334 atomic veterans who had filed disability claims with the VA. Gensler, the congressional aide probably most knowledgeable about the concerns of atomic veterans—on the staff of the senator most involved with these issues—has been unable to get reliable recent statistics. Gensler says, "VA statistics are meaningless. It's hard to separate the ineptness from the secrecy at the VA." Gensler was told that atomic vets were getting 99 percent compensation for their claims, but he discovered that these numbers had nothing to do with radiogenic problems. Rather, the statistics dealt with other physical problems such as disfigurement or flat feet.

Similar to the atomic veterans, sixty thousand American soldiers and sailors during World War II were used as human guinea pigs in secret tests involving chemical warfare.[71] Unaware of the danger and misled by their superiors, these participants thought they were serving their country by, for example, contributing to shortening the war or, more mundanely, testing summer uniforms. Instead, they were testing gases as lethal as sulfur mustard, nitrogen mustard, or lewisite, a gas containing arsenic.

Dr. Constance Pechura, director of a study by the National Academy of Sciences Institute of Medicine on the U.S. military's chemical warfare experiments, indicates that the level of exposure of the participants in these tests sometimes was as high as that experienced on the battlefield in World War I: "Despite the fact that it was well known by 1933 that there were serious long-term health effects from this kind of exposure, including emphysema, nothing was done to monitor or to follow up on these men's health. And, in fact, in some cases, symptoms that they had were deliberately recorded as something else." These World War II participants took their oath of silence so seriously that, almost without exception, they said nothing about these mustard gas tests for nearly fifty years. Not only did they keep the secret from their wives and families, but they also jeopardized their medical treatment and their compensation by concealing their experiences from their doctors and the VA.

In March 1993, when the Pentagon announced that it was declassifying test information and releasing the participants from their vows of secrecy, these World War II soldiers began speaking out. Still, their efforts to secure compensation—like their inability to redeem their suffering—were frustrating and demoralizing, as exemplified by Russell O'Berry, a veteran who attributes his repeated hospitalizations for chronic lung disease, emphysema, and asthma to his participation in mustard gas tests:

> When I filed for VA benefits, they told me that they didn't have anything on record. Then they said my records were burned up in St. Louis in a fire. So, I had to write to the Freedom of Information Act to get my records. And I do have those records now confirming the dates that I did go in the gas chambers, how long I stayed, so forth. . . . The monthly checks that I receive will never, never compensate me for what I've been through physically and mentally because it has certainly ruined my life. And I know of others that it's ruined, and there's a lot of others that have passed on, that's not here today to talk about this, and I'm speaking for them, too.

By April 1993, of the 295 veterans of mustard gas tests filing claims with the VA, only fifty-nine had been granted compensation. As for atomic veterans, current valid statistics for mustard gas veterans are becoming increasingly difficult to secure as the political impact of this aging and dying population continues to diminish.

Holding a Nation Accountable

Just as O'Berry's allegedly burnt records were resurrected when the mustard gas test participant employed the Freedom of Information Act, Gulf War combat logs—that the Defense Department claimed were

nonexistent—emerged when a Georgia veterans' group sought them under the same act.[72] Conceding that there were gaps in these otherwise meticulous logs, the Pentagon in 1996 announced its intention to investigate after veterans' groups pointed out that several pages were missing for key dates. Despite the denial of Pentagon spokesperson Brian Whitman, veterans' groups were suspicious that the government was concealing information about the detection of chemical or biological weapons during the Gulf War.

They were especially concerned about the period in 1991 when combat engineers blew up the Kamisiyah ammunition depot, possibly exposing nearly a hundred thousand U.S. military personnel to nerve gas as a result of explosions on March 4, March 10, and perhaps March 12.[73] The testimony of Gulf War veterans before congressional committees indicated that Kamisiyah was only one of many such events. In fact, while the Presidential Advisory Committee on Gulf War Veterans' Illnesses had counted fifteen similar occurrences, Pat Eddington, whistle-blower on the Central Intelligence Agency (CIA) and former CIA research analyst, claimed that there were "fifty or sixty solid incidents."[74] Although the Pentagon initially estimated that only four hundred soldiers were exposed, the figure later grew to five thousand and even later to twenty thousand.[75] James J. Tuite, a former senate staffer who led a congressional investigation into Gulf War illnesses, said in 1997 that "when the assessments are done and the analyses are finished, we're going to find out there was theater-wide exposure."

In the same year, DAV executive director Gorman urged the government to extend indefinitely the two-year time period that Persian Gulf War veterans with undiagnosed illnesses are allowed to prove that their disabilities emerged from their service in Southwest Asia.[76] Because the onset of these illnesses may take longer than two years, Gorman asserted that the regulation should be changed "until it can be determined what is making these men and women sick." He added:

> The need for the Department of Veterans Affairs to reconsider that eligibility period has been heightened by recent acknowledgments by the Department of Defense that many thousands of our troops in the Persian Gulf were likely exposed to depleted uranium, diseases endemic to Southwest Asia, and pesticides. In addition, U.S. troops were given vaccinations, inoculations, and anti-nerve agent pills without apparent regard for their side effects.... It is clear to the DAV that issues involving health care and compensation will never be resolved without the full disclosure and cooperation by all government agencies concerned.

Fearing a Pentagon whitewash, advocates for Gulf War veterans, such as Pat Eddington and Matt Puglisi, director of Gulf War Syndrome Research for the American Legion, in 1996 had called for comprehensive public hearings employing a special prosecutor and an oversight body independent of the Defense Department.[77]

"As a result of a 1950 lawsuit, *U.S. v. Feres,* the military cannot be held accountable legally for anything it does to people while they are on active service. This military immunity set a deadly precedent," Ensign asserts.[78] Although the U.S. government and the military are legally immune from financial obligation, theoretically corporations can be held accountable.[79] Not only have Gulf War veterans of New England and of Georgia used the Freedom of Information Act to acquire records, but also veterans brought a billion-dollar lawsuit (*Marshall Coleman et al. v. ABB Lumus Crest et al.*) in November 1994 against companies—including Bechtel, M. W. Kellogg, Dresser Industries, and Interchem, Inc.—that exported what the plaintiffs considered deadly technologies to Iraq.

Although they may have American subsidiaries, half of the companies that make up the sixty-nine defendants are not American.[80] Among them are three German companies: Degesch, manufacturer of cyclone B used in death camps in World War II; Preussag, producer of poison gas used in World War I; and Thyssen, whose founder, Fritz Thyssen, was one of the big financial backers of Adolph Hitler in the 1930s.

Originally filed in state district court of Brazoria County, Texas (Twenty-third Circuit) in 1994 and still pending in 1999, the *Coleman* case represents the efforts of between four and five thousand Gulf War veterans to circumvent legal prohibitions against government and military liability, uncover the causes of their ailments, gain compensation for their medical problems, and prevent companies from profiting from chemical and biological weapons of mass destruction. Frank Spagnoletti, a lawyer for the plaintiffs, describes the suit: "This is like a military operation we're engaged in. They'll stop at nothing to remain in the dark."[81] Among the investigators Spagnoletti has gathered to track down evidence regarding the shipment of weapons to Iraq is Admiral Elmo Zumwalt II, former chairman of the Joint Chiefs of Staff, the officer responsible for ordering the use of Agent Orange in Vietnam. One of the admiral's sons is assisting in the investigation; the other died as a result of Agent Orange-related cancer after the Vietnam War.[82]

Gary Pitts, another attorney for one of the four law firms representing the plaintiffs, refers to the suit as a David and Goliath affair since the defendants are represented by twenty-five or thirty law firms. Yet Pitts is optimistic about his chances of winning because of the strength of his case. Although he believes that the lawsuit may take up to three years to come to trial because of unresolved jurisdictional arguments, this case, he insists, is not just about the roughly one hundred thousand Gulf War veterans affected by dangerous exposures. "If these companies that made money off Saddam, if they're not chastened—and that means hit in the pocketbook—they will have all kinds of incentives to sell chemical and biological weapons to other dictators in the future, and that threatens everyone."[83]

In contrast to the veterans of World War II and the Korean War who unswervingly followed government orders even at the expense of their health and appropriate remuneration, veterans of more recent wars—a large percentage of Vietnam veterans and a much larger percentage of Gulf War veterans—have demanded full disclosure of the facts and just recompense for their sacrifices. The National Gulf War Resource Center was the leading organization that pushed through a major compensation bill, the 1998 Persian Gulf War Veterans Act, directly aimed at both diagnosed and undiagnosed conditions associated with toxic exposures connected with that conflict.[84] The law acknowledges that it is not fair that the government did not keep track of who was exposed to potential toxins, when, how much, and in what combinations. Since records were not kept, it should not be incumbent upon veterans to prove a biological link between exposure and illness, Sullivan points out.[85] Rather, if they have illnesses associated with such exposures, then, according to the law, they can be granted benefits such as health care and compensation. Sullivan suggests that the cost of these benefits may total as much as $6 billion.

"Because the country hired these soldiers and sent them off to war, the nation assumed a responsibility for returning each veteran to as whole a person as possible if that soldier should be wounded while serving," says Sullivan. "More than a legal commitment, it's a moral commitment. The fact that so many have their disability claims denied—and that it takes the most intense red tape in order to get assistance as a combat-wounded veteran—is unconscionable and tells us something about our society."[86]

Chapter Eleven

Education: Integration in the Least Restrictive Environment

THE FAILURE OF THE states, even as late as the 1960s, to provide many children with disabilities with the educational opportunities they required indicated the necessity for appropriate federal legislation. Two experts in the education of children with disabilities observe:

> While the nation was seeking to improve the quality of the minority child's schooling, the handicapped child's educational needs remained forgotten, even though these needs were easily as great as those of the most cruelly disadvantaged able-bodied children. At that time perhaps one handicapped child in eight— over one million handicapped children— received no education whatsoever, while more than half of all handicapped children did not receive the special instructional services that they needed.[1]

A "Quiet Revolution"

Although the U.S. Constitution does not guarantee every child the right to an education, the Fourteenth Amendment does affirm every person's right to equal protection under the law. Favoring the Pennsylvania Association for Retarded Children (PARC) in its suit against Pennsylvania, a federal court decision in Pennsylvania in 1971, invoking the Fourteenth Amendment, required that the state provide every "retarded" child with access to a free public education.[2] In *Mills v. Board of Education of the District of Columbia,* another district court in 1972 expanded the precedent established in the *PARC* case and ruled that every school-age child was entitled to a free public education regardless of the nature or severity of the individual's disability.[3]

The Developmental Disabilities and Bill of Rights Act and the Education for All Handicapped Children Act, passed by Congress in 1975, included principles stemming from federal court decisions—primarily *PARC* and *Mills*—concerning equal educational opportunities for students with disabilities. The former act provides funding "to assist and encourage states to improve care and training for developmentally disabled citizens,"[4] individuals with mental and/or physical impairments that manifested themselves at birth or in early childhood causing substantial functional limitations.[5] The latter law, renamed in 1990 the Individuals with Disabilities Education Act, required that each state find, identify, and assess all children with disabilities residing in that state, as well as tailor educational programs to suit each child's particular needs by means of an "individualized educational plan."[6] It extends to children with disabilities the principle of equality of educational opportunities underlying the landmark 1954 Supreme Court decision in *Brown v. Board of Education.*[7]

The disabilities of many of these children were "undiscovered or misclassified,"[8] as the story of Donald Snow illustrates:

> Once a patient at the old Willowbrook State Hospital, he was mistakenly diagnosed as mentally retarded when he was tested as a three-year-old child in 1965. Willowbrook employees noted that although he seemed very active, intelligent, and alert, he did appear to have a hearing problem. It was not until he was nine years old that doctors realized that his difficulties indeed were caused by hearing loss, not retardation. Soon after because of this misdiagnosis, Snow won a one and half million dollar lawsuit.[9]

Although many educational reformers referred to the IDEA as a "'quiet revolution' in special education," they also harbored reservations about the new legislation.[10] The IDEA provides "comprehensive procedural requirements, such as written notice, due process hearings, access to records, and right to counsel, permitting parental or guardian challenges to an IEP" in order to ensure that parents play a pivotal role in the child's education.[11] Reformers were concerned, however, about the primacy of the role of experts—physicians, psychologists, administrators, social workers, and educators—in devising the IEP, and the devaluation of the function of the parents, particularly when the parents were at a disadvantage because they were uneducated, non-English-speaking, poor, or minority.

One goal of the IDEA was to break the traditional patterns of segregation that were perpetuated by linking racial discrimination with disability discrimination. A study published in March 1971, four years before the passage of the IDEA, illustrates this tendency:

> The *prima facie* evidence that racial discrimination sometimes marched under the flag of special education in many school systems was especially compelling.... A particularly flagrant misuse of handicap classification was discovered in the Missouri school system. There virtually no black children were placed in classes for the learning disabled, whereas black children made up about one-third of the students in classes for the educably mentally retarded. Learning disability, it seemed, obeyed the color line in Missouri.[12]

Two precepts underlying the IDEA, individualizing the programs for students with disabilities and integrating them into the mainstream, militated against the continuation of segregation on the basis of race and disability. In fact, the IDEA specifies that "states must establish procedures to assure that the testing and evaluation materials and procedures used to evaluate and place children [with disabilities] are not racially or culturally discriminatory."[13]

Enforcing the IDEA: Early Efforts

Implementation of the IDEA, however, was difficult. For example, the Children's Defense Fund, led by Marian Wright Edelman, spent four years in the courts, from 1975 to 1979, obtaining a consent decree mandating that the state of Mississippi obey the provisions of the law.[14] Rims Barber, director of Human Services Agenda, who in 1979 served as director of the Mississippi Project of the Children's Defense Fund, refers to the consent decree as "a second-generation school desegregation issue."[15] He explains this characterization: "In the 1968/1969 school year, only white schools had special education classes in

Mississippi. After school desegregation in 1969/1970, only black children were in special education classes the following year, 1970/1971." The purpose of the consent decree was to prevent racial imbalance in special education and to provide remedies to assure that classroom placement was appropriate for each student. After implementation of the Mississippi consent decree in 1979, the *New York Times* pointed out that the policy of New York City's public school system allowed for greater segregation of children with disabilities from nondisabled children than would have been tolerated in Mississippi.[16]

A major reason that the IDEA was inadequately enforced was that many schools did not have the appropriate services, certainly not for children with severe or multiple disabilities. In order to fulfill the mandate of the IDEA, class action lawsuits were filed. One lawsuit—*Jose P. v. Board of Education*—filed by Brooklyn Legal Services chief counsel John C. Gray on behalf of a Puerto Rican student with a disability resulted in the appointment of a special master to oversee compliance with the IDEA by the New York City Board of Education.[17]

The amici curiae for the plaintiffs in the *Jose P.* lawsuit included Advocates for Children of New York, as well as the plaintiffs in *United Cerebral Palsy v. Board of Education* and in *Dyrcia S. v. Board of Education* (a related case on behalf of Hispanic children with disabilities who had limited English proficiency). The plaintiffs in the *Jose P.* case argued that the defendants, the New York City Board of Education and the New York State Education Department, failed to comply with the IDEA "in a timely manner" and with Section 504 of the Rehabilitation Act of 1973, which prohibited "discrimination against handicapped persons in any program which receives federal assistance." The IDEA—dealing only with primary and secondary school education—sets forth specific criteria, such as an IEP, for devising an appropriate education for each child with a disability between the ages of five and twenty-one.[18]

Judge Eugene H. Nickerson's December 1979 ruling in favor of the plaintiff in *Jose P.* ordered the New York City Board of Education to evaluate all children with disabilities and place them in an appropriate educational program by April 1, 1980. Consequently, the board had to accomplish a daunting task: to find and evaluate children with severe disabilities, to evaluate children with less severe disabilities, and to set up an IEP team for each one of these children with disabilities. In New York City in 1979, there were approximately thirty thousand children with severe disabilities and more than two hundred thousand with less severe disabilities.[19] Since most of the thirty thousand newly-found children with disabilities had severe impairments—and most of them had received no formal education whatsoever—many required special segregated educational services. On February 1, 1979, when *Jose P.* was filed, the prevailing view at the Board of Education was that most of the children covered by this lawsuit belonged in segregated special education classes.

The actual plaintiff, Jose P., was representative of the many educational problems concerning children with disabilities that the case addressed. Attorney John C. Gray described Jose P.: "A deaf child of a non-English speaking welfare mother, Jose P. was a mostly ignored pupil sitting in the back of a Bronx classroom in 1979. When his mother asked about her child, she was told to take him to an audiologist to be evaluated although she had no economic way of doing that."[20]

This situation demonstrates the obstacles faced by many children with disabilities whose impairments are compounded by the poverty and limited English proficiency of their parents or guardians. The *Jose P.*

requirement that the Board of Education provide bilingual tests, evaluations, instructions, programs, and services for those children whose native language was not English, as well as to ensure that parents of these children receive all information in their own language, was designed to deal with one of these issues.[21] Since many of the mandates in this watershed decision were not adequately implemented—especially with regard to children with developmental and learning disabilities, as well as emotional problems—the lawsuit remained unsettled by 2000.

Least Restrictive Environment

Because the *Jose P.* judgment necessitated *first* locating the unserved children with disabilities and developing IEPs, the "least restrictive environment" (LRE) requirement of the IDEA received little attention until the 1990s. The LRE stipulates that, whenever feasible, the child with a disability should be educated with nondisabled children to the maximum extent appropriate. A child with a disability may be removed "from the regular educational environment . . . only when the nature or degree [of the child's impairment] is such that education in regular classes cannot be accomplished satisfactorily even with the use of supplementary aids and services."[22] To illustrate, although a deaf child or a child with a severe developmental disability *may* be better served in a segregated special class than in an integrated regular class, inclusion in the general classroom is appropriate for *many* children with disabilities. Similar to the vision underlying school desegregation for children from racial and ethnic minorities, the desegregation of children with disabilities improves education "by breaking down the barriers of prejudice and misunderstanding" that have

excluded these children from "the mainstream of childhood."[23]

Gray points out that the two most significant factors determining whether a child was integrated or segregated was "the severity of the child's disability and the personality of the parents." Gray is referring to the degree to which the parents believe that the child needs special protection in the classroom, as well as to the understandable overprotectiveness of some of these parents. Also, because small towns usually have only a few children with disabilities, Gray notes that, where possible, these children have traditionally been accommodated in the mainstream.

In contrast, New York City was "supersegregated, for these children were not only segregated from nondisabled children but again segregated by specific disability." While some schools served children with mobility impairments, others served blind children, others served children with partial vision, others deaf and hard-of-hearing children, and still others children with developmental disabilities. Moreover, regular education and special education became separate entities in the New York City Board of Education, and within special education "feudal duchies," as Gray labels them, emerged.

Another factor reinforcing segregation was a funding formula by which districts received more money for a child in *special* education than for a child in *regular* education. Although schools were supposedly working toward integration of children with disabilities into regular classes, Gray calls attention to "the internal contradiction in rewarding districts for increasing the number of pupils placed in special education." Also, Gray states, the requirement in *Jose P.* that at least one elementary school and one intermediate school in each community district, and one high school in each high school region, be accessible proved to be inadequate to serve all the children with disabilities in New York City. Mary Somoza, member of School Board District 2 and parent of two children with severe disabilities, Alba and Anastasia, both wheelchair users, points out that "an accessible school in the same district may be so far from a child's neighborhood that the vital after-school social interaction of the child with a disability with his or her classmates may be precluded."[24] Gray indicates that the Section 504 mandate that all distinct programs in each district must be accessible—later reaffirmed with compliance dates in the ADA—necessitated even further retrofitting of school buildings.

Ironically, the children potentially easiest to integrate in the classroom, wheelchair users or other children with mobility impairments with at least normal intelligence, frequently could not get to schools or enter school buildings because of inaccessible school buses and school buildings. However understandable the board's inability to put the LRE immediately into effect given the enormity of the challenge posed by *Jose P.,* disability advocates criticized the board for its failure to develop an incremental plan to implement the LRE using the IDEA and Section 504. These activists conjectured that had they played a role in *Jose P.* equivalent to their participation in the 1980 *Dopico* transportation lawsuit, the LRE would have been given appropriate recognition by the early 1980s. While the *Dopico* suit—increasing accessibility to public transit—fostered integration of people with disabilities, *Jose P.* has been less successful in desegregating children with disabilities in the New York City public school system.[25]

An Appropriate Identity

At a 1996 panel discussion on special education, Professor Mark Alter, chair of the Department of Teaching and Learning at New York University, characterized the New York State educational establishment as unresponsive to the real needs of children with disabilities.[26] A disability activist, Paula Wolff, asked Professor Alter, "Why is New York ranked so low in the country in integrating children with special needs into general classrooms?" Alter replied, "Culture, a funding system that was in effect a bounty system, and historical justification for that system. When I went to school in the Bronx in the 1950s, I never saw a disabled kid." Alter was referring to the culture that stigmatized and concealed people with disabilities, and a funding process—violating the IDEA—that continues to reward schools for segregating children into special education classrooms, as well as an educational bureaucracy sanctioning these procedures. This approach—common in many parts of the country[27] and still practiced in New York City in 2000—serves neither children with disabilities who are isolated from the general population nor nondisabled children who are presented a false vision of the human condition.

A former New York City public school teacher in the early 1970s, who taught a class of children with physical disabilities, describes a protest initiated by the pupils themselves:

The approximately twenty children in my class, ranging in age from nine to sixteen, had a wide variety of motor impairments. Even though they were very different mentally, emotionally, physically, and socially, they were inappropriately segregated from the nondisabled kids and lumped together in one class. As a result, it was almost impossible to teach them. But they were very intelligent and high-spirited. So when the principal prohibited them from using the playground at the same time as their nondisabled peers, my class was outraged. While I was out of the room, they prepared signs expressing their indignation. Some wore them on their bodies; others attached them to the back of their wheelchairs. They planned to stage a demonstration, and I decided to encourage them. Exhibiting their signs, they marched around the inside foyer that served as the entrance to the school. They didn't change the principal's mind, but they made a statement, and they felt terrific about it. There were no curb cuts or wheelchair accessible buses at that time. But there was something in the air, and they sensed it.[28]

Assistant Secretary of Education Judith E. Heumann reflects on how even more than twenty years after the IDEA, as children with disabilities were being included in accessible general classrooms, educators too often resisted "accepting the reality of disability as one of the many ways of being and functioning in the world."[29] To illustrate, Heumann describes a teacher who measured the success of the integration of a wheelchair user by the degree to which the pupil *refrained* from using his wheelchair. " 'He's more like the other children now,' the teacher said. This teacher, and too many others like her," Heumann says, "see inclusion as assimilation rather than desegregation or integration of children with disabilities.[30] I would prefer that teachers encourage these children to acquire an appropriate identity, to accept and take pride in who they really are."

The IDEA in the Courts

The 1982 *Hendrick Hudson Central School District v. Rowley* decision, the first U.S. Supreme Court case interpreting the 1975 Individuals with Disabilities Education Act, held that the state was responsible for affording children with disabilities an adequate and meaningful education.[31] Amy Rowley, an elementary school girl with little residual hearing, was an "A" student mainstreamed into the general classroom. Although her parents requested a full-time sign language interpreter for their daughter, the district argued that its provision of a

hearing aid, a part-time interpreter, and tutors enabled the young student to function at a very high level. Her parents contended, however, that since Amy could hear only about half of what was said in class, granting the additional assistance they sought would allow their child to perform up to her maximum potential. "The issue was quickly framed as one of containing the costs, which would surely swamp all school systems if disabled people were allowed under this law to have just anything they wanted."[32]

Acknowledging that Congress intended for parents of children with disabilities to be involved with the development of their child's IEP throughout the educational process, the Court nonetheless ruled that the school had to provide a meaningful, but not necessarily the best, education. In his book about this case, R. C. Smith explains, "Amy was cursed in being deaf and bright because she would always get by and always be told she was doing fine. . . . And the courts would ultimately demand nothing more from educators than that they ensure that disabled children 'get by.' "[33] The Court's declaration that there was "no congressional intent to achieve strict equality of opportunity or services" contradicted a fundamental principle of the IDEA: "Each child requires an educational plan that is tailored to achieve his or her maximum potential."[34] Neither the Court nor the press seemed to understand that the Rowley case concerned appropriate accommodation, not guaranteed results: "A [full-time] sign language interpreter in her classes with hearing students was what the family wanted and all the family ever wanted. Never was there the least suggestion that the school be required to achieve certain results with Amy."[35]

In the 1980s, judicial decisions were inconsistent with regard to LRE cases. Some courts determined that placing children with disabilities in segregated "handicapped only" schools satisfied the legal requirements; others demonstrated a strong preference for integration and mainstreaming embodied in the mandates of the IDEA.[36] Disability rights attorney Diane Lipton maintains that "still other cases involved students with physical disabilities, such as cerebral palsy or deafness, in which federal courts concluded that the physical accommodations and methodologies related to these accommodations took precedence over 'the least restrictive environment' issues."[37] In a "precursor" to the 1989 to 1994 inclusion cases, the 1983 *Roncker v. Walters* decision, the U.S. Court of Appeals (Sixth Circuit)—rather than requiring a boy with a developmental disability to attend the school district's segregated "handicapped only" school—upheld his right to remain in a special classroom in a regular public school. In mandating the child's placement in the more integrated of the two schools, "the court in *Roncker* supported IDEA's presumption in favor of regular education placement."

From 1989 to 1994, four significant inclusion cases involving children with developmental disabilities—*Daniel R. R. v. State Board of Education* (Fifth Circuit) in 1989 in Texas, *Greer v. Rome City School District* (Eleventh Circuit) in 1991 in Georgia, *Oberti v. Board of Education of the Borough of Clementon School District* (Third Circuit) in 1993 in New Jersey, and *Sacramento City Unified School District v. Rachel Holland* (Ninth Circuit) in 1994 in California—resulted in consistent legal decisions that the IDEA mandated the integration of these children into regular classes with full supports.[38] In keeping with the IDEA, the courts found that children with disabilities must be educated in the least restrictive environment, employing the necessary supplementary aids. Moreover, academic grade level was not deemed an appropriate factor in determining whether or not children should be integrated into regular classrooms.

In arriving at these decisions, the courts compared academic and nonacademic benefits of regular and segregated education. Included among the nonacademic benefits were the availability of socialization and role models. Furthermore, the courts considered two pivotal questions: What is the effect on the other children in the class of having a child with a disability in the regular classroom? Does the presence of the child with the disability in the classroom detract from the education of the other children?

With regard to the *Greer* and *Holland* cases, a third question was added: Is the cost of services—itinerant special education teachers, supplementary aids, and paraprofessionals—so unreasonable as to impair the education of the other children in the district? Holland won her case against the school board at every level: at the administrative hearing, at the federal district court, and at the court of appeals. In 1994, the U.S. Supreme Court refused to hear the Holland case, thus upholding the court of appeals. The testimony of the teachers from the private school—in which Rachel Holland's parents placed their child during the five years of litigation in order to ensure her inclusion with nondisabled children—supported the plaintiff's case in the suit.

Lipton emphasizes that "the teachers were surprised at how Rachel thrived as a result of her inclusion in the regular classroom, how the other children benefited, and how delighted, as educators, they were to learn so much about teaching children with disabilities. The teachers said that they totally changed their minds about inclusion since it was great for Rachel and great for the other kids." Since children with developmental disabilities generally have been considered the most difficult to include in regular classrooms, these four appellate cases impacted on all children with disabilities. "If a child like Rachel Holland could be integrated so successfully," Lipton asserts, "educators began to recognize that inclusion could work for children with other disabilities, such as physical or learning disabilities."

A 1994 settlement between plaintiffs Alba and Anastasia Somoza, very bright ten-year-old twins with cerebral palsy, and the New York City Board of Education may have been affected by the uniformity of these four decisions, together with Anastasia's highly publicized interchange with President Clinton. The settlement affirmed the IDEA's provision of educational and related services for children with disabilities in the least restrictive environment. Because Anastasia had been placed in a mainstream class while Alba, who is nonverbal, was put in a special education class, Anastasia said to President Clinton in a February 1993 televised children's town meeting, "I have a twin sister, and we go to the same school. She's in a special class. Why can't she be in a regular class like me?" The twins' mother, Mary Somoza, recalls:

> I nearly fell off my seat. I had been working so hard to get Alba out of special education, where she was not being given anything, neither an education—since they had no real curriculum—nor appropriate supports. Also, I told Anastasia that she was the only child at that town meeting with a disability, so she would be speaking for all children with disabilities. But I never expected her to say what she did. The President had tears in his eyes, and they've been writing to each other ever since.[39]

Mary Somoza proudly exhibits President Clinton's response to a letter from Anastasia:

> Thank you so much for your great letter and for sending the book on water exercises. I'll certainly need it in the next few months.
> My knee is healing just fine, but being injured has humbled me and taught me a lot. Most especially, I have an even greater respect for anyone who uses a wheelchair.

> Keep your chin up and hang tough, especially when therapy gets rough! You'll be in my prayers.

Although the publicity resulted in the school board placing Alba in a regular class, she was not provided with the adaptive equipment or the trained school personnel that would allow her to benefit fully from this placement. Nor was Anastasia furnished with the equipment and services that she required to profit from her education on a level consistent with her ability. Representing both twins *pro bono* at special education hearings, a member firm of New York Lawyers for the Public Interest—Weil, Gotshal, & Manges—arrived at a settlement in which the board consented to several accommodations. The board agreed to give both girls motorized wheelchairs, to train Alba in the use of her adaptive equipment, to educate substitute paraprofessionals about the twins' medical needs, and to prepare the school's staff for the integration of children with disabilities into mainstream classes. In addition, the board offered to make periodic evaluations on the children's progress.

With the increasing acceptance of children with severe disabilities into regular classrooms, school districts are facing new challenges in the late 1990s.[40] Nicholas M.—an educator, disability rights advocate, and parent of M.M., an autistic child—believes that parents of children with disabilities should have three options: a segregated program, "partial inclusion," or total integration.[41] If all these alternatives were provided, children could move from one environment to the next as their development progressed. Since only two possibilities were available to his child in New York City in 1997, segregation or total inclusion, Nicholas M. was attempting to create a third choice, what he called "inclusion with a safety net" or "partial inclusion."

Having initiated a successful lawsuit in 1995 against the New York City Board of Education in order to obtain intervention services for two-year-old M.M., Nicholas M. had already experienced the challenge of confronting a bureaucracy. In 1995, when the cost of providing early intervention services for his child became economically prohibitive, Nicholas M. called on New York Lawyers for the Public Interest, which finds firms willing to offer pro bono legal assistance on specific issues. Using recommendations from psychologists and neurologists that M.M. receive Applied Behavioral Analysis (ABA), Weil, Gotshal & Manges—the law firm that represented M.M. in his case against the board—argued against the board's denial of early intervention services. Like M.M., many autistic children have responded well to ABA, an almost Pavlovian, forty-hour a week intensive therapeutic technique that prepares children for learning.[42]

"Before the ABA therapy, M.M. was in his own world; he did not make eye contact, and could not deal with physical contact," Nicholas M. recalls. "When I tried to pick him up, he would scream, arch his back, and sometimes even vomit. Now, he climbs into our bed and cuddles up to me, and he can imitate and learn from his peers." Although the firm won the lawsuit on appeal, employing the IDEA, Nicholas M. is concerned that too many parents of autistic children are neither aware of their children's needs, educational and social, nor their rights. Nicholas M., who is also a member of the Autism Advocacy Group—a Staten Island-based parents organization—insists that "programs must fit the child; the child must not be forced to fit into someone's theory."

In 1993, when the Ashburn Elementary School in Loudoun County, Virginia, attempted to accommodate autistic second-grader Mark Hartmann in a regular classroom with support services, school officials reported that the effort was not successful: "Still Mark had daily episodes of loud screeching and often hit, pinched, kicked, bit or removed his clothing," they said.[43] At the end of the school year, when officials determined that Mark should be placed in a special class for autistic children at Leeburg Elementary, Mark's parents sued.

They moved their son 230 miles away to attend a regular class in Blacksburg, Virginia, a town with a reputation for inclusionary policies. In fact, the Blacksburg middle school principal, who strongly endorsed inclusion, proudly claimed that the pupils in his school accepted children with disabilities as a natural part of the student body.[44] In order to avoid Mark's placement in a segregated class, Mrs. Hartmann and Mark spent Monday through Friday separated from the rest of the family. "We drive two thousand miles a month, and yes, I need a new car, but it's worth it." Mark is making progress now," Mrs. Hartmann observed. Mark's special education advisor at the Blacksburg school indicated that Mark demonstrated clear signs of improvement in school: "Besides becoming better adjusted socially, Mark is making academic progress....In social studies class, he participates and takes notes with all the other students. And he's getting ready to take a quiz, that we looked at this morning, that will be the same as the other students in the class."

After a Loudoun School local hearing officer agreed with the school that Mark belonged in a segregated class, the Hartmanns challenged the decision in federal district court. Ruling that the Loudoun School Board efforts were inadequate, the judge sided with the family. The court indicated that "given the strong presumption for inclusion under the Individuals with

Disabilities Education Act, disruptive behavior should not be the significant factor in determining the appropriate educational placement for a disabled child." In response to the 1997 U.S. Court of Appeals (Fourth Circuit) reversal of the district court's ruling, the Hartmanns commented, "We would like the Supreme Court to take the case, now that we've proven Mark [in 1997, a sixth grader in Blacksburg Middle School] can be successfully included."

Mark's father points out, "If you don't do this [include children with disabilities in regular classrooms], we know what happens. To pick a state, 189,000 Virginians with disabilities are in institutions at a cost of eighty-seven thousand dollars a year each to the taxpayers. If we can get Mark to be independent, earning a wage, being a productive member of society, that's a better way to go." Having spent two hundred thousand dollars on legal fees, the Hartmanns tried but failed to get the U.S. Supreme Court to rule on the degree to which the federal law requires inclusion in this case.

The U.S. Supreme Court did render a decision, however, in *Cedar Rapids v. Garret F.* (1999), a case in which a bright quadriplegic student with a ventilator required a trained aide in order to attend school.[45] Ruling for the student, Garret Frey, "the Court adhered to its view in a 1984 case that as long as a student's needs can be met by someone who is not a doctor, the required services do not fall within the excluded 'medical services' category." The decision, "a substantial victory" for families of children with severe disabilities, obligates school districts under the IDEA to pay for nonmedical services related to a student's education. Justice John Paul Stevens stated in the majority opinion, "A rule that limits the medical services exemption to physician services is unquestionably a reasonable and generally workable interpretation of the statute."

The Special Education Controversy

Examination of preschoolers in public schools in New York State—as well as students attending Dalton, a fashionable New York City private school—reveals that placement of students in special education is too often governed by financial incentives rather than serving the needs of children with disabilities. The *New York Times* reported that "at least two-thirds of the [preschoolers in New York State] are enrolled in the same school that evaluate their disability, a clear conflict of interest."[46] Since the same private nonprofit agency that receives payment for teaching these special education preschoolers has the responsibility of determining which children will be placed in their special education program, the incentive for these agencies to inflate the number of children who require special education is obvious.

The learning disability program from 1984 to 1992 initiated at Dalton demonstrated that "if there are thirty spots for learning disability students, you will magically have thirty learning disability students. If there are sixty, you'll have sixty."[47] Recognizing that "too many children were being given harmful and unreliable labels," the kindergarten teachers at Dalton refused to administer the screening tests for special education in Fall 1992. When the test for learning disability was first administered in 1984 at Dalton, the number of students requiring intervention of specialists soared; once the test was abandoned in 1992, the number plummeted. Dalton provided a valuable experiment for evaluating students with learning disabilities because fewer distorting socioeconomic variables tended to be present at this preeminent private school than at many other schools.

New York City Schools chancellor Rudolph Crew announced a proposal in 1996 to deal with the bloated segregated special education program in the New York City public school system, involving children with physical, sensory, or multiple disabilities, emotional or cognitive impairments, and chronic illnesses.[48] Consistent with programs in other cities, the plan was supposed to allow students with so-called minor learning disabilities as well as behavioral problems to receive extra help from teachers and therapists while remaining in regular classrooms.[49] Some of the stated purposes of the plan—cutting the cost of special education and preventing some children from inappropriately being designated as special education students—may have been achieved, but not to the benefit of many children with special needs. For example, by failing to test many students whom teachers recognized as having special needs, the system never included a significant number of these children in the statistics pertaining to special education. As a result, although the number of students in special education may have been limited, too many of them were permitted to flounder in general education without the programs or supports they required for success.

Still, Crew's plan did focus attention on the thorny issues inherent in special education. Disability advocates, parents of children with disabilities, and educators prophetically feared that if the driving force behind the changes in the New York City school system was budgetary, then children with "mild disabilities" would be "dumped" into general education without the support of the IDEA—which includes the protection of an IEP, designed specifically for each student.[50] As education professor Mark Alter explains: "If that youngster [a student with academic or behavioral problems] is to remain in general education, there must be appropriate supports for that kid. Right now, they don't have the resources, the teachers, the support systems to meet the needs of these youngsters."[51]

Some parents were apprehensive that their children suddenly would be transferred from a small special education class to a large general education class with neither forethought nor appropriate assistance, such as technical aids and paraprofessional help. Still other parents expressed skepticism about the preparation of teachers and students for diversity, involving not only pupils from different cultures, but also with various disabilities. Referring to the disproportionate number of non-English speaking students placed in special education in New York City, Advocates for Children attorney Roger Juan Maldanado wondered if evaluators who cannot understand the child's language or culture can accurately determine the student's disability status.

The 1997 reauthorization of the IDEA includes two requirements addressing some of the concerns of those who criticize the implementation of the law. First, the IEP must consider the language needs of the child with a disability; second, a state cannot have a funding formula that is a disincentive to integration of children with disabilities, referred to as "inclusion."[52] Attorney Diane Lipton suggests that although in some states the second requirement may be sufficient to eliminate the disincentive to inclusion, in other states a lawsuit may be necessary to make the second mandate effective.

The federal government's threat to deny a significant portion of education funding to states that do not comply with the IDEA may well serve as another effective implementation mechanism. For example, the 1999 New York State financing formula "encourages schools to put children in the most isolated environments, because they [schools] receive more money for a self-contained special-ed class than any other type of class."[53] Consequently, in 2000, New York State could lose $335 million in federal funds, money the federal government has warned New York would be withheld because of the state's noncompliance.

The two plans proposed to correct this situation demonstrate the difference between a genuine effort to educate children with special needs as opposed to a shortsighted, supposedly cost-saving approach, assuring failure. Allowing a "reasonable" seven-year phase-in period, the State Regents Plan provides incentives for school districts to place special education students in integrated environments with support service—"where students are more likely to improve their academic performance, communication, and socialization." In contrast, Governor George Pataki's plan offers practically no support services and proposes an unrealistic two-year phase-in.

The primary reason that special education has become controversial is because of its increasing costs. *New York Times* columnist Brent Staples argues, however, that despite such costs, special education is no "scandal" as some critics have claimed.[54] Concerned that "states have embarked on a campaign to define learning disabilities out of existence," Staples questions what he views as distorted priorities: "The central goal was always to educate children who had traditionally been viewed as ineducable. Integration was an important but distinctly secondary objective." He is especially worried about children with "abnormal activity in the parts of the brain that process phonemes," who are being labeled inappropriately as "mildly disabled." Since in a small percentage of children "the brain processing mechanism is off kilter,"[55] most educators and disability advocates believe that these students benefit from intensive and long-term supports.

Citing government data, he adds "that about 43 percent of learning-disabled children leave school without diplomas and that an enormous number of them end up in jail soon afterward. Fewer than 2 percent of them go on to four-year colleges—as compared with about 28 percent of students who are visually impaired and 15 percent of the deaf." Staples points out that the explosion in learning disabilities in the 1980s can be attributed to the move from teaching reading by the phonics method as opposed to "the 'whole language' craze."[56] Fearing that these children are being dragged "indiscriminately into the mainstream," he compares their plight to the experience of children with disabilities before the 1970s when many were institutionalized, hidden away, or even strapped into their chairs screaming.[57]

While "60 Minutes" commentator Leslie Stahl presents the issue as a contest between children with disabilities and nondisabled children, she acknowledges that "twenty-five years ago [many children with disabilities] probably wouldn't have had any kind of school. Unless parents could afford to pay for special care, disabled children were often ignored or institutionalized, sometimes in appalling conditions." Regardless of the cost, Stahl notes, "it's very hard to criticize the current system. No one wants to go back to the bad old days."[58]

Yet Stahl observes the increasing numbers of children designated as disabled: "One in every eight public school children in this country is now in special education.... That's more than five million children, and special education now costs taxpayers more than thirty-two billion dollars a year. That's one-quarter of all school money being spent on one-eighth of the kids." Therefore, Stahl indicates, parents of children in regular education are concerned that their children are being "shortchanged in order to pay for special ed."

Another parent complains that instruction for his nondisabled children was "being pared back to pay for special education," for example, by "the elimination of the program for gifted and talented children." This parent exhibits the same "either/or fallacy" in his thinking as does Philip K. Howard who states in *The Death of Common Sense:* "Gifted students, in contrast to disabled children, receive virtually no support or attention from America's school system."[59] Both comments—the parent's and Howard's—suggest that disability and intelligence are mutually exclusive.

The mother of a child with a severe disability sees the debate from another perspective:

> That's the kind of thing [special ed] I want my tax dollars to go for. I see it as an investment. . . . I see this school as a boot camp experience for him, a really intense time when he can gain as much skills as he can because in the long term, if he didn't learn how to brush his teeth by himself, and he didn't learn how to get around in an electric wheelchair, and he didn't learn how to effectively tell people that he needed to use the bathroom, then for the rest of his life we would have to be paying people to do that. Now we're not going to have to [pay for these services]. I don't want our child or any other child who has disabilities that they had no control over to be scapegoats for a much larger problem.

"The much larger problem" to which this mother referred is addressed in a *New York Times* editorial that reveals that while problems in special education are evident throughout the nation, New York has a far less successful program than many other localities.[60] For example, special education experts and parent advocates Barbara Fisher and Richard Spiegel, who "lobbied long and hard" for the IDEA, doubt that New York City's education system has the flexibility to deal with the variety of approaches necessary to serve children with special needs:

> We . . . believe that the most fragile of our children are best served and should remain in environments where instructional staff are trained to meet their special needs. And further, that disabled children who are not as severely impacted should be moved into the mainstream only when necessary support services have in fact been contracted and are in place at the school; when the administrative and educational staff have received the training to understand the rights, available services and learning styles of these students, and when the peers of these students, their parents, and the parents of the disabled students have been part of the transition planning process.[61]

Though educators agree that with proper preparation and supports "mainstreaming students with minor disabilities would be healthier and far less costly than the segregated approach," New York City has had a history of mainstreaming roughly one-fourth the percentage of special education preschoolers as compared to the nation as a whole.[62] The detrimental effects of misclassifying children and unnecessarily segregating them are compounded, for once designated as learning disabled or emotionally handicapped, children tend to retain the label and the stigma throughout their education. Even for children properly placed in special education, however, the IDEA's requirement that they be reassessed each year in order to be given the opportunity to be mainstreamed is generally ignored.[63]

Some educators, including Secretary of Education Richard S. Riley and Assistant Secretary of Education Judith E. Heumann, maintain that rather than ameliorating the educational situation for children who were not succeeding in school, special education has segregated and demoralized many of these students. A majority of children in New York City's special education program are classified as learning or emotionally disabled, often ambiguous and subjective designations that *still* lend themselves to racial and ethnic stereotyping:

> New York City's special education system . . . ensures a second-class education, particularly

for black boys, becoming a trap that incubates failure.... Nationwide, black students are twice as likely to be in special education programs as white children, with much higher rates in predominantly white districts, according to some academic studies. Yet, these same students perform better in regular classes with extra support, federal studies suggest.... While many agree on the need for specially geared classes for profoundly retarded children or those with other special needs, many advocates and educators say New York has gone too far.... The degree to which children identified as disabled are taught in regular classrooms varies widely from state to state. In Vermont [in 1994], 87 percent of special education students were in regular classes, compared with 7 percent in New York [City].[64]

Since 1989, when Vermont removed financial incentives for keeping children in segregated placements, the state has been the model for integration of children into regular classrooms.[65] The 85 percent of the annual budget for children with disabilities, formerly allocated for separate classes and separate schools, instead was spent on extra teachers, aides, therapists, and services in regular schools. "According to the current concept, special education is a service," Heumann explained to a disability studies colloquium, "not a place."[66] Heumann was pointing out that since each student should be educated in the least restricted environment appropriate for that individual student, the money for services should be connected to the learner, not limited to a special education classroom. Consistent with this approach, in Vermont after 1989 "special education money followed the children [with disabilities] to the regular classes."

Somnolent Samantha

Although with the passage of the IDEA, elementary and secondary schools systems were becoming increasingly aware of the numbers of students with invisible disabilities, especially learning disabilities, when these students entered college, they faced new challenges. In late 1995, the provost of Boston University (B.U.), Jon Westling, who was not a learning disabilities expert, "stiffened" the institution's policy regarding "reasonable accommodations" for students with these conditions.[67] To support his approach, on several public occasions he referred to Somnolent Samantha, a supposedly real student with a learning disability, who turned out to be fictitious. As a result of his policy changes at B.U., ten students with learning disabilities, encouraged by advocacy groups for such students, filed a class action lawsuit in federal district court in Boston in July 1996 against Boston University.

The university lawyer responsible for the case, Larry Elswit, argued that the suit "is about a university's right to set academic standards," for, he added, the ADA does not prevent an academic administrator from participating in judgments about academic modifications. On the other hand, the learning-disabled students contended that "the University and Mr. Westling have violated Federal laws requiring that educational institutions provide 'reasonable accommodations' to those with learning disabilities." Advocates for people with learning disabilities asserted that Westling's "dismissive words and actions" regarding this issue were tantamount to "illegal discrimination."

Boston University's Office of Learning Disabilities Support Services achieved national recognition for the services it provided for students with learning disabilities: a summer program, appropriate tutoring, relevant information, and special assistance. Of the twenty-nine thousand students registered at Boston University, only 480 were learning disabled. Many of these students specifically had chosen this school because it was reputed to have the supports they required. Elizabeth Guckenberger, a dyslexic third-year law student, describes her experience:

> I was drawn to B.U. because I thought there would be an attitude of understanding about learning disabilities. I have always had to work very hard. Things take me much longer than they take my twin sister, who is not dyslexic. I'm doing well in law school, but I need my accommodations. I get a reduced caseload, which means I'm not going to finish in the usual three years, and I get extended time on tests and a quiet room to take them in.

Applying the ADA definition of discrimination, this lawsuit was spearheaded by Anne Schneider, who claimed that her daughter, a B.U. student with learning disabilities, had not received the services she had expected from the university.[68] Having worked ten years with students with learning disabilities and their parents, Schneider labeled the implicit accusation that these students are frauds "the big lie." She insisted, "I haven't seen a phony yet"; the university has to "abide by the law and stop the harassment." Indicating that it would have been easy to have hired tutors and other personal accommodations for her daughter, Schneider noted that her concern "transcends the personal: I don't sleep at night because I worry about all the other kids [with learning disabilities], and not just the four hundred eighty [in the B.U. learning disabilities program]. B.U. became the national model. We were the example of how to do it right. [So] we're talking about three hundred fifty thousand kids [with learning disabilities] across the country."

Speaking for university administrators, however, Elswit claimed that the issue is basically academic: "Within our academic standards, we will do whatever we can to help students with learning disabilities over the bar. Time and a half on tests and notetakers can be fine efforts to help students over the bar. What we won't do is lower the bar." Yet Boston University Chancellor John Silber's comment was not supportive of students with learning disabilities: "Some of the things that pass for learning disabilities used to be called stupidity."[69] In her 1997 decision favoring the plaintiffs in *Elizabeth Guckenberger v. Boston University,* Judge Patti B. Saris stated:

> B.U.'s internally contentious, multitiered evaluation process involving evaluators who were not only inexperienced but also biased caused delay and denial of reasonable accommodations and much emotional distress for learning disabled students. The court concludes that the implementation of B.U.'s initial accommodations policy violated the ADA and Section 504 during the 1995–96 academic year.[70]

Too frequently, experienced educators like Westling are skeptical of "learning disabled" as a diagnosis, learning disabilities as bona fide conditions, and the experts who identify the symptoms. Familiar with neither these disabilities nor the appropriate techniques for dealing with them, educators may be suspicious of students who request special services designed for people with learning disabilities. Officials on campuses other than Boston University claimed that they were seeing students who paid for diagnoses that were "dubious" and then demanded services that they did not require.[71]

With a growing sensitivity to diverse learning styles and the development of new teaching strategies, educators—rather than merely weeding out "poor students"—have sought to educate an increasingly wide spectrum of learners. By the late 1990s, students with learning disabilities comprised roughly 51 percent of the students with disabilities from kindergarten through twelfth grade, and more than twice as many college students—3 percent since 1988—identified themselves as learning disabled. Since ADA detractors often cite people with invisible disabilities as examples of an unexpected population served by the ADA, individuals with conditions such as learning disabilities often bear the brunt of criticism against the law.

A Microcosm of the Real World

Just as accommodations for people with disabilities serve the general population (as curb cuts help many others besides those in wheelchairs), the approaches used in special education are valid for all students, observes special education expert Richard Spiegel.[72] "Rather than taking for granted that each student has to learn according to some arbitrary standard arrived at by somebody in a think tank," he adds, "educators could measure the growth of each student according to an individual evaluation. Using this approach, instead of just being a weeding-out process, the education system could serve all children." As Assistant Secretary of Education Heumann notes, "In a way you can see every child as having special needs. So the ideal is a system in which every child gets an individualized education."[73]

Born with cerebral palsy, Barak Stussman, a technology coordinator for ACCESS ERIC in Rockville, Maryland, demonstrates why inclusion, like an individualized education, benefits nondisabled students as well as students with disabilities.[74] Describing himself as "living the American dream—married, with two cars, two kids, and a mortgage on a townhouse," Stussman indicates that with the advent of new technology and new legislation, in the future "adults will have to deal with people of different limitations." Stussman asserts that this interaction fosters learning: "I believe the public school system should be a microcosm of the 'real world.' Education is more than just what you learn in books and are told by the teacher. Education is learning how to interact with others."

Heumann agrees with Stussman that "all students in inclusive environments benefit from learning that although human beings can vary greatly in appearance, background, and perspective, all people have their humanity in common."[75] Students with disabilities are served because, if they are provided with adequate supports and resources in the general classroom, they are more likely to be held to the highest standards of achievement than if they are segregated. Integration increases the probability that these students with disabilities will secure challenging jobs, earn good salaries, and participate fully in the community. "It is not the way people communicate, transport themselves from place to place, or sense the world that limits their ability to achieve," Heumann maintains; "it's the way society reacts to them."

By studying, working, and playing with peers with disabilities, nondisabled students also profit, "for they gain lasting lessons of character as valuable as academic knowledge," Heumann asserts. She offers an example that supports the findings that the achievement of nondisabled children may even improve when they have classmates with significant disabilities:

I have been told about a disabled child who had very few communications skills, who was placed in an inclusive class in Tulsa, Oklahoma. Before she got there, the children in the class had a reputation for being less than attentive in class. But when the disabled student arrived, the students took great pride in learning what she meant when she made various sounds and in interpreting her sounds to the teacher. In order to learn what their new classmate was saying, the students became quieter in class, and by the end of the semester, *everybody* was learning more.

Chapter Twelve

Identity and Culture

Three Strands of the Movement

Lex Frieden, former director of the National Council on Disability, refers to the two "strands" of the disability rights movement that came together in the effort to pass the Americans with Disabilities Act.[1] The *first* strand—made up of people with disabilities living independently in the community, *without personal assistance services*—emphasizes civil rights as a means of securing equal access to transportation, education, employment, housing, and health care. The *second* strand—composed of people with severe disabilities who *require personal assistance services* in order to live independently in the community—stresses the services they need for maintaining their independence.

Despite the different priorities embodied in these two strands, they share common goals, as the struggle for the ADA demonstrates. Many people who are now living independently in the community without personal assistance services recognize the inevitability of the decline that comes with advancing age, and hence, their eventual need for such services. Many people who now require personal assistance services need the access to society that disability rights legislation provides. Edward Roberts, Judith E. Heumann, Fred Fay, and Lex Frieden are examples of early leaders of the disability rights movement who were intrinsically involved in both of these two strands.

There is, however, a *third* strand—comprised of *institutionalized people* with significant disabilities—focusing on deinstitutionalization with all the supports necessary to allow them to live in the community. Wade Blank and members of the continuing ADAPT crusade, who are identified with this strand, brought the issues of institutionalized people with disabilities to the wider disability rights movement. Fred Fay of Justice For All observes, "Shamefully, here in America we have a couple of million people with disabilities incarcerated in institutions—many against their will, many drugged into silence, many strapped down in their beds—people who, with a little assistive technology and a little attendant care, could be living productive lives in the community."[2] Isolated not only from the greater society, but also until the 1980s from the disability community, this third strand infused the disability rights movement with a new radicalism and militancy.

Cheryl Marie Wade, 1994 recipient of a National Endowment for the Arts Solo Theatre Artist Fellowship, comments sardonically on the alienation of people associated with this third strand from the mainstream disability community: "OK. I admit it. I am weaker and more vulnerable than most nondisabled people and many disabled people, too. So throw me out of the movement. Take away my Crip Power button."[3] Yet she explains:

> We who are on the outside, living independently, using attendants for intimate care, owe to those of our brothers and sisters still dependent on family care or institutions to tell the truth about the pain and struggle of this life as well as the joy and freedom.... But if our shame tells us that our needs lack dignity, that we lack dignity, then the next thing we hear our shame say is that it is more dignified to die than to live with these basic needs that take away our privacy and seem like such a burden.

Nonetheless, Wade clearly positions herself on the side of life: "But it [personal assistance services] is the only deal in town. And no matter how difficult, well worth it when you consider the alternatives."

The contradictions, the "gnarled strands" of "the disability experience," have been characterized as a "hard to unravel ... tangled, knotted ball" of

> isolation and differentness versus a common identity; images of weakness, vulnerability, enforced childishness, learned helplessness versus defiance, willingness to make waves and change the status quo; pity, destroying dignity, fear of our differentness, our "imperfection," as if perfection were humanly achievable; and then our own fear, raw fear of attitudes that would destroy our kind, whether by genocide, selective abortion, euthanasia, assisted suicide or rationing of care.[4]

Disability Pride: Celebrating Difference

Disability activist Mary Jane Owen challenges the obvious impediment to the development of a group identity by people with disabilities: "It's hard to organize around having something in common—disability—that none of us really wants."[5] Yet she presents an analogy between people with disabilities and another minority group: "But the children of slavery came together around physical characteristics that the majority society taught were ugly. 'Black is beautiful' seemed an audacious assertion when it was first made." Similarly, Owen suggests that despite the marginalized status imposed on the disability population by the greater society, people with disabilities can bond with one another in mutual affirmation.

How can people with disabilities join with other people with disabilities unless they feel pride in themselves and a desire to identify with, and be among, others with disabilities? "When I was growing up, I was terrified of walking into a room of people with disabilities and admitting that I was one of them. Now I just love being in a community of people with disabilities," says Leslie Heller, who has cerebral palsy.[6] How do people who have been stigmatized, even ostracized, acquire this pride? Do they take the stigma and transform it into a badge of honor, as does Nadina LaSpina? "I would not trade my disability for anything. We will not change to fit the mold. Instead, we will destroy the mold and change the world to make sure there is room for everyone," insists LaSpina, who has polio. She is referring to her belief that by means of legislation, regulation, and technology the world should adapt to her needs.

LaSpina used analogy to explain her feelings:

I'm proud of being Italian. There are things I'm ashamed of, like the existence of the Mafia—but these things do not stop me from embracing my Italian-ness. I love being a woman, but I hate going through menopause. But I wouldn't want a sex-change operation just because of menopause. Certainly the pain and physical limitations of disability are not wonderful, yet that identity is who I am. And I am proud of it.[7]

Is this disability pride really a reflection of what Erik H. Erikson defines as "ego integrity," the last of his "eight ages of man": "the acceptance of one's one and only life cycle as something that had to be and that, by necessity, permitted of no substitutions"?[8] Especially for those born with a disability, or those who become disabled at an early age, their disability is as much a part of their "one and only life cycle" as any of their other characteristics. Therefore, the individual sense of pride that a person with a disability feels must refer to that self that evolved with a disability, not some substituted nondisabled self.

For an individual who becomes disabled after forming a sense of self as nondisabled, the new identity as a person with a disability may be nurtured by establishing relationships with other people in the disability community whose sensibilities have been shaped by similar experiences.[9] Daniel Robert, a movie prop man before he was diagnosed as having multiple sclerosis, forged a new self-image as a person with a disability by becoming a disability rights activist. "Once I stopped being what I had been, I needed to be part of a community," Robert explains.[10] "I see pride most strongly when I can be proud of others in the community," Robert notes, emphasizing his belief that disability pride cannot happen in isolation:[11]

Before my disability, I was a superficial person, caught up with competitiveness and machismo. The disability gave me the opportunity to find out who I really am. I had to start from square one to become a member of a community that from time immemorial has been discriminated against and viewed as defective by mainstream society. Transferred to a world of disability culture, I developed deep and meaningful relationships with people in the disability rights movement. Some became disabled early in life; some like me became disabled later in life, but they all took pride in who they were and what they were doing. They encouraged me to feel attractive and creative and powerful in my own way. I don't have to be angry or full of self-pity anymore. These are my people.[12]

Interweaving narrative, journal entries, letters, and poetry, Jean Stewart recounts in her autobiographical novel, *The Body's Memory,* her own personal transformation after becoming disabled at the age of twenty-eight—her discovery of her new identity as an activist in the disability rights movement:[13]

After surgery because a tumor on my hip left me motor impaired, I experienced profound depression. I lost my bearings entirely. When I went down the street, it seemed as if I was invisible. My disability had such a profound impact on my sense of self that I felt sexually erased. Before I became disabled, I had self-identified as a writer and a member of movements for social change. Now an issue of social change arrived on my doorstep with a resounding thud.[14]

She recalls that her introduction to disability rights made her aware of her kinship with "an oppressed minority, [her] own people," peers who understood her experiences and whose experiences she understood. Now that she had what she considered "a realistic frame of reference," she had reason to carry on despite chronic pain and demoralization. "My role models were indomitable. They were gutsy; they just bulldozed their way through obstacles. They showed me how to use my anger and indignation productively. In a no-nonsense way," she says, "they were changing the world." Since there seemed to be no such organization, in 1994 she founded the Disabled Prisoners Justice Fund to link prisoners with disabilities—one of the most vulnerable and abused populations in the country—with attorneys.[15]

As a result of a 1977 diving accident, Marca Bristo—president and CEO of Access Living, the Chicago independent living center, as well as chairperson of the National Council on Disability—became a wheelchair user as a young adult.[16] "My initial response was to go on with my old life," Bristo notes, "so I didn't try to extend my relationship with other people with disabilities. But two incidents pulled me out of my denial and started me on a journey that enabled me to meet many remarkable people with disabilities and to be involved in a time of historical change in the disability rights movement." The first incident occurred after her rehabilitation for a spinal cord injury. "I wanted to continue my work as a nurse by going into teaching and research," Bristo remembers. Because Vocational Rehabilitation considered her career goal unrealistic, the agency refused to support her in her effort to acquire a master's in nursing. She appealed and won.

Perceiving her struggle as "self advocacy," Bristo describes herself as "still feeling disconnected from the movement." She refers to the second incident, however, as "the one that made me self-identify as a person with a disability, that made me reach out to others with disabilities, that made me relate my disability to my work." While reviewing patient charts, she realized to her dismay that unlike all the other patients, none of the women with disabilities were asked questions regarding their sexuality. "I was struck by the way the sexuality of these women was being negated," Bristo indicates, "and I recognized that my own experience of disability and my observation of disability had a political dimension. It was about dis-crimination." Soon her work would center around independent living and disability policy development on a local and national level. "But these two events," Bristo points out, "provided the spark that connected me to my true identity as a woman with a disability and the emerging movement for the rights of people with disabilities."

Steven E. Brown, cofounder of the Institute on Disability Culture in Las Cruces, New Mexico, observes:

> People with disabilities have forged a group identity. We share a common history of oppression and a common bond of resilience. We generate art, music, literature, and other expressions of our lives and our culture, infused from our experience of disability. Most importantly, we are proud of ourselves as people with disabilities. We claim our disabilities with pride as part of our identity. We are who we are: we are people with disabilities.[17]

Robert F. Murphy in *The Body Silent* describes how his degenerative disability, a tumor of the spinal cord leading to atrophy of the body, impelled him to examine the society of people with disabilities with the same analytical tools that he used to study esoteric cultures in remote geographical areas, such as the southern Sahara and the Amazon.[18] His argument is that people with disabilities inhabit a separate culture inside the wider culture. As Murphy states:

> Just as an anthropologist gets a better perspective on his own culture through long and deep study of a radically different one, my extended sojourn in disability has given me, like it or not, a measure of estrangement far beyond the yield of any trip. I now stand somewhat apart from American culture, making me in many ways a stranger. And with this estrangement has come a greater urge to penetrate the veneer of cultural differences and reach an understanding of the underlying unity of all human experience.

Murphy recalls his protestations at the following comment made by a black anthropologist colleague: "I always think of myself as being black just as you always think of yourself as being white." With Murphy's disability came a realization that "I [Murphy] would no more have thought of myself as white than I would have thought of myself as walking on two legs." In other words, when one is within the so-called "normal" group, one does not know there is a classification; it is what ethnolinguists call an "unmarked category." When one feels compelled to defend oneself against a hostile environment, then the reality of both the environment and the individual's "embattled identity" becomes evident.

Murphy's dedication of his book, "To all those who cannot walk—and instead try to fly," underscores his conclusion:

> It takes a rare combination of intelligence, courage, and persistence to conquer the mental and physical quarantine thrown up around the disabled by a society that secretly sees in them its own epitaph.... The intensity of purpose required by the drive for autonomy makes the successful people [with serious disabilities] unusual. They have entered the mainstream of social life, and they have done this through great determination and unflagging effort.

Murphy explains how nonetheless, they have forged their own culture: "But no matter how well they become assimilated into society, their struggle sets them apart from their able-bodied fellows. They have a different history and follow a separate agenda; they remain part of the Other. Their otherness, however, is positive and creative, for their self-assertion is a profound celebration of life."[19]

The meaning of the term "culture" becomes so modified when linked with disability that until the 1990s many disability activists did not accept the authenticity of the concept of "disability culture." For example, in 1982, Cass Irvin of *The Disability Rag*, a newspaper devoted to recording and preserving the history of people with disabilities and their rights movement, registered her skepticism regarding this concept: "Unlike most minority groups, we [people with disabilities] do not have our own culture and traditions. But we do have a past and we should learn about it and feel pride in the accomplishments of our forebears and we should feel anguish at how badly our people have been treated."[20]

By 1994, however, Carol Gill, a quadriplegic psychologist who was one of the first to use the term "disability culture," referred to some of the "core values shared by people with disabilities" such as "tolerance for others' differences" and "highly developed skills at managing multiple problems."[21] Elaborating on her perception of the resourcefulness that people with disabilities are required to develop because of their differences, Gill describes her "ideal world":

> Society would accept my experience as "disability culture," which would in turn be accepted as part of "human diversity." There would be respectful curiosity about what I have learned from my differences that I could teach society. In such a world, no one would mind being called Disabled. Being unable to do something the way most people do it would not be seen as something bad that needed curing. It would be seen as just a difference.[22]

Gill reflects on the social value of diversity:

> Differences might make you proficient in some contexts, deficient in others, or not matter at all. For example, if I can't run, I might be an inferior messenger if time is critical. However, my inability to run might just as likely have stimulated me to address time more creatively or to develop ways to send messages swiftly that are as efficient

as running, or vastly superior. In other words, ideally, even if I had a difference that might impinge on me in some contexts, I wouldn't be judged *generally* deficient because a recognized feature of Disability culture would be the fact that such limitations can be fodder for innovation and for a rich and valuable human experience.

The well-known journalist John Hockenberry, who has a spinal cord injury, also describes disability as a cultural resource that the wider society ignores at its peril: "Suppose, when making his case for being allowed to use a golf cart, Casey Martin—the professional golfer with a disability—said, 'Yes, of course my disability constitutes an advantage because like other people with disabilities, I have expertise in adapting to change.' But no, he said needing the golf cart is a disadvantage, and so the market-driven homogeneous mainstream could say, 'all's right with the world.'"[23] Hockenberry asks, "Why aren't people with disabilities a source of reassurance to the general public that although life is unpredictable and circumstances may be unfavorable, versatility and adaptation are possible; they're built into the coding of human beings?"

"Why is it," Hockenberry continues, "that a person would not be considered educated or privileged if he went through school and never learned there was a France or a French language? But if a person went through school and knew nothing about disability, never met a disabled person, never heard of American Sign Language, he might be considered not only educated, but also lucky? Maybe we in the disability community," Hockenberry suggests, "need to get out of the clinical realm, even out of the equity realm, into the cultural realm, and show that a strategy that leads to inclusion makes a better community for everyone. That's really what the Declaration of Independence was about," Hockenberry asserts, "more than advantage—as if there was a lim-

ited amount of advantage to go around and disabled people will use it all up—more than fairness. The Declaration of Independence was really about a strategy to make the best community we can."

Deborah Ossoff Yanagisawa, a disability activist who is legally blind, remembers that she was always uncomfortable when people treated her disability as an unequivocal disaster.[24] Having grown up happily in a family in which congenital blindness was common, she wanted to say, "Maybe, but maybe not." Among her responses to her disability, she realized, were positive feelings like her sense of community and pride stemming from her connection to the culture of disability. "I knew," she adds, "that some folks' assumption that my life was spoiled by my disability was simplistic and incomplete." When Yanagisawa read the following parable, she was struck by how well it matched with her own experience. The story begins by acknowledging that although "being disabled is a deep wound, a source of pain," it is, similar to other wounds, also "a gift":

> As Eastern wisdom has always known, it is hard to tell good luck from bad luck. I recall the old story about the farmer who found a beautiful wild horse, and the neighbors said, "What good luck," and the farmer said, "Maybe." Then the farmer's son tried to tame the horse and fell off, breaking his leg. The neighbors all said, "What bad luck," and the farmer said, "Maybe." Then a war started and the army came to conscript all the young men, and they took everyone's son except the farmer's son with the broken leg. "What good luck," the neighbors said, and the farmer said, "Maybe." And on and on it goes. Life is the way it is, not the way we wish it was, and disability is a constant embodiment of this basic truth.[25]

Disability culture is gaining increased acceptance in the academic world as evidenced by the hundreds of disability studies courses nationwide,[26] such as Nadina LaSpina's "Celebrating Difference: Disability Culture," offered in class and on-line since Spring 1995 at New York City's New School for Social Research. A number of other scholars with disabilities, among them Paul Longmore at San Francisco State and Phyllis Rubenfeld at New York City's Hunter College, have been fostering an appreciation of disability culture by working toward the creation of disability studies programs in their respective institutions. At the University of Illinois in Chicago, a graduate program in disability studies was approved in Fall 1998.[27] Indicating that the topic of disability is slowly working its way into history, literature, political science, and sociology courses, David Pfeiffer, editor of the Society for Disability Studies' *SDS Quarterly,* likened disability studies to ethnic studies. Just as university departments are devoted to an examination of gender, race, or ethnicity, a disability studies program would treat disability as an "ordinary human variation," explains Rubenfeld.

Professor Simi Linton, a scholar and activist with a disability, and her colleagues at Hunter College have developed a working definition of disability studies.[28] Focusing on disability as a "social phenomenon, social construct, metaphor and culture," disability studies "reframes" the study of disability "utilizing a minority group model." Disability studies not only explores "ideas related to disability in all forms of cultural representation throughout history," but it also examines "the policies and practices of all societies to understand the social, rather than physical and psychological, determinants" of disability as experience:

> Disability Studies both emanated from and supports the Disability Rights Movement, which advocated for civil rights and self-determination. The focus shifts the emphasis away from a prevention/treatment/remediation paradigm, to a social/cultural/political paradigm. This shift does not signify a

denial of the presence of impairments, nor a rejection of the utility of intervention and treatment. Instead, Disability Studies has been developed to disentagle impairments from the myth, ideology and stigma that influence social interaction and social policy. The scholarship challenges the idea that the economic and social status and the assigned roles of people with disabilities are inevitable outcomes of their condition.

Disdainful of pity, disability culture—a major focus of disability studies—celebrates its heritage and sense of community, using the various forms of expression common to other cultures such as, for example film, literature, dance, and painting. Walter Brock's 1998 film *If I Can't Do It* evokes both the painful social alienation of Arthur Campbell Jr., a highly intelligent person with severe cerebral palsy, as well as his later exhilaration resulting from his political leadership in disability militancy.[29] Portraying the film as "ultimately less about disabled people than about viewers' own feelings," Mary Johnson, in her review of Brock's work, reiterates the film maker's own words that open the documentary:

> Mr. Brock says that Mr. Campbell had been described to him only as a disability rights activist. He wasn't prepared to meet a man with severe cerebral palsy and barely intelligible speech. He describes his response: "What kind of life could this guy have? Maybe the most merciful thing to do would be to put him out of his misery." Ten years later [after Brock got to know Campbell well], that response still shocks Mr. Brock. "Where does such prejudice come from?" he asks himself.[30]

"A slashingly dark humor,"[31] one of the characteristic qualities of disability art, is illustrated by Billy Golfus's view of the disability rights movement in his incisively witty film, *When Billy Broke His Head,* and by Lynn Manning's poem, "The Magic Wand," a sardonic comparison of two stereotypes—

one based on race, the other on disability. In this poem, the white cane belonging to a blind man, who happens to be African American, becomes the catalyst for a sudden transformation:

> Quick-change artist extraordinaire,
> I whip out my folded cane
> and change from black man to blind man
> with a flick of my wrist.
> It is a profound metamorphosis—
> From God-gifted wizard of roundball
> dominating backboards across America,
> To God-gifted idiot savant
> pounding out chart-busters on a cockeyed
>   whim;
> From sociopathic gangbanger with death for
>   eyes
> to all-seeing soul with saintly spirit;
> From rape driven misogynist
> to poor motherless child;
> From welfare-rich pimp
> to disability-rich gimp;
> And from "white man's burden"
> to every man's burden.
>
> It is always a profound metamorphosis.
> Whether from cursed by man to cursed by
>   God;
> or from scripture-condemned to God-
>   ordained;
> my final form is never of my choosing;
> I only wield the wand;
> You are the magician.[32]

Because of a spinal cord injury, a consequence of slipping on ice, Kitty Lunn became a wheelchair user after living as a nondisabled person for thirty-six years and working as an actor and dancer.[33] A ballerina since she was eight years old, Lunn not only teaches dance from her wheelchair to children with disabilities, but also founded her own dance company combining disabled and nondisabled dancers. She considers this connection of wheelchair dancing to traditional dancing a form of inclusion: "If we pursue this as professionals, if we set the standards like the African-American dancers who wanted to do classical ballet instead of modern dance, if we maintain

high professional standards, years from now mainstream dance companies may include dancers with disabilities."

A member of the Council of Actor's Equity since June 1990 and chair of its disability committee, Lunn has actively worked to increase access to theaters for all people with disabilities as well as to foster employment for actors with all kinds of impairments. Lunn declares, "If Actor's Equity supports nontraditional casting to encourage employing women and ethnic minorities, people with disabilities also must be included. Of course that means accessible audition spaces as well as all the required accommodations, and all these assumptions are accepted across the board now by all the performance unions."

Like Kitty Lunn, Dana Tozer—who had been "a stand-up dancer" for eighteen years before she broke her back in an automobile accident—feared the dancing chapter of her life was closed.[34] Nonetheless, Tozer is now a wheelchair-dancing member of the Cleveland Ballet Dancing Wheels, a company "creating a new vocabulary of dance" by featuring both "stand-up" and "sit-down" performers dancing together. Company director Mary Verdi-Fletcher, born with spina bifida, is challenging more than commonly-held assumptions about aesthetics. Verdi-Fletcher describes people's response to the company's work: "People have said, 'I totally changed my mind about my perceptions of disability and of dance. Next time I see a person rolling down the street in their wheelchair, I'm not going to say, that poor guy or that poor girl. I'm going to say, I wonder if they're a dancer, or I wonder if they're a lawyer or a doctor.'"

Changing Perceptions and the Media

Besides playing a critical role in the passage of major legislation from 1973 to 1990, the disability rights movement "has brought together people from all stations and backgrounds who share a common experience and a common interest that relate to disability, and inspired them to work for themselves and others," Lex Frieden points out.[35] "Because of the movement, there's been an enormous amount of progress," observes Eunice Fiorito, a pivotal force in the struggle for disability rights.[36] She adds:

> Many people with disabilities feel good about themselves now, and that has triggered their activities in the community, where they have been doing things along with nondisabled people. The effect has been not only much more consciousness-raising about disability issues among people with disabilities themselves, but also among nondisabled people. And in turn that has caused everyone to feel an unprecedented degree of comfort when talking about disability.

Susan Scheer, former deputy director of the Mayor's Office for People with Disabilities, indicates that the class of educated professionals with disabilities spawned by the movement are achieving influential positions: "They're becoming lawyers, judges, and doctors; they're entering the academy and politics. They are changing, and they will continue to change people's attitudes towards disability, professionally and socially."[37] When Edward Roberts became director of the California State Department of Rehabilitation in 1975, he was an anomaly; Judith E. Heumann's appointment as assistant secretary of the Office of Special Education and Rehabilitation Services at the U.S. Department of Education, though very meaningful to the disability community, was no surprise. Moreover, Heumann's role in the Clinton administration demonstrates how some former disability activists have moved from outside the power structure to inside the corridors of power. Also, the disability rights movement has been

well served by Justin Dart's relationship to three presidents: Reagan, Bush, and Clinton. When President Bush signed the ADA, Justin Dart was on one side of the president and Evan Kemp, another well-connected disability rights advocate, was on the other.

"One effect of having some access to insiders in government has been the increasingly sophisticated approach to the media that the disability community has been exhibiting in the late 1990s," Scheer adds. "Litigating cases and lobbying elected officials were the traditional techniques that the community used in the past. But now these techniques are used in combination with establishing connections with television, radio, and newspaper reporters and educating them." Scheer notes that "the language in the news accounts and editorials, although far from perfect, is much improved; for example, 'wheelchair user' is finally beginning to replace 'wheelchair bound.' Also, stories have more balance, and the result is that the public is beginning to understand disability issues."

James Weisman, counsel for Eastern Paralyzed Veterans Association, is scathingly critical of the editorial policy of the *New York Times* regarding issues affecting people with disabilities: "But it is the *Times* which has opposed accessible transportation, and the *Times* which opposed amending the building code to mandate access in new construction. And the *Times* opposed the Americans with Disabilities Act.... If a loophole can be found, or the law changed, believes the *New York Times,* people with disabilities can be excluded without moral consequence."[38] Ironically, Weisman points out, "When the *New York Times* opposed the Americans with Disabilities Act, Republican Senator Jesse Helms of North Carolina, an outspoken opponent of civil rights laws, told Congress that even 'this liberal New York newspaper' opposed the ADA."

To support his characterization of the newspaper, Weisman offers examples of *New York Times* editorials from November 1979 to May 1991. Responding to Section 504 of the Rehabilitation Act of 1973, one editorial stated: "The costs of rendering the handicapped 'equal' have threatened to become especially acute in publicly financed transportation."[39] Over four years later, another editorial reacted to a court injunction concerning subway station reconstruction: "The first object of a wise but concerned policy cannot be to make people with serious disabilities move as if they did not have them."[40] More than five and a half years after this editorial, another editorial expressed skepticism about the social value of the Americans with Disabilities Act: "With surprisingly narrow public scrutiny, Congress is moving swiftly to extend broad civil rights protection to the nation's 40 million disabled citizens. The sentiment is laudable.... But the legislation is vague...costs could be monumental....Predictions about the bill's projected benefits are obviously speculative."[41] And most surprisingly, less than two years later, an editorial attacked the concept of wheelchair accessibility: "Unfortunately...federal law requires newly constructed public facilities to be accessible to the handicapped."[42]

As Scheer states, "By 1997 the approach of the *New York Times,* as well as other newspapers, to disability issues showed signs of change. The *Times* gave increased prominence and serious treatment to the disability community." A sample of newspaper articles appearing since 1997 supports Scheer's observation. The June 1997 Sunday *New York Times* lead articles in the "Week in Review" and the "Real Estate" sections dealt thoughtfully with concerns important to the disability community. Although the first of these articles, "Disability Culture," tended to sensationalize the subject, the author made an effort to explain the "new

militant attitude among many of the disabled."[43] The second article, "Architecture in the Age of Accessibility," pointed out that "it [accessibility] is reshaping the entire built environment. And it is defining the architecture of the 1990s as much as any stylistic impulse."[44]

Without ignoring arguments against the accessibility laws, the article presented the reasons for the new architectural standards: "Advocates of barrier-free architecture are pursuing the even more ambitious goal of what they call universally accessible buildings; comfortable, usable and safe for anyone whose physical capabilities differ from those of an able-bodied, average-sized adult. As baby boomers go gray, the thinking goes, there will be more need than ever for environments that are easy to get around." Appearing about ten months later, a *New York Times* front page article, "New Needs for Retirement Complexes' Oldest," demonstrated how the meaning of accessibility has become painfully clear to retirees who, in their eighties, can no longer negotiate the one flight of steps to their Florida condominiums that they scarcely noticed when they were in their sixties.[45]

In "Disrupting Sales at Greyhound: Disabled Protest Bus Access," the *New York Times* offered an evenhanded account of how disability advocates—mostly wheelchair and scooter users—demonstrated against the inaccessibility of the over-the-road buses of the nation's largest interstate bus company.[46] Another example of a detailed and sympathetic report of a disability issue—by a newspaper not known for its support of the disability rights movement, the *Wall Street Journal*—was evident in "The Vision Thing: Mr. Magoo Watches U.S. Cultural History and Struggles to Adapt."[47] This article traced the background of this "comic" figure, revealing its inappropriateness as a representation of the experience of blindness. Although the Handicapped Adults Association protest in late 1997 against traffic hazards near a busy shopping center paralyzed Bronx rush-hour traffic, the New York *Daily News* gave an almost favorable description of the demonstration.[48]

Later in the same year, "Dateline NBC," featuring journalist John Hockenberry, honestly portrayed examples of illegal employment and housing discrimination frequently experienced by people with visible disabilities.[49] Still, Hockenberry concluded the program in a celebratory spirit, demonstrating the freedom that he enjoys as a wheelchair user on the Brooklyn Bridge accessible walkway—an accommodation secured by disability activism.[50] "Technologies That Enable the Disabled," a lengthy front-page article in the "Money and Business" section of the *New York Times,* presented with clarity and specificity illustrations of significant contributions to society that people with very severe disabilities are making because of technologies that allow them to express their considerable talents.[51]

By 1999, the *New York Times* featured a front-page article acknowledging the "Power of the Disabled" as a political force with regard to two seminal issues.[52] The first concerned the unreasonable requirement that many people with disabilities choose to be *either* workers *or* beneficiaries. The second dealt with "the highly unusual turnabout"—a product of effective disability activism—that resulted in nineteen of twenty-six states withdrawing from a U.S. Supreme Court brief supporting institutionalization of many people with disabilities.

Lex Frieden emphasizes what he considered the two most important media events related to the disability rights movement and "maybe the most important aspect of the ADA since laws are as much perception as reality."[53] First, he notes the decision made by CNN News president Ed

(not Ted) Turner the night before President Bush signed the ADA. "I happened to be there," Frieden remembers, "when Turner called the Washington Bureau of CNN and said the ADA signing ceremony should be covered live." Frieden continues:

> Since the ceremony was scheduled for 10 a.m., the Atlanta office argued that they could not preempt their 10 a.m. World News for what seemed to them an insignificant law. But the Washington staff insisted that this was the most important legislation since the 1964 civil rights law, and CNN would be negligent if it didn't show the world this news event. Atlanta finally resolved themselves to presenting the signing, and millions of people around the world saw and heard the President say about the ADA, "Let the shameful wall of exclusion come tumbling down."

The second most important event, Frieden explains, happened the day after the Senate's final passage of the law: "The ADA was the headline in the *New York Times,* the *Washington Post,* and every other major American newspaper. That was the first time that millions of people were exposed to disability rights as the number one story."

Alongside the mainstream media, in which twenty-two journalists write regular columns on disability issues, a disability media network has evolved so that by 2000, an estimated three thousand to thirty-five hundred newsletters, two hundred magazines, and fifty to sixty newspapers were regularly published.[54] Although most of these publications are devoted to a particular organization or disability, a few—covering cross-disability concerns—are broad-based, such as *New York Able* newspaper, and *Mainstream* and *We* magazines, as well as the politically activist *Ragged Edge* and *Mouth* magazines.[55] Given the increased number of people with disabilities appearing in advertisements, as well as in television and film, the emergence of glossy magazines, such as *We,* targeted to upper-income consumers with disabilities is not surprising. "*We,* a magazine that calls itself 'a lifestyle magazine for people with disabilities,' . . . has made the advertising department at the General Motors Corporation take notice."[56] A General Motors spokesperson said, "We're doing a lot of niche marketing to people with disabilities, and this publication is reaching them in a totally different way than they've ever been reached. It's more upscale." In addition, approximately forty radio programs and thirty-eight to forty television programs are broadcast throughout the nation. While most of these are local broadcasts, both Greg Smith's "On a Roll" and Bob Enteen's "Living Without Limits" are nationally syndicated radio programs.[57]

Between 1995 and 2000, the rapid growth in dial-in services, making approximately sixty mainstream newspapers—including the *New York Times, USA Today* and the *Chicago Tribune*—available to blind people by means of computer and telephone, has been "startling," declares Charles Winston, founder and director in 1990 of the National Telability Media Center. A nonprofit research organization created to promote the growth and development of mass media for people with disabilities, the center seeks to identify the media that serves people with disabilities and disseminate this information in all fifty states. Winston, who became blind while working in journalism and public relations, recognized the disability community's need for a clearinghouse to provide a resource base for the increasing number of disability publications and broadcasts emerging throughout the country.

Assessment of the Movement

Although welcoming the rise in newsletters, newspapers, magazines, radio and television broadcasts, and internet sites in the disability media, many disability advocates are concerned that they rarely get the opportunity to speak for themselves about their issues in the mainstream media. "Can you imagine the broadcast of a serious panel discussion on race relations in the United States without a person of color being present or a discussion of gender discrimination without a woman being present?" asks Anne Emerman, former director of the New York City Office of People with Disabilities.[58] "Our issues are always being discussed by people who are experts about us—politicians, policymakers, doctors, social workers—but not us. It's as if they thought, what do we know about ourselves? With all the enlightened thinking about disability, there's still that residue of paternalism." Emerman adds, "Sometimes disability advocates say, 'Well we're getting visibility in ads, and sometimes even an actor with a disability appears in a show.' That's good, but it's not the same as speaking for yourself in a serious public forum, like other people do, about the hard issues that affect not only your quality of life but maybe even your survival."

Eunice Fiorito, first president of the board of the American Coalition of Citizens with Disabilities, asserts, "What's missing is a strong unified public voice on disability issues, the kind of voice that can only emanate from a cross-disability national coalition that speaks for the nation's fifty-four million people with disabilities. That's what the American Coalition of Citizens with Disabilities once did, and we need an organization like that again."[59] "What's more," Fiorito continues, "people with disabilities need to know their rights. We need training sessions on the ADA and on the IDEA, like the ones we had on Section 504, because if we don't monitor compliance, nobody will. Eventually, we'll get enforcement with penalties for noncompliance, but that will take another generation." Fiorito was referring to the fact that although the ADA has clear-cut effective dates for its various provisions, there are no inspectors that check for ADA compliance. Both the ADA and the IDEA are complaint-driven, which means that enforcement most often occurs when individuals or organizations either threaten or actually file complaints or lawsuits. Legal fees are available for successful complaints and lawsuits, but there are no sanctions for noncompliance.

Although many disability advocates complain about the lack of ADA compliance, the Dole Foundation's Paul Hearne uses a wide lens to examine the ADA: "Is the ADA working?" he asks.[60] "Have we gotten rid of racism yet because of the 1964 Civil Rights Act or sexism because women were added to the law in 1972? Since the ADA became effective in 1992, it's preposterous to assume that all people with disabilities should have jobs by now, to which they arrive in their accessible vehicles." Hearne differentiates between the "easier issues," with which the disability community has achieved some success—transportation and accessibility—as opposed to the "harder issues," which present formidable challenges for the future—employment, education, personal assistance services, and health care, as well as institutionalization of and experimentation on people with disabilities.[61]

"Harder than passing the ADA," asserts Marca Bristo, chairperson of the National Council on Disability since May 1994, "is the struggle to take the promise of the ADA, and the values embedded in that law, and push them across public policy. We have the daunting challenge to look at all of our systems and to change them."[62] To illustrate, Bristo refers to the necessity for "an overarching national policy on employment for people with disabilities, a new way of thinking about the issue and committing to it, like the culture shift on smoking." The goal, for Bristo, is to make the percentage of employed working-age Americans with disabilities comparable to that of nondis-

abled people in the workforce.[63] "We won't see a huge shift in employment statistics for the disability population," Bristo adds, "until we can assure that the telecommunication systems that businesses use are developed in such a way that they don't cut out people with disabilities." Bristo is suggesting that these systems would have to be developed or altered, at reasonable costs, to be accessible to people with various disabilities, such as sensory or motor impairments.

In her capacity as NCD chairperson, Bristo describes herself as "a link between the disability grass roots and Washington." Yet she credits "the people in the savvy disability community with breathing life into the ADA with their activism." Fostering cohesion in the community, she encourages "passing the passion on to the next generation and to new groups yet untouched by the progress we have achieved." Despite the setbacks that Bristo anticipates, she maintains that "we of the disability community have set in motion something that can't be stopped."

The energy and commitment is evident "in the faces of the young and in the world's response," she observes:

At the NCD, I get calls many times a month from other governments or disability leaders in other countries for guidance around the disability rights agenda, the law, and other programmatic issues. And this gives me my greatest hope—the ripple effect, the still untapped impact on the whole world. When I travel to other countries, even though I can't speak the language, we can communicate because we speak the same language when it comes to disability.

Bristo acknowledges, however, the formidable task of coping with disability discrimination. To begin to deal with this obstacle, Bristo indicates that "we have to erase some of those very practical barriers for people with disabilities who want to work, as well as for their potential employers." Bristo's concern stems from the way the American health care system is designed. People with disabilities realize that the income they earn from their jobs may jeopardize their necessary health care benefits such as, for example, their personal attendant services or essential medication. Even though increases may often be unjustifiable, employers fear that their health insurance costs will rise precipitously if they hire people with disabilities.

Gay Men's Health Crisis (GMHC) counsel Susan Dooha refers to people with disabilities as the "canaries in the mine" in regard to the 1990s experiment with health care financing and delivery.[64] Compared to the needs of the general public, the medical requirements of people with disabilities tend to be more specialized, immediate, and acute. Not only do they frequently require a network to provide for their health care needs, but their problems are often more varied and extensive than those of nondisabled people. Since the weaknesses of a managed care system in providing health services become evident first in the disability population, many people with disabilities face changes in the delivery and financing of health care with trepidation. Dooha believes, however, that the regulations barring discrimination in the ADA ultimately may ensure that people with disabilities receive access to appropriate health care, including specialists, durable medical equipment, and medications, as well as long-term care and personal assistance services.[65]

Still, Frieden—pointing to the health care crisis that will erupt in about 2005 with the aging of the baby boomers—asks, "Where is the infrastructure they need for medical services, for assisted living in their own homes and communities?"[66] Frieden also is concerned about the future of the disability rights movement:

Independent living centers are not expanding enough for the people who need to be served. Annually, less than $100 million goes into the independent living centers that keep people productive at all stages of their lives, and one and a half billion dollars is spent for rehabilitation, which serves fewer people and provides fewer jobs. Also, ethnic and racial minorities and young people are not adequately involved in disability advocacy. It's our job in the movement to attract this underrepresented population.

Scheer suggests that young people are not attracted to the movement in the 1990s as they had been in the 1970s because—"like the civil rights movement and the women's movement—the disability rights movement seems to be a victim of its own success."[67] On the whole, mainstreaming has increased the participation of people with disabilities in the wider society, but it has diminished the sense of community, the bonding, between members of the disability population, Scheer observes. "They're willing to fight for themselves—get note-takers, access to libraries—but they're not as involved in the movement as people were in the 1970s." Also, she comments on how young people with disabilities are enjoying the benefits of accessibility that came out of the struggle of the generation that preceded them:

> They take these benefits for granted; they think they were always there, and they'll always be there. They don't realize that if they're not vigilant, they can lose what they've got. Clearly, the disability rights movement is not as visible, not as entrenched, as other civil rights movements. So, as a fringe movement, it's more vulnerable than the other movements. For example, if in flush times, like the 1990s, the expenditure of money can be used as an excuse against accessibility, special education, and health care, then what will happen in bad economic times?

Disability advocate Frank Bowe offers one reason that the legacy of the disability rights movement—more than other civil rights movements—is difficult to transfer from one generation to the next.[68] Since parents of children with disabilities usually are nondisabled, these children must, themselves, confront the stigma of disability and then emerge with self-esteem sufficient to allow them to discover and carry on the tradition of disability activism. "The process of moving toward assertiveness and independence, then, must begin anew with each child [with a disability]."

Judith E. Heumann proposes ways for the disability community to face the social and political realities of disability as well as counter the charitable model of cure: "We have to demystify who we are so people understand that disability is a natural part of life. The barriers to integration allow people to think disability is an unmitigated tragedy. But if the proper policies were implemented, we could make contributions that we're not able to make now because people assume we're not able to make them."[69] Calling for an increasingly strong, honest, and forthright dialogue with the American people, Heumann urges the disability community to make the effort to understand the fears of the wider society, and "put a face to those concerns."

The movement has not been as effective as it could be, Heumann believes, because disability advocates have not been strategic enough:

> We need to be more knowledgeable and analytical about what exists in other countries for people with disabilities—like on-the-job accommodations with government supports, modifications of apartments and homes, and appropriate health care. Clearly, health care is a disability issue for everyone because if you don't get the right coverage, a medical condition can become a disabling one. And what are we doing to educate the baby boomers, because they are us tomorrow?

In order to be seen as a constituency to be listened to, Heumann continues, the disability community will have to become increasingly political, consistently involved in party and elective politics:[70] "We're less political than other minority groups. We're mainly a middle-class movement, so we're not the rainbow we should be. And the fact that we're not representing a diversity is problematic because it means that some people are disenfranchised, and that limits our political clout." In fact, she asserts that the disability rights movement has to be an integral part of the overall movement for change:

> We have to appreciate what poverty means in this country because poverty is a significant cause of disability, and poverty adversely affects disability.[71] It is critically important that we look to our other civil rights partners and the larger economic picture. Then we can become a bigger player, and a diversified movement will naturally evolve. Though the gains of the disability rights movement over the last thirty years have been impressive, they are relatively few in relation to what we yet have to do.

"After all the accomplishments of the disability rights movement," Anne Emerman notes, "if in the late 1990s, the director of the Center for Independence of the Disabled in New York, Marilyn Saviola, can say, 'All the rights and all the programs we've fought for—the ones that keep people like me out of institutions—are back on the table,'[72] then I have grave concerns for the future."[73] Emerman raises the questions pivotal for the future of the disability rights movement:

> How do we educate young people with disabilities—like young people from racial and ethnic minorities—to learn about and embrace their heritage? How do we inspire them to translate that insight into more than sustaining—but even expanding—the hard-fought-for achievements of the disability rights movement? How do we encourage them to forge stronger connections to like-minded people from other communities and other movements?

And how do we get nondisabled people to understand that ours is truly a civil rights struggle, to realize that policies that serve people with disabilities tend to benefit everybody, politically, socially, and economically? How do we explain to nondisabled people that they are not in competition for programs and funding with the disability population, but rather people with disabilities are their friends, their families, and in all likelihood, at some point in their lives, themselves?

A Stealth Movement

"The disability rights movement is at the forefront of the human rights movement because it's one of the most serious—one of the toughest nuts to crack," observes wheelchair innovator Ralf Hotchkiss.[74] Why is this movement different from other rights movements? The movement comprises not only the largest minority—fifty-four million Americans with disabilities—but also impacts on their families and friends, who usually are nondisabled. People with disabilities is the only protected class that anyone can enter at any time through birth, accident, illness, or advanced age. Most individuals, at some point in their lives, will have a disability. With the aging of the American population and the advancement of medicine and technology, by 1994-1995 a fifth of the nation's population had some form of disability. The year 2020 will mark almost a revolution in medicine; chronic disease will predominate rather than infectious disease.[75] Dr. Joanne Lynn, director of George Washington University's Center to Improve Care of the Dying, emphasizes that "most women have eight years of disability before they die; most men, five or six."[76] However, unlike other civil rights movements—the African-American civil rights movement, the women's movement, the gay and lesbian rights movement—only the disability rights

movement has been referred to as a "stealth movement."

Perhaps one reason that even many politically sophisticated people are unaware of disability activism is the lack of a charismatic figure: no Martin Luther King Jr. nor Malcolm X, no Betty Frieden nor Gloria Steinem, to epitomize the movement. Certainly the movement has worked toward bringing the issues of people with disabilities before the public, for like Ralph Ellison's "Invisible Man," many members of the disability population, historically, were ignored, isolated, removed from the community. Sherry Lampert, a highly intelligent woman with cerebral palsy, describes her feelings when her parents—who experienced her disability as their shame[77]—tried to hide her by placing her in a hospital ward for children who were developmentally delayed: "I felt like I wasn't part of the human race."[78]

Yet disability, more than other movements, eludes embodiment in one figure. The reason is the inclusiveness of the movement, and its relevance to such a wide and varied spectrum of the population. And herein lies the movement's strength—its great and ever-increasing numbers—as well as its weakness. Shortly before her death in June 1997, Betty Shabazz reminded a group of students in Newark, New Jersey, that her husband, Malcolm X, often said that if you see a picture of the world and your face isn't in it, your job is to put your face there.

She might have added, is there one face with which a quadriplegic wheelchair user, a blind person, a deaf person, a frail elderly person, a person with AIDS, a person with a psychiatric disability, a person with diabetes or cancer, a veteran exposed to nerve gas, and a nondisabled parent of a child with a severe disability can identify? Disability activism has many faces; can one face be emblematic of all the faces of the disability rights movement?

Notes

Preface

1. Elisabeth Young-Bruehl, *The Anatomy of Prejudice* (Cambridge, Mass.: Harvard University Press, 1996).

2. Paul Robinson in "Intolerance," *New York Times,* Sunday, May 19, 1996, sec. 7, p. 41, reviewed Young-Bruehl's *The Anatomy of Prejudice*. Emphasis added. In their excellent history of the gay rights movement in America, *Out For Good* (New York: Simon & Schuster, 1999), authors Dudley Clendenin and Adam Nagomey refer to the movement as "the last great struggle for equal rights in American history to this point" (p. 13). AIDS is prominently discussed in their book, but there is no mention of the Americans with Disabilities Act or other disability legislation relevant to people with HIV or AIDS. The authors link the gay rights movement to other struggles for equal rights—by African Americans, women, Native Americans—but not to the disability community. Although they call the gay and lesbian population an "invisible people," equally invisible are people with disabilities whose goals are much the same.

3. R. C. Smith, *A Case About Amy* (Philadelphia: Temple University Press, 1996). See *Hendrick Hudson Central School District v. Rowley,* 102 S.Ct. 3034 (1982).

4. R. C. Smith, "An Audience for Amy," *Ragged Edge,* May/June 1998, 31-32.

5. In his catalogue of isms, comparable to racism, Andrew Hacker, professor of political science at Queens College of the City University of New York, includes handicapism. See Hacker, *Two Nations: Black and White, Separate, Hostile, Unequal* (New York: Scribners, 1992), 20.

6. Paul Longmore's presentation, Disability Studies Colloquium, New York City Hunter College School of Social Work, December 5, 1997. Longmore refers to *With a Song in My Heart* as an "inspirational" film, *Nightmare on Elm Street* as a "horror" film, and *My Left Foot* as a "realistic" film about a person with a disability, reflecting Christy Brown's "fierce lifelong battle against condescension and contempt." See also Martin F. Norden, *The Cinema of Isolation: The History of Physical Disability in the Movies* (New Jersey: Rutgers University Press, 1994).

7. Peter Hall, "Inventing the Poster Child," the first part of a four-part program, "Beyond Affliction: The Disability History Project," National Public Radio. The program was aired at different times in various parts of the country during the week of May 4, 1998.

8. John M. McNeil, "Current Population Reports: Americans with Disabilities 1994-95," published by U.S. Department of Commerce, Census Bureau, August 1997, 1-2. Unless otherwise indicated, statistical data is from this source.

9. "Follow-up to 1994 Research," *Ragged Edge,* September/October 1998, 5-6. Reference to the 1998 Harris Poll by Louis Harris and Associates for the National Organization on Disability from this source.

10. The three 1999 employment cases are *Sutton v. United Airlines, Inc.,* 119 S.Ct. 2139; *Murphy v. United Parcel Service, Inc.,* 119 S.Ct. 2133, and *Albertson's Inc. v. Kirkingburg,* 119 S.Ct. 2162. The U.S. Court of Appeals

in the *Garrett* case held for the plaintiff, 193 F3d 1214 (11th Cir 1999), but the State of Alabama has appealed to the Supreme Court. The Supreme Court's decision in the *Kimel* case can be found in 120 S.Ct. 631 (2000). In *City of Boerne v. Flores,* 521 U.S. 507 (1997), the Supreme Court held that under the Fourteenth Amendment, Congress may enact civil rights legislation only if the statute is designed to remedy a history of unconstitutional conduct and if the remedy is proportionate to the history of such violations. Prominent disability rights attorney Stephen Gold fears that the new federalism evident in the *Kimel* decision and other Supreme Court rulings does not bode well for disability rights advocates. References to threats to Title II of the ADA from conversations with John Gresham, senior litigation counsel at New York Lawyers for the Public Interest, May 12, 2000, and Stephen Gold, April 28, 2000.

11. Examples of "reasonable accommodations" include ramps for wheelchair users, computer voice synthesizers for blind people, and assistive listening devices for those who are hard of hearing. Because they are not prohibitively expensive, most "reasonable accommodations" are not difficult to provide.

12. Robert Pear, "Senate Approves Health Care for Disabled," *New York Times,* June 17, 1999, A28. References to Senator Edward M. Kennedy from this source. On October 19, 1999, the House passed the Work Incentives Improvement Act by an overwhelming vote (Justice For All, email jfa@jfanow.org, October 20, 1999). On December 17, 1999, WIIA (PL 106-170) was signed by President Clinton.

Chapter One

1. Judith E. Heumann, "Statement," *Civil Rights Issues of Handicapped Americans: Public Policy Implications* (Washington, D.C.: A Consultation Sponsored by the United States Commission on Civil Rights, May 13–14, 1980), 231. When Heumann—winner in 1993 of the first Betts Award for outstanding contribution to people with disabilities—made this statement in 1980, she was the deputy director of the Berkeley, California, Center for Independent Living. References to the postage stamp, "Hope for the Crippled," from this source.

2. Hugh Gregory Gallagher, *FDR's Splendid Deception,* rev. ed. (Arlington, Va.: Vandamere Press, 1994), 96.

3. Gallagher, *FDR's Splendid Deception,* 27.

4. Doris Kearns Goodwin, *No Ordinary Time* (New York: Simon & Schuster, 1994), 16–17.

5. Maureen Dowd, "Not-So-Splendid Deception," *New York Times,* May 2, 1996, A2.

6. Karl E. Meyer, "Editorial Notebook," *New York Times,* May 12, 1996, sec. 4, p. 13.

7. "Letters to the Editor," *New York Times,* May 16, 1996, 24.

8. Dowd, "Not-So-Splendid Deception," A2. At the April 19, 1998, New York City 504 Democratic Club dinner, Christopher Roosevelt, grandson of FDR, stated that the National Organization on Disability had pledged to raise private funds to add a statue of FDR in his wheelchair to the national memorial.

9. Though sympathetic to a historically accurate depiction of Roosevelt in the memorial, George F. Will exaggerates the importance of political correctness in the controversy. "The Only Thing To Fear: Political Incorrectness," *New York Post,* May 9, 1996, 33.

10. John Gliedman and William Roth, *The Unexpected Minority: Handicapped Children in America* (New York: Harcourt Brace Jovanovich, 1980).

11. Although his March 1, 1945, speech President Roosevelt made reference to his braces, "about ten pounds of steel around the bottom of my legs," the radio audience was hearing about, not seeing, evidence of his disability (Goodwin, *No Ordinary Time,* 586). The fatigue FDR was experiencing near the end of his life would be recognized by 1984 as post-polio syndrome, a continuous weakening of the muscles originally affected by the polio virus. He died on April 12, 1945.

12. Goodwin, *No Ordinary Time,* 533.

13. Goodwin, *No Ordinary Time,* 532.

14. Gallagher, *FDR's Splendid Deception,* 27.

15. In the Jim Crow South, African Americans who contracted polio were turned away from hospitals and facilities such as Warm Springs in Georgia. Although too many were inadequately treated, some were sent to Tuskegee Infantile Paralysis Institute in Alabama (*A Paralyzing Fear: The Story of Polio in America,*

the Center for History in the Media at George Washington University, Paul Wagner Productions, a Nina Gilden Seavey film).

16. Gallagher, *FDR's Splendid Deception*, 57. Winner of the 1996 Betts Award, Gallagher played a pivotal role in the development and passage of the federal Architectural Barriers Act of 1968.

17. Gallagher, *FDR's Splendid Deception*, 41.

18. Gallagher, *FDR's Splendid Deception*, 41-42, 154. References to Fred Botts from this source.

19. Mary Johnson quoted Longmore in "The Bargain," *The Disability Rag* (September–October 1989), 6. In 1961, Eleanor Roosevelt told Judith Heumann and her mother, Ilse, that if FDR were as young as Judith when he contracted polio, he would have dealt with it better than he did (interview with Ilse Heumann, June 22, 1996).

20. Goodwin, *No Ordinary Time*, 586-87.

21. Martha Fay, "Lungs of Iron," review of Katherine Black's *In the Shadow of Polio*, appeared in the *New York Times*, Sunday, June 2, 1996, sec. 7, p. 19.

22. As a 1996 presidential candidate with a clear physical impairment resulting from World War II wounds, Bob Dole—whose disability is much less severe than Roosevelt's was—appeared ambivalent regarding disability issues. Although he established the Dole Foundation (a nonprofit organization promoting employment for people with disabilities), Dole when campaigning for the presidency, seemed unsure how to position himself as a person with a disability.

23. Unless otherwise indicated, references to the League of the Physically Handicapped from interview with Florence Haskell, December 3, 1995, and Herman Joseph's interviews with Sylvia Bassoff, December 7, 1985, and Haskell, March 29, 1986.

24. "Crippled Pickets 'Torture' Harris," *New York Times*, June 21, 1935, 21.

25. Frances Lide, "Girl Leader of Cripples Asks Plan to End 'Discrimination,'" *Washington Star*, May 11, 1936.

26. References to slogan from the film *A Paralyzing Fear*.

27. Unless otherwise indicated, references to the Birthday Balls, the National Foundation for Infantile Paralysis, and the March of Dimes from Gallagher, *FDR's Splendid Deception*, 147-51.

28. Goodwin, *No Ordinary Time*, 575.

29. Stated in the film *A Paralyzing Fear*. References to Basil O'Connor from this source.

30. References to Eddie Cantor from the film *A Paralyzing Fear*.

31. Other means were used to raise funds to find a cure for polio. For example, in movie theaters, films would be stopped in the middle to allow collection cans for the March of Dimes to be passed up and down the aisles; the patrons did not seem to mind. Shown in the film *A Paralyzing Fear*.

32. The oral Sabin vaccine replaced the injected Salk vaccine throughout the world because not only is the Sabin vaccine cheaper and easier to administer than the injected vaccine, but with the oral vaccine the recipient's immunity also is transmittable even to those who have not swallowed it since the virus is alive. A small percentage of those receiving the oral vaccine, however, contract polio, so the federal Centers for Disease Control and Prevention recommended that beginning January 1, 2000, all four doses of the vaccine should be the injected inactivated form of the virus. Information on Sabin and Salk vaccines from "U.S. Panel Proposes a Change in Administering Polio Vaccine," *New York Times*, June 21, 1996, A14; "Morning Edition," National Public Radio, June 16, 1996; and Denise Grady, "Doctors Urge Polio Shots to Replace Oral Vaccine," *New York Times*, December 7, 1999, A21.

33. No longer a menace in the United States after the Salk and Sabin vaccines, polio did not disappear from the world. Ironically, because of the nature of the disease, improvement in sanitation—which prevented most other diseases—sometimes brought on polio epidemics as children never acquired the immunity to polio that they would have in a less sterilized environment. Discussed in the film *A Paralyzing Fear*.

34. Parents did play *some* role in combating polio; for example, in the Mothers' March on Polio—a campaign waged to raise money for the March of Dimes before Salk's successful polio vaccine—in the evening women went from house to house where lighted porches designated the residents' desire to make a contribution. Shown in the film *A Paralyzing Fear*.

35. Information concerning United Cerebral Palsy, the Association for the Help of Retarded Children,

and Association of Children with Retarded Mental Development from interview with Rachelle Grossman, August 20, 1997, former assistant director of the Department of Family and Clinical Services at AHRC.

36. "The Overdue Revolution" in "Beyond Affliction: The Disability History Project," National Public Radio, May 1998. The four-part program, "Inventing the Poster Child," "What's Work Got To Do with It," "The Overdue Revolution," and "Tomorrow's Children," was aired at different times in various parts of the country during the week of May 4, 1998.

37. Nora Groce, *The U.S. Role in International Disability Activities: A History and a Look Toward the Future* (Oakland, Calif.: International Disability Exchanges and Studies Project, 1992), 17-20. Unless otherwise indicated, information on Easter Seal from this source.

38. Interview with Eileen Healy, April 11, 1997, former director of the New York City office of Easter Seal.

39. Interview with Eileen Healy, April 11, 1997.

40. Gallagher, *FDR's Splendid Deception*, 146.

41. Leslie Bennetts, "Jerry vs. the Kids," *Vanity Fair* 56(8) (September 1993): 82.

42. John Hockenberry, *Moving Violations: War Zones, Wheelchairs, and Declarations of Independence* (New York: Hyperion, 1995), 33. Hockenberry apparently meant MD (muscular dystrophy), not MDA (Muscular Dystrophy Association).

43. Gliedman and Roth, *The Unexpected Minority*, 10.

44. Frank Bowe, "An Overview Paper on Civil Rights Issues of Handicapped Americans: Public Policy Implications," *Civil Rights Issues of Handicapped Americans: Public Policy Implications* (Washington, D.C.: A Consultation Sponsored by the United States Commission on Civil Rights, May 13-14, 1980), 8-9.

45. Paul K. Longmore, "The Life of Randolph Bourne and the Need for a History of Disabled People," *Reviews in American History* 13(4) (December 1985): 583-86. References to the life and times of Randolph Bourne, as well as to sterilization and mercy killing for people with disabilities, from this source.

46. Irving Zola is quoted in additional material prepared for the written transcript of "Beyond Affliction: The Disability History Project."

47. Bowe, "Overview Paper," 9. See chapter 10 for discussion of veterans and disability.

48. Bowe, "Overview Paper," 9.

49. "What's Work Got To Do with It" in "Beyond Affliction: The Disability History Project."

Chapter Two

1. Oliver Sacks, *Seeing Voices: A Journey into the World of the Deaf* (California: University of California Press, 1989; reprint, New York: HarperPerennial, 1990), 8-9.

2. Harlan Lane, *When the Mind Hears: A History of the Deaf* (New York: Random House, 1984; reprint, New York: Vintage, 1989), 93.

3. As late as July 1997, news sources as sophisticated as the *New York Times* and National Public Radio referred to deaf people as deaf-mutes without noting how offensive many in the deaf community consider this term—which reflects a lack of awareness of the authentic language of some deaf people, sign language.

4. Lane, *When the Mind Hears*, 111. Reference to Ponce de Leon from this source.

5. Andrew Solomon, "Defiantly Deaf," *New York Times* magazine, Sunday, August 28, 1994, sec. 6, 38-45, 62, 65-68.

6. Frances A. Koestler, *The Unseen Minority: A Social History of Blindness in America* (New York: David McKay Company, 1976), 23.

7. Koestler, *The Unseen Minority*, 18-19, 31-32, 90. Unless otherwise indicated, references to Henry Randolph Latimore and Robert Benjamin Irwin from this source.

8. Sacks, *Seeing Voices*, 26-27. Unless otherwise indicated, references to the Congress of Milan from this source.

9. John Dewey referred to Horace Mann with these words in "The Challenge of Democracy to Education," *The Later Works, 1925-1953,* vol. II, ed. Jo Ann Boydston (Carbondale: Southern Illinois University Press, 1991), 182.

10. Steven Pinker, *The Language Instinct: How the Mind Creates Language* (New York: William Morrow and Company, 1994), 237.

11. Nora Ellen Groce, *Everyone Here Spoke Sign Language: Hereditary Deafness on Martha's Vineyard* (Cambridge: Harvard University Press, 1985).

12. Sacks, *Seeing Voices*, 32.

13. Pinker, *The Language Instinct*, 293.

14. Ibid., 18–19.

15. Researchers discovered that deaf children in China and the United States follow the same patterns in learning and using sign language. "Morning Edition," National Public Radio News, January 15, 1998.

16. Carol Padden and Tom Humphries, *Deaf in America: Voices from a Culture* (Cambridge: Harvard University Press, 1988), 118–19.

17. Lane, *When the Mind Hears*, 53–54, 63.

18. Ibid., 162, 182–83.

19. Ibid., 199, 222.

20. Ibid., 6.

21. After the blind students of the Columbia Institution were transferred to another school in 1865, the Columbia Institution became known as the Institution for the Deaf and Dumb. The college division, then called the National Deaf-Mute College, was changed to Gallaudet College in 1893 in honor of Thomas Gallaudet, and later became Gallaudet University. See "The History of Gallaudet University," on the university's web site: http://www.depts.gallaudet.edu

22. Lane, *When the Mind Hears*, 397–99.

23. Sacks, *Seeing Voices*, 27.

24. "The Overdue Revolution" in "Beyond Affliction: The Disability History Project," National Public Radio, May 1998. The four-part program, "Inventing the Poster Child," "What's Work Got To Do with It," "The Overdue Revolution," and "Tomorrow's Children," was aired at different times in various parts of the country during the week of May 4, 1998.

25. Lane, *When the Mind Hears*, 394–95. References to the first meeting of the National Convention of Deaf-Mutes from this source.

26. Lane, *When the Mind Hears*, 404.

27. H-Dirksen L. Bauman, "Beyond Speech and Writing: Recognizing American Sign Language Literature in the MLA," *Profession*, The Modern Language Association of America, 1997, 174.

28. Sacks, *Seeing Voices*, 32.

29. Koestler, *The Unseen Minority*, 95–96.

30. Description of Braille from Hilarie Lynne Luxton, "Factors Affecting Rehabilitation Teachers' Braille Instruction of Adults Who Are Blind and Visually Impaired" (Ed.D. diss., Teachers College, Columbia University, 1993), 15–16.

31. Louis Braille was a student in Valentin Hauy's Parisian school (Koestler, *The Unseen Minority*, 397–98). Hauy was one of the three great founding fathers of education of blind people, along with Samuel Gridley Howe and Johann Wilhelm Klein (Koestler, *The Unseen Minority*, 303).

32. Koestler, *The Unseen Minority*, 96–98.

33. Ibid., 99–101.

34. Luxton, "Factors," 17–19.

35. According to the 1991–1992 Census, of the almost ten million Americans age fifteen and older who have difficulty reading words and letters even with glasses or contact lenses, approximately eighty-five thousand use Braille and only ten to fifteen thousand use Braille extensively. Statistical information provided by the American Foundation for the Blind. Because school systems used mainstreaming as an excuse to cut costs by reducing the number of Braille teachers, "in the past 30 years, the percentage of blind children learning Braille in the United States has fallen to less than 10 percent from about 50 percent," the National Federation of the Blind reported ("70% of Blind Lack Jobs; Computer Mouse Shares the Blame," *New York Times*, July 3, 1999), A12.

36. Koestler, *The Unseen Minority*, 130. References to long-playing records for blind people from this source.

37. Koestler, *The Unseen Minority,* 146.

38. Ibid., 209. Social reformers, such as Samuel Gridley Howe—and Dorothea Dix with whom he worked closely—were finding public funding for institutions that would provide care, education, and employment opportunities for individuals who were considered "mentally unfit," which included children and adults with birth defects, as well as those who were developmentally delayed, epileptic, dyslexic, deaf, autistic, and blind. Information on Howe and Dix from interview with Sandra Marlow, June 23, 1997, former librarian at Fernald State School for People with Mental Retardation, an institution established by Howe in the early 1850s.

39. Winifred Holt Mather, Edith Holt Bloodgood, and Rufus Graves Mather, *First Lady of the Lighthouse: A Biography of Winifred Holt Mather* (New York: The Lighthouse, The New York Association for the Blind, 1952), 110.

40. Ibid., 29, 84, 163, 165, 166, 171, 173, 206.

41. Koestler, *The Unseen Minority,* 315-16.

42. Unless otherwise indicated, information about the guide dog movement in the United States from Koestler, *The Unseen Minority,* 304-7. Although legally blind, Stephen Kuusisto, author of *Planet of the Blind* (New York: Dial Press, 1998), spent his childhood and young adulthood "passing" as sighted. Because of the stigma associated with each, the concept of "passing" is relevant to disability as it is to race.

43. Koestler, *The Unseen Minority,* 315. The story of the white cane movement from this source.

44. About twenty years ago, the passage of a federal law requiring localities, nationally, to permit cars to turn right on a red light, roused William Pickman—from the New York City chapter of the American Council of the Blind—to organize the Committee Against Right on Red (CARR), a citywide coalition representing blind people and others with disabilities, parents of young children, and older people. Consequently, the federal government did *not* mandate right on red in New York City.

45. Information on the difference between the pencil tip and rolling tip canes from interview with mobility instructor Marilyn Newman, May 2, 1998 and with one of her clients, Keisha Powell, December 8, 1996. Newman is the author of "Mobility Techniques that Affect Safety in Travel for Blind and Visually Impaired People," *Journal of Visual Impairment and Blindness,* January 1998. According to Newman, in the late 1980s Raymond Alaire, a Canadian, invented the rolling tip cane for his blind daughter.

46. Floyd Matson, *Walking Alone and Marching Together* (Baltimore, Maryland: National Federation of the Blind, 1990), 27.

47. Ibid., 23.

48. Ibid., 31-34. Unless otherwise indicated, references to Jacobus tenBroek from this source.

49. Matson, *Walking Alone and Marching Together,* 87-88.

50. Ibid., 109-10.

51. Ibid., 100.

52. Ibid., 798. Richard Severo, "Kenneth Jernigan, Advocate For the Blind, Is Dead at 71," *New York Times,* October 14, 1998, A21.

53. Matson quoted Jernigan in *Walking Alone and Marching Together,* 176. Authors' emphasis.

54. Interview with Rami Rabby, October 26, 1996.

55. "How Many More Must Die?" *DIA Activist,* March 1983, 2.

56. Richard K. Scotch, *From Goodwill to Civil Rights: Transforming Federal Disability Policy* (Philadelphia: Temple University Press, 1984), 54-55. References to John Nagle from this source.

57. References to Rami Rabby's lawsuit against the Foreign Service of the State Department from interview with Rabby, October 26, 1996.

58. Although other earlier types of "detectable warning strips" frequently were used, by the 1990s most blind people had indicated their preference for truncated domes.

59. References to Karen Luxton Gourgey, Ph.D., Director of the Computer Center for Visually Impaired People at Baruch College, from interview with Gourgey, September 26, 1996.

60. References to Guide Dog Users and Rosemarie McCaffrey from interview with McCaffrey, May 28, 1998. According to McCaffrey, Seeing Eye or Guiding Eye provides guide dogs free of charge to owners at least sixteen years old who take a training program of four weeks with the first dog and three weeks with any succeeding dogs.

61. Although Alice Crespo, founder and director of Independent Recreation of the Disabled, has had "very positive experiences" with her two guide dogs, she expressed doubt about getting a third: "I loved my two dogs, Xenta and Sunshine. But when each of them died, I really got depressed. I'm not sure I want to go through that pain again." Interview with Alice Crespo, April 11, 1996.

62. Philip K. Howard, *The Death of Common Sense: How Law is Suffocating America* (New York: Random House, 1994), 152.

63. Padden and Humphries, *Deaf in America,* 44.

64. Sacks, *Seeing Voices,* 153. The view that "Deaf" signifies a linguistic minority, not a disability, is the thesis of Harlen Lane's *The Mask of Benevolence: Disabling the Deaf Community* (San Diego: Dawn Sign Press, 1999).

65. Nadina LaSpina, "They Don't Want To Be Like Us," *DIA Activist,* June 1996, 15-16.

66. References to Frank Bowe's criticism of Deaf culture from Bowe's letter to the authors, January 3, 1993. Similar to advocates of Deaf culture, NFB expects to benefit from legislation prohibiting disability discrimination while at the same time denying that blindness is a disability.

67. Because of its historical roots, ASL, the sign language of the United States, is closer to the sign language of France than to the sign language of England.

68. Sacks, *Seeing Voices,* 143. Unless otherwise indicated, references to William Stokoe from this source. Stokoe, who "helped change the way deaf people are educated around the world," died on April 4, 2000 (Eric Nagourney, "William Stokoe Jr., Sign Language Advocate Dies at 80," *New York Times,* April 11, 2000, B10).

69. Sacks, *Seeing Voices,* 151. References to Barbara Kanapell from this source.

70. Padden and Humphries, *Deaf in America,* 2.

71. Frank Bowe letter to authors, January 3, 1993.

72. Edward Dolnick, "Deafness As Culture," *The Atlantic Monthly,* September 1993, 38. References to Roslyn Rosen from this source.

73. Dolnick, "Deaf As Culture," 39.

74. Statistics from the 1991-1992 Census provided by the League for the Hard of Hearing in New York City.

75. These three questions were suggested by a letter by Kate Gladstone in *New York Able,* October 1996, 2 and 13.

76. Sacks, *Seeing Voices,* 157.

77. Joseph P. Shapiro, *No Pity: People with Disabilities Forging a New Civil Rights Movement* (New York: Times Books, 1993), 75.

78. Sacks, *Seeing Voices,* 151.

79. Shapiro, *No Pity,* 74.

80. Erving Goffman, *Stigma: Notes on the Management of Spoiled Identity* (New York: Simon & Schuster, 1963), 138.

81. References to sign language and political organizing of black deaf people, minority interpreters for the deaf, and the comments of Celeste Owens from interview with Celeste Owens, September 30, 1996.

82. In order to be certified, interpreters must pass an examination and pay a fee.

83. A subset of interpreters who are not certified acquire the label "qualified" by accomplishing specific tasks.

84. Latino Deaf Advocates and Asian Deaf Advocates are *political* groups similar to Black Deaf Advocates.

85. References to Marcia Bernstein from interview with Bernstein, January 12, 1997.

86. Interview with Judith Cohen, March 20, 1997, author of *Disability Etiquette: Tips on Interacting with People with Disabilities,* illustrated by Yvette Silver and published by Eastern Paralyzed Veterans Association, in 1998.

87. Felicia R. Lee, "New York to Teach Deaf in Sign Language, Then English," *New York Times,* March 5, 1998, B3. Reference to recent instruction in ASL in schools for deaf students from this source. Deaf students were not taught to lip-read *or* speak; they were taught to lip-read *and* speak.

88. Bauman, "Beyond Speech and Writing," 175.

89. Henry Kisor, *What's That Pig Outdoors? A Memoir of Deafness* (New York: Penguin Books, 1990), 255-58. As a supplement to sign language, there are those who advocate "cued speech," breaking words into syllables and conveying these words with hand signals and lip-reading. Thus, these advocates argue, the academic achievement of deaf people would improve as they could link visual signs to language as it is spoken and written. See Lynette Holloway, "Among the Deaf: Ubiquitous Sign Language Faces a Challenge," *New York Times,* June 22, 2000, A1.

90. Lee, "New York to Teach," B3.

91. Walter Kendrick, "Her Hands Were a Bridge to the World," [Review of *Helen Keller: A Life* by Dorothy Hermann] *New York Times,* Sunday, August 30, 1998, sec. 7, p. 10.

92. Helen Keller, *The Story of My Life* (New York: Doubleday, 1991).

93. Cheryl Marie Wade, "Disability Culture Rap," *The Ragged Edge,* ed. Barrett Shaw (Louisville: The Advocado Press, 1994), 15-16.

Chapter Three

1. Interview with Anne Emerman, April 30, 1997.

2. Douglas Martin, "A Victor Fears For the Future," *New York Times,* April 29, 1997, B1, B6. References to the young adults' ward at Goldwater Memorial Hospital from this source.

3. References to Marilyn Saviola's education and career from interview with Saviola, June 27, 1997.

4. Edward D. Berkowitz, *Disabled Policy: America's Programs for the Handicapped* (Cambridge: Cambridge University Press, 1987), 179.

5. Incarceration is a term used by many disability rights activists to describe people who are unnecessarily institutionalized against their will.

6. Frieda Zames, "The Right To Choose," *Disabled In Action Advocate,* December 1978, 1. References to Lyn Thompson from this source.

7. References to the Independent Contractor Home Care System from material provided by Marvin Wasserman, July 7, 1997.

8. To preserve the rights of self-directing home care consumers, Victoria I. and Ira E. Holland and Edward Litcher established an organization in 1977 that developed into the program Concepts of Independence. References to the expansion of Concepts from conversations with Concepts Client Coordinator Carmen Silver, July 6, 1999, and February 7, 2000.

9. Interview with Marvin Wasserman, July 7, 1997. Concepts of Independence is so highly regarded that the son of Sandra Parrino, chair of the National Council on Disability from 1983 to 1993, travels from Westchester to New York City to hire his personal attendants from this innovative program.

10. Ed Shook, "A College Eases Handicaps of 56 Students by Removing Barriers to Active Campus Life," *The Kansas City Star,* October 4, 1959, 10A. (Material about Kansas State Teachers College provided by Keith Frank, Disabled Students Services Coordinator, Emporia State University, July 25, 1996.)

11. Duane F. Hetlinger, "Physically Handicapped College Graduates," *Vocational Guidance Quarterly,* Winter 1963, 85.

12. References to the University of Illinois at Champaign-Urbana from material provided by the university's Rehabilitation Education Center, April 29, 1996. The 1948 campus at Galesburg was moved to Champaign-Urbana in 1949.

13. The predecessor of Gallaudet College—the Columbia Institution for the Deaf, Dumb, and Blind—was established in 1864 to provide accessibility to higher education for deaf students and blind students. It became limited to deaf students in 1865.

14. Unless otherwise indicated, information about Edward Roberts from conversations with Roberts, May 23, 1994, and July 17, 1994.

15. Jon Oda (Edward Roberts's attendant for three years), "Highlights from Speeches by Ed Roberts" (unpublished manuscript), April 1995, 1. Oda manuscript provided by Bruce Alan Kiernan, board member of World Institute on Disability and close personal friend of Roberts.

16. Oda, "Highlights," 2.

17. Cheryl Marie Wade, "Disability Culture Rap," *The Ragged Edge,* ed. Barrett Shaw (Louisville: The Advocado Press, 1994), 17.

18. Douglas Martin, "Disability Culture: Eager to Bite the Hand That Would Feed Them," *New York Times,* Sunday, June 1, 1997, sec. 4, p. 1.

19. Oda, "Highlights," 3.

20. Unless otherwise indicated, references to Cowell Hospital from Berkowitz, *Disabled Policy,* 200.

21. Oda, "Highlights," 3-4.

22. Interview with Bruce Alan Kiernan, January 19, 1998.

23. Ed Roberts's comments on the relationship between disability rights and other civil rights movements, including the Women's Movement, as well as the Disabled Students Program, from Oda, "Highlights," 4-5.

24. Oda, "Highlights," 6.

25. Carr Massi, *National Paraplegia Foundation News,* January 1977, 1. Massi was president of the New York Metropolitan Chapter of the National Paraplegia Foundation in 1977.

26. Berkowitz, *Disabled Policy,* 201-2. Column by Georgie Ann Geyer, "Wheelchair Power! The Disabled Go Public," that appeared in the *New York Times* on July 5, 1975, was supplied by Judith E. Heumann's mother, Ilsa Heumann, to Berkowitz (p. 266, note 27).

27. Oda, "Highlights," 6.

28. Articles of both Simi Kelley and Jane Wifler appeared in the *National Paraplegia Foundation News,* November 1975, 3.

29. Oda, "Highlights," 7.

30. Judith E. Heumann, "Handicap and Disability," *Disability: Our Challenge,* John P. Hourihan, ed. (New York: Teachers College, Columbia University Press, 1979), 17.

31. Oda, "Highlights," 3.

32. Interview with Robert Levine, August 15, 1997.

33. Description of WID from *WID Blue Ribbon Panel Newsletter,* October 1992, 1: 1.

34. From Frank Bowe's May 28, 1996, letter to the authors.

35. Lucy Gwin, "True History," *Mouth,* January–March 1997, 7(5&6): 26-27. Partners in Policymaking is a group of disability activists who continue in 2000 to educate parents of children with disabilities about the disability rights movement and effective lobbying strategies.

36. Unless otherwise indicated, references to Fred Fay and the Boston Center for Independent Living from interview with Fay, July 5, 1996.

37. Unless otherwise indicated, references to Lex Frieden from interview with Frieden, July 16, 1997.

38. Berkowitz, *Disabled Policy,* 202.

39. Information about Independent Living Research Utilization from material provided by ILRU, July 24, 1997.

40. Information about Creative Living I and II, Columbus, Ohio, from material provided by Creative Living, April 26, 1996.

41. References to Rehabilitation Institute of Chicago and Marca Bristo, chairperson of the National Council on Disability since May 1994, from interview with Bristo, April 30, 1998.

42. Unless otherwise indicated, description of Access Living from conversation with Mary Delgado, May 6, 1998, Access Living information and referral administrator.

43. Adaptable design features are as follows: At least one building entrance must be on an accessible route. All public and common-use areas must be on readily accessible routes. All doors into and within all premises must be wide enough to allow passage by wheelchairs users. All premises must contain an accessible route into and through the dwelling unit. All light switches, electrical outlets, thermostats, and environmental controls must be in an accessible location. Reinforcements in the bathroom walls for later installation of grab bars around toilet, tub, and shower must be provided. Usable kitchens and bathrooms must be provided so that a wheelchair user can maneuver about the space. See Kleo King, *Know Your Fair Housing Rights,* Eastern Paralyzed Veterans Association, 1997, 7.

44. See Paul K. Longmore, "Introduction," in H. Stephen Kaye, *Disability Watch: The Status of People with Disabilities in the United States* (Volcano, Calif.: Volcano Press, 1997), 13.

45. Description of visitability from interview with Karen Tamley, Housing Policy coordinator with Access Living, June 3, 1998, and Eleanor Smith of Concrete Change in Atlanta, July 6, 2000, who developed the concept of visitability. This concept is defined by four basic features in the design of buildings: level access at one entrance, at least, although not necessarily at the front entrance; interior doorways no less than thirty-two inches in width (including bathroom doors); switches and outlets at heights reachable by people with different disabilities; and reinforced supports behind walls permitting the attachment of grab bars used in bathrooms. Although adaptable design is a legal term, visitability—not a legal term—is defined by Smith as a grass-roots movement to ensure that new housing is accessible to all people as visitors. The concept of visitability has been incorporated in legislation in Georgia and Texas.

46. Josie Byzek, "Living in the Past," *Ragged Edge,* May/June 1998, 13.

47. *Encyclopedia of Disability and Rehabilitation* (New York: Simon & Schuster Macmillan, 1995), 399.

48. Funds also were allocated specifically for counseling and training of elderly blind adults and independent living rehabilitation of people with disabilities. The legislation providing for these latter two programs contradicts the spirit of the independent living paradigm. The first is not consistent with the ILC cross-disability focus; the second is an oxymoron because independent living and rehabilitation reflect different approaches to disability. *Queens Independent Living Center, Inc.: A Timeline and History,* compiled by Susan Jouard (executive director from 1983 to 1988), 15.

49. *Encyclopedia of Disability and Rehabilitation,* 403.

50. Similar to the composition of the ILC boards, a majority of the Statewide Independent Living Council (SILC) boards had to be people with disabilities. To avoid conflict of interest, SILC members could not be staff members of ILCs nor employees of state agencies. The three-year plan required approval by the chair of the SILC and the head of the rehabilitation agency.

51. Christopher G. Bell and Robert L. Burgdorf, *Accommodating the Spectrum of Individual Abilities* (Washington, D.C.: U.S. Commission on Civil Rights, 1983), 84, footnote 95.

52. Gerben DeJong, "Independent Living: From Social Movement to Analytic Paradigm," *The Psychological and Social Impact of Physical Disability* (New York: Springer Publishing Company, 1984). Comparison of rehabilitation to independent living from this source.

53. Sandra Schnur's presentation at Summer 1979 conference of the New York State Coalition of People with Disabilities (NYSCPD) at New York University's Weinstein Hall.

54. Gwin, "True History," 27.

55. Patricio Figueroa's presentation at Summer 1979 NYSCPD conference.

56. Tom Clancy's presentation at Summer 1979 NYSCPD conference.

57. Justin Dart's references to Fred Fay from a 1992 unpublished version of Justin Dart, "The ADA: A Promise To Be Kept," p. 8, received May 27, 1997, from Dart.

58. In 1977, a few members of DIA agreed to work with the Mayor's Office for People with Disabilities on a conference. When told that Tom Clancy—the TV poster figure for a public service announcement to "hire the handicapped"—would be a major speaker, they went to see him, fearful that he would embarrass them. Although they found him charming, sensitive, and intelligent, they were not prepared for the stirring speech that he delivered.

Chapter Four

1. Christopher G. Bell and Robert L. Burgdorf, *Accommodating the Spectrum of Individual Abilities* (Washington, D.C.: U.S. Commission on Civil Rights, 1983), 47.

2. Chava Willig Levy, *A People's History of the Independent Living Movement* (Lawrence, Kans.: Research and Training Center on Independent Living, 1988), 15.

3. References to the May 1973 demonstrations at the Capitol and the Lincoln Memorial as well as the legislative and executive compromise resulting in the Rehabilitation Act of 1973 from Richard B. Treanor, *We Overcame: The Story of Civil Rights for Disabled People* (Falls Church, Va.: Regal Direct Publishing, 1993), 59–60.

4. References to James Cherry from interview with Cherry, October 16, 1996.

5. Richard K. Scotch, *From Goodwill to Civil Rights: Transforming Federal Disability Policy* (Philadelphia: Temple University Press, 1984), 52. See Scotch, pp. 51-52, for the names of congressional staff involved in adapting (from Title VI of the 1964 Civil Rights Act) and drafting the language that ultimately became Section 504 of the Rehabilitation Act of 1973. In addition, the key role of the staff of the Office of Civil Rights of the Department of Health, Education, and Welfare (the agency initially authorized to implement Section 504)—particularly Martin Gerry and John Wodatch—in drafting the Section 504 regulations cannot be overestimated. See Scotch, 59, and chap. 4.

6. *Cherry v. Mathews*, 419 F. Supp. 922 (D.D.C. 1976).

7. Scotch, *From Goodwill to Civil Rights*, 104.

8. References to Eunice Fiorito and her roles in the American Coalition of Citizens with Disabilities and the Section 504 demonstrations from interview, June 6, 1997. Fiorito died on November 22, 1999.

9. Levy, *A People's History*, 15.

10. References to Frank Bowe's letter to Joseph Califano from Treanor, *We Overcame*, 72.

11. Joseph P. Shapiro, *No Pity: People with Disabilities Forging a New Civil Rights Movement* (New York: Times Books, 1993), 66–69.

12. Levy, *A People's History*, 17.

13. Judith E. Heumann, "Handicap and Disability," *Disability: Our Challenge*, John P. Hourihan, ed. (New York: Teachers College, Columbia University Press, 1979), 20.

14. Shapiro, *No Pity*, 66.

15. Frank Bowe, "Handicapping America: Barriers to Disabled People," *Disability: Our Challenge*, John P. Hourihan, ed. (New York: Teachers College, Columbia University, 1979), 88–89.

16. William Coleman was Secretary of Transportation in the administration of President Ford.

17. These organizations included Disabled In Action of Pennsylvania, New York, New Jersey, and Baltimore, as well as the American Coalition of Citizens with Disabilities, the Center for Independent Living in Berkeley, Easter Seal of Pennsylvania, National Council of Senior Citizens, and Paralyzed Veterans of America.

18. The defendants in the case were the United States Department of Transportation (USDOT), the Urban Mass Transportation Administration (UMTA), and the Federal Aid Highway Administration (FAHA).

19. Interview with James Raggio, general counsel for the Access Board, July 25, 1997. In 1976, Raggio was an attorney in the Public Interest Law Center of Philadelphia, a nonprofit law firm that represented the plaintiffs in the Transbus lawsuit.

20. The laws to which the plaintiffs referred were Section 16(a) of the 1970 Urban Mass Transportation Assistance Act and Section 165(b) of the Federal-Aid Highway Act of 1973. In the late 1960s and early 1970s, Transbus was one of the prototypes developed as a result of the $27 million federal grant awarded to the Booz Allen Hamilton Company.

21. Frieda Zames, "Letter to the Membership," *DIA Advocate*, June 1977, 1.

22. References to the July 12, 1978, Transbus demonstrations from Disabled In Action press release packet.

23. In the early 1970s, both the General Motors lift-equipped bus and the discarded Transbus were developed in a contest to create an accessible "Bus of the Future."

24. Interview with Dennis Cannon, December 24, 1996. References to Stanford Research Institute and General Motors from this source.

25. Interview with James Raggio, July 25, 1997. Raggio's reference to low-floor buses from this source.

26. Interview with Dennis Cannon, December 24, 1996.

27. 99 S.Ct. 2361 (1979). See reference to *Southeastern Community College v. Davis* later in this chapter in "Mainstreaming Public Transit." See *EPVA Inc. et al. v. Metropolitan Transportation Authority et al.* 79 A.D.2d 516 (1980).

28. "Group for Disabled Sues on Bus Design," *New York Times*, August 23, 1980, sec. 2, p. 26.

29. "Key" refers to subway, trolley, and commuter rail stations, including all end stations and those serving major activity centers, as well as stations having specific characteristics, such as many riders or transfer opportunities to other trains and different transportation modes.

30. Twenty-four defendants were parties to *Dopico v. Goldschmidt,* including the following: New York State's Metropolitan Transportation Authority; New York City Transit; Mayor Edward Koch; New York State's and New York City's Departments of Transportation; and Carter's third Secretary of Transportation, Neil Goldschmidt. Although the case concerned New York City's public transportation system, state and federal agencies were involved because they had relevant supervisory and financial responsibilities. The plaintiffs include wheelchair users David and Rhea Dopico, Vincent and Muriel Zgardowski, as well as DIA of Metropolitan New York, the only organizational plaintiff.

31. 687 F2d 644. References to the U.S. Court of Appeals (2d Cir) decision in *Dopico* (1982) from Bell and Burgdorf, *Accommodating the Spectrum,* 137–38.

32. As a result of the 1981 *APTA v. Lewis* (D.C.) decision, retrofitting was not mandated.

33. 718 F2d 490 (1st Cir 1983).

34. Bell and Burgdorf, *Accommodating the Spectrum,* 138. The disparity between the *Dopico* and *Rhode Island* decisions may be attributed to the difference in expenditures for public transportation in the two localities. The cost for public transit accessibility in New York City in comparison to the total public transit budget was minimal. In Rhode Island, a locale with a comparatively small public transit budget, the cost of public transit accessibility was a significant percentage of that budget.

35. "Handicapped Block Elevators at M.T.A.," *New York Times,* November 22, 1980, sec. 2, p. 27.

36. Those who attended the strategy sessions at the office of EPVA purposely chose a variation on the abbreviation MTA.

37. Jean Stewart, "What Do We Want? Access! When Do We Want It? Now!!!" *DIA Advocate,* January 1981, 1–2. List of demands presented to MTA chairman Richard Ravitch from this source.

38. References to Anne Emerman's September 30, 1980, Ride the Bus Day experience from interview with Emerman, July 11, 1996.

39. Interview with Ellen Nuzzi, February 16, 1997.

40. References to Michael Imperiale's lawsuit from interview with Imperiale and his attorney, Diane Morrison, December 7, 1996.

41. Interview with EPVA attorney James Weisman, April 8, 1996. While *EPVA v. MTA* (1982) was a federal Section 504 lawsuit, *EPVA v. MTA* (1979) involved the New York State Building Code and Human Rights Law.

42. Susan Sugar Nathan, Esq., "The Cost of Accessible Transportation: Myth and Reality," *Disabled In Action Speaks,* May 1981, 6. References to Stephen Berger's role in MTA's purchase of Grumman buses from this source.

43. Interview with James Weisman, April 8, 1996. Weisman referred to the 1982 *New York Times* editorial "There's a Wheelchair on the Tracks." The Public Buildings Law, requiring that all newly-built or extensively renovated subway stations be wheelchair accessible, was suspended for subways for eight years.

44. Interview with Ellen Nuzzi, February 16, 1997.

45. Ellen Nuzzi, "The Battle for Accessible Public Transit in NYC Continues," *DIA Activist,* November 1984, 1.

46. Scotch, *From Goodwill to Civil Rights,* 188, note 18.

47. Anne Emerman, "We Won," *DIA Activist,* March 1985, 1–2. References to the 1984 New York State Handicapped Transportation Bill from this source.

48. References to Harold Willson and the development of the BART system from Robert Levine, *BART and the Handicapped,* Document No. WP 17-1-75, prepared by the Metropolitan Transportation Commission for the U.S. Department of Transportation and the U.S. Department of Housing and Urban Development.

49. Scotch, *From Goodwill to Civil Rights,* 29–30.

50. Bell and Burgdorf, *Accommodating the Spectrum,* 38, footnote 149.

51. Levine, *BART and the Handicapped,* 17.

52. The May 19, 1998, settlement of the class action lawsuit filed against BART on behalf of eight riders with mobility impairments revealed the necessity for constant vigilance by people with disabilities to maintain accessibility. Almost thirty years after the system was built, the plaintiffs were successful in requiring BART to make extensive renovations. "BART Settles Class Action Lawsuit," *Disability News Service,* June 1998, 1(5): 8.

53. References to the 1974 California policy resolution on accessible bus purchases from interview with Dennis Cannon, December 24, 1996.

54. Interview with Robert Levine, transportation planner for the Nine-County San Francisco Bay Area, August 16, 1996. During this period, not only were wheelchair-accessible buses purchased by this commission, but also a coordinated paratransit system was developed in the district.

55. Interview with Dennis Cannon, December 24, 1996.

56. 458 F2d 1277 (7th Cir 1977).

57. 99 S.Ct. 2361.

58. Bell and Burgdorf, *Accommodating the Spectrum*, 112, footnote 55.

59. 655 F2d 1272 (C.A.D.C. 1981). Drew Lewis was President Carter's second Secretary of Transportation.

60. The opinion of Third Circuit Court of Appeals Judge Carol Los Mansmann in *ADAPT (American Disabled for Accessible Public Transit) v. Burnley*, 867 F2d 1471 (1989), provides much valuable background information on this issue and is referred to here at length. The defendant in the original case was Transportation Secretary Elizabeth Dole, but was changed to James Burnley when he became Secretary, and then to Samuel Skinner when he succeeded Burnley in early 1989. Although the decision in the *Burnley* case was vacated not long after the ruling, in effect replaced by the holding by a larger Third Circuit Court in *ADAPT v. Skinner*, 881 F2d 1184 (1989), Judge Mansmann's comments in *Burnley* remain pertinent. In the *Skinner* decision, a divided court held that paratransit was a valid option, but that the 3 percent budget cap was not.

Since 1990, ADAPT, a national disability organization, has been known as American Disabled for Attendant Programs Today. "Special efforts" was referred to in the 1970 Urban Mass Transportation Assistance Act, an amendment to the 1964 Urban Mass Transportation Act, sponsored by Representative Mario Biaggi (D-N.Y.), that provided federal funds to local transit agencies.

61. Opinion of Judge Mansmann.

62. Ibid.

63. Ibid.

64. References to "equivalent service criteria" for paratransit and lift-equipped buses from interview with Dennis Cannon, December 24, 1996.

65. Opinion of Judge Mansmann.

66. Senator Alan Cranston, December 14, 1982, 128 Congressional Record S15.714, daily edition. The fact that in recent years transit authorities throughout the nation are encouraging their wheelchair users to ride fixed-route buses rather than paratransit reflects the lower costs of these buses.

67. Senator Donald Riegle, December 20, 1982, 128 Congressional Record S15.714, daily edition. The approximate 1998 cost figures for New York City (roughly the same as in 2000) are as follows: Buses cost from $271,000 to $41,000. Lifts cost from $5,000 to $11,000. Paratransit passengers cost the company $27.50 per one-way trip, while bus passengers (disabled or nondisabled) cost only $1.85 per trip. Passengers make use of bus lifts in over 50,000 one-way trips per month. Passengers with disabilities make use of paratransit in roughly 125,000 one-way trips per month. All figures from conversation with Stephen Nacho, Director, Bus Company Relations Center, June 22, 2000, except for the last figure supplied to the authors on the same day by an anonymous paratransit official. Because few New York City subway stations are accessible, few people with mobility impairments use this mode of transportation.

68. Opinion of Judge Mansmann.

69. 469 U.S. 287.

70. Opinion of Judge Mansmann.

71. 623 F. Supp. 920 (D.Me. 1985).

72. References to the final USDOT Section 504 regulations from opinion of Judge Mansmann.

73. The 3½ percent criteria in the interim regulations was reduced to 3 percent in the final Section 504 USDOT regulations.

74. Opinion of Judge Mansmann.

75. References to the District Court decision in *ADAPT v. Dole*, 676 F. Supp. 635 (1988), from opinion of Judge Mansmann.

76. Treanor, *We Overcame*, 304.

77. Because in November 1998 the New York City paratransit system (known as Access-A-Ride) was still not functioning in a manner consistent with "minimum service criteria," three paratransit users and five disability organizations sued the Metropolitan Transportation Authority and New York City Transit under the 1990 Americans with Disabilities Act. South Brooklyn Legal Services attorney Lee Ginsburg, who represented some of the plaintiffs, said that if the city adheres to the settlement, "disabled New Yorkers will have for the first time in history reliable transportation that will allow them to go to work, school and appointments. . . . This should have national repercussions" (Richard Weir, "Disabled Reach Pact with City in Transportation Suit," *New York Times,* Sunday, October 10, 1999, sec. 14, p. 9). The 1989 *ADAPT v. Skinner* decision relied on the U.S. Court of Appeals 1987 ruling in *Disabled in Action of Pennsylvania v. Sykes* (833 F2d 1333) in holding that Department of Transportation regulations mandated the purchase of accessible buses.

78. Dennis Cannon, "Statement," *Civil Rights Issues of Handicapped Americans: Public Policy Implications* (Washington, D.C.: A Consultation Sponsored by the U.S. Commission on Civil Rights, May 13-14, 1980), 329-30. References to Cannon's "Statement" from this source.

79. The authors have substituted "educational" for "attitudinal" because it is clear from the context that Cannon intended the former word rather than the latter.

80. Metropolitan areas of Atlanta, Boston, Chicago, Cleveland, Los Angeles, Miami, New York, Philadelphia, San Francisco, and Washington, D.C., have rapid transit—subway, elevated, and/or commuter trains—in 2000.

Chapter Five

1. Judith E. Heumann, "Statement," *Civil Rights Issues of Handicapped Americans: Public Policy Implications* (Washington, D.C.: A Consultation Sponsored by the United States Commission on Civil Rights, May 13-14, 1980), 234-35. Unless otherwise indicated, references to Heumann's experience with and lawsuit against the New York City Board of Education from this source.

2. Judith E. Heumann, "Handicap and Disability," *Disability: Our Challenge,* John P. Hourihan, ed. (New York: Teachers College, Columbia University Press, 1979), 12. References to Heumann's experience with the American Civil Liberties Union and with Ted Childs from this source.

3. Edward D. Berkowitz, *Disabled Policy: America's Programs for the Handicapped* (Cambridge: Cambridge University Press, 1987), 197.

4. Interview with Ilse Heumann, Judith Heumann's mother, June 22, 1996.

5. Andrew Hacker, *Two Nations: Black and White, Separate, Hostile, Unequal* (New York: Scribners, 1992), 20.

6. Frank Bowe, "Handicapping America: Barriers to Disabled People," *Disability: Our Challenge,* John P. Hourihan, ed. (New York: Teachers College, Columbia University, 1979), 90.

7. The founding of Disabled In Action occurred within a month of her rejection by the Board of Education (Berkowitz, *Disabled Policy,* 198). Again Heumann fought against disability discrimination when in 1975 she was arrested for refusing to leave a plane (that she had boarded unaccompanied) because the airline considered her a safety hazard (Ibid.). Her action propelled Senator Harrison Williams (D-N.J.) to publicly appeal for an end to such discrimination.

8. The following DIA chapters were formed after DIA of Metropolitan New York: DIA of Baltimore, DIA of Kentucky, DIA of New Jersey, DIA of Pennsylvania, DIA of Rockland (New York), DIA of Syracuse, DIA of Virginia, DIA of Western New York. By 2000, DIA of Metropolitan New York, Pennsylvania, and Syracuse were still actively engaged in political activity. Many of the leaders of other DIAs became employed in public or private agencies such as, for example, independent living centers.

9. From the album "Leap of Faith," Flying Fish Records, #90485.

10. In 1996, as a result of congressional action, the Legal Services Corporation (LSC) could no longer initiate class actions lawsuits. Hence, many of its most prominent attorneys, such as Jane Greengold Stevens, principal attorney representing the plaintiffs in *Dopico v. Goldschmidt* (1982), resigned from the LSC.

11. Philip K. Howard, *The Death of Common Sense: How Law is Suffocating America* (New York: Random House, 1994).

12. The purpose of *Hill v. New York City Board of Elections* (Supreme Court of Kings County) was to enforce Section 4-104 of the New York State Election Law.

13. Frieda Zames, "Accessible Polling Site Lawsuit Settled," *DIA Activist*, May 1995, 15-16.

14. Judge Herbert Kramer, "Memorandum to the Supreme Court of Kings County," June 10, 1986, 7.

15. 687 F2d 644 (2d Cir).

16. The Ford Foundation and the American Bar Association Special Committee on Public Interest Practice, "Public Interest Law: Five Years Later," 1976.

17. References to the history of NYLPI from Betty Hounslow, "New York Lawyers for the Public Interest Celebrating 15 Years" (New York: NYLPI, 1991).

18. New York Lawyers for the Public Interest Annual Luncheon Program, June 16, 1999.

19. References to Paul Hearne, the Legal Services Corporation, and DREDF start-up grant from interview with Hearne, June 25, 1997. From September 8, 1989, until his death, Paul Hearne was president of the Dole Foundation, a nonprofit organization created by then-Senator Bob Dole fostering the employment of people with disabilities.

20. Hearne (interview, June 25, 1997) indicated that New York City's Legal Services Corporation lost $250,000. The other $150,000, formerly earmarked for Handicapped Persons Legal Support Unit, was applied to fund a February 1980 conference in Minnesota, described by Hearne as "the first training program for lawyers in the country on the legal rights of people with disabilities." Hearne and attorney James Weisman presided over the conference.

21. Unless otherwise indicated, references to DREDF from "A Brief History" prepared by DREDF, 1-2.

22. Interview with DREDF attorney Diane Lipton, July 31, 1997.

23. References to DREDF's role in the education of children with disabilities from interview with DREDF attorney Diane Lipton, July 31, 1997.

24. "What DREDF Is and Does," prepared by DREDF, p. 1.

25. Rodman D. Griffin, "The Disabilities Act," *CQ Researcher*, December 27, 1991, 995.

26. 465 U.S. 555.

27. Interview with DREDF attorney Diane Lipton, July 31, 1997.

28. Interview with Bruce Alan Kiernan, January 19, 1998.

29. Unless otherwise indicated, all references to Sidney Wolinsky from interview with Wolinsky, April 22, 1998. One of Wolinsky's cases, *Elizabeth Guckenberger v. Boston University* (1997), is discussed in chapter 11. *Chabner v. United of Omaha*, 994 F. Supp. 1185 (N.D.Cal. 1998) is under appeal to the U.S. Court of Appeals for the Ninth Circuit.

30. Although sulphones are drugs that render a person with Hanson's disease noncontagious, these medications do not reverse the course of the disease.

31. Unless otherwise indicated, all references to Stephen Gold from interview with Gold, July 7, 1997. The cases referred to by Gold are *Strathie v. Department of Transportation*, 716 F2d 227 (3d Cir 1983) (dealing with the bus driver), *National Federation of the Blind v. LaPore*, settled in the Eastern District Court of Pennsylvania in 1982, and *Disabled in Action of Pennsylvania v. Sykes*, 833 F2d 1113 (3d Cir 1987), cert. denied, 108 S.Ct. 1293 (1988).

32. Interview with James Raggio, July 25, 1997.

33. Unless otherwise indicated, references to Michael Auberger and ADAPT demonstrations from interview with Auberger, July 11, 1996.

34. Unless otherwise indicated, references to Wade Blank from Laura Hershey, "Wade Blank's Liberated Community," *The Ragged Edge*, ed. Barrett Shaw (Louisville: The Advocado Press, 1994), 150-51.

35. Interview with Michael Auberger, July 11, 1996.

36. *APTA v. Lewis* (655 F2d 1272).

37. Brian Doherty, "Unreasonable Accommodation," *Reason*, August/September 1995, 22. References to ADAPT's protests against establishments that fail to provide ramps from this source.

38. Auberger is so anxious to do battle with the nursing home industry that he is willing to join forces with the HMOs to bring down powerful but vulnerable institutions. Fred Fay, on the other hand, sees the HMOs as the enemy to be eliminated.

39. Interview with Stephen Gold, July 7, 1997.

40. Unless otherwise indicated, references to Newt Gingrich from "Newt Sponsors CASA [later known as MiCasa]," *Mouth*, July/August 1997, 5. On November 16, 1999, Senators Tom Harkin (D-Iowa) and Arlen Specter (R-Pa.) introduced an updated version of this legislation now known as the Medicaid Community Attendant Services and Supports Act (MiCassa).

41. Garry Pierre-Pierre, "Disrupting Sales at Greyhound, Disabled Protest Bus Access," *New York Times*, August 9, 1997, 26. Reference to Thomas K. Small from this source.

42. Interview with Stephen Gold, July 7, 1997. See chapter 6, note 71, for details of Department of Justice settlement with Greyhound, April 1, 1999.

43. Disability activists such as Mary Johnson, former editor of *Disability Rag*; Anne Emerman, former director of the New York City Mayor's Office for People with Disabilities; and Robert Levine, coordinator of the New York City "One-Step" Campaign, though sensitive to ADAPT's goals, fear that the vision of individuals with disabilities crawling up steps may evoke images of powerlessness and dependency rather than pride and independence.

44. Jennifer Burnett, "Solidarity 200 Roars: Unity!" *Mouth*, January–March 1997, 4, 53.

45. Jean Dobbs, "And Justin for All," *New Mobility: Disability Culture and Lifestyle*, March 1998, 36. Reference to founding of JFA from this source. Dart has indicated that his disability activism also was spurred by the suicide of his brother, Peter, after his long struggle with polio and a head injury.

46. Burnett, "Solidarity 200 Roars," 53.

47. Burnett, "Solidarity 200 Roars," 53. Besides his role at JFA, Fred Fay also functions as chair of the Disability Advisory Committee to the Democratic National Committee as well as cofounder of the American Association of People with Disabilities (AAPD), modeled on the American Association of Retired People (AARP).

48. Unless otherwise indicated, references to Fred Fay's use of technology to perform his JFA activities from Deborah Ellen, "Lobbying for Rights of People with Disabilities," *Connections*, March 1998, 6. Though Fred Fay is required to lie supine, "his office [in his home] has sixty-four square feet of ceiling mirrors that allow him to maneuver easily" in his wheelbed.

49. Dobbs, "And Justice for All," 37. Justin Dart's reference to Ed Roberts from this source.

50. Burnett, "Solidarity 200 Roars," 4, 53.

Chapter Six

1. Joseph P. Shapiro, *No Pity: People with Disabilities Forging a New Civil Rights Movement* (New York: Times Books, 1993).

2. Unless otherwise indicated, references to efforts to defeat or threats to weaken the ADA from interview with Justin Dart, June 14, 1997.

3. Sandra Parrino, National Council on Disability chairperson from 1983 to 1993, said of Lex Frieden, who had served with Justin Dart on Governor William Clements's task force: "Frieden recruited and hired the staff; he organized the office, and he developed policy." Interview with Parrino, June 30, 1997.

4. Interview with Lex Frieden, July 16, 1997.

5. Ibid.

6. Interview with Justin Dart, June 14, 1997.

7. Edward D. Berkowitz, *Disabled Policy: America's Programs for the Handicapped* (Cambridge: Cambridge University Press, 1987), 13.

8. Nora Groce, *The U.S. Role in International Disability Activities: A History and a Look Toward the Future* (Oakland, Calif.: International Disability Exchanges and Studies Project, 1992), 136.

9. Interview with Justin Dart, June 14, 1997. References to President Carter NCD appointees from this source.

10. Justin Dart, "Introduction—The ADA: A Promise To Be Kept," *Implementing the Americans with Disabilities Act*, eds. Lawrence O. Gostin and Henry A. Beyer (Baltimore, Md.: Paul H. Brookes Publishing Co., 1993), xxii. References to a separate disability civil rights law from this source.

11. Interview with Paul Hearne, June 25, 1997. Title 9, the 1972 amendment to the Civil Rights Act of 1964, included women in the law.

12. The Switzer building was named for Mary Switzer, the innovative, forceful administrator of the Office of Vocational Rehabilitation in the 1950s and 1960s, who funded programs that led to the independent living and disability rights movements (Groce, *The U.S. Role in International Disability Activities,* 55, 128–31).

13. Interview with Lex Frieden, July 16, 1997.

14. Interview with Sandra Parrino, June 30, 1997.

15. Interview with Justin Dart, June 14, 1997.

16. *Toward Independence: An Assessment of Federal Laws and Programs Affecting Persons with Disabilities—With Legislative Recommendations* (Washington, D.C.: National Council on Disability, February 1986), 13. Paul Hearne says that many of the recommendations in *Toward Independence* were similar to those published in the report of the 1977 White House Conference on the Handicapped.

17. Interviews with Sandra Parrino, June 30, 1997, and Lex Frieden, July 16, 1997.

18. Unless otherwise indicated, references to the probability of civil rights legislation, such as the ADA, from Dart, "Introduction—The ADA," xxii.

19. Interview with Justin Dart, June 14, 1997.

20. Richard K. Scotch, *From Goodwill to Civil Rights: Transforming Federal Disability Policy* (Philadelphia: Temple University Press, 1984), 164.

21. Dart's view of the 1988 version of the ADA from interview with Justin Dart, June 14, 1997.

22. Interview with Paul Hearne, June 25, 1997.

23. Interview with Lex Frieden, July 16, 1997.

24. Interview with Justin Dart, June 14, 1997.

25. Interview with Paul Hearne, June 25, 1997.

26. Berkowitz, *Disabled Policy,* 208–9.

27. Interview with Justin Dart, June 14, 1997. References to Congressman Major Owens's 1988 Disability Task Force from this source.

28. References to Dale Brown and the National Network of Learning Disabled Adults, 1980 to 1994, from interview with Brown, April 26, 1998. This organization deals with the "internalized oppression," as well as the outright discrimination, experienced by learning disabled adults.

29. Fred Fay, "Empowerment: The Testament of Justin Dart Jr.," *Mainstream,* March 1998, 24.

30. From a 1992 unpublished version of "The ADA: A Promise To Be Kept," 4–5, received from Justin Dart, May 27, 1997. By 1997, there were fifty-four million people with disabilities in the United States.

31. Interview with Paul Hearne, June 25, 1997.

32. Dart, 1992 unpublished version of "The ADA: A Promise To Be Kept," 5.

33. Coelho, quoted in Rodman D. Griffin, "The Disabilities Act," *CQ Researcher,* December 27, 1991, 1004. By 1994–95, a fifth, not a sixth, of the nation's population had some form of disability according to the ADA definition (John M. McNeil, "Current Population Reports: Americans with Disabilities, 1994–1995," p. 1, published by U.S. Department of Commerce, Census Bureau, August 1997). Coelho's statistic was based on an earlier census.

34. Interview with Sandra Parrino, June 30, 1997.

35. Griffin, "The Disabilities Act," 1004.

36. Interview with Sandra Parrino, June 30, 1997.

37. Conversation with Arthur Wohl, April 1982.

38. References to Justin Dart's trip to England from interview, June 14, 1997.

39. 42 USC 12102 (2)(a)(b)(c).

40. Ibid.

41. The Section 504 definition of a person with a disability from Scotch, 69. In the ADA definition of a person with a disability, "drug addict" in Section 504 was changed to "recovered drug addict." See 42 USC 12114 (b)(1)(2)(3).

42. 42 USC 12114 (a). Disability advocates chose not to oppose North Carolina Senator Jesse Helms's insistence that disabilities such as pedophilia and kleptomania also be excluded from ADA coverage.

43. H. Stephen Kaye, *Disability Watch: The Status of People with Disabilities in the United States* (Volcano, Calif.: Volcano Press, 1997), 13.

44. References to the 1992 Health Interview Survey from Kaye, *Disability Watch*, 12–13.

45. Geanne Rosenberg, "When the Mind Is the Matter: Mental Disability Cases Pose Painful Workplace Issues," *New York Times*, November 7, 1998, C1–2.

46. Steve Gold's comment about the purpose of ADA.

47. "Follow-up to 1994 Research," *Ragged Edge*, September/October, 1998, 5–6.

48. Janet Reno and Dick Thornburgh, "ADA—Not a Disabling Mandate," *Wall Street Journal*, July 26, 1995, A13.

49. Peter Blanck, "Employment, Integration, Economic Opportunity, and the ADA: Empirical Study from 1990–1993," 79 *Iowa Law Review* (1994), 853–54.

50. 42 USC 12112 (a).

51. 42 USC 12111 (9).

52. 42 USC 12114.

53. The U.S. Court of Appeals for the Fourth Circuit affirmed the District Court's ruling in 77 F2d 470.

54. 62 F2d 1108 (1995).

55. The social work conference, "From Disability to Ability," was held at New York City's Fordham University on April 14, 1998.

56. 42 USC 12182.

57. 42 USC 12182 (b)(1)(B).

58. 42 USC 12181 (7).

59. 42 USC 12183 (a)(1)(2).

60. 42 USC 12183 (b).

61. 42 USC 12181 (9). In *Pascuiti v. New York Yankees* (98 Civ. 8186), Southern District (N.Y.) Judge Shira A. Scheindlin stated that the ADA is "silent as to who bears the burden of proving that [barrier] removal is readily achievable," and the courts have not yet dealt with the issue.

62. 42 USC 12182 (b)(2)(A)(v).

63. Matthew Diller, "Introduction: Civil Disturbances—Battles for Justice in New York City," *Fordham Urban Law Journal*, May 1999, 16(5): 1321.

64. References to the May 1996 Disability Rights Education and Defense Fund's ADA complaint against United Artists Theatre Circuit from interview with DREDF attorney Diane Lipton, July 31, 1997.

65. Furthermore, assistive listening devices for people who are hard of hearing became commonplace in legitimate theaters as well as movie theaters.

66. Frieda Zames, "Unseating People with Disabilities," *New York Able*, February 1999, 10. "Stadium seating" is described in Iver Peterson, "Catching On at the Movies: A Clear View for All," *New York Times*, Sunday, January 3, 1999, sec. 1, p. 27.

67. Unless otherwise indicated, references to the 1996 Justice Department suit against Days Inn from Betsy Wade, "Disabled Access to Inns at Issue," *New York Times*, Sunday, April 14, 1996, sec. 5, p. 4.

68. References to the settlement of the five lawsuits brought by the Justice Department against Days Inn Hotels and its parent company, and John Wodatch's response to the settlement, from http://www.nytimes.com/reuters/business/business-leisure-cend.html, posted December 2, 1999. (Cedant was formed through a 1997 merger between HFS, Inc., and CUC International, Inc.)

69. "Justice Department Agreement with Friendly's," *Washington Fax: President's Committee on Employment of People with Disabilities*, May 1997, 2. References to this agreement from this source.

70. See 42 USC 12184ff.

71. "Greyhound Must Comply," *New York Able*, November 1998, 1. The details of a Department of Justice settlement on April 1, 1999, with the over-the-road bus companies are as follows: new buses purchased or leased by over-the-road companies that gross over $5.3 million per year (such as Greyhound) must be wheelchair accessible by November 2000; new buses purchased or leased by over-the-road bus companies that gross under $5.3 million per year must be wheelchair accessible by October 2001. From a conversation with Terence Moakley, Associate Executive Director, Eastern Paralyzed Veterans Association, June 22, 2000.

72. Fixed-route vehicles seating sixteen or more must be accessible. Fixed-route vehicles seating less than sixteen, and demand-response vehicles seating sixteen or more, require either accessibility or equivalent service.

73. Public service refers to programs or activities of any state or local government such as police and fire departments. 42 USC 12131.

74. 42 USC 12132 sec. 202.

75. Furthermore, curb cuts provide access to sidewalks not only for wheelchair and scooter users, but also for older people and small children, as well as for people with baby carriages, strollers, and shopping carts.

76. *Kinney v. Yerusalim,* 812 F. Supp. 547 (E.D.Pa.), aff'd 9 F3d 1067 (3d Cir 1993), cert. denied, 114 S.Ct. 1545 (1994).

77. EPVA was still negotiating with New York City government on the curb-cut lawsuit as of this writing.

78. For example, Pietro Nivola of the Brookings Institution said that the disability laws—these unfunded federal mandates—are sapping federal money for transportation ("On the Line," WNYC-AM, February 18, 1999).

79. "TDD," *DIA Activist,* April 1992, 3.

80. Newspaper accounts include the following: Bob Liff, "Many Fire Boxes in Watered-Down Plan," New York *Daily News,* April 24, 1996; Dan Janison, "Hizzoner Gets Burned in Alarm-Box Firefight," *New York Post,* April 24, 1996; Paul Moses, "Fire Box Compromise," *New York Newsday,* April 24, 1996.

81. *Helen L. v. Didario,* 46 F3d 325 (3d Cir 1995).

82. In a class action ADA lawsuit, Center for Disability Advocacy Rights attorney Valerie Bogart—representing three plaintiffs threatened with being placed in a nursing home against their will—said, "Congress [in enacting the ADA] has made a very strong statement against institutionalization" (Jennifer Steinhauer, "Ruling in Favor of Patients Denied 24-Hour Home Care," *New York Times,* February 17, 1999, B4).

83. Conversation with ADAPT attorney Stephen Gold, February 2, 1997. There were two plaintiffs in the *Helen L.* case, Helen L. and ADAPT. The U.S. Department of Justice joined the plaintiffs in the *Helen L.* lawsuit as an amicus curiae.

84. The comparative costs appear in *Helen L.*

85. See 42 USC 12146ff. Commuter rail systems, such as Amtrak, provide transportation *between* rather than *within* cities.

86. See 47 USC 225 and 47 USC 611. For a description of the relay system, see "Teletypewriters and Relay Systems" in chapter 9 of this book.

87. See 42 USC 12201ff.

88. See 118 S.Ct. 2196. Linda Greenhouse, "Supreme Court Considers If Disabilities Act Covers HIV Case," *New York Times,* March 31, 1998, A19.

89. Ibid. "The Centers for Disease Control and Prevention has reported that there is no documented case of a dentist or hygienist being infected with HIV from a patient. Mr. McCarthy [the attorney for the dentist] said that there were seven such cases and that the risk was understated and underreported."

90. "NCD Bulletin," publication of the National Council on Disability, December 1997, 1.

91. Linda Greenhouse, "Court to Weigh Whether HIV Is a Disability," *New York Times,* March 23, 1998, A1.

92. Ibid., A13.

93. Linda Greenhouse, "Justices See HIV as Disability: Ruling on Bias Law," *New York Times,* June 26, 1998, A1.

94. Peter T. Kilborn, "Wide Impact Is Seen for Ruling on HIV," *New York Times,* June 27, 1998, A10.

95. See the June 22, 1999, Supreme Court rulings in *Sutton et al. v. United Air Lines, Inc., Murphy v. United Parcel Service, Inc.,* and *Albertsons, Inc. v. Kirkingburg* later in this chapter.

96. See 118 S.Ct. 1952. Unless otherwise indicated, references to *Pennsylvania Department of Corrections v. Yeskey* from Linda Greenhouse, "Federal Anti-Bias Law Protects States' Disabled Inmates, Court Says," *New York Times,* June 16, 1998, A18.

97. The court of appeals did not indicate the type of accommodation required for Yeskey.

98. From "U.S. Supreme Court Considers: Does the ADA Apply to State Prisons?" *Disability Network Newsletter* (published by New York Lawyers for the Public Interest), Spring 1998, 5. Comments of the U.S. Solicitor General on *Pennsylvania Department of Corrections v. Yeskey* from this source.

99. Although the Yeskey case established the intent of the ADA, a California lawsuit, *Wilson v. Armstrong*, dealt with a constitutional question that the U.S. Supreme Court had not yet heard as of this writing: Does Congress have "the authority to extend the law to the states and to breach state immunity from suit in federal court?" (Greenhouse, "Federal Anti-Bias Law Protects States' Disabled Inmates, Court Says," A18). The Supreme Court is expected to rule on this issue in 2001 in *Garrett v. Alabama*.

100. *Carolyn C. Cleveland v. Policy Management Systems Corp., et al.,* 199 S.Ct. 900 (1999).

101. 119 S.Ct. 633.

102. 119 S.Ct. 2139.

103. 119 S.Ct. 1331.

104. 119 S.Ct. 2162.

105. "Individuals Belong in the Community, Not Institutions, Says Supreme Court," The Center for an Accessible Society: Background Briefing, June 22, 1999, 1–2. Reference to William Stothers and Amici in *Olmstead* from this source. http://www.accessiblesociety.org/bkgdadatitle2.htm

106. Conversation with Stephen Gold, July 19, 1999. References to Gold's response to *Olmstead* from this source. The plaintiffs in *Olmstead* have both a psychiatric and a developmental disability. *Rodriguez v. City of New York* (2d Cir 1999) threatens *Olmstead*, as the defendants argued successfully that the type of care that people with cognitive disabilities (such as Alzheimer's disease) require to monitor their safety is a "different service" from the home care provided for those with physical disabilities.

107. Disability advocates are critical of some aspects of the *Olmstead* ruling: Only when "treatment professionals have determined that [it] is appropriate" is community placement required. "States can resist modifications that would fundamentally alter the nature of their services and programs." Without a definition of "a reasonable pace," states with "a waiting list that moves at a reasonable pace will have a defense against those who file suit."

108. The Supreme Court decision in *Sutton et al. v. United Air Lines, Inc.* References to Justice Sandra Day O'Connor's opinion in *Sutton* from this source. In writing the majority opinions for the Court in *Murphy v. United Parcel Service, Inc.,* and *Albertsons, Inc. v. Kirkingburg,* Justices O'Connor and David Souter, respectively, referred to the *Sutton* decision.

109. The Supreme Court dissent in *Sutton et al. v. United Air Lines, Inc.* Emphasis in original. Unless otherwise indicated, references to Justice John Paul Stevens's opinion in *Sutton* from this source.

110. Justice Stevens was pointing out that the Court's ruling that the ADA covers only those with existing unmitigated "substantial disabilities" was as if the Court had ruled that only African Americans could use the Civil Rights Act of 1964.

111. "Supreme Court Rules in Title I Cases," The Center for an Accessible Society background briefing, June 22, 1999, 1–2. http://www.accessiblesociety.org/bkgdadatitle1.htm

112. Justice For All action alert regarding June 22, 1999, Supreme Court decisions.

113. Nadina LaSpina, "Supreme Court Rulings: Victory and Defeats," *DIA Activist,* Summer 1999. References to LaSpina from this source.

114. "Morning Edition," National Public Radio, June 29, 1999. References to Peter Thompson from this source.

115. See "Mainstreaming Public Transit" section of chapter 4 in this book for *Davis* and "Litigating the IDEA" section of chapter 11 of this book for *Rowley.* The Supreme Court treated the three June 22, 1999, ADA employment cases as if they were based on a benefits—rather than a civil rights—law.

116. Philip K. Howard, *The Death of Common Sense: How Law is Suffocating America* (New York: Random House, 1994), 150.

117. Brian Doherty, "Unreasonable Accommodation," *Reason,* August/September 1995, 19–26. References to Doherty from this source.

118. Doherty, "Unreasonable Accommodation," 19. Emphasis added.

119. Interview with Harry Wieder, March 5, 1997.

120. Conversation with Justin Dart, July 22, 1997.

121. James Bovard, "The Lame Game," *American Spectator*, July 1995, 30–33.

122. Ibid., 31. John Stossel also treats this case as if it were covered by the ADA.

123. Conversation with Justin Dart, July 22, 1997.

124. Stated by Stossel on "20/20," July 19, 1996.

125. During the second presidential debate on October 16, 1996, when Republican candidate Bob Dole criticized affirmative action, President Clinton responded, "Again I say, think of the Americans with Disabilities Act. Make an effort to put a ramp up there so someone in a wheelchair can get up." The term "affirmative action," which does not appear in the ADA, refers to employment issues. The term in the ADA that applies to the requirement to build ramps is "readily achievable."

126. *Proceedings: U.S. Equal Employment Opportunity Commission (EEOC) Meeting*, March 12, 1996, 33.

127. Janet Reno and Dick Thornburgh, "ADA—Not a Disabling Mandate," A13. References to Reno and Thornburgh from this source.

128. "New Sears Report Shows Decrease in Accommodation Costs," *Washington Fax*, March 1996, 1. References from the *Sears Report* from this source.

129. "Four Years After the ADA," *Working Age: AARP Newsletter*, November/September 1996, 4.

130. Walter Olson, *The Excuse Factory: How Employment Law Is Paralyzing the American Workplace* (New York: Free Press, 1997). In his November 28, 1997, op-ed article in the *New York Times*, Olson, of the Manhattan Institute, again revealed his misunderstanding of the ADA when he contended that anesthesiologist Frank Ruhl Peterson's unethical act—stealing narcotics from his patients to feed his own drug habit while continuing to practice medicine—is protected by the ADA. The ADA does not sanction illegal behavior nor protect any unqualified workers, including professionals.

131. Reno and Thornburgh, "ADA—Not a Disabling Mandate," A13.

132. Interview with James Raggio, July 25, 1997.

133. *Proceedings*, 7.

134. Ibid., 8.

135. John Stossel of "20/20" (ABC-TV) and James Bovard of the *Wall Street Journal* are cited in *Proceedings* as telling "half truths about the ADA" (p. 34).

136. *Proceedings*, 81–82.

137. Ibid., 40.

Chapter Seven

1. Edward D. Berkowitz, *Disabled Policy: America's Programs for the Handicapped* (Cambridge: Cambridge University Press, 1987), 5.

2. The three ADA employment cases are *Sutton et al. v. United Air Lines, Inc., Murphy v. United Parcel Service, Inc.,* and *Albertsons, Inc. v. Kirkingburg.* See chapter 6.

3. Philip Shabecoff, quoting Frank Bowe, in "On the Job, Myths Are Reality and Damaging." *New York Times*, Sunday, May 13, 1979.

4. References to 1998 Harris Poll from "Follow-up to 1994 Research," *Ragged Edge*, September/October 1998, 5.

5. "Four Years After the ADA," *Working Age: AARP Newsletter*, 1996, 12(4): 3.

6. Caren Potoker, "Finding a Job Is a Job," *DIA Activist*, Summer 1999, 1–2. References to Potoker from this source.

7. Claiborne Haughton Jr., director for Civilian Equal Employment Opportunity for the Defense Department, *Proceedings: U.S. Equal Employment Opportunity Commission (EEOC) Meeting*, March 12, 1996, 74.

8. Daniel Robert's interview with Raphael Nisan, April 20, 1997.

9. *Proceedings*, 89. Dr. Margaret Nosek, director of the Center for Research on Women with Disabilities, said, "Previous research indicated that women with disabilities constitute our nation's most severely oppressed minority" (press release, Baylor College of Medicine in Houston, July 7, 1997).

10. *Proceedings*, 21.

11. Ibid., 71–72.

12. Interview with James Weisman, April 8, 1996.

13. Interview with Terence Moakley, April 8, 1996. References to Moakley from this source.

14. Speech by John Wingate at a celebration of the ADA at Gracie Mansion, August 10, 1993. References to Wingate from this source.

15. Goals and timetables refer to an effort to hire a determined number of qualified members of a specific population within a specified time period.

16. Interview with Anne Emerman, July 18, 1996.

17. "Part Three: Core Implications for the Twenty-First Century," *Sears Report*, 1–2. References to the *Sears Report* from this source.

18. Nancy Anne Longhurst, *The Self-Advocacy Movement by People with Developmental Disabilities: A Demographic Study and Directory of Self-Advocacy Groups in the United States* (Washington, D.C.: American Association on Mental Retardation, 1994), 1–6. References to the definition of "self-advocacy" and the evolution of the "self-advocacy movement" throughout the United States and British Columbia from this source.

19. Mary Hayden, "Absence of Justice," *Mouth,* March/April 1998, 34.

20. *Achieving Independence: The Challenge for the 21st Century* (Washington, D.C.: National Council on Disability, 1996), 99.

21. Interview with Harvey Pacht, April 3, 1998. References to Pacht from this source.

22. As Bernard Carabello indicates in his job resumé, "With nearly six thousand inmates, Willowbrook typified the overcrowded, understaffed institutions relied on to 'handle the problem' of the developmentally disabled." Carabello has championed the movement for self-advocacy for people with developmental disabilities in New York State and across the nation.

23. The statistic was cited by Charles Lakin, director of the Research and Training Center on Community Living in Minneapolis. See Dirk Johnson, "Tight Labor Supply Creates Jobs for the Mentally Disabled," *New York Times,* November 15, 1999, A1, A22.

24. Robert Pear, "Employees Told To Accommodate the Mentally Ill," *New York Times,* April 30, 1997, A1, D22. Unless otherwise indicated, description of *EEOC Enforcement Guidance* from this source.

25. "EEOC Releases Policy Guidance Concerning the ADA and People with Psychiatric Disabilities," *New York Able,* May 1997, 3.

26. "Americans with Disabilities Update," *National Council on Disability Bulletin,* March 1997, 1.

27. *EEOC Enforcement Guidance: The Americans with Disabilities Act and Psychiatric Disabilities,* March 27, 1997, 1.

28. Ann Davis, "Courts Reject Many Mental-Disability Claims," *Wall Street Journal,* July 22, 1997, B6. References to outcome of these claims in trial courts from this source.

29. Geanne Rosenberg cites John Parry, director of the American Bar Association's Commission on Mental and Physical Disabilities Law, in "When the Mind Is the Matter: Mental Disability Cases Pose Painful Workplace Issues," *New York Times,* November 7, 1998, C1. Darryl Van Duch indicated in the *National Law Journal* (June 29, 1998, B01) that employers won 86 percent of the disability cases resolved by the EEOC. Van Duch quoted a study of the American Bar Association Commission on Mental and Physical Disability Law in which twelve hundred cases filed since 1992 were reviewed.

30. Darryl Van Duch, "Employment and Labor Law" web site http://www.ljextra.com/practice/labor-employment/0629ada.html, posted June 29, 1998, 1. EEOC recommendations from this source.

31. *EEOC Enforcement Guidance,* 1.

32. Pear, "Employers Told To Accommodate the Mentally Ill," A1. References to the National Institute of Mental Health from this source.

33. Rosenberg, "When the Mind Is the Matter," C1–2. Rosenberg pointed out that "preliminary numbers for the 1998 fiscal year show yet another increase" for psychiatric disability claims.

34. Sheryl Gay Stolberg, "Breaks for Mental Illness: Just What the Government Ordered," *New York Times,* Sunday, May 4, 1997, sec. 4, p. 1. Unless otherwise indicated, references to parity for psychiatric disabilities from this source.

35. Robert Pear, "Insurance Plans Skirt Requirement on Mental Health," *New York Times,* December 26, 1998, A20. Reference to Ronald E. Bachman from this source.

36. Sally L. Satel, "When Work Is the Cure," *New York Times,* May 10, 1997, A19. References to Satel from this source.

37. Professor Michael Dorf of Columbia University Law School and former Supreme Court clerk to Justice Anthony Kennedy commented on the Supreme Court's June 1997 ruling that states may confine sex offenders to mental institutions after they have already completed criminal sentences: "In some ways that reflects a prejudice against people with mental illness, not just some concern about society" ("On the Line," WNYC-AM Radio, June 27, 1997).

38. Stolberg, "Breaks for Mental Illness," sec. 4, p. 5, quoting Peter D. Kramer.

39. Peter D. Kramer, "The Mentally Ill Deserve Job Protection," *New York Times,* May 6, 1997, A21. Unless otherwise indicated, references to Kramer from this source.

40. Kip Opperman, "Confidentiality: Who Needs To Know?" *Connections,* February 1997, 8. Opperman, who describes the requirements for an employee requesting disability accommodation, notes that they pertain also to college applicants and students.

41. *EEOC Enforcement Guidance,* 17.

42. *Proceedings,* 58–61. References to Claudia Center from this source.

43. Fox Butterfield, "Prisons Replace Hospitals for the Nation's Mentally Ill," *New York Times,* March 5, 1998, A1, A26. Unless otherwise indicated, references to the criminalization of people with psychiatric disabilities from this source.

44. "Morning Edition," National Public Radio, June 10, 1997. In response to the ADA, the Police Executive Research Forum, a coalition of progressive police chiefs, is working with the Justice Department to create a comprehensive training curriculum and model policy for police departments to deal with people with "mental illness."

45. Butterfield, "Prisons Replace Hospitals," A1, A26. The Mental Health Bell, symbol of the National Mental Health Association, was forged out of metal melted down from "barbaric" chains and shackles formerly used to restrain people with psychiatric disabilities (Michael Faenza, "Chains and Shackles Replaced with Programs and Services," *New York ABLE,* January 2000, 26M–27M. Faenza is president and CEO of the National Mental Health Association).

46. In *9 Highland Road* (New York: Vintage Books, 1995), *New York Times* reporter Michael Winerip makes a compelling case for the benefits of group homes for people with psychiatric disabilities.

47. References to the July 24, 1998, shooting of two Capitol police officers by John Weston Jr. from Frank Rich, "This Way Lies Madness," *New York Times,* July 29, 1998, A19.

48. Michael Winerip, "Bedlam on the Streets," *New York Times,* Sunday, May 23, 1999, sec. 6, pp. 45–46. The numbers in the 1950 to 1998 comparison were adjusted for inflation and population growth. Winerip adds, "Fewer than half of Americans with schizophrenia receive adequate care according to a 1998 national survey" (p. 45).

49. Rich, "This Way Lies Madness," A19.

50. Erica Goode, "With Help, Climbing Back from Schizophrenia's Isolation," *New York Times,* January 30, 1999, A1. Kendra Webdale's violent death, which occurred on January 3, 1999, prompted the adoption in August 1999 of the Assisted Outpatient Treatment Act in New York State, providing for court-ordered, involuntary treatment of almost any person at least eighteen years old who has a history of serious mental illness. The *New York Times* featured a front-page series of four articles (April 9–12, 2000) on "Rampage Killers," people with serious psychiatric problems who went on shooting sprees. Given the sensational examples presented, readers easily could have missed the following statement buried in the jump page of the third article: "Few of these people [with psychiatric disabilities] commit murder, of course, and shootings by the mentally ill account for only a tiny fraction of all homicides" (Fox Butterfield, "Hole in Gun Control Law Lets Mentally Ill Through," *New York Times,* April 11, 2000, A24).

51. Winerip, "Bedlam on the Streets," 42–44, 70. That the Assisted Outpatient Treatment Act is known as Kendra's Law is misleading, for as John Gresham, senior litigation counsel for New York Lawyers for the Public Interest, notes, "It is extremely unlikely that the tragedy of Kendra Webdale would have been prevented if such a law had existed at the time of her death" (conversation with Gresham, November 18, 1999).

52. Rich, "This Way Lies Madness," A19. Rich refers to Sylvia Nasar, *A Beautiful Mind: A Biography of John Forbes Nash, Jr.* (New York: Simon & Schuster, 1998).

53. Unless otherwise indicated, references to Clifford W. Beers and the NMHA from Faenza, "Chains and Shackles Replaced with Programs and Services," 26M–27M and the Association web site http://www.nmha.org. Beers's *Mind That Found Itself: An Autobiography,* which is out of print, is available from Reprint Services Corporation.

54. Interview with Patrick Cody, vice president for Communications of the NMHA, January 26, 2000.

55. Interview with Judi Chamberlin, March 26, 1998. Unless otherwise indicated, references to Chamberlin and the organization *of* people with psychiatric disabilities ("psychiatric survivors") from this source.

56. Interview with Marvin Spieler, consumer advocate for Mental Health Association of New York City, January 25, 2000.

57. Judi Chamberlin, "Psychiatric Survivors: Are *We* Part of the Disability Movement?" *The Disability Rag,* March/April 1995, 1, 4–6.

58. Interview with Marvin Spieler, January 25, 2000.

59. Chamberlin, "Psychiatric Survivors," 4. In *Transforming Madness: New Lives for People Living with Mental Illness* (New York: William Morrow and Company, Inc., 1999), Jay Neugeboren describes people who, though they have experienced long-term, serious psychiatric disorders, have emerged with meaningful lives. Yet, as Neugeboren recounts, his own brother has not recovered from this illness.

60. National Public Radio News, May 15, 1998. References to the *Archives of General Psychiatry* study from this source.

61. Interview with Richard Greer, March 24, 1998. Unless otherwise indicated, references to Greer and the National Alliance *for* the Mentally Ill from this source.

62. The National Alliance for the Mentally Ill, which has fostered biochemical approaches to mental illness, has accepted over $11 million from the pharmaceutical industry, as reported in *Mother Jones* (Ken Silverstein, "Prozac.org," November/December, 1999, 22–23).

63. Interview with Patrick Cody, January 26, 2000.

64. Interview with Marvin Spieler, January 25, 2000. The rebel Connecticut Chapter of the National Alliance for the Mentally Ill opposes "involuntary outpatient commitment" laws, as indicated by a statement issued by the chapter's board of directors in February 2000. The position of the National Council on Disability regarding "involuntary outpatient commitment" is consistent with that of NMHA and "psychiatric survivors" ("From Privileges to Rights: People Labeled with Psychiatric Disabilities Speak for Themselves," the NCD Report, January 20, 2000).

65. "Talk of the Nation," National Public Radio, July 31, 1997. Joseph Rogers is executive director of the Mental Health Association of Southeastern Pennsylvania and of the affiliated National Mental Health Consumers' Self-Help Clearinghouse, both in Philadelphia.

66. References to Ken Steele from "Talk of the Nation," National Public Radio, October 25, 1999, and from Michael Faenza, "Voter Project Goes National," and Ken Steele, "The Making of the Voter Empowerment Project," both articles in *New York City Voices: A Consumer Journal for Mental Health Advocacy,* September/October 1999, 1, 4, 7.

67. Surgeon General Dr. David Satcher reported that "while 22 percent of the population has a diagnosable mental disorder" and "a range of effective treatments exist for nearly all mental disorders, including the most severe, . . . nearly two-thirds of all people [with such disorders] do not seek treatment" because of lack of information and appropriate insurance coverage as well as fear of stigma. Satcher's definition of mental disorders includes not only psychiatric but also cognitive disabilities such as Alzheimer's disease, attention-deficit disorder, or hyperactivity. Robert Pear, "Mental Disorders Common, U.S. Says; Many Not Treated," *New York Times,* Sunday, December 13, 1999, A1.

68. The Fair Housing Amendments Act of 1988 prohibits discrimination against people with disabilities in housing sales, rentals, or financing; requires reasonable modifications of existing premises; and mandates basic accessibility in newly constructed multi-family dwellings (Kleo King, *Know Your Fair Housing Rights,* published by Eastern Paralyzed Veterans Association, 1997).

69. "60 Minutes: HMO—Managed or Mangled," CBS-TV, January 5, 1997. References to Keith Dixon and James Wrich from this source.

70. A capitation payment is the fixed price that a managed care organization determines is appropriate to provide all health care per managed care consumer for a specific year.

71. Robert Pear, "Elderly and Poor Do Worse Under HMO Plans' Care," *New York Times,* October 2, 1996, A10.

72. Information about the Fall 1998 changes in the Medicare system from "All Things Considered," National Public Radio, June 9, 1998.

73. *Rebuilding Medicare for the 21st Century,* The National Campaign to Protect, Improve, and Expand Medicare, 1999, 13.

74. Interview with Lani Sanjek, March 4, 1999. Unless otherwise indicated, references to Sanjek, Medicare Plus Choice, a two-tier health care system, the Kyl Amendment, and HMO client recruitment strategies from this source.

75. "All Things Considered," National Public Radio, June 9, 1998. By February 1999, there were forty million Medicare beneficiaries (*Rebuilding Medicare for the 21st Century,* 7).

76. Robert Pear, "Panel Finds Medicare Costs Are Underestimated by U.S.," *New York Times,* June 3, 1998, A23. Reference to Gray Panthers, a national grass-roots organization of older people, from this source.

77. *Achieving Independence,* 81.

78. Interview with Elisabeth Benjamin, New York City Legal Aid Attorney, April 16, 1998. References to the 1993 Tennessee Medicaid plan, which included people with incomes up to three times the poverty level, from this source.

79. Linda Peeno, "What Is the Value of a Voice?" *U.S. News and World Report,* March 9, 1998, 40–46. Reference to "Cadillac care" from this source.

80. "Frontline," Public Broadcasting System, April 14, 1998.

81. Interview with Susan Scheer, June 19, 1998. References to Scheer's work at the New York City Public Advocate's office from this source.

82. Interview with Alexander Wood, June 18, 1998. Reference to the Oxford HMO response to Wood's request for a pillow from this source. On June 23, 1998, Wood's struggle with Oxford to get an appropriate wheelchair was described on NBC-TV News.

83. Milt Freudenheim, "Pioneering State for Managed Care Considers Change," *New York Times,* July 14, 1997, A1, D8. Unless otherwise indicated, references to HMO consumer rights bills from this source.

84. Examples of consumer bill of rights mandates described by Representative Frank Pallone (D-N.J.) in "On the Line," WNYC-AM, June 9, 1998.

85. David E. Rosenbaum, "House Hears Grim Tales about Managed Care," *New York Times,* October 8, 1999, A23. While California enacted similar legislation less than two weeks before the House vote, the House bill still required reconciliation with the Senate version before becoming federal law. See also James Sterngold, "Trailblazing California Broadens the Rights of Its HMO Patients," *New York Times,* September 28, 1999, A1, A20. The *New York Times* stated in an editorial (June 14, 2000), "The Supreme Court's unanimous decision [on June 12, 2000 in *Pegram v. Herdrich,* No. 98–1949] that patients cannot sue health maintenance organizations for giving their doctors financial incentives to hold down costs is a reasoned analysis of the state of federal law. But the decision also underscores the need for Congress to set standards for how the managed-care industry operates and to expand the rights of patients who have been harmed by managed-care decisions, including the denial of care" (p. A26).

86. Betsy McCaughey Ross, "One Man's Battle with Managed Care," *New York Times,* December 28, 1996, A27.

87. Bob Herbert quoted Dr. Finley in "A Chance to Survive," *New York Times,* July 4, 1997, A19.

88. Ross, "One Man's Battle," A27.

89. Interview with Robert Fasano, December 31, 1996. Oregon state officials have been rethinking the concept of health care rationing since 1994; nonetheless, doctors and federal Medicaid regulators have doubts about the program (Peter T. Kilborn, "Oregon Falters on a New Path to Health Care," *New York Times,* Sunday, January 3, 1999, A1).

90. Robert Fasano, a social worker, and his wife, an attorney, were forced to reduce their savings precipitously—a requirement known as "spending down"—so that he would be eligible for Medicaid.

91. References to the exclusion of medication from Medicare from "Morning Edition," National Public Radio, February 5, 1999.

92. "Medical Equipment," *New York Times,* January 20, 1999, A12. *DeSario v. Thomas,* 97-6027 (2d Cir 1998) became *Slekis v. Thomas,* 98-5070 (S.Ct. 1999) when the case was reviewed by the U.S. Supreme Court. References to the September 1998 Health Care Financing Administration letter to Medicaid directors from this source.

93. Unless otherwise indicated, references to *DeSario v. Thomas* from Jonathan Rabinowitz, "Court Panel's Ruling Limiting Medicaid Services Is Appealed," *New York Times,* April 7, 1998, B6.

94. Justice For All email jfa@mailbot.com, January 22, 1999. Reference to the amicus brief of the coalition of eighty-one state and national organizations (represented by the Greater Upstate New York Law Project and the Legal Aid Society of New York City) supporting the plaintiffs from this source.

95. Interview with Melinda Dutton, February 24, 1999. References to the effect of the Balanced Budget Act of 1997 on the safety net for children with disabilities from this source.

96. Peter T. Kilborn, "Disabled Children Feel Pain of Cuts," *New York Times,* March 24, 1997, A10.

97. Robert Pear, "Fearing Errors, U.S. Will Review Cutoff in Aid to Disabled Youth," *New York Times,* December 18, 1997, A21.

98. Accepted by members of Congress such as former House Speaker Newt Gingrich (R-Ga.), Representative Gerald Klecxka (D-Wisc.) and news commentators such as Sam Donaldson, Diane Sawyer, and Mike Wallace, the 1994 bizarre accusation—that poor parents were coaching their children to feign "mental disorders" in order to receive SSI benefits—was totally discredited by Joyce Purnick in "Throwing Out the Disabled, Or the Fraud?" *New York Times,* August 8, 1996, B1. Names of legislators and news commentators who accepted this discredited charge from Ken Silverstein and Alexander Cockburn, *Counterpunch,* July 15, 1995, 1.

99. Pear, "Fearing Errors," A21. References to the Zebley ruling from Marta Russell's *Beyond Ramps: Disability at the End of the Social Contract* (Monroe, Maine: Common Courage Press, 1998), 156. See *Sullivan v. Zebley,* 493 U.S. 521 (1990).

100. This Medicaid waiver program, known as the Katie Beckett program, was established in the late 1970s and early 1980s for children with severe disabilities or illnesses by Family Voices, the national advocacy organization founded by Katie Beckett's mother, Julie Beckett.

101. Children with disabilities whose immigrant status prevent them from receiving Medicaid generally do not receive CHIP benefits.

102. For example, in 1997 in New York State, 77 percent of uninsured children who were eligible for Medicaid or CHIP were not enrolled.

103. *Achieving Independence,* 85.

104. Melvyn R. Tanzman, "Work Incentives and Long Term Care Programs Proposed by President Clinton," *New York Able,* February 1999, 8.

105. *Achieving Independence,* 81.

106. Robert Pear, "Medicare Cuts Would Reduce At-Home Care for Patients," *New York Times,* February 9, 1997, A30. Unless otherwise indicated, references to complex medical services provided in the home from this source.

107. Ian Fisher, "Families Provide Medical Care, Tubes and All," *New York Times,* June 7, 1998, A1.

108. Although in "Medicare Cuts Would Reduce At-Home Care for Patients," A30, Pear discusses the threat to only Medicare recipients of long-term home health care, Medicaid beneficiaries are also threatened.

109. "MarketPlace," National Public Radio, March 12, 1998. References to 1997 cuts in home health care from this source.

110. Interview with New York City comptroller Alan Hevesi, July 21, 1997.

111. Unless otherwise indicated, references to recommendations of the NCD regarding Medicare and Medicaid from *Achieving Independence,* 90–91.

112. Sections 503 and 504 apply to federal contractors and recipients of federal funds.

113. Berkowitz, *Disabled Policy,* 106.

114. Interview with Lani Sanjek, March 4, 1999.

115. Anne Emerman, "Testimony on the Future of Medicare," *New York Able,* January 1999, 7.

116. *Achieving Independence,* 86.

117. Tanzman, "Work Incentives," 8.

118. References to the NCD recommendations regarding Medicaid and health care ombudsman from *Achieving Independence*, 90–92.

119. *Achieving Independence*, 89. The federal Health Care Financing Administration (HCFA), the agency that oversees Medicare and Medicaid, is the largest purchaser of managed care in the country ("Rising Medicare Standards," *New York Times*, Sunday, December 29, 1996, sec. 4, p. 8).

120. *Achieving Independence*, 88–90.

121. Former employees on SSDI receive Medicare after two years, even if they have not reached the age of sixty-five. For a nine-month trial period, a person on SSDI may earn more than seven hundred dollars a month and still remain on SSDI. If that person earns more than seven hundred dollars a month for longer than nine months, then that individual may lose SSDI and therefore Medicare.

122. *Achieving Independence*, 83.

123. Ibid., 74.

124. *Proceedings*, 30–31. Rebecca Ogle also points out the need for intensive education, habilitation, and rehabilitation services to prepare young people with disabilities for mainstream employment.

125. References to WIIA from John F. Harris, "House Passes Job Benefit for Disabled," *Washington Post*, October 20, 1999, A02, and "WIIA Vote Counts," email justice@jfanow.org, November 22, 1999.

126. Supplemental Security Income, a federal welfare program initiated in 1974, is provided to disabled or older individuals, ineligible for Social Security Disability Insurance, who cannot work. Unless people have worked under the social security system for no less than ten years (forty three-month periods, not necessarily consecutively), they are ineligible for SSDI.

127. References to Paul Longmore's employment problems from "Beyond Affliction: What's Work Got To Do with It" (aired at different times in various parts of the country on National Public Radio during the week of May 4, 1998).

128. President Clinton's January 14, 1999, remarks on his Disability Initiative to encourage employment of people with disabilities. See Suzanne Christy, "President Includes Disabled: $2 Billion Budgeted to Bolster Employment Opportunities," *New York Able*, March 1999, 1 and 12.

129. *Proceedings*, 13.

130. Sections 501 and 503 of the Rehabilitation Act of 1973 require affirmative action to employ qualified people with disabilities in the federal government. Some local governments have affirmative action requirements similar to that of the federal government. The ADA, which applies to employment in the private sector, however, does not mandate affirmative action.

131. *Proceedings*, 75.

Chapter Eight

1. Nat Hentoff quoted Margaret Mead in "We Hear the Death Train Coming," *Village Voice*, February 4, 1997, 12. See also Michael Specter, "The Dangerous Philosopher," *The New Yorker*, September 6, 1999, 46–55. For a comprehensive analysis of some of the cases and issues discussed in this chapter, see Gregory E. Pence, *Classic Cases in Medical Ethics* (New York: McGraw Hill, 2000).

2. "People with physical and mental disabilities . . . still continue to be segregated, institutionalized, tortured in the name of behavior management, abused, raped, euthanized and murdered" (Norman Kunc and Emma Van Der Klift, "A Credo For Support," *Moebius Syndrome News*, 1995).

3. Although he is frequently referred to as Dr. Jack Kevorkian, not only was his Michigan medical license revoked in 1991, but also "the only remedies he 'prescribes' are poisons" (Michael Betzold, "The Selling of Dr. Death," *The New Republic*, May 26, 1997, 22–23).

4. Mark O'Brien, "Maybe You'd Rather Die Than Be Me," *DIA Activist*, January 1997, 3.

5. Nadina LaSpina quoted Diane Coleman and Stephen Gold in "We Want To Live," *New York Able*, January 1997, 7.

6. The CBS program "60 Minutes" presented Jack Kevorkian's videotape of his euthanasia of Thomas Youk. Although in their response to this "60 Minutes" broadcast producers of the November 23, 1998,

ABC program "Nightline" decided against disability representation, on February 28, 1999, "60 Minutes" presented people living meaningful lives with ALS.

7. Diane Coleman, letter to Not Dead Yet Members and Supporters, January 25, 1999.

8. Pam Belluck, "Dr. Kevorkian Is a Murderer, the Jury Finds," *New York Times,* March 27, 1999, A1, A9. Jack Kevorkian was found guilty of murder in Pontiac, Michigan, on March 26, 1999.

9. Michael Betzold, *Appointment with Dr. Death* (Troy, Mich.: Momentum Books, 1993). References to Jack Lessenberry from Michael Betzold, "The Selling of Dr. Death," *New Republic,* May 26, 1997, 22–28.

10. "Lessenberry has also published pieces flattering toward Kevorkian and Fieger in *Esquire, George, Vanity Fair* and other publications" (Betzold, "The Selling of Dr. Death," 25).

11. Betzold, "The Selling of Dr. Death," 22.

12. Nat Hentoff, "Class Warfare to the Death," *Village Voice,* May 21, 1996, 12.

13. John Gresham of New York Lawyers for the Public Interest provided information about *Vacco v. Quill,* 117 S.Ct. 2293 (1997). See *Washington v. Glucksberg,* 117 S.Ct. 2258 (1997).

14. LaSpina, "We Want To Live," 7.

15. Nat Hentoff, "Death's Enemy: Yale Kamisar," *Village Voice,* May 28, 1996, 10. Hentoff paraphrased from Kamisar's *Minnesota Law Review* article, "Some Non-Religious Views Against Proposed 'Mercy Killing' Legislation."

16. Hentoff, "Death's Enemy." Hentoff quoted from Kamisar's essay that appeared in the *University of Detroit Mercy Law Review.*

17. Hentoff, "Death's Enemy." Hentoff quoted Robert Beezer.

18. Information from annotated list of participating law firms distributed at June 19, 1997, luncheon of New York Lawyers for the Public Interest.

19. "Excerpts from Court's Decision Upholding Bans on Assisted Suicide," *New York Times,* June 27, 1997, A18.

20. David France, quoting Larry Kramer, in "A Life-and-Death Decision," *New York Times,* January 13, 1997, 26–27. Discussion of *The Normal Heart* as a spur to Larry Kramer's support of Jack Kevorkian's assisted suicides from this source.

21. "Small Group of Doctors Supports Concept of Assisting in Suicide," *New York Times,* October 31, 1996, A20.

22. "60 Minutes," CBS Television, January 5, 1997. References to publications by Timothy Quill and Lonnie Shavelson in the *New England Journal of Medicine* from this source. See Timothy Quill, "Death and Dignity: A Case of Individualized Decision Making," *NEJM,* 324(10) (March 7, 1991): 691–94.

23. "A Poll of AIDS Doctors Finds That Many Help in Suicides," *New York Times,* February 6, 1997, A18. *New York Times* reference to this survey of San Francisco Bay Area physicians from February 5, 1997, article published in the *New England Journal of Medicine.*

24. References to Sheila Diamond and Dr. Ira Byock from "Nightline," ABC-TV, January 9, 1997.

25. References to Kathleen Foley from Paul Wilkes, "The Next Pro-Lifers," *New York Times Magazine,* Sunday, July 21, 1996, 45.

26. Daniel Carr and Nelson Hendler stated their views on pain management on the WNYC-AM program "On the Line," March 24, 1997. References to Carr and Hendler from this source.

27. Robert Pear, "Clinton Names Panel to Draft Health Consumer Bill of Rights," *New York Times,* March 27, 1997, B11.

28. Brian Lehrer, well-informed radio host of "On the Line" (WNYC-AM), offered this observation during his interview with Carr and Hendler.

29. "Reeve Feels Others Show As Much Courage," *Brainerd Daily Dispatch,* October 28, 1996, 6A.

30. David Peterson, "Reeve's Honesty Charms His Audience," *Minneapolis Star Tribune,* October 28, 1996, A12. When a television commercial using computer animation showed Reeve walking, "many advocates for the handicapped were aghast, maintaining that no such cure is in the offing, and that the spot cruelly offered false hope to people who should be concentrating on adapting to life with their disabilities" (Bernard Stamler, "Christopher Reeve Is Sanguine about His Madison Avenue Connections, but Some Are Skeptical," *New York Times,* June 15, 2000, C10).

31. Information about and comments of Marca Bristo from authors' April 30, 1998, interview with Bristo.

32. "Superman's Telethon," *Ragged Edge*, May/June 1998, 27.

33. "Reeve Feels Others Show As Much Courage," 6A.

34. Christopher Reeve, *Still Me* (New York: Random House, 1998).

35. John Hockenberry, *Moving Violations: War Zones, Wheelchairs, and Declarations of Independence* (New York: Hyperion, 1995), 204.

36. Daniel Robert, "A Rock and A Hard Place—Superman, Dr. Death and You and Me," *New York Able*, February 1997, 11.

37. Martin S. Pernick, *The Black Stork: Eugenics and the Death of "Defective" Babies in American Medicine and Motion Pictures* (New York: Oxford University Press, 1996).

38. Stated by Martin S. Pernick in "Tomorrow's Children: Beyond Affliction: The Disability History Project," National Public Radio, May 1998.

39. Pernick, *The Black Stork*, 5-6.

40. Ibid., 7. Although the *New York Times* supported Haiselden on eugenics, the newspaper eventually took issue with his publicity-seeking.

41. Pernick, *The Black Stork*, 16.

42. Robert J. Lifton, *The Nazi Doctors: Medical Killing and the Psychology of Genocide* (New York: Basic Books, 1986), 23.

43. Ibid., 23. Unless otherwise indicated, references to Fritz Lenz from this source. Lenz was referring to the research, such as that at Cold Spring Harbor, New York, guided by Charles B. Davenport and financed by the Carnegie Institution in Washington and by Mary Harriman.

44. Virginia Kallianes and Phyllis Rubenfeld, "Disabled Women and Reproductive Rights," *Disability and Society*, 1997, 12(2): 212.

45. Quoted in footnote in Lifton, *The Nazi Doctors*, 23. Reference to "national degeneration" from this source.

46. Diane Coleman, J.D., and Carol Gill, Ph.D., testified before the Constitution Subcommittee of the U.S. House Judiciary Committee on April 29, 1996. References to Coleman and Gill from this source.

47. The 1996 Israeli documentary *Healing by Killing*, produced and directed by Nitzan Aviram, pointed out that without "the technical know-how from euthanasia" and "euthanasia teams" already in place, the Holocaust may not have been possible.

48. In *By Trust Betrayed* (Arlington, Va.: Vandamere Press, 1995, 202-3), Hugh Gregory Gallagher credited this reversal to many people who risked their lives: disabled people themselves, as well as others, including some clergy, some doctors and nurses, and even some Nazi party members. While the execution of Jews, gypsies, homosexuals, and others was not condemned by most German people, many were troubled by the killing of what they considered to be "German" people with disabilities.

49. Marta Russell, *Beyond Ramps: Disability at the End of the Social Contract* (Monroe, Maine: Common Courage Press, 1998), 27-28. References to the Nuremberg Court from this source.

50. In *Freedom To Die* (New York: St. Martin's Press, 1998), authors Derek Humphry and Mary Clement imply that there indeed is a duty to die: "Is there, in fact, a duty to die—a responsibility within the family unit—that should remain voluntary but expected nevertheless?" (p. 313).

51. Michael Betzold in a letter published in the June 30, 1997, *New Republic*—commenting on his May 26, 1997, *New Republic* article, "The Selling of Dr. Death"—described Kevorkian as "a man who advocates medical experiments as part of euthanasia for people who are disabled and depressed."

52. Coleman and Gill, testimony before the Constitution Subcommittee of the House Judiciary Committee on April 29, 1996. In her July 14, 1998, testimony before the Constitution Subcommittee of the House Judiciary Committee, Coleman indicated that although Kevorkian's acts violate Michigan law according to the state Supreme Court, he is "still killing people with non-terminal disabilities, and now even harvesting their organs."

53. John Hess, formerly of the *New York Times*, argued on WNYC-AM on "New York and Company," June 6, 1996, that in the United States, the economy is currently booming, and therefore scarcity is a manufactured product of a conservative social agenda.

54. Humphry and Clement, *Freedom to Die*, 313.

55. John Hardwig, "Is There a Duty to Die?" *Hastings Center Report*, March—April 1997, 27(2): 80. Emphasis added.

56. Unless otherwise indicated, references to Anne Emerman's views on physician-assisted suicide from her January 10, 1997, conversation with authors. Wilkes, "The Next Pro-Lifers," 42. Wilkes quoted Yale Kamisar.

57. Ezekiel J. Emanuel, associate professor of ethics and medicine at Harvard Medical School, and Linda L. Emanuel, vice president for ethical standards at the American Medical Association, "Assisted Suicide? Not In My State," *New York Times,* July 24, 1997, A21. This article appeared before the referendum victory for physician-assisted suicide in Oregon on November 4, 1997. See Timothy Egan, "Right To Die: In Oregon, Opening a New Front in the World of Medicine," *New York Times,* November 6, 1997, A26.

58. Neil A. Lewis, "Reno Lifts Barrier to Oregon's Law on Aided Suicide," *New York Times,* June 6, 1998, A1.

59. Emanuel and Emanuel, "Assisted Suicide?", A21. References to the Emanuels from this source.

60. France, "A Life-and-Death Decision," 26. Sheryl Gay Stolberg, in "Assisted Suicides Are Rare, Survey of Doctors Finds," *New York Times,* April 23, 1998, A1. Stolberg, offering statistics that conflicted with those presented in France's article, indicated that although only 5 percent of physicians admitted that they have given lethal injections, more say they would do so if such action were legally sanctioned.

61. Timothy Egan, "Right to Die," A26.

62. Lewis, "Reno Lifts Barrier," A1. References to Reno's ruling on Oregon's assisted suicide law from this source. Although according to the Associated Press, November 11, 1997, "Administrator Thomas Constantine [of the Drug Enforcement Administration] warned that doctors who take part in assisted suicides would be violating federal narcotics law and risk losing their licenses to prescribe drugs," Reno reversed that position on June 5, 1998.

63. Interview with Anne Emerman, November 8, 1997.

64. Because on October 27, 1999, the U.S. House of Representatives passed a bill that would make prescribing lethal drugs for terminally-ill patients a federal crime, elected Oregon officials considered a legal challenge that could bring the issue to the U.S. Supreme Court. See Robert Pear, "House Backs Ban on Using Medicine To Aid in Suicide," *New York Times,* A1, A29; and Sam Howe Verhovek, "Oregon Considers Challenge," *New York Times,* October 28, 1999, A29.

65. Summary of the warning posed by Herbert Hendin—author of *Seduced by Death: Doctors, Patients and the Dutch Cure* (New York: W. W. Norton, 1996)—from Charles E. Rosenberg's "Slippery Slope," *New York Times,* Sunday, November 24, 1996, sec. 7, p. 33. In "Kevorkian on Trial," *Psychiatric Times,* February 1999, 16(2), Hendin related the "slippery slope" danger to Kevorkian's euthanasia of Thomas Youk.

66. Coleman, letter to Not Dead Yet Members and Supporters, January 25, 1999. References to Compassion In Dying from this source.

67. Diane Coleman, testimony before the Constitution Subcommittee of the House Judiciary Committee, July 14, 1998.

68. Interview with Diane Coleman, March 11, 1999.

69. Coleman's 1998 Congressional testimony.

70. Humphry and Clement, *Freedom to Die,* 313.

71. Coleman's 1998 Congressional testimony.

72. Editorial, *New York Times,* February 27, 1999. References to this comparison from this source.

73. Joseph Shapiro, "Casting a Cold Eye on 'Death with Dignity,'" *U.S. News & World Report,* March 1, 1999, 56. References to Shapiro's discussion of the 1999 Oregon report from this source. Shapiro quoted Kathleen Foley.

74. Unless otherwise indicated, discussion of legalizing disability discrimination from Diane Coleman's July 14, 1998, testimony before the Constitution Subcommittee of the House Judiciary Committee.

75. 42 USC 12101 (a)(7); emphasis added.

76. Interview with Coleman, March 11, 1999.

77. Ezekiel Emanuel, "Whose Right To Die?" *Atlantic Monthly,* March 1997, 73–79. Emanuel's references to the danger of the legalization of physician-assisted suicide for vulnerable populations from this source.

78. David E. Rosenbaum, "Americans Want a Right To Die or So They Think," *New York Times,* Sunday, June 8, 1997, sec. 4, p. 3. "The better off financially and the better educated . . . the more likely [people] were to favor legal assisted suicide," Rosenbaum noted.

79. Emanuel discusses the effect of budgetary pressures on decisions regarding physician-assisted suicide. Both Dr. Kathleen Foley and Dr. Joanne Lynn (editor of *Handbook for Mortals: Guidance for People Facing Serious Illness* [New York: Oxford University Press, 1999]) stated on "The Open Mind" (PBS-TV, aired November 11, 1998, and March 3, 1999) that these demographics will forge a cultural shift in attitudes toward death and dying. As Lynn indicated, two generations ago people died suddenly, but now they tend to "die by inches."

80. Rosenbaum, "Americans Want a Right to Die," 3. References to Michael J. Sandel from this source.

81. Wilkes, "The Next Pro-Lifers," 26.

82. Coleman's 1998 congressional testimony.

83. Rosenbaum, "Americans Want a Right to Die," 3.

84. Nancy Rolnick, "The Right to Live/The Right To Die," *New York Able,* December 1995, 12, 19. References to Rolnick from this source.

85. References to the Latimer case from "Murder of Disabled Daughter Draws 1-year Sentence," *Ragged Edge,* January/February, 1998, 5. Bioethicist Adrienne Asch at a December 5, 1997, Disabilities Studies Colloquium at New York City's Hunter College School of Social Work stated, "A father killing his twelve-year-old daughter is neither personal assistance services nor physician-assisted suicide; we have other words for that."

86. Mary Jane Owen, "The Elizabeth Bouvia Suicide Case: Is Psychiatry Only for Able-Bodied?" *The Detroit News,* February 6, 1984, sec. A, p. 11.

87. While Joseph P. Shapiro in *No Pity: People with Disabilities Forging a New Civil Rights Movement* (New York: Times Books, 1993), 274, indicated that in 1988 Bouvia was wishing for death, Richard B. Treanor in *We Overcame: The Story of Civil Rights for Disabled People* (Falls Church, Va.: Regal Direct Publishing, 1993), 264, stated that she was a happy person in 1988.

88. Mary Jane Owen, "We're Cowards to Think This Suicide Is Right," *The Washington Post,* February 12, 1984, B05 (in "Sunday Outlook").

89. Mary Johnson, "Life and Death: Unanswered Questions," *The Ragged Edge* (Louisville: The Advocado Press, 1994), 187–93. References to comments on this case by Kenneth Bergstedt and Edward Roberts from this source.

90. "Around the Nation," *Incitement,* July 1992, 8(2): 15. In chapter 9 of *No Pity,* Joseph Shapiro offers a thorough discussion of this case.

91. Republic Bank funded these yearly awards ceremonies honoring two or three students for their accomplishments, as well as several adults, who have served the disability community in New York City.

92. Frank Bowe, "Handicapping America: Barriers to Disabled People," *Disability: Our Challenge,* John P. Hourihan, ed. (New York: Teachers College, Columbia University, 1979), 90.

93. Michael White and John Gribbin, *Stephen Hawking: A Life in Science* (New York: Penguin Books, 1993), 15. White and Gribbin quoted from Dennis Overbye's *Lonely Hearts of the Cosmos* (New York: Little Brown, 1999).

94. *A Brief History of Time,* 84 min., 1992, Paramount Pictures Corporation. Comments of Hawking's colleague from this source.

95. Howard B. Hain, quoting Stephen Nachtheim, in "Light Years Ahead: One-on-One with Stephen Hawking," *We,* October 1997, 14.

96. Malcolm W. Browne, "A Bet on a Cosmic Scale and a Concession, Sort Of," *New York Times,* February 12, 1997, A1, A22.

97. Hain, "Light Years Ahead," 14, quoting Hawking.

98. Diane Coleman's mention of "Final Exit" is a reference to Derek Humphry's bestseller, the right-to-die movement's call to arms, *Final Exit* (Eugene, Ore.: Hemlock Society, 1991).

Chapter Nine

1. Richard B. Treanor in *We Overcame: The Story of Civil Rights for Disabled People* (Falls Church, Va.: Regal Direct Publishing, 1993), 122, quoted Steven A. Holmes, *New York Times,* March 18, 1990. Holmes

described technological innovations for "people with severe handicaps." Some discussion of the impact of technology on veterans is included in chapter 10.

2. Wolfgang Saxon, Obituaries, "Ronald L. Mace, 58, Designer of Buildings Accessible to All," *New York Times,* July 13, 1998, B9. References to Mace—who was instrumental in the passage of the 1988 Fair Housing Amendments Act and the 1990 ADA—from this source.

3. Definition of universal design (memorandum by Scott Shanklin-Peterson, senior deputy chairman of the National Endowment for the Arts) from an accessibility project initiated in September 1997 at The Millay Colony for the Arts.

4. Ralf Hotchkiss is quoted in *Report on the "American Creativity at Risk" Symposium,* Rhode Island, November 1996, 16.

5. Description of universal design from *Beyond Access,* a film about the Millay Colony for the Arts.

6. From material distributed—by the Center for Universal Design at North Carolina State University— at the June 19-20, 1998, New York City conference. See also Jim Davis, "Design for the 21st Century Starts Now," *Ragged Edge,* November/December 1998, 10-14; and Jim Davis, "Developing an Accessible Penn Station," *New York Able,* March 1998, 3, 16.

7. Frank Bowe, "Handicapping America: Barriers to Disabled People," *Disability: Our Challenge,* John P. Hourihan, ed. (New York: Teachers College, Columbia University, 1979), 91.

8. Editorial, *New York Times,* November 13, 1992.

9. Peter Hellman, "Toilet Wars," *New York* magazine, May 3, 1993, 38-43.

10. "20/20," ABC-TV, March 12, 1993.

11. Philip K. Howard, *The Death of Common Sense: How Law is Suffocating America* (New York: Random House, 1994), 116-17. Howard's references to the New York City street toilet issue from this source.

12. A German company placed one of its accessible street toilets near City Hall in Manhattan for about six months in 1995. Although this experiment complied with the ADA, the company did not contract with New York City to set up street toilets throughout the five boroughs.

13. References to *Bravin v. Mount Sinai Medical Center,* 1999, (S.D.N.Y.) from Barbara Stewart, "Judge Finds Bias at Hospital in Dealings with Deaf Man," *New York Times,* April 17, 1999, B4. Stewart quoted the Bravins' lawyer. Just as interpreters are required for people who speak foreign languages, the ADA mandates sign language interpreters for deaf people in hospitals. Disability advocates have suggested that hospitals and private doctors should have access to a service providing a pool of sign language interpreters.

14. References to this grant from information provided by Eileen Healy, president of the board of CIDNY; Marilyn Saviola, executive director of CIDNY; and Gerry Zuzze, CIDNY coordinator of Outreach and Training.

15. The exact number of major cities with accessible taxis is difficult to determine because they are springing up continually. The June 29, 2000, proposal by New York City Taxi and Limousine Commissioner Diane Magrath McKechnie states that as of July 1, 2001, all vehicles purchased for use as yellow taxis must be accessible to people with disabilities, including wheelchair users. By July 1, 2001, the livery services provided to wheelchair users must be equivalent to the services available to others. Taxi and livery companies are exempted from this requirement if they offer an alternative accepted by the Taxi and Limousine Commission. From Taxi and Limousine Commission hearing, June 29, 2000.

16. According to deaf advocate Martin Leff, the reason it took so long for the TTY to be used in great numbers was "sleepy people and no money. Business woke up when it saw the financial potential. By 2000, approximately two million TTYs have been sold at an average price of two hundred dollars each."

17. Howard, *The Death of Common Sense,* 5. Howard's discussion of the incident is incomplete. The New York City Department of Buildings and the Missionaries of Charity accepted a compromise: the elevator, paid for by the city, would go only to the second floor, where all necessary services for homeless people who could not negotiate steps would be provided.

18. As Anne Emerman—the director of the Mayor's Office for People with Disabilities at that time— revealed in a August 17, 1997, interview, Mother Teresa's Missionaries of Charity stated their reason for leaving New York City in a letter to Emerman.

19. Usually, it is easier to attain compliance in Title II ADA issues like curb cuts than Title III ADA issues like One-Step. In the former, it is necessary to deal with one municipal agency whereas in the latter, it

is necessary to deal with each individual entity, one by one. Richard Connette—winner of the first Richard Gelman award conferred on an individual who has made a major contribution benefiting the disability population in New York State—reorganized the One-Step Campaign in New York City in 1994.

20. Ralf D. Hotchkiss, "Ground Swell on Wheels," *The Sciences* (July/August 1993), 16.

21. Unless otherwise indicated, references to wheelchair technology and the work of Ralf D. Hotchkiss is based on an interview with Hotchkiss and his wife, Deborah Kaplan, an attorney formerly at World Institute on Disability, aired in 1993 on "Disabled In Action Speaks," WBAI-FM.

22. Ralf Hotchkiss is quoted in "Pioneering Mobility," *Graduating Engineer* (December 1994), 31. The need for a new approach to wheelchairs and scooters even in the United States is evident to most mobility-impaired drivers since they can much more easily get their cars repaired than their wheelchairs or scooters.

23. More appropriate for most quadriplegics than computerized walking stimulators, motorized wheelchairs are required by many in this population.

24. Andrew Wyeth, "Christina's World," exhibited at the Museum of Modern Art in New York City since 1973.

25. John Hockenberry, *Moving Violations: War Zones, Wheelchairs, and Declarations of Independence* (New York: Hyperion, 1995). *Spoke Man* was presented at the American Place Theater in New York City, from February 21 to March 24, 1996.

26. References to Ira Colchin from Walter H. Waggoner, "Blind Are Trained to Read Instruments in Newark Program," *New York Times,* Sunday, December 18, 1977, sec. 11, pp. 12–13, and to William Skawinski from interview, June 19, 2000. References to multiple chemical sensitivity from Ben Van Wagner, "Science for People with Disabilities—President's Column," *Science Is for Everyone,* Fall 1995, 1–2.

27. Hofstra professor Frank Bowe, who is deaf and a disability advocate, uses similar terminology to indicate the remarkable benefits of technology to people with sensory impairments. The Kurzweil reader changes print on paper to speech while the voice synthesizer changes print on the computer screen to speech.

28. Dolores King, "Changing Attitudes," *Disabled In Action Activist,* Spring 1999.

29. References to the computer as an accommodation for autism and comments of Temple Grandin from Harvey Blume, "Autism & the Internet" http://www.media-in-transition.mit.edu/articles/blume.html, 10–11.

30. Temple Grandin, *Thinking in Pictures: And Other Reports from My Life with Autism* (New York: Vintage, 1996).

31. In order for Dragon Dictate to work properly, not only must the individual learn the appropriate computer commands, but also the computer must become familiar with the individual's voice patterns, vocabulary, and phrasing.

32. The increased use of computers, especially since the mid-1980s, has resulted in a growing number of professionals with disorders that were formerly associated only with blue-collar workers—for example, repetitive strain injuries such as carpal tunnel syndrome and tendinitis (from interview with Michael McCann, Ph.D., board member of the New York Committee on Occupational Safety and Health, April 23, 1997).

33. Bruce Felton, "Technologies That Enable the Disabled," *New York Times,* Sunday, September 14, 1997, sec. 3, p. 11.

34. "In Virtual Reality, Tools for the Disabled," *New York Times,* April 13, 1994, C1, C6.

35. References to Judy Brewer, the May 1998 New Orleans Conference of the President's Council on Employment of People with Disabilities, Paul Schrader, and the cost of add-on computer technology, from "Talk of the Nation, Science Friday," National Public Radio, May 8, 1998. Although "people with disabilities are perhaps the single segment of society with the most to gain from the new technologies of the electronic age . . . , only one-quarter of people with disabilities own computers, and only one- tenth ever make use of the internet." H. Stephen Kaye, "Computer and Internet Use among People with Disabilities," Disability Statistics Center: Report 13, March 2000 http://www.dsc.uscf.edu. Kaye says the reason for the problem is that many people with disabilities are poor, and so they cannot afford the kind of computer they need, the specialized software to make it accessible to them, and the monthly charges of an internet service provider.

36. One of the services provided by the American Foundation for the Blind is the evaluation of

assistive technology for blind people. The National Federation of the Blind filed an ADA lawsuit in Boston Federal District Court against America Online for failing to provide blind people with accessible services compatible with "screen access programs that convert text into synthesized speech or Braille" (Pamela Mendels, "Advocates for Blind, in Suit, Say AOL Impedes Access to Internet," *New York Times,* November 5, 1999, A25).

37. Peter D. Kramer, *Listening to Prozac* (New York: Viking, 1993). In "New and Old Depression Drugs Are Found Equal," Erica Goode reports that a new government study revealed that "Prozac and other drugs of its generation are not any better—or any worse—than older compounds in treating major depression" (*New York Times,* March 19, 1999, A1).

38. Peter D. Kramer, *Should You Leave* (New York: Simon & Schuster, 1997). Kramer begins chapter 10 with this observation.

39. Peter R. Breggin, *Toxic Psychiatry* (New York: St. Martin's Press, 1991). Dr. Sherwin B. Nulands is concerned about the assumption of "a psychopharmacological fantasy that, in the name of science, offers . . . simple, painless self-transformation if you take the right pill" ("The Pill of Pills," *New York Review of Books,* June 9, 1994, 4).

40. Barbara Strauch, "Use of Antidepression Medicine for Young Patients Has Soared," *New York Times,* Sunday, August 10, 1997, A1, 24. References to Dr. Leon Eisenberg from this source. The Journal of the American Medical Association reported that between 1991 and 1995, the number of teenagers taking antidepressants doubled and the number of two- to four-year-old children taking some form of Ritalin (a psychostimulant used to treat children with Attention Deficit Hyperactivity Disorder) tripled ("Nightline," ABC-TV News, February 24, 2000).

41. "All Things Considered," National Public Radio News, May 26, 1998.

42. References to experiments with drugs that provoke psychotic symptoms from Philip J. Hilts, "Psychiatric Researchers Under Fire." *New York Times,* May 19, 1998, F1, F5. On January 19, 1999, Lynda Richardson ("New Rules Proposed for Medical Experiments on Mentally Ill," *New York Times,* B4) reported that "a [New York State] advisory panel had proposed new rules that would allow medical experiments involving some risk to be performed on mentally ill patients and others incapable of giving consent."

43. References to Peter Weiden, author of *Conquering Schizophrenia: A Father, His Son, and a Medical Breakthrough* (New York: Knopf, 1998), from New York and Company, WNYC-AM, February 10, 1998.

44. Marvin Spieler, "A Car Ride to Hell," *New York City Voices: A Consumer Journal for Mental Health Advocacy,* July/August 1999, 14.

45. Interview with Samuel W. Anderson, Ph.D., Associate Research Scientist, Columbia University and Director of Communication Sciences Laboratory, New York Psychiatric Institute, August 13, 1997.

46. Interview with audiologist Dr. Ernest Zelnick, Ph.D., December 23, 1997. Zelnick points out that cochlear implants are appropriate only for the small population for whom even the extremely sensitive and programmable digital hearing aids are ineffective. He adds that digital hearing aids are far more effective, though considerably more expensive, than the older technology—analogue or linear hearing aids.

47. Dr. Randolph Mallory, "On the Line," WNYC-AM, July 23, 1997. In their study, Mario Svirsky and his colleagues at Indiana School of Medicine at Indianapolis discovered that the language proficiency of children who received cochlear implants developed at a rate similar to that of hearing children. The National Association for the Deaf (NAD) is reassessing its skeptical view of cochlear implants. References to Svirsky and the NAD from http://www.abcnews.com, March 2, 2000.

48. Statistics provided by the League for the Hard of Hearing in New York City.

49. Natalie Angier, "Joined for Life, and Living Life to the Full," *New York Times,* December 23, 1997, F5. References to Dr. Alan Fleischman from this source.

50. One of the coauthors provided Nat Hentoff—who has written articles on the Baby Jane Doe case—with a copy of the amicus brief filed on the side of the government by several disability rights organizations. Significant Hentoff articles on the subject appeared in the *Village Voice* of January 3 and January 10, 1984. See also Gregory E. Pence, *Classic Cases in Medical Ethics* (New York: McGraw Hill, 2000), chap. 8.

51. References to Dixie Lawrence's parent-directed therapy for Down syndrome from "ABC News Nightline," December 20, 1996.

52. References to transplants from Sheryl Gay Stolberg, "Live and Let Die Over Transplants," *New*

York Times, Sunday, April 5, 1998, sec. 4, p. 3. The question of who should get preference in receiving "the nation's scarcest medical resource," human organs, continues to be a controversial issue as the country moves toward a policy in which "organs are shared broadly across regional lines, with sickest patients being given first priority" (Sheryl Gay Stolberg, "Agreement on Plan to Revamp Organ Distribution," *New York Times,* November 12, 1999, A1, A31).

53. Spina bifida means "open spine" in Latin. Once amniocentesis became routine for high-risk pregnant women, only economically deprived pregnant women gave birth to babies with spina bifida. As a result, the racial and ethnic profile of babies with spina bifida altered dramatically, and funding for the Spina Bifida Association declined precipitously.

54. Interview with Susan Scheer, July 26, 1997. References to Scheer and "the miracle baby" from this source.

55. Milt Freudenheim, "Corporate-Paid Psychotherapy: At What Price?" *New York Times,* April 12, 1994, D2. The article is appropriately subtitled, "Therapy Isn't Quantifiable." References to Dr. Harold Eist from this source.

56. "Morning Edition," National Public Radio, March 4, 1997. References to Larry Gostin and Robert Gelman from this source.

57. Gina Kolata, "Advent of Testing for Breast Cancer Genes Leads to Fears of Disclosure and Discrimination," *New York Times,* February 4, 1997, C1, C3. The new rules that President Clinton announced to ensure the privacy of personal medical records initiated a vigorous debate involving physicians, health care providers, insurance companies, and HMOs (Robert Pear, "Rules on Privacy of Patient Data Stir Hot Debate," *New York Times,* October 30, 1999, A1, A10).

58. Gina Kolata, "Biology's Big Project Turns into Challenge for Computer Experts," *New York Times,* June 11, 1996, C1. Two teams have been competing in a race to decode the human genome: one the public consortium that wishes to make information freely available and the other a private company, Celera, seeking "enough proprietary safeguards to make a profit" (Nicholas Wade, "Genome Decoding Plan Is Derailed by Conflict," *New York Times,* March 9, 2000, A20). On June 19, 2000, the two teams jointly announced that they have mapped a rough draft of the human genome. University of Pennsylvania professor Arthur Kaplan notes that bioethicists are concerned that DNA information could be secured without an individual's knowledge and that tests and drugs resulting from genetic mapping may not be affordable by a significant number of people (CNN News, June 19, 2000).

59. Interview with Jeremy Rifkin regarding *The Biotech Century: Harnessing the Gene and Remaking the World* (New York: J. P. Tarcher, 1999), Pacifica Radio Archives. In this book Rifkin considered the potentially dangerous consequences of granting any institution or group the authority to redesign the planet's genetic blueprint.

60. Adrienne Asch, "The Human Genome and Disability Rights," *The Disability Rag and ReSource,* January/February 1994, 12.

61. "The Newshour with Jim Lehrer," Public Broadcasting System, January 1, 1997. References to Patricia King from this source.

62. Kolata, "Advent of Testing for Breast Cancer Gene," C1. References to discrimination based on genetic tests from this source. Although Dr. Susan Love does not consider prophylactic mastectomy good medical procedure, Denise Grady of the *New York Times* reported in opposition on January 14, 1999, in "Removal of Healthy Breasts Is Found to Cut Cancer Risk" (p. A1).

63. See David L. Wheeler, "Scientists Worry about the Implications of Genetic Testing for Inherited Disease," Nancy R. MacKenzie, ed. *Science and Technology Today* (New York: St. Martin's Press, 1995), 324. Hoping his policy would be replicated by the private sector, President Clinton prohibited "the misuse of genetic tests to discriminate against any American" by federal agencies ("President Acts to Bar Genetic Discrimination," Associated Press, *New York Times* web site http://www.nytimes.com, February 8, 2000).

64. References to DNA patenting from "Weekend Edition," National Public Radio, June 23, 1996.

65. "On the Line," April 16, 1997, WNYC-AM, interview with Karen Stabiner, who referred to Susan Love's terminology.

66. Stated by Stabiner, "On the Line," April 16, 1997. References to the "potential paradigm shift" in breast cancer treatment from this source. Nicholas Wade ("Scientists Cultivate Cells at Root of Human

Life," *New York Times,* November 6, 1998, A1) reported that researchers hope to "introduce genes into the body to remedy inherited disease." Other researchers—such as biologist Sandra Steingraber, author of *Living Downstream: A Scientist's Personal Investigation of Cancer and the Environment* (New York: Vintage Books, 1998)—stress environmental toxins rather than genetic predisposition as the major cause of cancer.

67. Susan Bolotin in "Slash, Burn, and Poison" (review of Karen Stabiner's *To Dance with the Devil: The New War on Breast Cancer* [New York: Delacorte Press, 1997]), *New York Times,* Sunday, April 13, 1997, sec. 7, p. 8, quoted Stabiner.

68. "Premarin, an estrogen product . . . is already the biggest-selling drug in the United States" (Susan Love, "Sometimes Mother Nature Knows Best," *New York Times,* March 20, 1997, A25).

69. "The American College of Obstetrics and Gynecology recommends that postmenopausal women be on 'replacement' hormones for the rest of their lives unless they have a compelling reason not to be" (Love, "Sometimes Mother Nature Knows Best," A25). This hormone replacement has been recommended to help women stave off osteoporosis, heart disease, and some discomforts of menopause, as well as possibly Alzheimer's disease (Alexis Jetter, "Should You Trust Her?" *Health,* July/August 1997, 104).

70. Love, "Sometimes Mother Nature Knows Best," A25. "In Drug Marketing Starts Legal Battle: Makers of Postmenopausal Products Clash with Regulators," Denise Grady reported, "Two drug companies seeking to tap the vast market of postmenopausal women at risk for breast cancer, heart disease and bone loss have clashed with each other and run afoul of the Food and Drug Administration over their marketing practices, prompting a flurry of lawsuits, government warning letters and accusations that inaccurate assertions could endanger women's health" (*New York Times,* Sunday, March 28, 1999, A28).

71. References to Dr. Christiane Northrup from Jetter, "Should You Trust Her?", 103-4.

72. Love, "Sometimes Mother Nature Knows Best," A25. In this article, Love refers to "Graham Colditz, one of the authors of the Nurse's Health Study [a definitive fourteen-year study of 120,000 nurses issued in 1995], who estimated that 90 percent of heart disease cases could be eliminated if people changed their life style; this means encouraging women to exercise, watch their diet, and quit smoking." Love believes that "a healthier life style" decreases not only the probability of heart disease in postmenopausal women, but also osteoporosis and breast cancer, "with less risk" than estrogen replacement ("On the Line," WNYC-AM, May 8, 1997). Love's and Northrup's skepticism has been supported by the results of "a huge federal study" indicating that estrogen replacement therapy—with or without progestin—for postmenopausal healthy women may result in increased probability for heart attacks, strokes, and blood clots" (Gina Kolata, "Estrogen Question Gets Tougher," *New York Times,* April 6, 2000, A22).

73. "Sunday Morning," May 11, 1997. References to Fran Visco from this source. See also Sheryl Gay Stolberg, "Now, Prescribing Just What the Patient Ordered," *New York Times,* Sunday, August 10, 1997, sec. 4, p. 3, concerning how, with regard to women's health issues, feminism—together with the movement toward patient self-education and activism—countered medical paternalism and the cost-cutting excesses of managed care.

74. Stated by Stabiner, "On the Line," April 16, 1997. Stabiner offered another reason for the new militancy: "Gender bias played a terrific role in the sense that we weren't doing any research on women's disease until the early part of this decade. . . . You have a lot of very angry women, and you have a lot of baby boomers, who grew up with social change and with this notion that they could do things that would affect the way the world worked" ("Sunday Morning," CBS Television, May 11, 1997).

75. Steven Epstein, *Impure Science* (Berkeley: University of California Press, 1997).

76. Jeffrey Goldberg, in "Breakthrough," *New York Times,* Sunday, January 12, 1997, sec. 7, p. 16, described Epstein's work.

77. Frank Bruni, "Act-Up Doesn't Much, Anymore," *New York Times,* March 21, 1997, B1.

78. AIDS activists' guidance in producing new drugs, from Goldberg, "Breakthrough," 17. There were five dramatic Act-Up demonstrations from 1987 to 1992 at the following sites: two pharmaceutical companies, the Food and Drug Administration headquarters, the New York Stock Exchange, and the White House lawn (Bruni, "Act-Up Doesn't Much, Anymore," B1).

79. Christine Gorman, "The Disease Detective," *Time,* December 30, 1996/January 6, 1997, 62.

80. Frank Rich, "Not If, But When," *New York Times,* August 3, 1996, 19, quoted Dr. Jerome Groopman. References to Groopman from this source.

81. Gorman, "The Disease Detective," 58.

82. Bruce G. Weniger and Max Essex, "Clearing the Way for an AIDS Vaccine," *New York Times,* January 4, 1997, A23. References to Weniger and Essex's criticism of the National Institutes of Health approach to the AIDS crisis from this source.

83. Lawrence K. Altman, "Some Scientists Are Hopeful Again for an AIDS Cure," *New York Times,* July 1, 1998, A19. Bob Jaffe, Director of State Affairs, Gay Mens' Health Crisis in New York City, indicated to authors on January 7, 1998, that in 1997 scientists discovered the latent reservoir of HIV in supposedly cured patients.

84. Altman, "Some Scientists Are Hopeful," A19.

85. Dr. David Ho, "Too Much Pessimism on AIDS Therapies," *New York Times,* June 27, 1998, A15. In a report released ahead of the Thirteenth International AIDS Conference (which began July 9, 2000), the United Nations projected that "about half of all 15-year-olds in the African countries worst affected by AIDS will eventually die of the disease even if the rates of infection drop substantially in the next few years. . . . And if infection rates remain high, the odds are that more than two-thirds of the 15- year-olds will die from AIDS in countries like Botswana." Lawrence K. Altman, "U.N. Warning AIDS Imperils Africa's Youth," *New York Times,* June 28, 2000, A1, A12.

86. Lawrence K. Altman, "AIDS Meeting Ends with Little Hope of Breakthrough," *New York Times,* Sunday, July 5, 1998, A1, A11. References to the prohibitive cost of AIDS medication from this source.

87. "Morning Edition," National Public Radio, August 31, 1999.

88. Gabriel Rotello, "The Risk in a 'Cure' for AIDS," *New York Times,* 14 July 1996, sec. 4, p. 17; and *Sexual Ecology: AIDS and the Destiny of Gay Men* (New York: E. P. Dutton, 1997).

89. "National Public Radio News," March 30, 1998. Although in 1988 African Americans made up only 13 percent of the U.S. population, they accounted for 57 percent of all new infections of the virus that causes AIDS, and AIDS was the leading cause of death of African Americans between twenty-five and forty-four years of age (Sheryl Gay Stolberg, "Eyes Shut, Black America Is Being Ravaged by AIDS," *New York Times,* June 29, 1998, A1). AIDS in the United States has become "increasingly a disease of the poor and disadvantaged" (editorial, *New York Times,* Sunday, December 5, 1999, A16).

90. See Randy Shilts, *And the Band Played On: Politics, People, and the AIDS Epidemic* (New York: Viking Penguin, 1988), an exposé of the political expediency and irresponsibility of members of the government, health, and science establishment during the early 1980s while AIDS was allowed to spread unchecked.

91. Dinitia Smith, "Viewing AIDS Writing through Prism of Hope," *New York Times,* January 13, 1997, C11, C15. References to Literature in the Days of AIDS from this source.

92. Mammogram machines accessible to most women—like the Bennet Contour-Plus in Berkeley, California—have been produced, but they are few in number. See Dr. Debra Shabas, "Knowledge Is Empowerment: Breast Cancer Prevention for Women with Disabilities," *We,* September—October 1999, 47.

Chapter Ten

1. Howard A. Rusk, *A World To Care For: The Autobiography of Howard A. Rusk, M.D.* (New York: Random House, 1977), 89–90. References to Herb Klinefeld from this source.

2. "Wars & Scars: A Diamond Anniversary History of the Disabled American Veterans," *DAV Magazine,* July/August 1995, 1–2. References to obstacles to securing services faced by World War I veterans from this source.

3. Frances A. Koestler, *The Unseen Minority: A Social History of Blindness in America* (New York: David McKay Company, 1976), 251. References to the War Risk Insurance Act and the establishment of the U.S. Veterans Bureau in 1921 from this source.

4. Richard B. Treanor, *We Overcame: The Story of Civil Rights for Disabled People* (Falls Church, Va.: Regal Direct Publishing, 1993), 11. Richard K. Scotch, *From Goodwill to Civil Rights: Transforming Federal Disability Policy* (Philadelphia: Temple University Press, 1984), 20.

5. "Wars & Scars," 2–4. Unless otherwise indicated, references to DAVWW from this source.

6. Treanor, *We Overcame,* 15. "Wars & Scars," 10.

7. Treanor, *We Overcame,* 15.

8. Edward D. Berkowitz, *Disabled Policy: America's Programs for the Handicapped* (Cambridge: Cambridge University Press, 1987), 169. See also Koestler, *The Unseen Minority,* 259.

9. Koestler, *The Unseen Minority,* 260, refers to Public Law 78-16.

10. Rodman D. Griffin, "The Disabilities Act," *CQ Researcher,* December 27, 1991, 1001. The Smith-Fess Vocational Rehabilitation Act covering civilians with disabilities was passed two years after the 1918 Smith-Sears Veterans Rehabilitation Act covering disabled veterans. Scotch, *From Goodwill to Civil Rights,* 20.

11. *Paraplegia News,* September 1956, 4. Rusk, *A World To Care For,* 99.

12. Nora Groce, *The U.S. Role in International Disability Activities: A History and a Look Toward the Future* (Oakland, Calif.: International Disability Exchanges and Studies Project, 1992), 123-24. See also Henry H. Kessler, *The Knife is Not Enough* (New York: W. W. Norton, 1968).

13. Groce, *The U.S. Role in International Disability Activities,* 28. References to the Kessler's comprehensive approach to rehabilitation from this source.

14. Discussion of "the whole man" from Rusk, *A World To Care For,* 66.

15. Rusk, *A World To Care For,* 52. References to the Air Force Rehabilitation Center at Pawling, New York, from this source.

16. Rusk, *A World To Care For,* 43, 149.

17. Ibid., 77-78.

18. The institute was known first as The Red Cross Institute for Crippled and Disabled Men in 1917, then as the Institute for the Crippled and Disabled by 1919, and finally as the International Center for the Disabled by 1981, retaining the abbreviation ICD.

19. Rusk, *A World To Care For,* 48-49.

20. Ibid., 66.

21. *Paraplegia News,* December 1950, 4-5.

22. *Paraplegia News,* August 1949, 3. References to the September 1947 anti-segregation PVA resolution from this source.

23. *Paraplegia News,* August 1946, 1, and August 1949, 3.

24. *Paraplegia News,* October 1946, 1, 3. PVA's goals from this source.

25. *Paraplegia News,* December 1950, 4.

26. Rusk, *A World To Care For,* 42-43.

27. Ibid., 76. Numbers of surviving paraplegics of World Wars I and II from this source.

28. *Paraplegia News,* April 1949, 3; April 1950, 4; June 1950, 4; March 1952, 4; August 1957, 8-9 and 12-13; and September 1961, 13. Although in the November 1946 *Paraplegia News* (p. 1), automobiles for triplegics and quadriplegics were considered appropriate only for rehabilitation because they were regarded as unemployable, by the later 1940s this restrictive assumption was less prevalent in the newspaper.

29. *Paraplegia News,* March 1948, 1.

30. *Paraplegia News,* August 1948, 5.

31. *Paraplegia News,* March/April 1953, 3.

32. *Paraplegia News,* September 1950, 3.

33. *Paraplegia News,* November 1946, 1. Mobility-impaired veterans were also granted the cost of outfitting their cars with hand controls.

34. *Paraplegia News,* October 1946, 3.

35. Automatic transmission was introduced by General Motors as an option in the 1940 Oldsmobile (*Guinness Book of Car Facts and Feats* [Middlesex, England: Guinness Superlatives Limited, 1980], 252). This technology, however, was not commonplace in cars until over five years later.

36. Advertisements for different models of hand controls appeared in *Paraplegia News* throughout the late 1940s and the 1950s.

37. *Paraplegia News,* April 1950, 4.

38. Advertisements for the following appeared in *Paraplegia News:* the Hoyer Kartop-Lift in April 1959, the hydraulic lift in June 1961, and the portable ramp in February 1964.

39. *Paraplegia News,* June 1961, 12.

40. Groce, *The U.S. Role in International Disability Activities,* 156–57. References to Henry Viscardi from this source.

41. For example, the failure of the administration of New York City Mayor John Lindsay in 1966 to limit the use of special parking permits by people with disabilities can be credited to the organized drivers with disabilities.

42. Wilber J. Scott, *The Politics of Readjustment: Vietnam Veterans Since the War* (Hawthorne, N.Y.: Aldine de Gruyter, 1993). Scott notes that the strategies and determination of the ostracized gay activists were instructive to veterans who became activists as a result of their experience in Vietnam.

43. Description of veterans bureaucracy from interview with Paul Camacho (Joiner Center for the Study of War and Social Consequences, University of Massachusetts, Boston), June 12, 1997.

44. Paul Camacho, "The Future of the Veterans' Lobby and Its Potential Impact for Social Policy," *The American War in Vietnam,* ed. Jayne Werner and David Hunt (Ithaca, N.Y.: Cornell University [Southeast Asia Program], 1993), 116–17. Efforts of Vietnam veterans to gain visibility from this source.

45. Interview with Paul Camacho, June 12, 1997.

46. Unless otherwise indicated, references to Gulf War-related disabilities from "America's Defense Monitor," Center for Defense Information, Program Number 634: "War May Be Hazardous To Your Health," (initial broadcast, Public Broadcasting System, May 9, 1993).

47. Tod Ensign described Citizen Soldier in interview, June 18, 1997. Ensign coauthored, with Michael Uhl, *GI Guinea Pigs: How the Pentagon Exposed Our Troops to Dangers More Deadly Than War* (New York: Wideview Books, 1980).

48. Philip Shenon, "Two Studies Seem To Back Veterans Who Trace Illnesses to Gulf War," *New York Times,* November 26, 1996, A1, A16. References to these studies from this source.

49. "Studies on Gulf War Illnesses Are Faulted," *New York Times,* Sunday, June 15, 1997, A18.

50. Interview with Paul Sullivan, April 26, 1999. Sullivan's references to the complex and potentially lethal nature of Gulf War syndrome from this source.

51. Steven Lee Myers, "Drug May Be Cause of Veterans Illnesses," *New York Times,* October 19, 1999, A18. The chemical involved, pyridostigmine bromide, was used as a pretreatment for soman, a nerve agent that Iraq never used in the Gulf War. See also Steven Lee Myers, "Study of Ill Gulf War Veterans Points to Chemical Damage," *New York Times,* December 1, 1999, A18, for scientific study revealing "signs of brain damage" in Gulf War veterans "caused by exposure to toxic chemicals."

52. The National Gulf War Resource Center is a coalition of fifty-eight veterans and other groups involved in promoting health care for Gulf War veterans. Patricia Axelrod, military scientist who specializes in weapons systems analysis and winner of a MacArthur grant to do research on depleted uranium, insists that the term "depleted uranium" is an oxymoron, a convenient way for the Department of Defense to marginalize the toxic effects of what is called depleted uranium but is in reality Uranium 238. From Amy Goodman's interview with Patricia Axelrod, "Democracy Now," WBAI, May 30, 2000.

53. In his interview on May 5, 1999, Gary Pitts referred to the recent discovery by Howard Urenovitz at the University of California in Berkeley that chromosome 22 was damaged by exposure to toxins in half of the twenty-four Gulf War veterans that he examined while no such damage was evident in any of those in the control group.

54. Philip Shenon, "Chemical Arms in Gulf War: Medical Mystery and Credibility Crisis," *New York Times,* January 2, 1997, A14. In 1989, when the Veterans Administration became a cabinet level agency, the name was changed to the Department of Veterans Affairs.

55. Even as late as January 20, 1999, "Frontline: The Last Battle of the Gulf War," aired on PBS-TV, suggested that evidence of Gulf War syndrome was inconclusive. "The program was primarily based on an interview with Stephen Joseph, Assistant Secretary for Health at the Department of Defense, whose poor handling of the Gulf War illness issue was cited in the press as the reason he is no longer at the Department," said Paul Sullivan in a May 18, 1999, interview in which he referred to "Thanks of a Grateful Nation," the 1998 cable television mini-series, as offering a valid, though popularized, account of the injustice done to Gulf War veterans.

56. Interview with Paul Sullivan, April 26, 1999.

57. Shenon, "Chemical Arms in Gulf War," A14.

58. Shenon, "Two Studies," A16.

59. Unless otherwise indicated, references to Vietnam and World War II related disabilities and illnesses from "America's Defense Monitor," Program Number 634. For discussion of post-traumatic stress disorder, see Robert J. Lifton's *Home From the War* (New York: Basic Books, 1973).

60. William A. Buckingham, "Operation Ranch Hand: Herbicides in Southeast Asia, 1961–1971," posted October 18, 1997, http://cpcug.org/user/billb/ranchhand/ranchhand.html (Buckingham is author of *Operation Ranch Hand: The Air Force and Herbicide in Southeast Asia, 1961–1971* [Washington, D.C.: U.S. Government Printing Office, 1982].) Not only has Dr. Joel E. Michalek, U.S. Air Force statistician for the Ranch Hand study, observed a persistent connection between diabetes and dioxin among Vietnam veterans, but also Dr. Michael Gough, chairperson of a federal advisory panel for this study from 1990–1995, said that he is certain that "diabetes will be turned into a compensable disease" for these veterans. Gina Kolata, "Agent Orange and Diabetes: Diving into Murky Depths," *New York Times,* March 30, 2000, A16.

61. Ensign is quoted in "America's Defense Monitor," Program Number 634. In *Ok-Lee v. Dow Chemical Co. et. al.*—a class action suit filed in U.S. District Court in Philadelphia (December 3, 1999)—more than one thousand American veterans who served in Korea in the late 1960s claim that defoliants such as Agent Orange have had a delayed toxic effect on them.

62. Interview with Dr. Steven Stellman, March 26, 1997. References to Dr. Steven Stellman and Dr. Jeanne Stellman, professor of public health at Columbia University, from this source. The Stellmans' work was drawn upon heavily by the National Academy of Sciences report on Agent Orange.

63. Dr. Steven Stellman added, "Although this coverup was whispered about for a long time, in 1991 New York City Congressman Ted Weiss held a series of oversight hearings resulting in documentation that implicated the Reagan White House in an attempt to conceal the facts. According to the House Report, when Ed Meese was the Attorney General, he used the Domestic Policy Council as a political tool for delaying and suppressing research efforts into Agent Orange."

64. Unless otherwise indicated, references to "atomic guinea pigs" from "America's Defense Monitor," Program Number 634.

65. Michael D'Antonio, "Atomic Guinea Pigs," *New York Times,* August 31, 1997, Sunday, sec. 6, p. 38. References to Anthony Guarisco from this source.

66. See also Eileen Welsome, *The Plutonium Files: America's Secret Medical Experiments in the Cold War* (New York: Delacorte Press, 1999).

67. Interview with Sandra Marlow, June 23, 1997.

68. Sandra Marlow, "A Daughter's Story," *The Bulletin of the Atomic Scientists,* January 1983, 30.

69. "DAV Targets Aid to Vets Who Took Part in Nuclear Testing," *New York Able,* March 1997, 6. Reference to David W. Gorman from this source.

70. Interview with Dr. Martin Gensler, May 25, 1999. References to Gensler and his explanation for the denial of compensation to atomic vets from this source. The views expressed by Gensler do not necessarily reflect those of Senator Paul Wellstone. The Pentagon's October 21, 1999, reiteration of its claim that the cancer rate of atomic veterans did not differ significantly from other veterans who served during the same time period drew media attention as well as skepticism from atomic veteran supporters.

71. References to World War II chemical warfare tests from "America's Defense Monitor," Program Number 634.

72. Philip Shenon, "Pentagon Says Gulf War Data Seem To Be Lost," *New York Times,* December 5, 1996, A1, B18. References to the gaps in the logs from this source.

73. Philip Shenon, "Study Sharply Raises Estimate of Troops Exposed to Nerve Gas," *New York Times,* July 24, 1997, A18.

74. "On the Line," WNYC-AM, December 13, 1996.

75. Shenon, "Study Sharply Raises Estimate," A18. Reference to James J. Tuite from this source.

76. "DAV Supports Easing Burden of Proof for Gulf War Vets," *New York Able,* March 1997, 3. References to extending time period for regulations governing proof of Gulf War-related illnesses from this source.

77. "On the Line," WNYC-AM, December 13, 1996. See *Feres v. United States* 340 U.S. 135 (1950).

78. Interview with Tod Ensign, June 18, 1997.

79. Dennis Bernstein, "Gulf War Syndrome Coverup," *Covert Action Quarterly,* No. 53, Summer 1995, 9. Unless otherwise indicated, references to *Coleman v. Alcolac* from this source.

80. Interview with Gary Pitts, one of the attorneys for the plaintiffs, May 5, 1999. References to Pitts and foreign companies that are defendants in *Marshall Coleman et al. v. ABB Lymus Crest Inc. et al.* from this source. Pitts indicates that companies use subsidiaries in a "shell game" in order to hide what they have done.

81. References to attorney Frank Spagnoletti from *Newsletter of the Gulf War Veterans of Massachusetts,* December 17, 1997, 1(3): 3.

82. In a case of life imitating art, the story of Admiral Elmo Zumwalt II is reminiscent of the plot of Arthur Miller's play, *All My Sons.*

83. Although following the Gulf War the Chemical Weapons Convention prohibited the sale of dangerous chemicals, Pitts explained (in his interview of May 5, 1999) that companies can get around this prohibition by selling two or more benign chemicals that form a lethal compound when combined.

84. Interview with Paul Sullivan, April 26, 1999. References to the 1998 Persian Gulf War Veterans Act (PL 105-277) from this source. This act followed on the heels of a similar 1994 Act (PL 103-446), which veterans groups had almost written off as ineffective.

85. When many variables prevent statistically establishing cause and effect with regard to, for example, Gulf War syndrome, the phenomenon is referred to as "confounding."

86. Interview with Paul Sullivan, April 26, 1999. As Representative Christopher Shays (R-Conn.) stated (March 4, 1999), because military men and women have become "understandably distrustful of the Pentagon on medical matters," some have resisted mandatory anthrax vaccinations jeopardizing "their military careers and even their liberty." As a result, Representative Benjamin Gilman (R-N.Y.) and others introduced (on July 19, 1999) HR 2548, a bill to suspend further implementation of the Department of Defense anthrax vaccination program.

Chapter Eleven

1. John Gliedman and William Roth, *The Unexpected Minority: Handicapped Children in America* (New York: Harcourt Brace Jovanovich, 1980), 173.

2. *Pennsylvania Association for Retarded Children v. Pennsylvania,* 344 F. Supp. 1257 (E.D. Pa. 1971) and 343 F. Supp. 279 (E.D. Pa. 1972) from Christopher G. Bell and Robert L. Burgdorf, *Accommodating the Spectrum of Individual Abilities* (Washington, D.C.: U.S. Commission on Civil Rights, 1983), 57.

3. References to *Mills v. Board of Education of the District of Columbia,* 348 F. Supp. 866 (D. D.C. 1972) from Gliedman and Roth, *The Unexpected Minority,* 176-77.

4. Bell and Burgdorf, *Accommodating the Spectrum,* 59.

5. Edward D. Berkowitz, *Disabled Policy: America's Programs for the Handicapped* (Cambridge: Cambridge University Press, 1987), 207.

6. Gliedman and Roth, *The Unexpected Minority,* 466, note 1.

7. Bell and Burgdorf, *Accommodating the Spectrum,* 27, footnote 73.

8. Ibid., 57.

9. "The One and a Half Million Dollar Goof," *Disabled People Speak to Medical People,* February 1990, 20.

10. Gliedman and Roth, *The Unexpected Minority,* 174.

11. Bell and Burgdorf, *Accommodating the Spectrum,* 57-58.

12. Gliedman and Roth, *The Unexpected Minority,* 179, 467 (note 10).

13. Bell and Burgdorf, *Accommodating the Spectrum,* 57.

14. Gliedman and Roth, *The Unexpected Minority,* 466, note 4.

15. Interview with Rims Barber, May 28, 1999. Unless otherwise indicated, references to the 1979 Mississippi consent decree from this source.

16. Gene I. Maeroff, "Suit Spurring Mississippi Efforts To Teach Handicapped Children," *New York Times,* April 5, 1979, A13. Comparison between mainstreaming children with disabilities in Mississippi and New York City from this source.

17. References to the *Jose P.* lawsuit from *Jose P. v. Board of Education,* 79 C 270, December 14, 1979, 2-6.

18. After assessing the child's present level of education, the IEP establishes annual goals, special education and related services to be provided, and projected dates for and anticipated duration of services, as well as objective criteria and evaluation procedures and schedules appropriate for the child (Gliedman and Roth, *The Unexpected Minority,* 182-83).

19. The authors arrived at these estimates by calculations based on the population of the United States, approximately 225 million, and the population of New York City, about 7 million. The authors also included in their calculations estimates of the number of children with severe disabilities nationwide that required identification, around 1 million, and the total number of children with disabilities nationwide, roughly 8 million.

20. Interview with John C. Gray, May 16, 1997. References to Gray from this source.

21. The *Jose P.* judgment of December 13, 1979, mandated that the language requirements for this population be consistent with the consent decree in *Aspira of New York, Inc. v. Board of Education.*

22. Bell and Burgdorf, *Accommodating the Spectrum,* 58.

23. Gliedman and Roth, *The Unexpected Minority,* 218.

24. Interview with Mary Somoza, July 29, 1997.

25. Both the 1979 *Jose P.* education lawsuit and the 1980 *Dopico* transportation lawsuit were Brooklyn Legal Services cases.

26. Panel discussion on special education, New York City Bar Association, December 5, 1996. References to this panel discussion from this source.

27. Interview with attorney Diane Lipton, director of the Children with Disabilities and Families Advocacy Program for the Disability Rights Education and Defense Fund, July 31, 1997.

28. Interview with former New York City public school teacher, August 1, 1997. The school to which she referred was on 96th Street and Park Avenue in Manhattan.

29. Disability Studies Colloquium, "Inclusion: The Challenge, the Opportunity," New York City Hunter College School of Social Work, December 5, 1997. Judith E. Heumann's reference to the resistance of some educators to "accepting the reality of disability" from this source.

30. Rather than "inclusion," Heumann favors the terms "desegregation" and "integration" because of the political connotations of the two latter words.

31. Interview with Diane Lipton, July 31, 1997. See *Hendrick Hudson Central School District v. Rowley,* 102 S.Ct. 3034 (1982). Unless otherwise indicated, references to the Rowley case from the Lipton interview.

32. Mary Johnson, "Amy and the Supremes," *Ragged Edge,* May/June 1998, 29.

33. Johnson, "Amy and the Supremes," 29. Johnson is quoting from R. C. Smith, *The Case About Amy: Health, Society and Policy* (Philadelphia: Temple University Press, 1996).

34. A 1975 House Committee on Education and Labor Report quoted in Kipp Watson, "The Rowley Case: A Broken Promise," *DIA Activist,* January 1983, 8.

35. R. C. Smith, "An Audience for Amy," *Ragged Edge,* May/June 1998, 31.

36. Diane Lipton, "The 'Full Inclusion' Court Cases: *1989-1994,*" Presented at Wingspread Conference, Racine, Wisconsin, April 28 to May 1, 1994, 2.

37. Ibid., 3. References to *Roncker v. Walters,* 700 F2d 1058 (6th Cir 1983) from this source.

38. Interview with Diane Lipton, July 31, 1997. See *Daniel R. R. v. State Board of Education,* 874 F2d 1036 (5th Cir 1989); *Greer v. Rome School District,* 950 F2d 688 (11th Cir 1991); *Oberti v. Board of Education,* 995 F2d 1204 (3d Cir 1993); and *Sacramento City Unified School District v. Holland,* 14 F3d 1398 (9th Cir 1994). References to these cases from interview with Diane Lipton.

39. Interview with Mary Somoza, July 28, 1997. President Clinton's letter to Anastasia as well as the description of the Somoza settlement with the New York City Board of Education from this source.

40. Interview with Barbara Zitcer, director of the Nursery School of the Young Men and Women's Hebrew Association of North New Jersey, December 21, 1997. Zitcer observed that children identified as autistic began to be included with supports into her regular nursery school classrooms between 1994 and 1995.

41. Interview with Nicholas M., December 21, 1997. References to Nicholas M. and M.M. from this source. Catherine Maurice's *Let Me Hear Your Voice: A Family's Triumph Over Autism* (New York: Fawcett Books, 1994) profoundly impacted Nicholas M.'s response to autism.

42. In her book *Targeting Autism: What We Know, Don't Know, and Can Do to Help Young Children with Autism and Related Disorders* (Los Angeles: University of California Press, 1997), Shirley Cohen, professor of special education at Hunter College, referred to another technique that has been successful with some autistic children—Dr. Stanley I. Greenspan's emotionally-based approach, designed to re-ignite the autistic child's developmental processes.

43. Tamar Lewin, "Family Tests Law on the Meaning of Inclusion," *New York Times,* Sunday, December 28, 1997, sec. 1, p. 20. References to Ashburn Elementary School officials and the Hartmanns' legal fees from this source. See *Hartman v. Loudoun County Board of Education,* 962809P (4th Cir 1997).

44. "The NewsHour with Jim Lehrer," Public Broadcasting System, March 24, 1998. Unless otherwise indicated, references to the Hartmann "inclusion" case from this source.

45. References to *Cedar Rapids v. Garrett F.* from Linda Greenhouse, "Court Says School Must Pay for Needs of Disabled Pupils," *New York Times,* March 4, 1999, 1 and 18. See *Cedar Rapids School District v. Garret F.,* 119 S.Ct. 37 (1997).

46. Editorial, "The Special Education Nightmare," *New York Times,* June 24, 1996, A14.

47. Michael Winerip, "A Disabilities Program That 'Got Out of Hand,'" *New York Times,* April 8, 1994, B6. References to Dalton from this source.

48. Pam Belluck, "A Plan To Revamp Special Education," *New York Times,* November 26, 1996, A1. See Ann Colin, *Willie: Raising and Loving a Child with Attention Deficit Disorder* (New York: Viking Press, 1997).

49. Interview with Barbara Fisher, May 31, 1999. "Special education" has at least three different meanings: full-time segregated education, part-time segregated education, and education in the general classroom with supports. References to the difference between the stated intention of the Crew plan and the actual results from this source.

50. Panel Discussion on Special Education, New York City Bar Association, December 5, 1996. Unless otherwise indicated, references to concerns of advocates, parents, educators, and of attorney Roger Juan Maldanado, regarding special education in New York City from this source.

51. Belluck, "A Plan To Revamp Special Education," B4.

52. Interview with DREDF attorney Diane Lipton, July 31, 1997. References to the Reauthorization of the IDEA from this source.

53. Jill Chaifetz, "Saving Special Ed: System Dooms Too Many Children, but There's a Chance to Fix It," *New York Times,* Sunday, May 30, 1999, sec. 14, p. 13. References to the State Regents Plan and Governor George Pataki's plan from this source.

54. Brent Staples, "Special Education Is Not a Scandal," *New York Times,* Sunday, September 21, 1997, sec. 6, pp. 64-65. References to Staples from this source.

55. Winerip, "A Disabilities Program That 'Got Out of Hand,'" B6. Winerip notes that the learning disability most often mentioned, dyslexia—in which the brain processes letters and symbols backwards— accounts for only a small portion of learning problems.

56. Brent Staples states, "Whole-language enthusiasts thought that children were naturally disposed to reading and writing and learned those skills just as they learned to speak." Unlike the phonics method, the whole-language method—emphasizing words and phrases as clusters of meaning independent of sounds— does not stress connecting letters to sounds, sounds to syllables, and syllables to words, and so forth.

57. Conversation with Edward Lewinson, Ph.D., December 5, 1996. Retired Seton Hall history professor Lewinson, blind from birth, received an excellent integrated public school education in Detroit in the 1930s and 1940s. Even before the passage of the IDEA, some schools mainstreamed children with disabilities who were able to function in an integrated setting. Mainstreaming tended to be most successful when parents were assertive advocates for their children.

58. "60 Minutes," CBS-TV, June 9, 1996. Remarks of commentator Leslie Stahl, as well as those of parents of both nondisabled and disabled children who appeared on this segment, "Special Ed," from this source.

59. Philip K. Howard, *The Death of Common Sense: How Law is Suffocating America* (New York: Random House, 1994), 151.

60. Editorial, *New York Times,* June 24, 1996, A14.

61. Barbara Fisher and Richard Spiegel, "Diaspora: Special Education—NYC," *DIA Activist,* January

1997, 8. In an interview on May 31, 1999, Fisher and Spiegel pointed out that because many teachers do not know how to deal with students with disabilities, an increasing number of "consultative teachers" should be provided on-site to train general classroom teachers by modeling teaching techniques appropriate for a wide spectrum of learning styles.

62. Editorial, *New York Times,* June 24, 1996, A14.

63. Lynda Richardson, "Minority Students Languish in Special Education System," *New York Times,* April 6, 1994, A2, B7.

64. Richardson, "Minority Students Languish," A2, B7. References to segregation and racial and ethnic stereotyping in New York City's special education program from this source. This article was still relevant in 2000.

65. Tamar Lewin, "Where All Doors Are Open For Disabled Students," *New York Times,* Sunday, December 28, 1997, sec. 1, p. 20. References to the 1989 shift in special education in Vermont from this source.

66. Disability Studies Colloquium, New York City Hunter College School of Social Work, December 5, 1997. Reference to Judith E. Heumann's view that special education money should follow the student from this source.

67. Tamar Lewin, "Fictitious Learning-Disabled Student Is at Center of Lawsuit against College," *New York Times,* April 8, 1997, B9. Unless otherwise indicated, references to this lawsuit, attorney Larry Elswit, plaintiff Elizabeth Guckenberger, and services provided by Boston University for students with learning disabilities from this source.

68. Debra Ellen, "Taking the Case to Court," *Connections,* September 1996, 3(4): 3, 11. References to Anne Schneider from this source.

69. Joseph P. Shapiro, "The Strange Case of Somnolent Samantha," *U.S. News and World Report,* April 14, 1997, p. 31.

70. Reference to the August 15, 1997, decision in *Elizabeth Guckenberger v. Boston University,* 957 F. Supp. 306 (D.C. Mass.) from disability rights attorney Frank Laski, Disability Rights Advocates of Oakland, and lawyers from the firm Clark, Hunt & Embry of Cambridge, Massachusetts, who represented the plaintiffs. A second *Guckenberger* decision, 974 F. Supp. 106 (D.C. Mass. 1997), further clarified the issue of "reasonable accommodation." By the time the lawsuit was decided, Jon Westling had become president of Boston University.

71. Shapiro, "The Strange Case of Somnolent Samantha," 31. Statistics on the number of students with learning disabilities from this source.

72. Interview with Richard Spiegel, May 31, 1999. Unless otherwise indicated, references to Spiegel from this source. Spiegel indicates that techniques used in special education—students' preparation of portfolios and oral presentations, as well as their performance of job-related tasks—are valid educational strategies for all those in the general classroom.

73. Lewin, "Where All Doors Are Open For Disabled Students," sec. 1, p. 20.

74. "Inclusion: It's Not All Academic," *The Eric Review,* Fall 1996, 4(3): 17. References to Barak Stussman from this source.

75. Disability Studies Colloquium, New York City Hunter College School of Social Work, December 5, 1997. Judith E. Heumann's references to the benefits of inclusion to both nondisabled students and students with disabilities from this source.

Chapter Twelve

1. Interview with Lex Frieden, July 16, 1997.

2. "Talk of the Nation, Science Friday," National Public Radio, May 8, 1998.

3. Cheryl Marie Wade, "It Ain't Exactly Sexy," *The Ragged Edge* (Louisville: The Advocado Press, 1994), 89–90. References to Wade from this source.

4. Barrett Shaw, "Introduction," *The Ragged Edge,* ed. Barrett Shaw (Louisville: The Advocado Press, 1994), xi.

5. Mary Jane Owen, "Like Squabbling Cubs," *The Ragged Edge,* ed. Barrett Shaw (Louisville: The Advocado Press, 1994), 7. References to Owens from this source.

6. Douglas Martin, "Disability Culture: Eager to Bite the Hand That Would Feed Them," *New York Times,* Sunday, June 1, 1997, sec. 4, pp. 1, 6. Unless otherwise indicated, references to Leslie Heller and Nadina LaSpina from this source.

7. Nadina LaSpina and Daniel Robert, "Pride and Identity," *Ragged Edge,* March/April 1998, 13.

8. Erik H. Erikson, *Childhood and Society* (New York: W. W. Norton, 1950), 268.

9. Leonard Kriegel, author of *Flying Solo: Re-imagining Manhood, Courage and Loss* (New York: Beacon Press, 1998), is an example of a person living a fulfilling and successful life with a disability, who has little or no involvement with disability politics. Having contracted polio at eleven years old, he does appear to feel a kinship with other *writers* with disabilities. Yet his positive sense of self and his creativity as a writer seem to stem from his capacity to mine his experiences as a person with a disability.

10. Martin, "Disability Culture," sec. 4, p. 6.

11. LaSpina and Robert, "Pride and Identity," 3.

12. Interview with Daniel Robert, August 14, 1997.

13. Jean Stewart, *The Body's Memory* (New York: St. Martin's Press, 1989). In 1981, the International Year of Disabled Persons, Stewart—as program director of the Clearwater Great Hudson River Revival—received the go-ahead from Pete Seeger to create a fully accessible festival for people with all kinds of disabilities. The annual Clearwater Revival was one of the first outdoor festivals in the world to become accessible to the disability community and has continued to serve as a model for other such festivals.

14. Interview with Jean Stewart, January 12, 1998. Unless otherwise indicated, references to Stewart from this source.

15. Further information on people with disabilities in prisons is available in Jean Stewart's unpublished manuscript, *Inside Abuse: Disability Oppression Behind Bars.*

16. Interview with Marca Bristo, April 30, 1998. References to Bristo from this source.

17. Steven E. Brown, "We Are Who We Are . . . So Who Are We?" *Mainstream,* August 1996, 31.

18. Robert F. Murphy, *The Body Silent* (1987; reprint, New York: W. W. Norton, 1990). References to Murphy's treatment of disability as "a separate culture," as well as the "unmarked category" and "embattled identity" from Murphy, *The Body Silent,* 102–3.

19. Ibid., 160–61.

20. Cass Irvin, "Preface: Why We Do What We Do," *The Ragged Edge* (Louisville: The Advocado Press, 1994), xiv.

21. Martin, "Disability Culture," sec. 4, p. 6. Quotations are Martin's paraphrase of Gill's remarks.

22. Carol Gill, "Questioning Continuum," *The Ragged Edge* (Louisville: The Advocado Press, 1994), 45. Unless otherwise indicated, references to Gill from this source.

23. John Hockenberry's discussion of disability as a cultural resource from his presentation at the International Center for the Disabled in New York City on March 18, 1998. The U.S. Court of Appeals in the Seventh and Ninth Circuits came to opposite conclusions in cases involving accommodations for professional golfers with disabilities. In *Martin v. PGA,* 204 F3d 994 (9th Cir 2000), the court held that golfer Casey Martin could use a golf cart in competition and that using such a vehicle did not alter tournament play. In *Olinger v. U.S. Golf Association,* 205 F3d 1001 (7th Cir 2000), however, the Seventh Circuit came to a different conclusion, ruling that the use of such a cart would fundamentally alter the nature of the tournament. The PGA has asked the U.S. Supreme Court to review the decision of the Ninth Circuit in light of the two interpretations of the ADA. It is also likely that golfer Ford Olinger will appeal to the Supreme Court on the Seventh Circuit ruling against him. See Marcia Chambers, "PGA Seeks a Review of Cart Suit," *New York Times,* July 4, 2000, D4.

24. Interview with Deborah Yanagisawa, April 29, 1998. References to Yanagisawa from this source.

25. Joan Tollifson, "Imperfection is a Beautiful Thing: On Disability and Meditation," *Staring Back: The Disability Experience from the Inside Out,* ed. Kenny Fries (New York: A Plume Book, 1997), 110.

26. "Disability Studies," *Ragged Edge,* January/February 1998, 18. Reference to David Pfeiffer from this source.

27. Anthony Ramiriz, "Disability As a Field of Study?" *New York Times,* December 21, 1997, sec. 14, p. 8. References to Phyllis Rubenfeld from this source.

28. Definition of Disability Studies quoted in Paul Longmore, "The Second Phase: From Disability Rights to Disability Culture," *The Disability Rag & ReSource*, September/October 1995, 16(5): 4–11.

29. For Arthur Campbell Jr., the most frustrating and limiting aspect of his disability is his difficulty making his speech understood. The weakness of the otherwise effective film is its failure to distinguish between the final personal depression of its protagonist and the state of the disability rights movement.

30. Mary Johnson, "Just One Man's Story, But It Speaks for Many," Sunday, *New York Times*, sec. 2, p. 23.

31. Martin, "Disability Culture," sec. 4, p. 1.

32. Lynn Manning, "The Magic Wand," ed. Kenny Fries, *Staring Back: The Disability Experience from the Inside Out* (New York: A Plume Book, 1997), 165.

33. Interview with Kitty Lunn, July 2, 1997. References to Lunn from this source.

34. "Sunday Morning," CBS-TV, May 23, 1999. References to Dana Tozer and the Cleveland Ballet Dancing Wheels from this source. Severe cerebral palsy has not prevented Daniel Keplinger (subject and writer of the 2000 Oscar winner for best documentary, *King Gimp*) from painting—"using a specially designed headpiece to hold a brush"—works that are "fierce, almost defiant, but also strangely beautiful" (Julie Solomon, "A Painter Happily Emerges from a Determined Battle," *New York Times*, Sunday, June 5, 2000, E5).

35. Interview with Lex Frieden, July 16, 1997.

36. Interview with Eunice Fiorito, June 6, 1997. References to Fiorito from this source.

37. Interview with Susan Scheer, July 26, 1997. References to Scheer from this source. By continuing to serve as attorney general while living with Parkinson's disease, Janet Reno is helping to change the public perception of disability. See Sheryl Gay Stolberg, "Reno Puts a Face on an Often Private Disease," *New York Times*, Sunday, August 15, 1999, A14.

38. James Weisman, "Myth & Media: Bigoted," *The Disability Rag*, September/October 1991. Weisman's criticism of the *New York Times* from this source.

39. Editorial, *New York Times*, November 18, 1979.

40. Editorial, *New York Times*, January 3, 1984.

41. Editorial, *New York Times*, September 6, 1989.

42. Editorial, *New York Times*, May 28, 1991.

43. Martin, "Disability Culture," sec. 4, p. 1.

44. David W. Dunlap, "Architecture in the Age of Accessibility," *New York Times*, Sunday, June 1, 1997, sec. 9, p. 1. References to new architectural standards from this source.

45. Sara Riner, "New Needs for Retirement Complexes' Oldest," *New York Times*, March 23, 1998, A1.

46. Garry Pierre-Pierre, "Disrupting Sales at Greyhound, Disabled Protest Bus Access," *New York Times*, August 9, 1997, 26.

47. Lisa Bannon, "The Vision Thing: Mr. Magoo Watches U.S. Cultural History and Struggles to Adapt," *Wall Street Journal*, July 31, 1997, A1, A8. References to Mr. Magoo from this source. On July 2, 1997, the NFB urged the Disney organization to halt production of its live-action film, "Mr. Magoo," calling the stereotyped figure as offensive to blind people as *Little Black Sambo* and "Amos 'n Andy" are to black people. See Roxana Hegeman, "No More Mr. Magoo Say Blind Group," New York *Daily News*, July 3, 1997, 3.

48. Greg Gittrich, "Disabled Rip Bay Plaza Traffic Peril," New York *Daily News*, August 7, 1997, Metro sec., 2.

49. In Walter Goodman's September 9, 1997, *New York Times* review of "Dateline NBC," aired the same day, he condescendingly indicated that John Hockenberry's reference to his inability to enter the Ziegfeld Theatre or the new Armani store, because of their inaccessibility, trivialized the program. Also, Goodman stated, "the program presents evidence that a law [ADA] is being widely violated, at least in spirit." On the contrary, the program presented evidence that the law is being widely violated *in fact*, not just "in spirit."

50. When a renovation was required on the Brooklyn Bridge walkway in the 1980s, New York City considered building an inaccessible modification. Urged by bicyclists and joggers to insist on accessibility, Disabled In Action struggled to secure a walkway available to wheelchair users, bicyclists, and joggers. Early in August 1985, DIA members from Brooklyn and Manhattan met in the middle of the modified Brooklyn

Bridge accessible promenade to toast with champagne the newly renovated walkway. See Maria Fugate, "Disabled Bridge Gap," New York *Daily News,* August 10, 1985.

51. Bruce Felton, "Technologies That Enable the Disabled," *New York Times,* Sunday, September 14, 1997, sec. 3, pp. 1, 10, 11.

52. David E. Rosenbaum, "Health Benefits Bill Shows Power of the Disabled," *New York Times,* June 7, 1999, A1, A18. Reference to the "turnabout" in nineteen states from this source.

53. Interview with Lex Frieden, July 16, 1997. References to two major media events related to the ADA from this source.

54. Interviews with Charles Winston, director of the National Telability Media Center, August 16, 1997, and June 14, 1999. References to disability media, dial-in services, and the National Telability Media Center from this source.

55. Publisher and editor Angela Melledy founded *New York Able,* the only cross-disability newspaper in New York City, in June 1995. Mary Johnson, long-time editor of the *Disability Rag,* now editor of the *Ragged Edge,* and Lucy Gwin, editor of *Mouth,* are nationally-known disability activists.

56. Constance L. Hays, "Niche Magazines on Maladies Take a Peppier and Glossier Route," *New York Times,* June 9, 1997, D23. Reference to General Motors response to *We* from this source. The fact that *We* placed Jerry Lewis on its front cover in an issue (March/April 1999) lauding his Muscular Dystrophy telethons reveals that this publication stresses marketing rather than politics. For magazines devoted to disability politics, Lewis has been a representation of the unacceptable "charitable model."

57. Greg Smith's program emanates from Dayton, Ohio, and Bob Enteen's program from New York City.

58. Interview with Anne Emerman, August 17, 1997. References to Emerman from this source.

59. Interview with Eunice Fiorito, June 6, 1997. References to Fiorito from this source.

60. Interview with Paul Hearne, June 25, 1997. References to Hearne from this source.

61. Hearne is referring to medical practices such as the experiment conducted in Children's Hospital of Oklahoma, between 1977 and 1982, in which twenty-four spina bifida babies lost their lives. John R. Woodward, "It Can Happen Here," *The Ragged Edge* (Louisville: The Advocado Press, 1994), 230-35.

62. Interview with Marca Bristo, April 30, 1998. References to Bristo from this source.

63. Issued by Presidential Executive Order on March 13, 1998, the Task Force on Employment of Adults with Disabilities was recommended in the 1996 *Achieving Independence,* a publication of the NCD under Marca Bristo.

64. Interview with Susan Dooha, August 15, 1997. References to Dooha from this source.

65. These requirements for people with disabilities were listed in the "ADA Compliance Work Group Agenda," developed by the New York City Task Force on Medicaid Managed Care, February 18, 1997.

66. Interview with Lex Frieden, July 16, 1997. References to Frieden from this source.

67. Interview with Susan Scheer, July 26, 1997. References to Scheer from this source.

68. Frank Bowe, "An Overview Paper on Civil Rights Issues of Handicapped Americans: Public Policy Implications," *Civil Rights Issues of Handicapped Americans: Public Policy Implications* (Washington, D.C.: A Consultation Sponsored by the United States Commission on Civil Rights, May 13-14, 1980), 11. Reference to transferring the legacy of the disability rights movement from this source.

69. Interview with Judith E. Heumann, January 16, 1998. References to Heumann from this source.

70. Marvin Wasserman, president of the New York City 504 Democratic Club—founded in 1983 and named after Section 504 of the Rehabilitation Act of 1973—refers to his political club as the only one in the country that focuses primarily on issues of people with disabilities.

71. The connection between disability and poverty is illustrated by homeless children who lack access "to vital preventive care and the management of chronic conditions." For example, "an astonishing 38 percent of the . . . kids in the city's [New York] shelter system have asthma," a condition that is life-threatening for children. Even in its milder forms as a chronic condition, asthma adversely affects functioning in school. See Bob Herbert, "Children in Crisis," *New York Times,* June 10, 1999, A31. (Herbert quoted from a report by the president of the Children's Health Fund, Dr. Irwin Redlener.)

72. Douglas Martin, "A Victor Fears for the Future," *New York Times,* April 29, 1997, B1.

73. Interview with Emerman, April 30, 1997. Emerman's references to the future of the disability rights movement from this source.

74. Ralf Hotchkiss is quoted in *Report on the "American Creativity at Risk" Symposium,* Rhode Island, November 1996, 16.

75. "National Public Radio News," June 20, 1997.

76. Sheryl Gay Stolberg, "The Good Death: Embracing a Right to Die Well," *New York Times,* Sunday, June 29, 1997, sec. 4, p. 4.

77. Interview with Sherry Lampert, May 10, 1997.

78. Martin, "Disability Culture," sec. 4, p. 6.

Index